Strategies of Qualitative Inquiry

4 EDITION

Strategies of Qualitative Inquiry

4

EDITION

Norman K. Denzin
University of Illinois

Yvonna S. Lincoln
Texas A&M University

Editors

SAGE

Los Angeles | London | New Delhi
Singapore | Washington DC

Los Angeles | London | New Delhi
Singapore | Washington DC

FOR INFORMATION:

SAGE Publications, Inc.
2455 Teller Road
Thousand Oaks, California 91320
E-mail: order@sagepub.com

SAGE Publications Ltd.
1 Oliver's Yard
55 City Road
London EC1Y 1SP
United Kingdom

SAGE Publications India Pvt. Ltd.
B 1/I 1 Mohan Cooperative Industrial Area
Mathura Road, New Delhi 110 044
India

SAGE Publications Asia-Pacific Pte. Ltd.
3 Church Street
#10-04 Samsung Hub
Singapore 049483

Acquisitions Editor: Helen Salmon
Editorial Assistant: Kaitlin Perry
Production Editor: Laura Stewart
Typesetter: C&M Digitals (P) Ltd.
Proofreader: Stefanie Storholt
Indexer: Naomi Linzer
Cover Designer: Candice Harman
Marketing Manager: Nicole Elliott
Permissions Editor: Karen Ehrmann

Printed in the United States of America

Library of Congress Cataloging-in-Publication Data

10 07243 180

Strategies of qualitative inquiry / editors, Norman K. Denzin, University of Illinois, Urbana-Champaign, Yvonna S. Lincoln, Texas A&M University.—Fourth Edition.

pages cm
Includes bibliographical references and index.

ISBN 978-1-4522-5805-8 (pbk.)

1. Social sciences—Methodology.
2. Social sciences—Research—Methodology.
I. Denzin, Norman K. II. Lincoln, Yvonna S.

H61.S8823 2013
300.72′1—dc23   2012035580

This book is printed on acid-free paper.

Certified Chain of Custody
Promoting Sustainable Forestry
www.sfiprogram.org
SFI-01268

SFI label applies to text stock

12 13 14 15 16 10 9 8 7 6 5 4 3 2 1

Contents

Preface

For nearly five decades, a quiet methodological revolution has been taking place in the social sciences. A blurring of disciplinary boundaries has occurred. The social sciences and humanities have drawn closer together in a mutual focus on an interpretive, qualitative approach to research and theory. Although these trends are not new, the extent to which the "qualitative revolution" has overtaken the social sciences and related professional fields has been nothing short of amazing.

Reflecting this revolution, a host of textbooks, journals, research monographs, and readers have been published in recent years. In 1994 we published the first edition of the *Handbook of Qualitative Research* in an attempt to represent the field in its entirety, to take stock of how far it had come and how far it might yet go. The immediate success of the first edition suggested the need to offer the *Handbook* in terms of three separate volumes. So in 1998 we published a three-volume set, *The Landscape of Qualitative Research: Theories and Issues*; *Strategies of Inquiry*; *Collecting and Interpreting Qualitative Materials*. In 2013 we offer a new three-volume set, based on the fourth edition of the handbook.[1]

By 2005 we had published the third edition of the *Handbook*. Although it became abundantly clear that the "field" of qualitative research is still defined primarily by tensions, contradictions, and hesitations—and that they exist in a less-than-unified arena—we believed that the handbook could and would be valuable for solidifying, interpreting, and organizing the field in spite of the essential differences that characterize it.

The first edition attempted to define the field of qualitative research. The second and third editions went one step further. Building on themes in the first edition we asked how the practices of qualitative inquiry could be used to address issues equity and of social justice. The fourth edition continues where the third edition ended. The transformations that were taking place in the first decade of this new century continue to gain momentum in the second decade.

Not surprisingly, this quiet revolution has been met by resistance. In many quarters, a resurgent, scientifically based research paradigm has gained the upper hand.

---

[1]To review: the first three-volume set was offered in 1998, the second in 2003, and the third in 2008.

Borrowing form the field of biomedical research, the National Research Council (NRC) has appropriated neo-positivist, evidence-based epistemologies. Calls for Randomized Control Trials and mixed-methods designs are now common. Interpretive methods are read as being unsuitable for those who legislate social policy.

The days of value-free inquiry based on a God's-eye of reality are over. Today many agree that inquiry is moral, and political. Experimental, reflexive ways of writing and performing first-person autoethnographic texts are now commonplace. There continues to be a pressing need to show how the practices of qualitative research can help change the world in positive ways. It is necessary to reengage the promise of qualitative research as a form of radical democratic practice. At the same time there is an urgent need to train students in the new qualitative methodologies.

We have been enormously gratified and heartened by the response to the *Handbook* since its publication. Especially gratifying has been that it has been used and adapted by such a wide variety of scholars and graduate students in precisely the way we had hoped: as a starting point, a springboard for new thought and new work.

The Paperback Project

The fourth edition of the *Handbook of Qualitative Research* is virtually all new. Over half of the authors from the first edition have been replaced by new contributors. Indeed there are 33 new chapter authors or co-authors. There are fifteen totally new chapter topics, including contributions on: mixed methods, the sacred and the spiritual, critical humanism and queer theory, Asian epistemologies, disability communities and transformative research, performance ethnography, participatory action inquiry, oral history focus groups in feminist research, applied ethnography, and anthropological poetics. All returning authors have substantially revised their original contributions, in many cases producing a totally new and different chapter.

A handbook, we were told by our publisher, should ideally represent the distillation of knowledge of a field, a benchmark volume that synthesizes an existing literature, helping to define and shape the present and future of that discipline. In metaphoric terms, if you were to take one book on qualitative research with you to a desert island (or for a comprehensive graduate examination), a handbook would be the book.

It was decided that the part structure of the *Handbook* could serve as useful point of departure for the organization of the paperbacks. Thus Volume 1, titled *The Landscape of Qualitative Research: Theories and Issues*, takes a look at the field from a broadly theoretical perspective, and is composed of the *Handbook*'s Parts I ("Locating the Field"), II ("Major Paradigms and Perspectives"), and VI ("The Future of Qualitative Research"). Volume 2, titled *Strategies of Qualitative Inquiry*, focuses on just that, and consists of Part III of the *Handbook*. Volume 3, titled *Collecting and Interpreting Qualitative Materials*, considers the tasks of collecting, analyzing, and interpreting empirical materials, and comprises the *Handbook*'s Parts IV ("Methods of Collecting and Analyzing Empirical Materials") and V ("The Art of Interpretation, Evaluation, and Presentation").

As with the first edition of the Landscape series, we decided that nothing should be cut from the original *Handbook*. Nearly everyone we spoke to who used the *Handbook* had his or her own way of using it, leaning heavily on certain chapters and skipping others altogether. But there was consensus that this reorganization made a great deal of sense both pedagogically and economically. We and Sage are committed to making this iteration of the *Handbook* accessible for classroom use. This commitment is reflected in the size, organization, and price of the paperbacks, as well as in the addition of end-of-book bibliographies.

It also became clear in our conversations with colleagues who used the *Handbook* that the single-volume, hard-cover version has a distinct place and value, and Sage will keep the original version available until a revised edition is published.

ORGANIZATION OF THIS VOLUME

Strategies of Qualitative Theory isolates the major strategies—historically, the research methods—that researchers can use in conducting concrete qualitative studies. The question of methods begins with questions of design and the matters of money and funding, issues discussed by Julianne Cheek. These questions always begin with a socially situated observer who moves from a research question to a paradigm or perspective, and then to the empirical world. So located, the researcher then addresses a range of methods that can be employed in any study. The history and uses of these strategies are explored extensively in this volume. The chapters move from forms (and problems with) mixed methods inquiry to case study, performance and narrative ethnography, to constructionist analytics to grounded theory strategies, testimonies, participatory action research, and clinical research.

Acknowledgments

This *Handbook* would not be without its authors, and the editorial board members who gave freely, often on very short notice, of their time, advice and ever courteous suggestions. We acknowledge *en masse* the support of the authors, and the editorial board members, whose names are listed facing the title page. These individuals were able to offer both long-term, sustained commitments to the project and short-term emergency assistance.

There are other debts, intensely personal and closer to home. The *Handbook* would never have been possible without the ever present help, support, wisdom, and encouragement of our editors and publishers at Sage: Michele Sordi, Vicki Knight, Sean Connelly, and Lauren Habib. Their grasp of this field, its history, and diversity is extraordinary. Their conceptions of what this project should look like were extremely valuable. Their energy kept us moving forward. Furthermore, whenever we confronted a problem Michele, Vicki and Lauren were there with their assistance and good natured humor.

We would also like to thank the following individuals, and institutions for their assistance, support, insights and patience: our respective universities, administrations and departments. In Urbana James Salvo, Melba Velez, Koeli Goel, and Katia Curbelo were the *sine qua non*. Their good-humor and grace kept our ever -growing files in order, and everyone on the same timetable. Without them, this project would never have been completed!

Laura Stewart at SAGE Publications helped move this project through production. We are extremely grateful to her, as well as to Stefanie Storholt and Naomi Linzer for their excellent work during the proofreading and indexing phases of production. Our spouses, Katherine Ryan and Egon Guba, helped keep us on track, listened to our complaints, and generally displayed extraordinary patience, forbearance and support.

Finally, there is another group of individuals who gave unstintingly of their time and energy to provide us with their expertise and thoughtful reviews when we needed additional guidance. Without the help of these individuals we would often have found ourselves with less than complete understandings of the various traditions, perspectives and methods represented in this volume. We would also like to acknowledge the important contributions of the following special readers to this project: Bryant Alexander, Susan Chase, Michele Fine, Susan Finley, Andrea Fontana, Jaber Gubrium, James Holstein, Alison Jones, Stacy Holman Jones, Tony Kuzel, Luis Miron, Ron Pelias, John Prosser, Johnny Saldana, Harry Torrance.

Norman K. Denzin
University of Illinois at Urbana-Champaign

Yvonna S. Lincoln
Texas A & M University
24 April 2012

About the Editors

Norman K. Denzin is Distinguished Professor of Communications, College of Communications Scholar, and Research Professor of Communications, Sociology and Humanities, at the University of Illinois, Urbana-Champaign. He is the author, editor, or coeditor of numerous books, including *The Qualitative Manifesto; Qualitative Inquiry Under Fire; Flags in the Window: Dispatches From the American War Zone; Searching for Yellowstone: Identity, Politics and Democracy in the New West; Performance Ethnography: Critical Pedagogy and the Politics of Culture; Screening Race: Hollywood and a Cinema of Racial Violence; Performing Ethnography;* and *9/11 in American Culture.* He is past editor of *The Sociological Quarterly;* coeditor of *The SAGE Handbook of Qualitative Research,* Fourth Edition; coeditor of *Qualitative Inquiry;* editor of *Cultural Studies <=> Critical Methodologies;* editor of *International Review of Qualitative Research,* editor of *Studies in Symbolic Interaction,* and founding President of the International Association of Qualitative Inquiry.

Yvonna S. Lincoln is Ruth Harrington Chair of Educational Leadership and Distinguished Professor of Higher Education at Texas A&M University, where she also serves as Program Chair for the higher education program area. She is the coeditor, with Norman K. Denzin, of the journal *Qualitative Inquiry,* and of the first and second, third and now fourth editions of *the SAGE Handbook of Qualitative Research* and the *Handbook of Critical and Indigenous Methodologies.* As well, she is the coauthor, editor, or coeditor of more than a half dozen other books and volumes. She has served as the President of the Association for the Study of Higher Education and the American Evaluation Association, and as the Vice President for Division J (Postsecondary Education) for the American Educational Research Association. She is the author or coauthor of more than 100 chapters and journal articles on aspects of higher education or qualitative research methods and methodologies. Her research interests include development of qualitative methods and methodologies, the status and future of research libraries, and other issues in higher education. And, she's fun.

About the Contributors

Mary Brydon-Miller, PhD, directs the University of Cincinnati's Action Research Center and is Professor of Educational Studies and Urban Educational Leadership in the College of Education, Criminal Justice, and Human Services. She is a participatory action researcher who engages in both community-based and educational-action research. She coedited the volumes *Traveling Companions: Feminism, Teaching, and Action Research* (with Patricia Maguire and Alice McIntyre), *From Subjects to Subjectivities: A Handbook of Interpretive and Participatory Methods* (with Deborah Tolman), and *Voices of Change: Participatory Research in the United States and Canada* (with Peter Park, Budd Hall, and Ted Jackson). Her other publications include work on participatory action research methods, academic writing in the social sciences, refugee resettlement, elder advocacy, and disability rights. Her current scholarship focuses on ethics and action research.

Kathy Charmaz is Professor of Sociology and Director of the Faculty Writing Program at Sonoma State University, a program she designed to help faculty complete their research and scholarly writing. She has written, coauthored, or coedited nine books including *Constructing Grounded Theory: A Practical Guide Through Qualitative Analysis,* which has been translated into Chinese, Japanese, Polish, and Portuguese and received a Critics' Choice Award from the American Educational Studies Association. Among her recent writings are two multi-authored books, *Developing Grounded Theory: The Second Generation,* and *Five Ways of Doing Qualitative Analysis: Phenomenological Psychology, Grounded Theory, Discourse Analysis, Narrative Research, and Intuitive Inquiry.* She served as the 2009–2010 president of the Society for the Study of Symbolic Interaction and has been an officer in several other professional societies. Kathy Charmaz gives many workshops on qualitative methods, grounded theory, and writing for publication around the globe.

Julianne Cheek is Professor at Atlantis Medical College, Oslo, Norway. She is an associate editor of *Qualitative Health Research,* a past coeditor of *Health: An*

Interdisciplinary Journal for the Social Study of Health, Illness and Medicine, and an editorial board member of a number of journals related to qualitative inquiry and/or social health. Julianne has attracted funding for many qualitative health-related projects. She has also reviewed funding applications for a number of funding schemes including the Australian Research Council and National Health and Medical Research Council. Her books, book chapters, and journal articles reflect her ongoing interest in qualitative inquiry and the politics of that inquiry as it relates to the world of health and social care. In addition, she has a long interest in the mentoring and development of qualitative inquirers, including the development of postdoctoral programs. In 2010, she had the honor of serving as the vice president of the International Association of Qualitative Inquiry, as well as on the advisory board of the International Congress of Qualitative Inquiry, held annually at the University of Illinois.

John W. Creswell is a Professor of Educational Psychology and teaches courses and writes about mixed methods research, qualitative methodology, and general research design. He has been at the University of Nebraska at Lincoln for 30 years and has authored 12 books, many of which focus on alternative types of research designs, comparisons of different qualitative methodologies, and the nature of and use of mixed methods research. His books are read around the world by audiences in the social sciences, education, and the health sciences. In addition, he has codirected for the last five years the Office of Qualitative and Mixed Methods Research at Nebraska that provides support for scholars incorporating qualitative and mixed methods research into projects for extramural funding. He serves as the founding coeditor for the *Journal of Mixed Methods Research,* and he has been an Adjunct Professor of Family Medicine at the University of Michigan and assisted investigators in the health sciences and education on the research methodology for National Institutes of Health and National Science Foundation projects. He is a Senior Fulbright Scholar to South Africa and lectured during 2008 at five universities to faculty in education and the health sciences.

Bent Flyvbjerg is BT Professor and Chair of Major Programme Management at Oxford University's Saïd Business School and Founding Director of Oxford's BT Centre for Major Programme Management. He works for better management of megaprojects and cities. He also writes about phronetic social science and case study research. Bent Flyvbjerg was twice a Visiting Fulbright Scholar to the United States, where he did research at UCLA, the University of California, Berkeley, and Harvard University. His books include *Making Social Science Matter, Rationality and Power, Megaprojects and Risk, and Decision-Making on Mega-Projects.* His books and articles have been translated into 18 languages and his research covered by *Science, The Economist,* the *Financial Times,* the *New York Times,* the BBC, NPR, and many other media. Bent Flyvbjerg has served as adviser to the United Nations, the EU Commission, and government and business in many countries.

Jaber E. Gubrium is Professor and Chair of Sociology at the University of Missouri. He has had a long-standing program of research on the social organization of care in human service institutions and pioneered in the reconceptualization of qualitative methods and the development of narrative analysis. His publications include numerous books and articles on aging, the life course, medicalization, and representational practice in therapeutic context. Collaborating for over 25 years, Gubrium and James Holstein have authored and edited dozens of books, including *Analyzing Narrative Reality, The New Language of Qualitative Method, The Active Interview, Handbook of Constructionist Research, Handbook of Interview Research, The Self We Live By, Constructing the Life Course, and What is Family?*

Judith Hamera is Professor and Head of the Department of Performance Studies at Texas A&M University. Her scholarship is interdisciplinary, contributing to American, communication, and cultural studies, as well as performance studies. Her most recent book is the *Cambridge Companion to American Travel Writing* (2009), coedited with Alfred Bendixen; and she has completed a monograph examining the cultural work of the American home aquarium, to be published by the University of Michigan Press. She is the author of *Dancing Communities: Performance, Difference and Connection in the Global City* (2007), which received the Book of the Year award from the National Communication Association's Ethnography Division. Other books are *Opening Acts: Performance In/As Communication and Cultural Studies* (2006); and, coedited with D. Soyini Madison, *The SAGE Handbook of Performance Studies* (2006). Her essays have appeared in *Communication and Critical/Cultural Studies, Cultural Studies, TDR: The Drama Review, Modern Drama, Text and Performance Quarterly, Theatre Topics,* and *Women and Language.*

James A. Holstein is Professor of Sociology in the Department of Social and Cultural Sciences at Marquette University. His research and writing projects have addressed social problems, deviance and social control, family, and the self, all approached from an ethnomethodologically informed, constructionist perspective. His publications include numerous books and articles on qualitative research methods. Collaborating for over 25 years, Holstein and Jaber Gubrium have authored and edited dozens of books, including *Analyzing Narrative Reality, The New Language of Qualitative Method, The Active Interview, Handbook of*

Constructionist Research, Handbook of Interview Research, The Self We Live By, Constructing the Life Course, and *What is Family?*

Michael Kral, PhD, is Assistant Professor of Psychology and Anthropology at University of Illinois at Urbana-Champaign, and in the Department of Psychiatry, University of Toronto. He works primarily with Inuit in Arctic Canada on suicide prevention, community wellness, and community-based participatory action research. He has coedited *Suicide in Canada* (with Antoon Leenaars, Susanne Wenkstern, Isaac Sakinofsky, Ron Dyck, and Roger Bland), *About Psychology: Essays at the Crossroads of History, Theory, and Philosophy* (with Darryl Hill), and a special issue of the *American Journal of Community Psychology* (with Mark Aber and Jorge Ramirez Garcia) on culture and community psychology. Michael's current research is on indigenous youth resilience in the circumpolar north, indigenous community action and success stories, and urban indigenous well-being.

Antjie Krog is teaching at the University of Western Cape, South Africa. She has published 12 poetry volumes and 3 nonfiction books in English: *Country of my Skull,* on the South African Truth and Reconciliation Commission; *A Change of Tongue,* about the transformation in South Africa after 10 years of democracy; and recently *Begging to be Black,* about living with a Black majority. Krog has been awarded all the main prizes available in South Africa for poetry and nonfiction, as well as the Hiroshima Foundation Award for Peace and Culture (2000); the Open Society Prize (2006) from the Central European University (previous winners were Jürgen Habermas and Vaclav Havel); and a research fellowship at Wissenschaftskolleg zu Berlin in 2007–2008.

Patricia Maguire, EdD, Professor of Education and Counseling, is the Chairperson of Western New Mexico University, Gallup Graduate Studies Center. She has worked as a school and mental health counselor, international development trainer (Africa, Jamaica), and community activist. Since 1987, Maguire has been a member of a collaborative team developing transformative-oriented graduate education programs in a rural community on the edge of the Navajo Nation and Pueblo of Zuni. Her networking, research, and publication interests include the interface between feminisms and participatory action research and teacher action research, building on her 1987 book, *Doing Participatory Research: A Feminist Approach* and *Traveling Companions: Feminism, Teaching, and Action Research* (2004), coedited with Mary-Brydon Miller and Alice McIntyre. Maguire's activist interests include working against sexual and interpersonal violence, supporting community efforts to address hunger and food insecurity, and promoting transformative teacher action research.

Janice M. Morse, PhD (Nursing), PhD (Anthropology), FAAN, is a Professor and Presidential Endowed Chair at the University of Utah College of Nursing, and Professor Emeritus, University of Alberta, Canada. She was the founding director of the International Institute for Qualitative Methodology (IIQM, 1997–2007), University of Alberta; founding editor for the *International Journal of Qualitative Methods;* and since 1991 has served as the founding editor for *Qualitative Health Research.* Morse is the recipient of the Episteme Award (Sigma Theta Tau) and honorary doctorates from the University of Newcastle (Australia) and Athabasca University (Canada). She is the author of 370 articles and 15 books on qualitative research methods, suffering, comforting, and patient falls. Her most recent book (with Linda Niehaus) is *Mixed Method Design: Principles and Procedures* (2009).

Susan Noffke is Associate Professor of Curriculum & Instruction at the University of Illinois at Urbana-Champaign. She taught in public elementary and middle schools for a decade, and has led preservice and inservice teachers and doctoral students in courses in action research for the past 25 years. She has also worked with teachers in school-based action research projects, and has used action research to study her own practice as a teacher educator. Her major scholarship has addressed the history of action research, its existing and theoretical foundations, international variations, as well as studies using action research in community school settings.

Anu Sabhlok, PhD, is Assistant Professor of Humanities and Social Sciences at the Indian Institute of Science Education and Research in Mohali, India. She is also deeply involved with a local NGO, CEVA: Center for Education and Voluntary Action where she integrates her work on gender, education, and urban environments with community concerns related to social and economic development. As part of her dissertation research on disaster-relief, she volunteered with SEWA (Self-Employed Women's Association) in Gujarat, India, and conducted community-based research in order to address issues of identity and justice. Her previous training is as an architect and her design works to embody the participatory ethic.

Abbas Tashakkori (PhD, Social Psychology, University of North Carolina at Chapel Hill) is a Professor and Chair of Educational Psychology Department at the University of North Texas, Denton. He has been a Mellon Post-Doctoral Fellow of the Carolina Population Center and a faculty member at various universities in the United States and abroad for almost three decades. He has published more than 70 articles and book chapters, and authored or edited five books, including the *Handbook of Mixed Methods in the Social & Behavioral Research* (2nd ed., 2010, with Charles Teddlie). He has a rich and diverse history of research, program evaluation, and writing on attitude change, self-perceptions and efficacy, planning and evaluation of school improvement programs, and utilization of mixed methods in educational, social, and behavioral research.

Charles Teddlie (PhD, Social Psychology, University of North Carolina at Chapel Hill) is a Distinguished Professor Emeritus in the College of Education at Louisiana State University. He has been an investigator on several mixed methods research studies internationally and in the United States. Professor Teddlie has taught research methods courses for over 25 years, including statistics, qualitative methods, and mixed methods and was awarded the Excellence in Teaching Award from the LSU College of Education. He has been the co-owner and evaluation director of K. T. Associates, a consulting company specializing in mixed methods research and evaluation, since 1986. He has produced numerous articles and chapters in education, psychology, and evaluation and coauthored or coedited a dozen books including two editions of the *Handbook of Mixed Methods Research in Social & Behavioral Research* (2003, 2010) and *Foundations of Mixed Methods Research* (2009) with Abbas Tashakkori.

Barbara Tedlock is Distinguished Professor of Anthropology at the State University of New York at Buffalo. She served as editor-in-chief of the *American Anthropologist* (1993–1998). She received the 2003 SUNY Chancellor's Research Recognition Award for "Overall Excellence of Research in the Social Sciences." Tedlock is a former president of the Society for Humanistic Anthropology and a member of PEN (Poets-Essayists-Novelists). Her publications include six books and more than 120 articles and essays.

Introduction

The Discipline and Practice of Qualitative Research

Norman K. Denzin and Yvonna S. Lincoln

The global community of qualitative researchers is midway between two extremes, searching for a new middle, moving in several different directions at the same time.[1] Mixed methodologies and calls for scientifically based research, on the one side, renewed calls for social justice inquiry from the critical social science tradition on the other. In the methodological struggles of the 1970s and 1980s, the very existence of qualitative research was at issue. In the new paradigm war, "every overtly social justice-oriented approach to research . . . is threatened with de-legitimization by the government-sanctioned, exclusivist assertion of positivism . . . as the 'gold standard' of educational research" (Wright, 2006, pp. 799–800).

The evidence-based research movement, with its fixed standards and guidelines for conducting and evaluating qualitative inquiry, sought total domination: one shoe fits all (Cannella & Lincoln, Chapter 5, volume 1; Lincoln, 2010). The heart of the matter turns on issues surrounding the politics and ethics of evidence and the value of qualitative work in addressing matters of equity and social justice (Torrance, Chapter 11, volume 3).

In this introductory chapter, we define the field of qualitative research, then navigate, chart, and review the history of qualitative research in the human disciplines. This will allow us to locate this handbook and its contents within their historical moments. (These historical moments are somewhat artificial; they are socially constructed, quasi-historical, and overlapping conventions. Nevertheless, they permit a "performance" of developing ideas. They also facilitate an increasing sensitivity to and sophistication about the pitfalls and promises of ethnography and qualitative research.) A conceptual framework for reading the qualitative research act as a multicultural, gendered process is presented.

We then provide a brief introduction to the chapters, concluding with a brief discussion of qualitative research. We will also discuss the threats to qualitative human-subject research from the methodological conservatism movement, which was noted in our Preface. As indicated there, we use the metaphor of the bridge to structure what follows. This volume provides a bridge between historical moments, politics, the decolonization project, research methods, paradigms, and communities of interpretive scholars.

History, Politics, and Paradigms

To better understand where we are today and to better grasp current criticisms, it is useful to return to the so-called paradigm wars of the 1980s, which resulted in the serious crippling of quantitative research in education. Critical pedagogy, critical theorists, and feminist analyses fostered struggles to acquire power and cultural capital for the poor, non-whites, women, and gays (Gage, 1989).

Charles Teddlie and Abbas Tashakkori's history is helpful here. They expand the time frame of the 1980s war to embrace at least three paradigm wars, or periods of conflict: the postpositivist-constructivist war against positivism (1970–1990); the conflict between competing postpositivist, constructivist, and critical theory paradigms (1990–2005); and the current conflict between evidence-based methodologists and the mixed methods, interpretive, and critical theory schools (2005–present).[2]

Egon Guba's (1990a) *The Paradigm Dialog* signaled an end to the 1980s wars. Postpositivists, constructivists, and critical theorists talked to one another, working through issues connected to ethics, field studies, praxis, criteria, knowledge accumulation, truth, significance, graduate training, values, and politics. By the early 1990s, there was an explosion of published work on qualitative research; handbooks and new journals appeared. Special interest groups committed to particular paradigms appeared, some with their own journals.[3]

The second paradigm conflict occurred within the mixed methods community and involved disputes "between individuals convinced of the 'paradigm purity' of their own position" (Teddlie & Tashakkori, 2003b, p. 7). Purists extended and repeated the argument that quantitative and qualitative methods and postpositivism and the other "isms" cannot be combined because of the differences between their underlying paradigm assumptions. On the methodological front, the incompatibility thesis was challenged by those who invoked triangulation as a way of combining multiple methods to study the same phenomenon (Teddlie & Tashakkori, 2003a, p. 7). This ushered in a new round of arguments and debates over paradigm superiority.

A soft, apolitical pragmatic paradigm emerged in the post-1990 period. Suddenly, quantitative and qualitative methods became compatible, and researchers could use both in their empirical inquiries (Teddlie & Tashakkori, 2003a, p. 7). Proponents made appeals to a "what works" pragmatic argument, contending that "no incompatibility between quantitative and qualitative methods exists at either the level of practice or that of epistemology . . . there are thus no good reasons for educational researchers to fear forging ahead with 'what works'" (Howe, 1988, p. 16). Of course, what works is more than an empirical question. It involves the politics of evidence.

This is the space that evidence-based research entered. It became the battleground of the third war, "the current upheaval and argument about 'scientific' research in the scholarly world of education" (Clark & Scheurich, 2008; Scheurich & Clark, 2006, p. 401). Enter Teddlie and Tashakkori's third moment: Mixed methods and evidence-based inquiry meet one another in a soft center. C. Wright Mills (1959) would say this is a space for abstracted empiricism. Inquiry is cut off from politics. Biography and history recede into the background. Technological rationality prevails.

RESISTANCES TO QUALITATIVE STUDIES

The academic and disciplinary resistances to qualitative research illustrate the politics embedded in this field of discourse. The challenges to qualitative research are many. To better understand these criticisms, it is necessary to "distinguish analytically the political (or external) role of [qualitative] methodology from the procedural (or internal) one" (Seale, Gobo, Gubrium, & Silverman, 2004, p. 7). Politics situate methodology within and outside the academy. Procedural issues define how qualitative methodology is used to produce knowledge about the world (Seale et al., 2004, p. 7).

Often, the political and the procedural intersect. Politicians and hard scientists call qualitative researchers *journalists* or "soft" scientists. Their work is termed unscientific, only exploratory, or subjective. It is called criticism and not theory, or it is interpreted politically, as a disguised version of Marxism or secular humanism (see Huber, 1995; also Denzin, 1997, pp. 258–261).

These political and procedural resistances reflect an uneasy awareness that the interpretive traditions of qualitative research commit one to a critique of the positivist or postpositivist project. But the positivist resistance to qualitative research goes beyond the "ever-present desire to maintain a distinction between hard science and soft scholarship" (Carey, 1989, p. 99). The experimental (positivist) sciences (physics, chemistry, economics, and psychology, for example) are often seen as the crowning achievements of Western civilization, and in their practices, it is assumed that "truth" can transcend opinion and personal bias (Carey, 1989, p. 99; Schwandt, 1997b, p. 309). Qualitative research is seen as an assault on this tradition, whose adherents often retreat into a "value-free objectivist science" (Carey, 1989, p. 104) model to defend their position. The positivists seldom attempt to make explicit, and critique the "moral and political commitments in their own contingent work" (Carey, 1989, p. 104; Lincoln, Lynham, & Guba, Chapter 6, volume 1).

Positivists further allege that the so-called new experimental qualitative researchers write fiction, not science, and have no way of verifying their truth statements. Ethnographic poetry and fiction signal the death of empirical science, and there is little to be gained by attempting to engage in moral criticism. These critics presume a stable, unchanging reality that can be studied with the empirical methods of objective social science (see Huber, 1995). The province of qualitative research, accordingly, is the world of lived experience, for this is where individual belief and action intersect with culture. Under this model, there is no preoccupation with discourse and method as material interpretive practices that constitute representation and description. This is the textual, narrative turn rejected by the positivists.

The opposition to positive science by the poststructuralists is seen, then, as an attack on reason and truth. At the same time, the positivist science attack on qualitative research is regarded as an attempt to legislate one version of truth over another.

THE LEGACIES OF SCIENTIFIC RESEARCH

Writing about scientific research, including qualitative research, from the vantage point of the colonized, a position that she chooses to privilege, Linda Tuhiwai Smith states that "the term 'research' is inextricably linked to European imperialism and colonialism." She continues, "the word itself is probably one of the dirtiest words in the indigenous world's vocabulary . . . It is "implicated in the worst excesses of colonialism" (p. 1), with the ways in which "knowledge about indigenous peoples was collected, classified, and then represented back to the West" (Smith, 1999, p. 1). This dirty word stirs up anger, silence, distrust. "It is so powerful that indigenous people even write poetry about research " (Smith, 1999, p. 1). It is one of colonialism's most sordid legacies, she says.

Frederick Erickson's Chapter 3 of volume 1 charts many key features of this painful history. He notes with some irony that qualitative research in sociology and anthropology was born out of concern to understand the exotic, often dark-skinned "other." Of course, there were colonialists long before there were anthropologists and ethnographers. Nonetheless, there would be no colonial— and now no neo-colonial—history, were it not for this investigative mentality that turned the dark-skinned other into the object of the ethnographer's gaze. From the very beginning, qualitative research was implicated in a racist project.[4]

Definitional Issues

Qualitative research is a field of inquiry in its own right. It crosscuts disciplines, fields, and subject matter.[5] A complex, interconnected family of terms, concepts, and assumptions surrounds the term. These include the traditions associated with foundationalism, positivism, postfoundationalism, postpositivism, post-structuralism, postmodernism, post-humanism, and the many qualitative research perspectives and methods connected to cultural and interpretive studies.[6] There are separate and detailed literatures on the many methods and approaches that fall under the category of qualitative research, such as case study, politics and ethics, participatory inquiry, interviewing, participant observation, visual methods, and interpretive analysis.

In North America, qualitative research operates in a complex historical field that crosscuts at least eight historical moments. These moments overlap and simultaneously operate in the present.[7] We define them as the traditional (1900–1950), the modernist or golden age (1950–1970), blurred genres (1970–1986), the crisis of representation (1986–1990), the postmodern, a period of experimental and new ethnographies (1990–1995), postexperimental inquiry (1995–2000), the methodologically contested present (2000–2010), and the future (2010–), which is now. The future, the eighth moment, confronts the methodological backlash associated with the evidence-based social movement. It is concerned with moral discourse, with the development of sacred textualities. The eighth moment asks that the social sciences and the humanities become sites for

critical conversations about democracy, race, gender, class, nation-states, globalization, freedom, and community.[8]

The postmodern and postexperimental moments were defined in part by a
concern for literary and rhetorical tropes and the narrative turn, a concern for
storytelling, for composing ethnographies in new ways (Ellis, 2009; and in this
volume, Hamera, Chapter 6; Tedlock, Chapter 7; Spry, Chapter 7, volume 3; Ellingson, Chapter 13, volume 3; St.Pierre, Chapter 14, volume 3; and Pelias, Chapter 17, volume 3).

Successive waves of epistemological theorizing move across these eight
moments. The traditional period is associated with the positivist, foundational
paradigm. The modernist or golden age and blurred genres moments are connected to the appearance of postpositivist arguments. At the same time, a variety
of new interpretive, qualitative perspectives were taken up, including hermeneutics, structuralism, semiotics, phenomenology, cultural studies, and feminism.[9]
In the blurred genre phase, the humanities became central resources for critical,
interpretive theory and the qualitative research project broadly conceived. The
researcher became a *bricoleur* (as discussed later), learning how to borrow from
many different disciplines.

The blurred genres phase produced the next stage, the crisis of representation.
Here researchers struggled with how to locate themselves and their subjects in reflexive texts. A kind of methodological diaspora took place, a two-way exodus. Human-
ists migrated to the social sciences, searching for new social theory and new ways to
study popular culture and its local ethnographic contexts. Social scientists turned to
the humanities, hoping to learn how to do complex structural and poststructural
readings of social texts. From the humanities, social scientists also learned how to
produce texts that refused to be read in simplistic, linear, incontrovertible terms. The
line between a text and a context blurred. In the postmodern experimental moment,
researchers continued to move away from foundational and quasifoundational criteria (in this volume, see Altheide & Johnson, Chapter 12, volume 3; St.Pierre, Chapter 14, volume 3). Alternative evaluative criteria were sought, ones that might prove
evocative, moral, critical, and rooted in local understandings.

Any definition of qualitative research must work within this complex historical field. Qualitative research means different things in each of these moments.
Nonetheless, an initial, generic definition can be offered. *Qualitative research* is a
situated activity that locates the observer in the world. Qualitative research consists of a set of interpretive, material practices that make the world visible. These
practices transform the world. They turn the world into a series of representations, including fieldnotes, interviews, conversations, photographs, recordings,
and memos to the self. At this level, qualitative research involves an interpretive,

naturalistic approach to the world. This means that qualitative researchers study things in their natural settings, attempting to make sense of or interpret phenomena in terms of the meanings people bring to them.[10]

Qualitative research involves the studied use and collection of a variety of empirical materials—case study, personal experience, introspection, life story, interview, artifacts, and cultural texts and productions, along with observational, historical, interactional, and visual texts—that describe routine and problematic moments and meanings in individuals' lives. Accordingly, qualitative researchers deploy a wide-range of interconnected interpretive practices, hoping always to get a better understanding of the subject matter at hand. It is understood, however, that each practice makes the world visible in a different way. Hence, there is frequently a commitment to using more than one interpretive practice in any study.

The Qualitative Researcher-as-Bricoleur and Quilt Maker

Multiple gendered images may be brought to the qualitative researcher: scientist, naturalist, fieldworker, journalist, social critic, artist, performer, jazz musician, filmmaker, quilt maker, essayist. The many methodological practices of qualitative research may be viewed as soft science, journalism, ethnography, *bricolage*, quilt making, or montage. The researcher, in turn, may be seen as a *bricoleur*, as a maker of quilts, or in filmmaking, a person who assembles images into montages (on montage, see Cook, 1981, pp. 171–177; Monaco, 1981, pp. 322–328; and discussion below; on quilting, see hooks, 1990, pp. 115–122; Wolcott, 1995, pp. 31–33).

Douglas Harper (1987, pp. 9, 74–75, 92); Michel de Certeau (1984, p. xv); Cary Nelson, Paula A. Treichler, and Lawrence Grossberg (1992, p. 2); Claude Lévi-Strauss (1962/1966, p. 17); Deena and Michael Weinstein (1991, p. 161); and Joe L. Kincheloe (2001) clarify the meaning of bricolage and bricoleur.[11] A bricoleur makes do by "adapting the bricoles of the world. Bricolage is 'the poetic making do'" (de Certeau, 1984, p. xv), with "such bricoles—the odds and ends, the bits left over" (Harper, 1987, p. 74). The bricoleur is a "Jack of all trades, a kind of professional do-it-yourself[er]" (Lévi-Strauss, 1962/1966, p. 17). In Harper's (1987) work, the bricoleur defines herself and extends herself (p. 75). Indeed, her life story, her biography, "may be thought of as bricolage" (Harper, 1987, p. 92).

There are many kinds of bricoleurs—interpretive, narrative, theoretical, political. The interpretive bricoleur produces a bricolage; that is, a pieced-together set of representations that are fitted to the specifics of a complex situation. "The solution (bricolage) which is the result of the bricoleur's method is an [emergent] construction" (Weinstein & Weinstein, 1991, p. 161), which changes and takes new forms as different tools, methods, and techniques of representation and interpretation are added to the puzzle. Nelson et al. (1992) describe the methodology of cultural studies "as a bricolage. Its choice of practice, that is, is pragmatic, strategic, and self-reflexive" (p. 2). This understanding can be applied, with qualifications, to qualitative research.

The qualitative-researcher-as-bricoleur or a maker of quilts uses the aesthetic and material tools of his or her craft, deploying whatever strategies, methods, or empirical materials are at hand (Becker, 1998, p. 2). If new tools or techniques have to be invented or pieced together, then the researcher will do this. The choice of which interpretive practices to employ is not necessarily set in advance. The "choice of research practices depends upon the questions that are asked, and the questions depend on their context" (Nelson et al., 1992, p. 2), what is available in the context, and what the researcher can do in that setting.

These interpretive practices involve aesthetic issues, an aesthetics of representation that goes beyond the pragmatic or the practical. Here the concept of *montage* is useful (see Cook, 1981, p. 323; Monaco, 1981, pp. 171–172). Montage is a method of editing cinematic images. In the history of cinematography, montage is associated with the work of Sergei Eisenstein, especially his film, *The Battleship Potemkin* (1925). In montage, a picture is made by superimposing several different images on one another. In a sense, montage is like *pentimento,* where something painted out of a picture (an image the painter "repented," or denied) now becomes visible again, creating something new. What is new is what had been obscured by a previous image.

Montage and pentimento, like jazz, which is improvisation, create the sense that images, sounds, and understandings are blending together, overlapping, and forming a composite, a new creation. The images seem to shape and define one another; an emotional gestalt effect is produced. Often, these images are combined in a swiftly run sequence. When done, this produces a dizzily revolving collection of several images around a central or focused picture or sequence; such effects signify the passage of time.

Perhaps the most famous instance of montage is given in the Odessa Steps sequence in *The Battleship Potemkin.*[12] In the climax of the film, the citizens of Odessa are being massacred by tsarist troops on the stone steps leading down to the city's harbor. Eisenstein cuts to a young mother as she pushes her baby's carriage across the landing in front of the firing troops. Citizens rush past her, jolting the carriage, which she is afraid to push down to the next flight of stairs. The troops are above her firing at the citizens. She is trapped between the troops and the steps. She screams. A line of rifles pointing to the sky erupts in smoke. The mother's head sways back. The wheels of the carriage teeter on the edge of the steps. The mother's hand clutches the silver buckle of her belt. Below her, people are being beaten by soldiers. Blood drips over the mother's white gloves. The baby's hand reaches out of the carriage. The mother sways back and forth. The troops advance. The mother falls back against the carriage. A woman watches in horror as the rear wheels of the carriage roll off the edge of the landing. With accelerating speed, the carriage bounces down the steps, past the dead citizens. The baby is jostled from side to side inside the carriage. The soldiers fire their rifles into a group of wounded citizens. A student screams, as the carriage leaps across the steps, tilts, and overturns (Cook, 1981, p. 167).[13]

Montage uses sparse images to create a clearly defined sense of urgency and complexity. Montage invites viewers to construct interpretations that build on one another as a scene unfolds. These interpretations are built on associations based on the contrasting images that blend into one another. The underlying assumption of montage is that viewers perceive and interpret the shots in a "montage sequence not *sequentially,* or one at a time, but rather *simultaneously*" (Cook, 1981, p. 172, italics in original). The viewer puts the sequences together into a meaningful emotional whole, as if at a glance, all at once.

The qualitative researcher who uses montage is like a quilt maker or a jazz improviser. The quilter stitches, edits, and puts slices of reality together. This process creates and brings psychological and emotional unity to an interpretive experience. There are many examples of montage in current qualitative research. Using multiple voices and different textual formations, voices, and narrative styles, Marcelo Diversi and Claudio Moreira (2009) weave a complex text about race, identity, nation, class, sexuality, intimacy, and family. As in quilt making and jazz improvisation, many different things are going on at the same time: different voices, different perspectives, points of views, angles of vision. Autoethnographic performance texts use montage simultaneously to create and enact moral meaning. They move from the personal to the political, the local to the historical and the cultural. These are dialogical texts. They presume an active audience. They create spaces for give and take between reader and writer. They do more than turn the other into the object of the social science gaze (in volume 3, see Spry, Chapter 7; Pelias, Chapter 17).

Of course, qualitative research is inherently multimethod in focus (Flick, 2002, pp. 226–227; 2007). However, the use of multiple methods, or triangulation, reflects an attempt to secure an in-depth understanding of the phenomenon in question. Objective reality can never be captured. We know a thing only through its representations. Triangulation is not a tool or a strategy of validation but an alternative to validation (Flick, 2002, p. 227; 2007). The combination of multiple methodological practices, empirical materials, perspectives, and observers in a single study is best understood, then, as a strategy that adds rigor, breadth complexity, richness, and depth to any inquiry (see Flick, 2002, p. 229; 2007, pp. 102–104).

Laura L. Ellingson (Chapter 13, volume 3; also 2009) disputes a narrow conception of triangulation, endorsing instead a postmodern form (2009, p. 190). It asserts that the central image for qualitative inquiry is the crystal—multiple lenses—not the triangle. She sees crystallization as embodying an energizing, unruly discourse, drawing raw energy from artful science and scientific artwork (p. 190). Mixed-genre texts in the postexperimental moment have more than three sides. Like crystals, Eisenstein's montage, the jazz solo, or the pieces in a quilt, the mixed-genre text combines "symmetry and substance with an infinite variety of shapes, substances, transmutations . . . crystals grow, change, alter . . . crystals are prisms that reflect externalities and refract within themselves, creating different colors, patterns, arrays, casting off in different directions" (Richardson, 2000, p. 934).

In the crystallization process, the writer tells the same tale from different points of view. Crystallized projects mix genres and writing formats, offering partial, situated, open-ended conclusions. In *Fires in the Mirror* (1993) Anna Deavere Smith presents a series of performance pieces based on interviews with people involved in a racial conflict in Crown Heights, Brooklyn, on August 19, 1991. Her play has multiple speaking parts, including conversations with gang members, the police, and anonymous young girls and boys. There is no correct telling of this event. Each telling, like light hitting a crystal, gives a different reflection of the racial incident.

Viewed as a crystalline form, as a montage, or as a creative performance around a central theme, triangulation as a form of, or alternative to, validity thus can be extended. Triangulation is the display of multiple, refracted realities simultaneously. Each of the metaphors "works" to create simultaneity rather than the sequential or linear. Readers and audiences are then invited to explore competing visions of the context, to become immersed in and merge with new realities to comprehend.

The methodological bricoleur is adept at performing a large number of diverse tasks, ranging from interviewing to intensive self-reflection and introspection. The theoretical bricoleur reads widely and is knowledgeable about the many interpretive paradigms (feminism, Marxism, cultural studies, constructivism, queer theory) that can be brought to any particular problem. He or she may not, however, feel that paradigms can be mingled or synthesized. If paradigms are overarching philosophical systems denoting particular ontologies, epistemologies, and methodologies, one cannot move easily from one to the other. Paradigms represent belief systems that attach the user to a particular worldview. Perspectives, in contrast, are less well developed systems, and it can be easier to move between them. The researcher-as-bricoleur-theorist works between and within competing and overlapping perspectives and paradigms.

The interpretive bricoleur understands that research is an interactive process shaped by one's personal history, biography, gender, social class, race, and ethnicity and those of the people in the setting. Critical bricoleurs stress the dialectical and hermeneutic nature of interdisciplinary inquiry, knowing that the boundaries between traditional disciplines no longer hold (Kincheloe, 2001, p. 683). The political bricoleur knows that science is power, for all research findings have political implications. There is no value-free science. A civic social science based on a politics of hope is sought (Lincoln, 1999). The gendered, narrative bricoleur also knows that researchers all tell stories about the worlds they have studied. Thus, the narratives or stories scientists tell are accounts couched and framed within specific storytelling traditions, often defined as paradigms (e.g., positivism, postpositivism, constructivism).

The product of the interpretive bricoleur's labor is a complex, quilt-like bricolage, a reflexive collage or montage; a set of fluid, interconnected images and representations. This interpretive structure is like a quilt, a performance text, or a sequence of representations connecting the parts to the whole.

Qualitative Research as a Site of Multiple Interpretive Practices

Qualitative research, as a set of interpretive activities, privileges no single methodological practice over another. As a site of discussion or discourse, qualitative research is difficult to define clearly. It has no theory or paradigm that is distinctly its own. Multiple theoretical paradigms claim use of qualitative research methods and strategies, from constructivism to cultural studies, feminism, Marxism, and ethnic models of study. Qualitative research is used in many separate disciplines, as we will discuss below. It does not belong to a single discipline.

Nor does qualitative research have a distinct set of methods or practices that are entirely its own. Qualitative researchers use semiotics, narrative, content, discourse, archival, and phonemic analysis—even statistics, tables, graphs, and numbers. They also draw on and use the approaches, methods, and techniques of ethnomethodology, phenomenology, hermeneutics, feminism, rhizomatics, deconstructionism, ethnographies, interviews, psychoanalysis, cultural studies, survey research, and participant observation, among others.[14] All of these research practices "can provide important insights and knowledge" (Nelson et al., 1992, p. 2). No specific method or practice can be privileged over another.

Many of these methods or research practices are used in other contexts in the human disciplines. Each bears the traces of its own disciplinary history. Thus, there is an extensive history of the uses and meanings of ethnography and ethnology in education (Erickson, Chapter 3, volume 1); of participant observation and ethnography in anthropology (Tedlock, Chapter 7, this volume); sociology (Holstein & Gubrium, Chapter 8, this volume); communications (in this volume, Hamera, Chapter 6; Spry, Chapter 7, volume 3); cultural studies (Giardina & Newman, Chapter 10, volume 1); textual, hermeneutic, feminist, psychoanalytic, arts-based, semiotic, and narrative analysis in cinema and literary studies (in volume 1, Olesen, Chapter 7; Chase, Chapter 2, volume 3; Finley, Chapter 3, volume 3); and narrative, discourse, and conversational analysis in sociology, medicine, communications, and education (in this volume, Chase, Chapter 2, volume 3; Peräkylä & Ruusuvuori, Chapter 9, volume 3).

The many histories that surround each method or research strategy reveal how multiple uses and meanings are brought to each practice. Textual analyses in literary studies, for example, often treat texts as self-contained systems. On the other hand, a cultural studies or feminist perspective reads a text in terms of its location within a historical moment marked by a particular gender, race, or class ideology. A cultural studies use of ethnography would bring a set of understandings from feminism, postmodernism, and poststructuralism to the project. These understandings would not be shared by mainstream postpositivist sociologists. Similarly, postpositivist and poststructural historians bring different understandings and uses to the methods and findings of historical research. These tensions and contradictions are evident in many of the chapters in this handbook.

These separate and multiple uses and meanings of the methods of qualitative research make it difficult to agree on any essential definition of the field, for it is never just one thing.[15] Still, a definition must be made. We borrow from and paraphrase Nelson et al.'s (1992, p. 4) attempt to define cultural studies:

> Qualitative research is an interdisciplinary, transdiciplinary, and sometimes counterdisciplinary field. It crosscuts the humanities, as well as the social and the physical sciences. Qualitative research is many things at the same time. It is multiparadigmatic in focus. Its practitioners are sensitive to the value of the multimethod approach. They are committed to the naturalistic

perspective and to the interpretive understanding of human experience. At the same time, the field is inherently political and shaped by multiple ethical and political positions.

Qualitative research embraces two tensions at the same time. On the one hand, it is drawn to a broad, interpretive, postexperimental, postmodern, feminist, and critical sensibility. On the other hand, it is drawn to more narrowly defined positivist, postpositivist, humanistic, and naturalistic conceptions of human experience and its analysis. Furthermore, these tensions can be combined in the same project, bringing both postmodern and naturalistic, or both critical and humanistic, perspectives to bear.

This rather awkward statement means that qualitative research is a set of complex interpretive practices. As a constantly shifting historical formation, it embraces tensions and contradictions, including disputes over its methods and the forms its findings and interpretations take. The field sprawls between and crosscuts all of the human disciplines, even including, in some cases, the physical sciences. Its practitioners are variously committed to modern, postmodern, and postexperimental sensibilities and the approaches to social research that these sensibilities imply.

POLITICS AND REEMERGENT SCIENTISM

In the first decade of this new century, the scientifically based research movement (SBR) initiated by the National Research Council (NRC) created a new and hostile political environment for qualitative research (Howe, 2009). Connected to the No Child Left Behind Act of 2001 (NCLB), SBR embodied a reemergent scientism (Maxwell, 2004), a positivist evidence-based epistemology. Researchers are encouraged to employ "rigorous, systematic, and objective methodology to obtain reliable and valid knowledge" (Ryan & Hood, 2004, p. 80). The preferred methodology has well-defined causal models using independent and dependent variables. Causal models are examined in the context of randomized controlled experiments, which allow replication and generalization (Ryan & Hood, 2004, p. 81).

Under this framework, qualitative research becomes suspect. There are no well-defined variables or causal models. Observations and measurements are not based on random assignment to experimental groups. Hard evidence is not generated by these methods. At best, case study, interview, and ethnographic methods offer descriptive materials that can be tested with experimental methods. The epistemologies of critical race, queer, postcolonial, feminist, and postmodern theories are rendered useless, relegated at best to the category of scholarship, not science (Ryan & Hood, 2004, p. 81; St.Pierre & Roulston, 2006, p. 132).

Critics of the evidence movement are united on the following points. The movement endorses a narrow view of science (Lather, 2004; Maxwell, 2004), celebrating a "neoclassical experimentalism that is a throwback to the Campbell-Stanley era and its dogmatic adherence to an exclusive reliance on quantitative methods" (Howe, 2004, p. 42). There is "nostalgia for a simple and ordered universe of science that never was" (Popkewitz, 2004, p. 62). With its emphasis on only one form of scientific rigor, the NRC ignores the need for and value of complex historical, contextual, and political criteria for evaluating inquiry (Bloch, 2004).

Neoclassical experimentalists extol evidence-based "medical research as the model for educational research, particularly the random clinical trial" (Howe, 2004, p. 48). But the random clinical trial—dispensing a pill—is quite unlike "dispensing a curriculum" (Howe, 2004, p. 48), nor can the "effects" of the educational experiment be easily measured, unlike a "10-point reduction in diastolic blood pressure" (Howe, 2004, p. 48).

Qualitative researchers must learn to think outside the box as they critique the NRC and its methodological guidelines (Atkinson, 2004). We must apply our critical imaginations to the meaning of such terms as *randomized design, causal model, policy studies,* and *public science* (Cannella & Lincoln, 2004; Weinstein, 2004). At a deeper level, we must resist conservative attempts to discredit qualitative inquiry by placing it back inside the box of positivism.

CONTESTING MIXED METHODS EXPERIMENTALISM

Kenneth R. Howe (2004) observes that the NRC finds a place for qualitative methods in mixed methods experimental designs. In such designs, qualitative methods may be "employed either singly or in combination with quantitative methods, including the use of randomized experimental designs" (Howe, 2004, p. 49; also Clark & Creswell, 2008; Hesse-Biber & Leavy, 2008). Clark, Creswell, Green, and Shope (2008) define mixed methods research "as a design for collecting, analyzing, and mixing both quantitative and qualitative data in a study in order to understand a research problem" (p. 364).[16] Mixed methods are direct descendants of classical experimentalism and the triangulation movement of the 1970s (Denzin, 1989b). They presume a methodological hierarchy, with quantitative methods at the top, relegating qualitative methods to "a largely auxiliary role in pursuit of the *technocratic* aim of accumulating knowledge of 'what works'" (Howe, 2004, pp. 53–54).

The *incompatibility thesis* disputes the key claim of the mixed methods movement, namely that methods and perspectives can be combined. Recalling the paradigm wars of the 1980s, this thesis argues that "compatibility between quantitative and qualitative methods is impossible due to incompatibility of the paradigms that underlie the methods" (Teddlie & Tashakkori 2003a, pp. 14–15; 2003b). Others disagree with this conclusion, and some contend that the incompatibility thesis has been largely discredited because researchers have demonstrated that it is possible to successfully use a mixed methods approach.

There are several schools of thought on this thesis, including the four identified by Teddlie and Tashakkori (2003a); that is, the complementary, single paradigm, dialectical, and multiple paradigm models. There is by no means consensus on these issues. Morse and Niehaus (2009) warn that ad hoc mixing of methods can be a serious threat to validity. Pragmatists and transformative emancipatory action researchers posit a dialectical model, working back and forth between a variety of tension points, such as etic–emic, value neutrality–value committed. Others (Guba & Lincoln, 2005; Lather, 1993) deconstruct validity as an operative term. Sharlene Nagy Hesse-Biber and Patricia Leavy's (2008) emphasis on emergent methods pushes and blurs the methodological boundaries between quantitative and qualitative methods.[17] Their model seeks to recover subjugated knowledges hidden from everyday view.

The traditional mixed methods movement takes qualitative methods out of their natural home, which is within the critical interpretive framework (Howe, 2004, p. 54; but see Teddlie and Tashakkori, 2003a, p. 15). It divides inquiry into dichotomous categories, exploration versus confirmation. Qualitative work is assigned to the first category, quantitative research to the second (Teddlie & Tashakkori, 2003a, p. 15). Like the classic experimental model, this movement excludes stakeholders from dialogue and active participation in the research process. Doing so weakens its democratic and dialogical dimensions and decreases the likelihood that previously silenced voices will be heard (Howe, 2004, pp. 56–57).

Howe (2004) cautions that it is not just

[the] "methodological fundamentalists" who have bought into [this] approach. A sizeable number of rather influential . . . educational researchers . . . have also signed on. This might be a compromise to the current political climate; it might be a backlash against the perceived excesses of postmodernism; it might be both. It is an ominous development, whatever the explanation. (p. 57; also 2009, p. 438; Lincoln, 2010, p. 7)

The hybrid dialogical model, in contrast, directly confronts these criticisms.

THE PRAGMATIC CRITICISMS OF ANTI-FOUNDATIONALISM

Clive Seale et al. (2004) contest what they regard as the excesses of an anti-methodological, "anything goes," romantic postmodernism that is associated with our project. They assert that too often the approach we value produces "low quality qualitative research and research results that are quite stereotypical and close to common sense" (p. 2). In contrast they propose a practice-based, pragmatic approach that places research practice at the center. Research involves an engagement "with a variety of things and people: research materials . . . social theories, philosophical debates, values, methods, tests . . . research participants" (p. 2). (Actually this approach is quite close to our own, especially our view of the bricoleur and bricolage).

Their situated methodology rejects the antifoundational claim that there are only partial truths, that the dividing line between fact and fiction has broken down (Seale et al., 2004, p. 3). They believe that this dividing line has not collapsed and that we should not accept stories if they do not accord with the best available facts (p. 6). Oddly, these pragmatic procedural arguments reproduce a variant of the evidence-based model and its criticisms of poststructural performative sensibilities. They can be used to provide political support for the methodological marginalization of many of the positions advanced in this handbook.

This complex political terrain defines the many traditions and strands of qualitative research: the British and its presence in other national contexts; the American pragmatic, naturalistic, and interpretive traditions in sociology, anthropology, communications, and education; the German and French phenomenological, hermeneutic, semiotic, Marxist, structural, and poststructural perspectives; feminist, African American, Latino, and queer studies; and studies of indigenous and aboriginal cultures. The politics of qualitative research create a tension that informs each of the above traditions. This tension itself is constantly being reexamined and interrogated, as qualitative research confronts a changing historical world, new intellectual positions, and its own institutional and academic conditions.

To summarize, qualitative research is many things to many people. Its essence is two-fold: (1) a commitment to some version of the naturalistic, interpretive approach to its subject matter and (2) an ongoing critique of the politics and methods of postpositivism. We turn now to a brief discussion of the major differences between qualitative and quantitative approaches to research. We will then discuss ongoing differences and tensions within qualitative inquiry.

QUALITATIVE VERSUS QUANTITATIVE RESEARCH

The word *qualitative* implies an emphasis on the qualities of entities and on processes and meanings that are not experimentally examined or measured (if measured at all) in terms of quantity, amount, intensity, or frequency. Qualitative researchers stress the socially constructed nature of reality, the intimate relationship between the researcher and what is studied, and the situational constraints that shape inquiry. Such researchers emphasize the value-laden nature of inquiry. They seek answers to questions that stress *how* social experience is created and given meaning. In contrast, quantitative studies emphasize the measurement and analysis of causal relationships between variables, not processes. Proponents claim that their work is done from within a value-free framework.

RESEARCH STYLES: DOING THE SAME THINGS DIFFERENTLY?

Of course, both qualitative and quantitative researchers "think they know something about society worth telling to others, and they use a variety of forms, media, and means to communicate their ideas and findings" (Becker, 1986, p. 122). Qualitative research differs from quantitative research in five significant ways (Becker, 1996). These points of difference turn on different ways of addressing the same set of issues. They return always to the politics of research and who has the power to legislate correct solutions to these problems.

Using Positivism and Postpositivism: First, both perspectives are shaped by the positivist and postpositivist traditions in the physical and social sciences (see discussion below). These two positivist science traditions hold to naïve and critical realist positions concerning reality and its perception. Proponents of the positivist version contend that there is a reality out there to be studied, captured, and understood, whereas the postpositivists argue that reality can never be fully apprehended, only approximated (Guba, 1990a, p. 22). Postpositivism relies on multiple methods as a way of capturing as much of reality as possible. At the same time, emphasis is placed on the discovery and verification of theories. Traditional evaluation criteria like internal and external validity are stressed, as are the use of qualitative procedures that lend themselves to structured (sometimes statistical) analysis. Computer-assisted methods of analysis, which permit frequency counts, tabulations, and low-level statistical analyses, may also be employed.

The positivist and postpositivist traditions linger like long shadows over the qualitative research project. Historically, qualitative research was defined within the positivist paradigm, where qualitative researchers attempted to do good positivist research with less rigorous methods and procedures. Some mid-century qualitative researchers (Becker, Geer, Hughes, & Strauss, 1961) reported findings from participant observations in terms of quasi-statistics. As recently as 1999 (Strauss & Corbin, 1999), two leaders of the grounded theory approach to qualitative research attempted to modify the usual canons of good (positivistic) science to fit their own postpositivist conception of rigorous research (but see Charmaz, Chapter 9, this volume; also see Glaser, 1992). Some applied researchers, while claiming to be atheoretical, often fit within the positivist or postpositivist framework by default.

Uwe Flick (2002, pp. 2–3) usefully summarizes the differences between these two approaches to inquiry. He observes that the quantitative approach has been used for purposes of isolating "causes and effects . . . operationalizing theoretical relations . . . [and] measuring and . . . quantifying phenomena . . . allowing the generalization of findings" (p. 3). But today, doubt is cast on such projects.

> Rapid social change and the resulting diversification of life worlds are increasingly confronting social researchers with new social contexts and perspectives . . . traditional deductive methodologies . . . are failing . . . thus research is increasingly forced to make use of inductive strategies instead of starting from theories and testing them . . . knowledge and practice are studied as local knowledge and practice. (Flick, 2002, p. 2)

George and Louise Spindler (1992) summarize their qualitative approach to quantitative materials.

> Instrumentation and quantification are simply procedures employed to extend and reinforce certain kinds of data, interpretations and test hypotheses across samples. Both must be kept in their place. One must avoid their premature or overly extensive use as a security mechanism. (p. 69)

While many qualitative researchers in the postpositivist tradition will use statistical measures, methods, and documents as a way of locating a group of subjects within a larger population, they will seldom report their findings in terms of the kinds of complex statistical measures or methods that quantitative researchers are drawn to (i.e., path, regression, log-linear analyses).

Accepting Postmodern Sensibilities: The use of quantitative, positivist methods and assumptions has been rejected by a new generation of qualitative researchers who are attached to poststructural or postmodern sensibilities. These researchers argue that positivist methods are but one way of telling a story about society or the social world. They may be no better or no worse than any other method; they just tell a different kind of story.

This tolerant view is not shared by everyone. Many members of the critical theory, constructivist, poststructural, and postmodern schools of thought reject positivist and postpositivist criteria when evaluating their own work. They see these criteria as being irrelevant to their work and contend that positivist and postpositivist research reproduces only a certain kind of science, a science that silences too many voices. These researchers seek alternative methods for evaluating their work, including verisimilitude, emotionality, personal responsibility, an ethic of caring, political praxis, multivoiced texts, dialogues with subjects, and so on. In response, positivist and postpositivists argue that what they do is good science, free of individual bias and subjectivity. As noted above, they see postmodernism and poststructuralism as attacks on reason and truth.

Capturing the Individual's Point of View: Both qualitative and quantitative researchers are concerned with the individual's point of view. However, qualitative investigators think they can get closer to the actor's perspective by detailed interviewing and observation. They argue that quantitative researchers are seldom able to capture the subject's perspective because they have to rely on more remote, inferential empirical methods and materials. Many quantitative researchers regard empirical materials produced by interpretive methods as unreliable, impressionistic, and not objective.

Examining the Constraints of Everyday Life: Qualitative researchers are more likely to confront and come up against the constraints of the everyday social world. They see this world in action and embed their findings in it. Quantitative researchers abstract from this world and seldom study it directly. They seek a nomothetic or etic science based on probabilities derived from the study of large numbers of randomly selected cases. These kinds of statements stand above and outside the constraints of everyday life. Qualitative researchers, on the other hand, are committed to an emic, ideographic, case-based position, which directs their attention to the specifics of particular cases.

Securing Rich Descriptions: Qualitative researchers believe that rich descriptions of the social world are valuable, whereas quantitative researchers, with their etic, nomothetic commitments, are less concerned with such detail. They are deliberately unconcerned with such descriptions because such detail interrupts the process of developing generalizations.

These five points of difference described above (using positivism and postpositivism, accepting postmodern sensibilities, capturing the individual's point of view, examining the constraints of everyday life, securing thick descriptions) reflect commitments to different styles of research, different epistemologies, and different forms of representation. Each work tradition is governed by a different set of genres, and each has its own classics and its own preferred forms of representation, interpretation, trustworthiness, and textual evaluation (see Becker, 1986, pp. 134–135). Qualitative researchers use ethnographic prose, historical narratives, first-person accounts, still photographs, life history, fictionalized "facts," and biographical and autobiographical materials, among others. Quantitative researchers use mathematical models, statistical tables, and graphs and usually write in an impersonal, third-person prose.

Tensions Within Qualitative Research

It is erroneous to presume that qualitative researchers share the same assumptions about these five points of difference. As the discussion below will reveal, positivist, postpositivist, and poststructural differences define and shape the discourses of qualitative research. Realists and postpositivists within the interpretive, qualitative research tradition criticize poststructuralists for taking the textual, narrative turn. These critics contend that such work is navel-gazing. It produces the conditions "for a dialogue of the deaf between itself and the community" (Silverman, 1997, p. 240). Those who attempt to capture the point of view of the interacting subject in the world are accused of naïve humanism, of reproducing a Romantic impulse that elevates the experiential to the level of the authentic (Silverman, 1997, p. 248).

Still others argue that lived experience is ignored by those who take the textual, performance turn. David Snow and Calvin Morrill (1995) argue that

> This performance turn, like the preoccupation with discourse and storytelling, will take us further from the field of social action and the real dramas of everyday life and thus signal the death knell of ethnography as an empirically grounded enterprise. (p. 361)

Of course, we disagree.

According to Martyn Hammersley (2008, p. 1), qualitative research is currently facing a crisis symbolized by an ill-conceived postmodernist image of qualitative research, which is dismissive of traditional forms of inquiry. He feels that "unless this dynamic can be interrupted the future of qualitative research is endangered" (p. 11).

Paul Atkinson and Sara Delamont (2006), two qualitative scholars in the traditional, classic Chicago School tradition,[18] offer a corrective. They remain committed to qualitative (and quantitative) research *"provided that they are conducted rigorously and contribute to robustly useful knowledge"* (p. 749, italics in original). Of course, these scholars are committed to social policy initiatives at some level. But, for them, the postmodern image of qualitative inquiry threatens and undermines the value of traditional qualitative inquiry. Atkinson and Delamont exhort qualitative researchers to "think hard about whether their investigations are the best social science they could be" (p. 749). Patricia and Peter Adler (2008) implore the radical postmodernists to "give up the project for the good of the discipline and for the good of society" (p. 23).

Hammersley (2008, pp. 134–136, 144), extends the traditional critique, finding little value in the work of ethnographic postmodernists and literary ethnographers.[19] This new tradition, he asserts, legitimates speculative theorizing, celebrates obscurity, and abandons the primary task of inquiry, which is to produce truthful knowledge about the world (p. 144). Poststructural inquirers get it from all sides. The criticisms, Carolyn Ellis (2009, p. 231) observes, fall into three overlapping categories. Our work (1) is too aesthetic and not sufficiently realistic; it does not provide hard data; (2) is too realistic and not mindful of poststructural criticisms concerning the "real" self and its place in the text; and (3) is not sufficiently aesthetic, or literary; that is, we are second-rate writers and poets (p. 232).

THE POLITICS OF EVIDENCE

The critics' model of science is anchored in the belief that there is an empirical world that is obdurate and talks back to investigators. This is an empirical science based on evidence that corroborates interpretations. This is a science that returns to and is lodged in the real, a science that stands outside nearly all of the turns listed above; this is Chicago School neo-postpositivism.

Contrast this certain science to the position of those who are preoccupied with the politics of evidence. Jan Morse (2006), for example, says: "Evidence is not just something that is out there. Evidence has to be produced, constructed, represented. Furthermore, the politics of evidence cannot be separated from the ethics of evidence" (pp. 415–416). Under the Jan Morse model, representations of empirical reality become problematic. Objective representation of reality is impossible. Each representation calls into place a different set of ethical questions regarding evidence, including how it is obtained and what it means. But surely a middle ground can be found. If there is a return to the spirit of the paradigm dialogues of the 1980s, then multiple representations of a situation should be encouraged, perhaps placed alongside one another.

Indeed, the interpretive camp is not antiscience, per se. We do something different. We believe in multiple forms of science: soft, hard, strong, feminist, interpretive, critical, realist, postrealist, and post-humanist. In a sense, the traditional and postmodern projects are incommensurate. We interpret, we perform, we interrupt, we challenge, and we believe nothing is ever certain. We want performance texts that quote history back to itself, texts that focus on epiphanies; on the intersection of biography, history, culture, and politics; on turning point moments in people's lives. The critics are correct on this point. We have a political orientation that is radical, democratic, and interventionist. Many postpositivists share these politics.

CRITICAL REALISM

For some, there is a third stream between naïve positivism and poststructuralism. Critical realism is an antipositivist movement in the social sciences closely associated with the works of Roy Bhaskar and Rom Harré (Danermark, Ekstrom, Jakobsen, & Karlsson, 2002). Critical realists use the word *critical* in a particular way. This is not Frankfurt School critical theory, although there are traces of social criticism here and there (Danermark et al., 2002, p. 201). *Critical,* instead, refers to a transcendental realism that rejects methodological individualism and universal claims to truth. Critical realists oppose logical positivist, relativist, and antifoundational epistemologies. Critical realists agree with the positivists that there is a world of events out there that is observable and independent of human consciousness. Knowledge about this world is socially constructed. Society is made up of feeling, thinking human beings, and their interpretations of the world must be studied (Danermark et al., 2002, p. 200). A correspondence theory of truth is rejected. Critical realists believe that reality is arranged in levels. Scientific work must go beyond statements of regularity to the analysis of the mechanisms, processes, and structures that account for the patterns that are observed.

Still, as postempiricist, antifoundational, critical theorists, we reject much of what is advocated here. Throughout the last century, social science and philosophy were continually tangled up with one another. Various "isms" and philosophical movements criss-crossed sociological and educational discourse, from positivism to postpositivism to analytic and linguistic philosophy, to hermeneutics, structuralism, and poststructuralism; to Marxism, feminism, and current post-post-versions of all of the above. Some have said that the logical positivists steered the social sciences on a rigorous course of self-destruction.

We do not think critical realism will keep the social science ship afloat. The social sciences are normative disciplines, always already embedded in issues of value, ideology, power, desire, sexism, racism, domination, repression, and control. We want a social science committed up front to issues of social justice, equity, nonviolence, peace, and universal human rights. We do not want a social science that says it can address these issues if it wants to do so. For us, this is no longer an option.

Qualitative Research as Process

Three interconnected, generic activities define the qualitative research process. They go by a variety of different labels, including theory, method, and analysis; or ontology, epistemology, and methodology. Behind these terms stands the personal biography of the researcher, who speaks from a particular class, gendered, racial, cultural, and ethnic community perspective. The gendered, multiculturally situated researcher approaches the world with a set of ideas, a framework (theory, ontology) that specifies a set of questions (epistemology), which are then examined (methodology, analysis) in specific ways. That is, empirical materials bearing on the question are collected and then analyzed and written about. Every researcher speaks from within a distinct interpretive community, which configures, in its special way, the multicultural, gendered components of the research act.

In this volume, we treat these generic activities under five headings or phases: the researcher and the researched as multicultural subjects, major paradigms and interpretive perspectives, research strategies, methods of collecting and analyzing empirical materials, and the art of interpretation. Behind and within each of these phases stands the biographically situated researcher. This individual enters the research process from inside an interpretive community. This community has its own historical research traditions, which constitute a distinct point of view. This perspective leads the researcher to adopt particular views of the "other" who is studied. At the same time, the politics and the ethics of research must also be considered, for these concerns permeate every phase of the research process.

The Other as Research Subject

From its turn-of-the-century birth in modern, interpretive form, qualitative research has been haunted by a double-faced ghost. On the one hand, qualitative researchers have assumed that qualified, competent observers could, with objectivity, clarity, and precision, report on their own observations of the social world, including the experiences of others. Second, researchers have held to the belief in a real subject or real individual who is present in the world and able, in some form, to report on his or her experiences. So armed, researchers could blend their own observations with the self-reports provided by subjects through interviews, life story, personal experience, and case study documents.

These two beliefs have led qualitative researchers across disciplines to seek a method that would allow them to record accurately their own observations while also uncovering the meanings their subjects brought to their life experiences. This method would rely on the subjective verbal and written expressions of meaning given by the individuals, which are studied as windows into the inner life of the person. Since Wilhelm Dilthey (1900/1976), this search for a method has led to a perennial focus in the human disciplines on qualitative, interpretive methods.

Recently, as noted above, this position and its beliefs have come under assault. Poststructuralists and postmodernists have contributed to the understanding that there is no clear window into the inner life of an individual. Any gaze is always filtered through the lenses of language, gender, social class, race, and ethnicity. There are no objective observations, only observations socially situated in the worlds of—and between—the observer and the observed. Subjects, or individuals, are seldom able to give full explanations of their actions or intentions; all they can offer are accounts or stories about what they did and why. No single method can grasp the subtle variations in ongoing human experience. Consequently, qualitative researchers deploy a wide-range of interconnected interpretive methods, always seeking better ways to make more understandable the worlds of experience that have been studied.

Table 1.1 depicts the relationships we see among the five phases that define the research process (the researcher; major paradigms; research strategies; methods of collecting and analyzing empirical materials; and the art, practices, and politics of interpretation). Behind all but one of these phases stands the biographically situated researcher. These five levels of activity, or practice, work their way through the biography of the researcher. We take them up in brief order here, for each phase is more fully discussed in the transition sections between the various parts of this volume.

Table 1.1 The Research Process

Phase 1: The Researcher as a Multicultural Subject	Historical method
	Action and applied research
History and research traditions	Clinical research
Conceptions of self and the other	
The ethics and politics of research	*Phase 4: Methods of Collection and Analysis*
Phase 2: Theoretical Paradigms and Perspectives	Interviewing
	Observing
Positivism, postpositivism	Artifacts, documents, and records
Interpretivism, constructivism, hermeneutics	Visual methods
	Autoethnography
Feminism(s)	Data management methods
Racialized discourses	Computer-assisted analysis
Critical theory and Marxist models	Textual analysis
Cultural studies models	Focus groups
Queer theory	Applied ethnography
Post-colonialism	
	Phase 5: The Art, Practices, and Politics of Interpretation and Evaluation
Phase 3: Research Strategies	
Design	Criteria for judging adequacy
Case study	Practices and politics of interpretation
Ethnography, participant observation, performance ethnography	Writing as interpretation
	Policy analysis
Phenomenology, ethnomethodology	Evaluation traditions
Grounded theory	Applied research
Life history, ***testimonio***	

PHASE 1: THE RESEARCHER

Our remarks above indicate the depth and complexity of the traditional and applied qualitative research perspectives into which a socially situated researcher enters. These traditions locate the researcher in history, simultaneously guiding and constraining work that will be done in any specific study. This field has been constantly characterized by diversity and conflict, and these are its most enduring traditions (see Levin & Greenwood, Chapter 2, volume 1). As a carrier of this complex and contradictory history, the researcher must also confront the ethics and politics of research (Christians, Chapter 4, volume 1). It is no longer possible for the human disciplines to research the native, the indigenous other, in a spirit of value-free inquiry. Today researchers struggle to develop situational and transsituational ethics that apply to all forms of the research act and its human-to-human relationships. We no longer have the option of deferring the decolonization project.

PHASE 2: INTERPRETIVE PARADIGMS

All qualitative researchers are philosophers in that "universal sense in which all human beings . . . are guided by highly abstract principles" (Bateson, 1972, p. 320). These principles combine beliefs about *ontology* (What kind of being is the human being? What is the nature of reality?), *epistemology* (What is the relationship between the inquirer and the known?), and *methodology* (How do we know the world or gain knowledge of it?) (see Guba, 1990a, p. 18; Lincoln & Guba, 1985, pp. 14–15; and Lincoln, Lynham, & Guba in Chapter 6 of volume 1). These beliefs shape how the qualitative researcher sees the world and acts in it. The researcher is "bound within a net of epistemological and ontological premises which—regardless of ultimate truth or falsity—become partially self-validating" (Bateson, 1972, p. 314).

The net that contains the researcher's epistemological, ontological, and methodological premises may be termed a *paradigm* (Guba, 1990a, p. 17) or interpretive framework, a "basic set of beliefs that guides action" (Guba, 1990a, p. 17). All research is interpretive: guided by a set of beliefs and feelings about the world and how it should be understood and studied. Some beliefs may be taken for granted, invisible, or only assumed, whereas others are highly problematic and controversial. Each interpretive paradigm makes particular demands on the researcher, including the questions that are asked and the interpretations that are brought to them.

At the most general level, four major interpretive paradigms structure qualitative research: positivist and postpositivist, constructivist-interpretive, critical (Marxist, emancipatory), and feminist-poststructural. These four abstract paradigms become more complicated at the level of concrete specific interpretive communities. At this level, it is possible to identify not only the constructivist but also multiple versions of feminism (Afrocentric and poststructural),[20] as wellas specific ethnic, feminist, endarkened, social justice, Marxist, cultural studies, disability, and non-Western-Asian paradigms.

The paradigms work against or alongside (and some within) the positivist and postpositivist models. They all work within relativist ontologies (multiple constructed realities), interpretive epistemologies (the knower and known interact and shape one another), and interpretive, naturalistic methods.

Table 1.2 presents these paradigms and their assumptions, including their criteria for evaluating research, and the typical form that an interpretive or theoretical statement assumes in the paradigm.[21]

Each paradigm is explored in considerable detail in chapters 6 through 10. The positivist and postpositivist paradigms were discussed above. They work from within a realist and critical realist ontology and objective epistemologies, and they rely on experimental, quasi-experimental, survey, and rigorously defined qualitative methodologies.

The *constructivist paradigm* assumes a relativist ontology (there are multiple realities), a subjectivist epistemology (knower and respondent co-create understandings), and a naturalistic (in the natural world) set of methodological procedures. Findings are usually presented in terms of the criteria of grounded theory or pattern theories (in this volume, see Lincoln, Lynham, & Guba, Chapter 6 , volume 1; Creswell, Chapter 3; Teddlie & Tashakkori, Chapter 4; Charmaz, Chapter 9; Morse, Chapter 12; Altheide & Johnson, Chapter 12, volume 3; and St.Pierre, Chapter 14, volume 3). Terms like credibility, transferability, dependability, and confirmability replace the usual positivist criteria of internal and external validity, reliability, and objectivity.

Feminist, ethnic, Marxist, cultural studies, queer theory, Asian, and disability models privilege a materialist-realist ontology; that is, the real world makes a material difference in terms of race, class, and gender. Subjectivist epistemologies and naturalistic methodologies (usually ethnographies) are also employed. Empirical materials and theoretical arguments are evaluated in terms of their emancipatory implications. Criteria from gender and racial communities (e.g., African American) may be applied (emotionality and feeling, caring, personal accountability, dialogue).

Poststructural feminist theories emphasize problems with the social text, its logic, and its inability to ever represent the world of lived experience fully. Positivist and postpositivist criteria of evaluation are replaced by other terms, including the reflexive, multivoiced text, which is grounded in the experiences of oppressed people.

The cultural studies and queer theory paradigms are multifocused, with many different strands drawing from Marxism, feminism, and the postmodern sensibility (in volume 1, Giardina & Newman, Chapter 10; Plummer, Chapter 11; St.Pierre, Chapter 14, volume 3). There is a tension between a humanistic cultural studies, which stresses lived experiences (meaning), and a more structural cultural studies project, which

Table 1.2 Interpretive Paradigms

Paradigm/ Theory	Criteria	Form of Theory	Type of Narration
Positivist/ postpositivist	Internal, external validity	Logical-deductive, grounded	Scientific report
Constructivist	Trustworthiness, credibility, transferability, confirmability	Substantive-formal, standpoint	Interpretive case studies, ethnographic fiction
Feminist	Afrocentric, lived experience, dialogue, caring, accountability, race, class, gender, reflexivity, praxis, emotion, concrete grounding, embodied	Critical, standpoint	Essays, stories, experimental writing
Ethnic	Afrocentric, lived experience, dialogue, caring, accountability, race, class, gender	Standpoint, critical, historical	Essays, fables, dramas
Marxist	Emancipatory theory, falsifiability, dialogical, race, class, gender	Critical, historical, economic	Historical, economic, sociocultural analyses
Cultural studies	Cultural practices, praxis, social texts, subjectivities	Social criticism	Cultural theory-as-criticism
Queer theory	Reflexivity, deconstruction	Social criticism, historical analysis	Theory-as-criticism, autobiography

stresses the structural and material determinants and effects (race, class, gender) of experience. Of course, there are two sides to every coin; both sides are needed and are indeed critical. The cultural studies and queer theory paradigms use methods strategically, that is, as resources for understanding and for producing resistances to local structures of domination. Such scholars may do close textual readings and discourse analysis of cultural texts (in volume 1, Olesen, Chapter 7; Chase, Chapter 2, volume 3), as well as local, online, reflexive, and critical ethnographies; open-ended interviewing; and participant observation. The focus is on how race, class, and gender are produced and enacted in historically specific situations.

Paradigm and personal history in hand, focused on a concrete empirical problem to examine, the researcher now moves to the next stage of the research process, namely working with a specific strategy of inquiry.

PHASE 3: STRATEGIES OF INQUIRY AND INTERPRETIVE PARADIGMS

Table 1.1 presents some of the major strategies of inquiry a researcher may use. Phase 3 begins with research design, which broadly conceived involves a clear focus on the research question, the purposes of the study, "what information most appropriately will answer specific research questions, and which strategies are most effective for obtaining it" (LeCompte & Preissle with Tesch, 1993, p. 30; see also Cheek, Chapter 2, this volume). A research design describes a flexible set of guidelines that connect theoretical paradigms, first, to strategies of inquiry and, second, to methods for collecting empirical material. A research design situates researchers in the empirical world and connects them to specific sites, people, groups, institutions, and bodies of relevant interpretive material, including documents and archives. A research design also specifies how the investigator will address the two critical issues of representation and legitimation.

A strategy of inquiry refers to a bundle of skills, assumptions, and practices that researchers employ as they move from their paradigm to the empirical world. Strategies of inquiry put paradigms of interpretation into motion. At the same time, strategies of inquiry also connect the researcher to specific methods of collecting and analyzing empirical materials. For example, the case study relies on interviewing, observing, and document analysis. Research strategies implement and anchor paradigms in specific empirical sites or in specific methodological practices, for example, making a case an object of study. These strategies include the case study, phenomenological and ethnomethodological techniques, the use of grounded theory, and biographical, autoethnographic, historical, action, and clinical methods. Each of these strategies is connected to a complex literature; each has a separate history, exemplary works, and preferred ways for putting the strategy into motion.

PHASE 4: METHODS OF COLLECTING
AND ANALYZING EMPIRICAL MATERIALS

The researcher has several methods for collecting empirical materials.[22] These methods are taken up in Part IV. They range from the interview to direct observation, the use of visual materials or personal experience. The researcher may also use a variety of different methods of reading and analyzing interviews or cultural texts, including content, narrative, and semiotic strategies. Faced with large amounts of qualitative materials, the investigator seeks ways of managing and interpreting these documents, and here data management methods and computer-assisted models of analysis may be of use. In volume 3, David L. Altheide and John M. Johnson (Chapter 12), Laura L. Ellingson (Chapter 13), and Judith Davidson and Silvana diGregorio (Chapter 15) take up these techniques.

PHASE 5: THE ART AND POLITICS OF
INTERPRETATION AND EVALUATION

Qualitative research is endlessly creative and interpretive. The researcher does not just leave the field with mountains of empirical materials and easily write up his or her findings. Qualitative interpretations are constructed. The researcher first creates a field text consisting of fieldnotes and documents from the field, what Roger Sanjek (1992, p. 386) calls "indexing" and David Plath (1990, p. 374) "filework." The writer-as-interpreter moves from this text to a research text; notes and interpretations based on the field text. This text is then re-created as a working interpretive document that contains the writer's initial attempts to make sense out of what has been learned. Finally, the writer produces the public text that comes to the reader. This final tale from the field may assume several forms: confessional, realist, impressionistic, critical, formal, literary, analytic, grounded theory, and so on (see Van Maanen, 1988).

The interpretive practice of making sense of one's findings is both artistic and political. Multiple criteria for evaluating qualitative research now exist, and those we emphasize stress the situated, relational, and textual structures of the ethnographic experience. There is no single interpretive truth. As argued earlier, there are multiple interpretive communities, each having its own criteria for evaluating an interpretation.

Program evaluation is a major site of qualitative research, and qualitative researchers can influence social policy in important ways. Applied, qualitative research in the social sciences has a rich history (discussed in volume 1 by

Levin & Greenwood, Chapter 2 , volume 1; Brydon-Miller, Kral, Maguire, Noffke, & Sabhlok, Chapter 11; Morse, Chapter 12; Torrance, Chapter 11, volume 3; Abma & Widdershoven, Chapter 18, volume 3). This is the critical site where theory, method, praxis, action, and policy all come together. Qualitative researchers can isolate target populations, show the immediate effects of certain programs on such groups, and isolate the constraints that operate against policy changes in such settings. Action and clinically oriented qualitative researchers can also create spaces for those who are studied (the other) to speak. The evaluator becomes the conduit for making such voices heard.

BRIDGING THE HISTORICAL MOMENTS: WHAT COMES NEXT?

St.Pierre (2004) argues that we are already in the post "post" period—post-poststructuralism, post-postmodernism, post-experimental. What this means for interpretive, ethnographic practices is still not clear. But it is certain that things will never again be the same. We are in a new age where messy, uncertain multivoiced texts, cultural criticism, and new experimental works will become more common, as will more reflexive forms of fieldwork, analysis, and intertextual representation. In a complex space like this, pedagogy becomes critical—that is, How do we teach qualitative methods? Judith Preissle (Chapter 14, volume 1) and Margaret Eisenhart and S. Jurow (Chapter 15, volume 1) offer insights on the future. It is true, as the poet said, the center no longer holds. We can reflect on what should be in this new center.

Thus, we come full circle. And returning to our bridge metaphor, the chapters that follow take the researcher back and forth through every phase of the research act. Like a good bridge, the chapters provide for two-way traffic, coming and going between moments, formations, and interpretive communities. Each chapter examines the relevant histories, controversies, and current practices that are associated with each paradigm, strategy, and method. Each chapter also offers projections for the future, where a specific paradigm, strategy, or method will be 10 years from now, deep into the formative years of the next century.

In reading this volume, it is important to remember that the field of qualitative research is defined by a series of tensions, contradictions, and hesitations. This tension works back and forth between and among (1) the broad, doubting, postmodern sensibility; (2) the more certain, more traditional positivist, post-positivist, and naturalistic conceptions of this project; and (3) an increasingly conservative, neoliberal global environment. All of the chapters that follow are caught in and articulate these tensions.

Notes

1. The following paragraphs draw from Denzin (2010, pp. 19–25).

2. They contend that our second moment, the Golden Age (1950–1970), was marked by the debunking of positivism, the emergence of postpositivism, and the development of designs that used mixed quantitative and qualitative methods. Full-scale conflict developed throughout the 1970–1990 period, the time of the first "paradigm war."

3. Conflict broke out between the many different empowerment pedagogies: feminist, anti-racist, radical, Freirean, liberation theology, postmodernists, poststructuralists, cultural studies, and so on (see Guba & Lincoln, 2005; also, Erickson, Chapter 3, volume 1).

4. Recall bell hooks's reading of the famous cover photo on *Writing Culture* (Clifford & Marcus, 1986), which consists of a picture of Stephen Tyler doing fieldwork in India. Tyler is seated some distance from three dark-skinned people. A child is poking its head out of a basket. A woman is hidden in the shadows of the hut. A male, a checkered white and black shawl across his shoulder, elbow propped on his knee, hand resting along the side of his face, is staring at Tyler. Tyler is writing in a field journal. A piece of white cloth is attached to his glasses, perhaps shielding him from the sun. This patch of whiteness marks Tyler as the white male writer studying these passive brown and black people. Indeed, the brown male's gaze signals some desire or some attachment to Tyler. In contrast, the female's gaze is completely hidden by the shadows and by the words in the book's title, which cross her face (hooks, 1990, p. 127).

5. Qualitative research has separate and distinguished histories in education, social work, communications, psychology, history, organizational studies, medical science, anthropology, and sociology.

6. Definitions: *positivism:* Objective accounts of the real world can be given; *postpositivism:* Only partially objective accounts of the world can be produced, for all methods are flawed; *foundationalism:* We can have an ultimate grounding for our knowledge claims about the world, and this involves the use of empiricist and positivist epistemologies (Schwandt, 1997a, p. 103); *nonfoundationalism:* We can make statements about the world without "recourse to ultimate proof or foundations for that knowing" (Schwandt, 1997a, p. 102); *quasifoundationalism:* Certain knowledge claims about the world based on neorealist criteria can be made, including the correspondence concept of truth. There is an independent reality that can be mapped.

7. Jameson (1991, pp. 3–4) reminds us that any periodization hypothesis is always suspect, even one that rejects linear, stage-like models. It is never clear to what reality a stage refers. What divides one stage from another is always debatable. Our seven moments are meant to mark discernible shifts in style, genre, epistemology, ethics, politics, and aesthetics.

8. See Denzin and Lincoln (2005, pp. 13–21) for an extended discussion of each of these phases. This model has been termed a progress narrative by Alasuutari (2004, pp. 599–600) and Seale, Gobo, Gubrium, and Silverman (2004, p. 2). The critics assert

that we believe that the most recent moment is the most up-to-date, the avant-garde, the cutting edge (Alasuutari, 2004, p. 601). Naturally, we dispute this reading. Teddlie and Tashakkori (2003a, pp. 5–8) have modified our historical periods to fit their historical analysis of the major moments in the emergence of mixed methods in the last century.

9. *Definitions: structuralism*: Any system is made up of a set of oppositional categories embedded in language; *semiotics*: the science of signs or sign systems—a structuralist project; *poststructuralism:* Language is an unstable system of referents, making it impossible to ever completely capture the meaning or an action, text, or intention; *postmodernism:* a contemporary sensibility, developing since World War II, which privileges no single authority, method, or paradigm; *hermeneutics:* An approach to the analysis of texts that stresses how prior understandings and prejudices shape the interpretive process; *phenomenology:* A complex system of ideas associated with the works of Edmund Husserl, Martin Heidegger, Jean-Paul Sartre, Maurice Merleau-Ponty, and Alfred Schutz; *cultural studies:* a complex, interdisciplinary field that merges with critical theory, feminism, and poststructuralism.

10. Of course, all settings are natural, that is, places where everyday experience takes place. Qualitative researchers study people doing things together in the places where these things are done (Becker, 1986). There is no field site or natural place where one goes to do this kind of work (see also Gupta & Ferguson, 1997, p. 8). The site is constituted through our interpretive practices. Historically, analysts have distinguished between experimental (laboratory) and field (natural) research settings; hence the argument that qualitative research is naturalistic. Activity theory erases this distinction (Keller & Keller, 1996, p. 20; Vygotsky, 1978).

11. "The meaning of *bricoleur* in French popular speech is 'someone who works with his (or her) hands and uses devious means compared to those of the craftsman . . . the bricoleur is practical and gets the job done" (Weinstein & Weinstein, 1991, p. 161). These authors provide a history of this term, connecting it to the works of the German sociologist and social theorist Georg Simmel, and by implication to Charles Baudelaire. Martyn Hammersley (2000) disputes our use of this term. Following Claude Lévi-Strauss, he reads the bricoleur as a myth maker. He suggests it be replaced with the notion of the boat builder. Hammersley also quarrels with our "moments" model of qualitative research, contending it implies some sense of progress.

12. Brian De Palma reproduces this baby carriage scene in his 1987 film, *The Untouchables*.

13. In the harbor, the muzzles of the Potemkin's two huge guns swing slowly into the camera. Words on screen inform us: "The brutal military power answered by guns of the battleship." A final famous three-shot montage sequence shows, first, a sculptured sleeping lion, then the lion rising from his sleep, and finally the lion roaring, symbolizing the rage of the Russian people (Cook, 1981, p. 167). In this sequence, Eisenstein uses montage to expand time, creating a psychological duration for this horrible event. By drawing out this sequence, by showing the baby in the carriage, the soldiers firing on the citizens, the blood on the mother's glove, the descending carriage on the steps, he suggests a level of destruction of great magnitude.

14. Here it is relevant to make a distinction between techniques that are used across disciplines and methods that are used within disciplines. Ethnomethodologists, for example, employ their approach as a method, whereas others selectively borrow that method-as-technique for their own applications. Harry Wolcott (in conversation) suggests this distinction. It is also relevant to make a distinction between topic, method, and resource. Methods can be studied as topics of inquiry; that is how a case study gets done. In this ironic, ethnomethodological sense, method is both a resource and a topic of inquiry.

15. Indeed any attempt to give an essential definition of qualitative research requires a qualitative analysis of the circumstances that produce such a definition.

16. They identify four major mixed methods designs: triangulation, embedded, explanatory, and exploratory (Clark et al., 2008, p. 371).

17. Their emergent model focuses on methods that break out of traditional frameworks and exploit new technologies and innovations; this is a process model that works between politics, epistemology, theory, and methodology.

18. There are several generations of the Chicago School, from Robert Park and Ernest Burgess, Herbert Blumer, and Everett Hughes (1920–1950) period, to second (Becker, Strauss, Goffman), to third (Hammersley, Atkinson, Delamont, Snow, Anderson, Fine, Adler and Adler, Prus, Maines, Flaherty, Sanders et al).

19. His blanket term for auto, performance, poststructural ethnography.

20. Olesen (Chapter 7, volume 1) identifies three strands of feminist research: mainstream empirical; standpoint and cultural studies; and poststructural, postmodern; placing Afrocentric and other models of color under the cultural studies and postmodern categories.

21. These, of course, are our interpretations of these paradigms and interpretive styles.

22. *Empirical materials* is the preferred term for what are traditionally described as data.

References

Adler, P. A., & Adler, P. (2008). Of rhetoric and representation: The four faces of ethnography. *Sociological Quarterly, 49*(4), 1–30.

Alasuutari, P. (2004). The globalization of qualitative research. In C. Seale, G. Gobo, J. F. Gubrium, & D. Silverman (Eds.), *Qualitative research practice* (pp. 595–608). London: Sage.

Atkinson, E. (2004). Thinking outside the box: An exercise in heresy. *Qualitative Inquiry, 10*(1), 111–129.

Atkinson, P., & Delamont, S. (2006). In the roiling smoke: Qualitative inquiry and contested fields. *International Journal of Qualitative Studies in Education, 19*(6), 747–755.

Bateson, G. (1972). *Steps to an ecology of mind.* New York: Ballantine.

Becker, H. S. (1986). *Doing things together.* Evanston, IL: Northwestern University Press.

Becker, H. S. (1996). The epistemology of qualitative research. In R. Jessor, A. Colby, & R. A. Schweder (Eds.), *Ethnography and human development* (pp. 53–71). Chicago: University of Chicago Press.

Becker, H. S. (1998). *Tricks of the trade.* Chicago: University of Chicago Press.

Becker, H S., Geer, B., Hughes, E. C., & Strauss, A. L. (1961). *Boys in white.* Chicago: University of Chicago Press.

Bloch, M. (2004). A discourse that disciplines, governs, and regulates: On scientific research in education. *Qualitative Inquiry, 10*(1), 96–110.

Cannella, G. S. (2004). Regulatory power: Can a feminist poststructuralist engage in research oversight? *Qualitative Inquiry, 10*(2), 235–245.

Cannella, G. S., & Lincoln, Y. S. (2004a). Dangerous discourses II: Comprehending and countering the redeployment of discourses (and resources) in the generation of liberatory inquiry. *Qualitative Inquiry, 10*(2), 165–174.

Cannella, G. S., & Lincoln, Y. S. (2004b). Epilogue: Claiming a critical public social science—reconceptualizing and redeploying research. *Qualitative Inquiry, 10*(2), 298–309.

Carey, J. W. (1989). *Culture as communication.* Boston: Unwin Hyman.

Cicourel, A. V. 1964. *Method and measurement in sociology.* New York: Free Press.

Clark, C., & Scheurich, J. (2008). Editorial: The state of qualitative research in the early twenty-first century. *International Journal of Qualitative Research in Education, 21*(4), 313.

Clark, V. L. P., & Creswell, J. W. (2008). Introduction. In V. L. Plano Clark & J. W. Creswell (Eds.), *The mixed methods reader* (pp. xv–xviii). Thousand Oaks: Sage.

Clark, V. L. P., Creswell, J. W., Green, D. O., & Shope, R. J. (2008). Mixing quantitative and qualitative approaches: An introduction to emergent mixed methods research. In S. N. Hesse-Biber & P. Leavy (Eds.), *Handbook of emergent methods* (pp. 363–388). New York: Guilford.

Clifford, J. (1988). *Predicament of culture.* Cambridge: Harvard University Press.

Clifford, J. (1997). *Routes: Travel and translation in the late twentieth century.* Cambridge: Harvard University Press.

Clifford, J., & Marcus, G. E. (Eds.). (1986). *Writing culture.* Berkeley: University of California Press.

Clough, P. T. (1992). *The end(s) of ethnography.* Newbury Park, CA: Sage.

Clough, P. T. (1998). *The end(s) of ethnography* (2nd ed.). New York: Peter Lang.

Clough, P. T. (2000). Comments on setting criteria for experimental writing. *Qualitative Inquiry, 6,* 278–291.

Cook, D. A. (1981). *A history of narrative film.* New York: W. W. Norton.

Creswell, J. W. (1998). *Qualitative inquiry and research design: Choosing among five traditions.* Thousand Oaks, CA: Sage.

Danermark, B., Ekstrom, M., Jakobsen, L., & Karlsson, J. C. (2002). *Explaining society: Critical realism in the social sciences.* London: Routledge.

de Certeau, M. (1984). *The practice of everyday life.* Berkeley: University of California Press.

Denzin, N. K. (1970). *The research act.* Chicago: Aldine.

Denzin, N. K. (1978). *The research act* (2nd ed.). New York: McGraw-Hill.

Denzin, N. K. (1989a). *Interpretive interactionism.* Newbury Park, CA: Sage.

Denzin, N. K. (1989b). *The research act* (3rd ed.). Englewood Cliffs, NJ: Prentice Hall.

Denzin, N. K. (1997). *Interpretive ethnography.* Thousand Oaks, CA: Sage.

Denzin, N. K. (2003). *Performance ethnography: Critical pedagogy and the politics of culture.* Thousand Oaks, CA: Sage.

Denzin, N. K. (2009). *Qualitative inquiry under fire: Toward a new paradigm dialogue.* Walnut Creek, CA: Left Coast Press.

Denzin, N. K. (2010). *The qualitative manifesto: A call to arms.* Walnut Creek, CA: Left Coast Press.

Denzin, N. K., & Lincoln, Y. S. (2005). Introduction: The discipline and practice of qualitative research. In N. K. Denzin & Y. S. Lincoln (Eds.), *The SAGE handbook of qualitative research* (3rd ed., pp. 1–32). Thousand Oaks, CA: Sage.

Dilthey, W. L. (1976). *Selected writings.* Cambridge, UK: Cambridge University Press. (Original work published 1900)

Diversi, M. (1998). Glimpses of street life: Representing lived experience through short stories. *Qualitative Inquiry, 4,* 131–137.

Diversi, M., & Moreira, C. (2009). *Betweener talk: Decolonizing knowledge production, pedagogy, and praxis.* Walnut Creek, CA: Left Coast Press.

Ellingson, L. L. (2009). *Engaging crystallization in qualitative research.* Thousand Oaks, CA: Sage.

Ellis, C. (2009). *Revision: Autoethnographic reflections on life and work.* Walnut Creek, CA: Left Coast Press.

Ellis, C., & Bochner, A. P. (Eds.). (2000). *Ethnographically speaking: Autoethnography, literature, and aesthetics.* Walnut Creek, CA: AltaMira Press.

Filstead, W. J. (Ed.). (1970). *Qualitative methodology.* Chicago: Markham.

Flick, U. (1998). *An introduction to qualitative research.* London: Sage.

Flick, U. (2002). *An introduction to qualitative research* (2nd ed.). London: Sage.

Flick, U. (2007). *Designing qualitative research.* London: Sage

Gage, N. L. (1989). The paradigm wars and their aftermath: A "historical" sketch of research and teaching since 1989. *Educational Researcher, 18*(7), 4–10.

Geertz, C. (1973). *Interpreting cultures.* New York: Basic Books.

Geertz, C. (1983). *Local knowledge.* New York: Basic Books.

Geertz, C. (1988). *Works and lives.* Stanford, CA: Stanford University Press.

Geertz, C. (1995). *After the fact: Two countries, four decades, one anthropologist.* Cambridge: Harvard University Press.

Glaser, B. G. (1992). *Emergence vs. forcing: Basics of grounded theory.* Mill Valley, CA: Sociology Press.

Glaser, B., & Strauss, A. (1967). *The discovery of grounded theory.* Chicago: Aldine.

Goodall, H. L., Jr. (2000). *Writing the new ethnography.* Walnut Creek, CA: AltaMira.

Gordon, D. A. (1988). Writing culture, writing feminism: The poetics and politics of experimental ethnography. *Inscriptions, 3/4* (8), 21–31.

Gordon, D. A. (1995). Conclusion: Culture writing women: Inscribing feminist anthropology. In R. Behar & D. A. Gordon (Eds.), *Women writing culture* (pp. 429–441). Berkeley: University of California Press.

Greenblatt, S. (1997). The touch of the real. In S. B. Ortner (Ed.), The fate of "culture": Geertz and beyond [Special issue]. *Representations, 59,* 14–29.

Grossberg, L., Nelson, C., & Treichler, P. (Eds.) (1992). *Cultural studies.* New York: Routledge.

Guba, E. G. (1990a). The alternative paradigm dialog. In E. G. Guba (Ed.), *The paradigm dialog* (pp. 17–30). Newbury Park, CA: Sage.

Guba, E. G. (1990b). Carrying on the dialog. In Egon G. Guba (Ed.), *The paradigm dialog* (pp. 368–378). Newbury Park, CA: Sage.

Guba, E., & Lincoln, Y. S. (1989). *Fourth generation evaluation.* Newbury Park, CA: Sage.

Guba, E., & Lincoln, Y. S. (2005). Paradigmatic controversies and emerging confluences. In N. K. Denzin & Y. S. Lincoln (Eds.), *The SAGE handbook of qualitative research* (3rd ed., pp. 191–216). Thousand Oaks, CA: Sage.

Gupta, A., & Ferguson, J. (Eds.). (1997). Discipline and practice: "The field" as site, method, and location in anthropology. In A. Gupta & J. Ferguson (Eds.), *Anthropological locations: Boundaries and grounds of a field science* (pp. 1–46). Berkeley: University of California Press.

Hammersley, M. (1992). *What's wrong with ethnography?* London: Routledge.

Hammersley, M. (2000). Not bricolage but boatbuilding. *Journal of Contemporary Ethnography, 28,* 5.

Hammersley, M. (2008). *Questioning qualitative inquiry: Critical essays.* London: Sage.

Harper, D. (1987). *Working knowledge: Skill and community in a small shop.* Chicago: University of Chicago Press.

Hesse-Biber, S. N., & Leavy, P. (2008). Introduction: Pushing on the methodological boundaries: The growing need for emergent methods within and across the disciplines. In S. N. Hesse-Biber & P. Leavy (Eds.), *Handbook of emergent methods* (pp. 1–15). New York: Guilford Press.

Holman-Jones, S. H. (1999). Torch. *Qualitative Inquiry, 5,* 235–250.

hooks, b.(1990). *Yearning: Race, gender, and cultural politics.* Boston: South End Press.

Howe, K. (1988). Against the quantitative-qualitative incompatibility thesis (Or dogmas die hard). *Educational Researcher, 17*(8), 10–16.

Howe, K. R. (2004). A critique of experimentalism. *Qualitative Inquiry, 10*(1), 42–61.

Howe, K. R. (2009). Positivist dogmas, rhetoric, and the education science question. *Education Researcher, 38* (August/September), 428–440.

Huber, J. (1995). Centennial essay: Institutional perspectives on sociology. *American Journal of Sociology, 101,* 194–216.

Jackson, M. (1998). *Minima ethnographica.* Chicago: University of Chicago Press.

Jameson, F. (1991). *Postmodernism, or the cultural logic of late capitalism.* Durham, NC: Duke University Press.

Keller, C. M., & Keller, J. D. (1996). *Cognition and tool use: The blacksmith at work.* New York: Cambridge University Press.

Kincheloe, J. L. (2001). Describing the bricolage: Conceptualizing a new rigor in qualitative research. *Qualitative Inquiry, 7*(6), 679–692.

Lather, P. (1993). Fertile obsession: Validity after poststructuralism. *Sociological Quarterly, 35,* 673–694.

Lather, P. (2004). This *is* your father's paradigm: Government intrusion and the case of qualitative research in education. *Qualitative Inquiry, 10*(1), 15–34.

Lather, P., & Smithies, C. (1997). *Troubling the angels: Women living with HIV/AIDS.* Boulder, CO: Westview Press.

LeCompte, M. D., & Preissle, J. with R. Tesch. (1993). *Ethnography and qualitative design in educational research* (2nd ed.). New York: Academic Press.

Lévi-Strauss, C. (1966). *The savage mind.* Chicago: University of Chicago Press. (Original work published 1962)

Lincoln, Y. S. (1997). Self, subject, audience, text: Living at the edge, writing in the margins. In W. G. Tierney & Y. S. Lincoln (Eds.), *Representation and the text: Re-framing the narrative voice* (pp. 37–56). Albany: SUNY Press.

Lincoln, Y. S. (1999, June 3–6). *Courage, vulnerability, and truth.* Paper presented to the Reclaiming Voice II Conference, University of California-Irvine, Irvine, CA.

Lincoln, Y. S. (2010). What a long, strange trip it's been . . . : Twenty-five years of qualitative and new paradigm research. *Qualitative Inquiry, 16*(1), 3–9.

Lincoln, Y. S., & Cannella, G. S. (2004a). Dangerous discourses: Methodological conservatism and governmental regimes of truth. *Qualitative Inquiry, 10*(1), 5–14.

Lincoln, Y. S., & Cannella, G. S. (2004b). Qualitative research, power, and the radical right. *Qualitative Inquiry, 10*(2), 175–201.

Lincoln, Y. S., & Guba, E. G. (1985). *Naturalistic inquiry.* Beverly Hills, CA: Sage.

Lincoln, Y. S., & Tierney, W. G. (2004). Qualitative research and institutional review boards. *Qualitative Inquiry, 10*(2), 219–234.

Lofland, J. (1971). *Analyzing social settings.* Belmont, CA: Wadsworth.

Lofland, J. (1995). Analytic ethnography: Features, failings, and futures. *Journal of Contemporary Ethnography, 24,* 30–67.

Lofland, J., & Lofland, L. H. (1984). *Analyzing social settings.* Belmont, CA: Wadsworth.

Lofland, J., & Lofland, L. H. (1995). *Analyzing social settings* (3rd ed.). Belmont, CA: Wadsworth.

Lofland, L. (1980). The 1969 Blumer-Hughes talk. *Urban Life and Culture, 8,* 248–260.

Malinowski, B. (1948). *Magic, science and religion, and other essays.* New York: Natural History Press. (Original work published 1916)

Malinowski, B. (1967). *A diary in the strict sense of the term.* New York: Harcourt.

Marcus, G., & Fischer, M. (1986). *Anthropology as cultural critique.* Chicago: University of Chicago Press.

Maxwell, J. A. (2004). Reemergent scientism, postmodernism, and dialogue across differences. *Qualitative Inquiry, 10*(1), 35–41.

Mills, C. W. (1959). *The sociological imagination.* New York: Oxford University Press.

Monaco, J. (1981). *How to read a film: The art, technology, language, history and theory of film* (Rev. ed.). New York: Oxford University Press.

Morse, J. M. (2006). The politics of evidence. In N. Denzin & M. Giardina (Eds.), *Qualitative inquiry and the conservative challenge* (pp. 79–92). Walnut Creek, CA: Left Coast Press.

Morse, J. M., & Niehaus, L. (2009). *Mixed method design: Principles and procedures.* Walnut Creek, CA: Left Coast Press.

Nelson. C., Treichler, P. A., & Grossberg, L. (1992). Cultural studies. In L. Grossberg, C. Nelson, & P. A. Treichler (Eds.), *Cultural studies* (pp. 1–16). New York: Routledge.

Ortner, S. B. (1997). Introduction. In S. B. Ortner (Ed.), The fate of "culture": Clifford Geertz and beyond [Special issue]. *representations, 59,* 1–13.

Pelias, R. J. (2004). *A methodology of the heart: Evoking academic & daily life.* Walnut Creek, CA: AltaMira.

Plath, David. (1990). Fieldnotes, filed notes, and the conferring of note. In R. Sanjek (Ed.), *Fieldnotes* (pp. 371–384). Albany: SUNY Press.

Popkewitz, T. S. (2004). Is the National Research Council committee's report on scientific research in education scientific? On trusting the manifesto. *Qualitative Inquiry, 10*(1), 62–78.

Richardson, L. (1991). Postmodern social theory. *Sociological Theory, 9,* 173–179.

Richardson, L. (1992). The consequences of poetic representation: Writing the other, rewriting the self. In C. Ellis & M. G. Flaherty (Eds.), *Investigating subjectivity: Research on lived experience.* Newbury Park, CA: Sage.

Richardson, L. (1997). *Fields of play.* New Brunswick, NJ: Rutgers University Press.

Richardson, L. (2000). Writing: A method of inquiry. In N. K. Denzin & Y. S. Lincoln (Eds.), *Handbook of qualitative research* (2nd ed., pp. 923–948). Thousand Oaks, CA: Sage.

Richardson, L., & Lockridge, E. (2004). *Travels with Ernest: Crossing the literary/sociological divide.* Walnut Creek, CA: AltaMira.

Roffman, P., & Purdy, J. (1981). *The Hollywood social problem film.* Bloomington: Indiana University Press.

Ronai, C. R. (1998). Sketching with Derrida: An ethnography of a researcher/erotic dancer. *Qualitative Inquiry, 4,* 405–420.

Rosaldo, R. (1989). *Culture & truth.* Boston: Beacon.

Ryan, K. E., & Hood, L. K. (2004). Guarding the castle and opening the gates. *Qualitative Inquiry, 10*(1): 79–95.

Sanjek, R. (1992). *Fieldnotes.* Albany: SUNY Press.

Scheurich, J. & Clark, M. C. (2006). Qualitative studies in education at the beginning of the twenty-first century. *International Journal of Qualitative Studies in Education, 19*(4), 401.

Schwandt, T. A. (1997a). *Qualitative inquiry.* Thousand Oaks, CA: Sage.

Schwandt, T. A. (1997b). Textual gymnastics, ethics, angst. In W. G. Tierney & Y. S. Lincoln (Eds.), *Representation and the text: Re-framing the narrative voice* (pp. 305–313). Albany: SUNY Press.

Seale, C., Gobo, G., Gubrium, J. F., & Silverman, D. (2004). Introduction: Inside qualitative research. In C. Seale, G. Gobo, J. F. Gubrium, & D. Silverman (Eds.), *Qualitative research practice* (pp. 1–11). London: Sage.

Semaili, L. M., & Kincheloe, J. L. (1999). Introduction: What is indigenous knowledge and why should we study it? In L. M. Semaili & J. L. Kincheloe (Eds.), *What is indigenous knowledge? Voices from the academy* (pp. 3–57). New York: Falmer Press.

Silverman, D. (1997). Towards an aesthetics of research. In D. Silverman (Ed.), *Qualitative research: Theory, method, and practice* (pp. 239–253). London: Sage.

Smith, A. D. (1993). *Fires in the mirror.* New York: Anchor Books.

Smith, L. T. (1999). *Decolonizing methodologies: Research and indigenous peoples.* Dunedin, NZ: University of Otago Press.

Snow, D., & Morrill, C. (1995). Ironies, puzzles, and contradictions in Denzin and Lincoln's vision of qualitative research. *Journal of Contemporary Ethnography, 22,* 358–362.

Spindler, G., & Spindler, L. (1992). Cultural process and ethnography: An anthropological perspective. In M. D. LeCompte, W. L. Millroy, & J. Preissle (Eds.), *The handbook of qualitative research in education* (pp. 53–92). New York: Academic Press.

Stocking, G. W., Jr. (1986). Anthropology and the science of the irrational: Malinowski's encounter with Freudian psychoanalysis. In *History of anthropology: Vol. 4. Malinowski, Rivers, Benedict, and others: Essays on culture and personality* (pp. 13–49). Madison: University of Wisconsin Press.

Stocking, G. W., Jr. (1989). The ethnographic sensibility of the 1920s and the dualism of the anthropological tradition. In *History of anthropology: Vol. 6. Romantic Motives: Essays on anthropological sensibility* (pp. 208–276). Madison: University of Wisconsin Press.

Stoller, P., & Olkes, C. (1987). *In sorcery's shadow.* Chicago: University of Chicago Press.

St.Pierre, E. A. (2004). Refusing alternatives: A science of contestation. *Qualitative Inquiry, 10*(1), 130–139.

St.Pierre, E. A., & Roulston, K. (2006). The state of qualitative inquiry: A contested science. *International Jouranl of Qualitative Studies in Education, 19*(6), 673–684.

Strauss, A. (1987). *Qualitative analysis for social scientists.* New York: Cambridge.

Strauss, A., & Corbin, J. (1999). *Basics of qualitative research* (2nd ed.). Thousand Oaks, CA: Sage.

Taylor, S. J., & Bogdan, R. (1998). *Introduction to qualitative research methods: A phenomenological approach to the social sciences* (3rd ed.). New York: Wiley.

Teddlie, C., & Tashakkori, A. (2003a). Major issues and controversies in the use of mixed methods in the social and behavioral sciences. In A. Tashakkori & C. Teddlie (Eds.), *Handbook of mixed-methods in social and behavioral research* (pp. 3–50). Thousand Oaks, CA: Sage.

Teddlie, C., & Tashakkori, A. (2003b). Preface. In A. Tashakkori & C. Teddlie (Eds.), *Handbook of mixed-methods in social and behavioral research* (pp. ix-xv). Thousand Oaks, CA: Sage.

Turner, V., & Bruner, E. (Eds.). (1986). *The anthropology of experience.* Urbana: University of Illinois Press.

Van Maanen, J. (1988). *Tales of the field.* Chicago: University of Chicago Press.

Vygotsky, L. S. (1978). *Mind in society.* Cambridge, MA: Harvard University Press.

Weinstein, D., & Weinstein, M. A. (1991). Georg Simmel: Sociological *flaneur bricoleur. Theory, Culture & Society, 8,* 151–168.

Weinstein, M. (2004). Randomized design and the myth of certain knowledge: Guinea pig narratives and cultural critique. *Qualitative Inquiry, 10*(2), 246–260.

West, C. (1989). *The American evasion of philosophy.* Madison: University of Wisconsin Press.

Wolcott, H. F. (1990). *Writing up qualitative research.* Newbury Park, CA: Sage.

Wolcott, H. F. (1992). Posturing in qualitative research. In M. D. LeCompte, W. L. Millroy, & J. Preissle (Eds.), *The handbook of qualitative research in education* (pp. 3–52). New York: Academic Press, Inc.

Wolcott, H. F. (1995). *The art of fieldwork.* Walnut Creek, CA: AltaMira Press.

Wolfe, M. (1992). *A thrice-told tale.* Stanford, CA: Stanford University Press.

Wright, H. K. (2006). Are we there yet? Qualitative research in education's profuse and contested present. *International Journal of Qualitative Studies in Education, 19*(6), 793–802.

Part I

Strategies of Inquiry

The civic-minded qualitative researcher thinks historically, interactionally, and structurally. He or she attempts to identify the many persuasions, prejudices, injustices, and inequities that prevail in a given historical period (Mills, 1959, p. 7). Critical scholars seek to examine the major public and private issues and personal troubles that define a particular historical moment. In doing so, qualitative researchers self-consciously draw upon their own experience as a resource in such inquiries. They always think reflectively and historically, as well as biographically. They seek strategies of empirical inquiry that will allow them to make connections between lived experience, social injustices, larger social and cultural structures, and the here and now. These connections will be forged out of the interpretations and empirical materials that are generated in any given inquiry.

Empirical inquiry, of course, is shaped by paradigm commitments and by the recurring questions that any given paradigm or interpretive perspective asks about human experience, social structure, and culture. More deeply, however, the researcher always asks how the practices of qualitative inquiry can be used to help create a free, democratic society. Critical theorists, for example, examine the material conditions and systems of ideology that reproduce class and economic structures. Queer, constructivist, cultural studies, critical race, and feminist researchers examine the stereotypes, prejudices, and injustices connected to race, ethnicity, and gender. There is no such thing as value-free inquiry, although in qualitative inquiry this premise is presented with more clarity. Such clarity permits the value-commitments of researchers to be transparent.

The researcher-as-interpretive-bricoleur is always already in the material world of values and empirical experience. This world is confronted and constituted through the lens that the scholar's paradigm or interpretive perspective provides. The world so conceived ratifies the individual's commitment to the paradigm or perspective in question. This paradigm is connected at a higher ethical level to the values and politics of an emancipatory, civic social science.

As specific investigations are planned and carried out, two issues must be immediately confronted: research design and choice of strategy of inquiry. We take them up in order. Each devolves into a variety of related questions and issues that must also be addressed.

Research Design[1]

The research design, as discussed in our Introduction and analyzed by Julianne Cheek in this part of the *Handbook,* situates the investigator in the world of experience. Five basic questions structure the issue of design:

1. How will the design connect to the paradigm or perspective being used?

That is, how will empirical materials be informed by and interact with the paradigm in question?

2. How will these materials allow the researcher to speak to the problems of praxis and change?

3. Who or what will be studied?

4. What strategies of inquiry will be used?

5. What methods or research tools for collecting and analyzing empirical materials will be utilized?

These questions are examined in detail in Part IV of the *Handbook.*

Paradigm, Perspective, and Metaphor

The positivist, postpositivist, constructionist, and critical paradigms dictate, with varying degrees of freedom, the design of a qualitative research investigation. This can be viewed as a continuum moving from rigorous design principles on one end to emergent, less well-structured directives on the other. Positivist research designs place a premium on the early identification and development of a research question, a set of hypotheses, a research site, and a statement concerning sampling strategies, as well as a specification of the research strategies and methods of analysis that will be employed. A research proposal laying out the stages and phases of the study may be written. In interpretive research, a priori design commitments may block the introduction of new understandings. Consequently, while qualitative researchers may design procedures beforehand, designs always have built-in flexibility, to account for new and unexpected empirical materials and growing sophistication.

The stages of a study can be conceptualized as involving reflection, planning, entry, data collection, withdrawal from the field, analysis, and write-up. Julianne Cheek (Chapter 2) observes that the degree of detail involved in the proposal will vary, depending on the funding agency. Funding agencies fall into at least six categories: local community funding units, special purpose, family-sponsored, corporate or national foundations, and federal governmental agencies. Depending on the requirements of the funder, proposals may also include a budget, a review of the relevant literature, a statement concerning human subjects protection, a copy of consent forms, interview schedules, and a timeline. Positivist designs attempt to anticipate all of the problems that may arise in a qualitative study (although interpretivist designs do not). Such designs provide rather well-defined road maps for the researcher. The scholar working in this tradition hopes to produce a work that finds its place in the literature on the topic being studied.

In contrast, much greater ambiguity and flexibility are associated with post-positivist and nonpositivist designs, those based, for example, on the constructivist or critical theory paradigms, or the critical race, feminist, queer, or cultural studies perspectives. In studies shaped by these paradigms and perspectives, there will be less emphasis on formal grant proposals, well-formulated hypotheses, tightly defined sampling frames, structured interview schedules, and predetermined research strategies and methods and forms of analysis. The researcher may follow a path of discovery, using as a model qualitative works that have achieved the status of classics in the field. Enchanted, perhaps, by the myth of the Lone Ethnographer, the scholar hopes to produce a work that has the characteristics of a study done by one of the giants from the past (Bronislaw Malinowski, Margaret Mead, Gregory Bateson, Erving Goffman, Ernest Becker, Claude Lévi-Strauss, Harry Wolcott). As a result, qualitative researchers often at least begin by undertaking studies that can be completed by one individual after prolonged engagement.

The Politics and Practices of Funding Qualitative Inquiry

Cheek's chapter complicates and deconstructs the relationship between money, ethics, and research markets. She examines the politics and practices involved in funding qualitative inquiry, including seeking, gaining, and accepting funding. The politics of funding privileges certain forms of inquiry. A concern for the politics of evidence—what is evidence—leads to problems surrounding research design and sample size. Pressures to employ mixed methods procedures can complicate matters.

Cheek shows how qualitative research is a commodity that circulates and is exchanged in this political economy. Funding involves selling one's self to a funding agency. Such agencies may not understand the nuances of qualitative research practice. She discusses the problems associated with institutional review boards (IRBs) and ethics committees. In Australia, researchers cannot conduct research on human subjects until they have formal ethics approval from the University Research Ethics Committee. In the United States and the United Kingdom, as well as Australia, the original focus of IRBs and the context from which they emerged was medicine. Qualitative research is often treated unfairly by ethics committees. Such research, it may be charged, is unscientific. In effect, IRBs have become methodological review boards, institutionalizing only one brand, or version, of science. In the United Kingdom, the Royal College of Physicians' guidelines make the point that badly designed research is unethical. This means that judgment is being passed on the scientific as well as the ethical merits of research. Cheek observes that in too many instances "it seems that qualitative researchers have become the fall guys for ethical mistakes in medical research." Cheek notes that many times qualitative researchers are unable to answer in advance all of the questions that are raised by such committees. Issues of control over the research are also central. As she observes, "taking money from a sponsor [in order to conduct research] is not a neutral activity." This issue shades into another, namely, what happens when the researcher's findings do not please the funder?

There are problems in accepting external funding. Faculty are increasingly under pressure to secure external funding for their research. Such pressures turn research into a commodity that is bought and sold. Cheek observes that these are dangerous times. The conservative discourse of the marketplace has become preeminent. It is the market, not the judgment of stakeholders and peers, that now determines the worth of what we do. Are we writing for inquiry purposes, or for funding reasons?

CHOREOGRAPHING THE DANCE OF DESIGN

V. J. Janesick (2000, 2010) presents a fluid view of the design process. She observes that the essence of good qualitative research design requires the use of a set of procedures that are at once open-ended and rigorous. Influenced by Martha Graham, Merce Cunningham, Alvin Ailey, Elliot Eisner, and John Dewey, she approaches the problem of research design from an aesthetic, artistic, and metaphorical perspective. With Dewey and Eisner, she sees research design as a work of improvisational, rather than composed, art—as an event, a process, with phases connected to different forms of problematic experience, and their interpretation and representation. Art molds and fashions experience. In its dance form, art is a choreographed, emergent production with distinct phases: warming up, stretching exercises, and design decisions, cooling down, interpretation, and writing the narrative.

WHO AND WHAT WILL BE STUDIED?

The who and what of qualitative studies involve cases, or instances, of phenomena and/or social processes. Three generic approaches may be taken to the question of who or what will be studied. First, a single case, or single process, may be studied, what Robert Stake (2005) calls the intrinsic case study. Here, the researcher examines in detail a single case or instance of the phenomenon in question, for example, a classroom, an arts program, or a death in the family.

Second, the researcher may focus on a number of cases. Stake (2005) calls this the collective case approach. These cases are then analyzed in terms of specific and generic properties. Third, the researcher can examine multiple instances of a process as that process is displayed in a variety of different cases. Denzin's (1993) study of relapse in the careers of recovering alcoholics examined types of relapses across several different types of recovering careers. This process approach is then grounded or anchored in specific cases.

Research designs vary, of course, depending on the needs of multi-, or single-focused case and process inquiries. Different sampling issues arise in each situation. These needs and issues also vary by the paradigm that is being employed. Every instance of a case or process bears the stamp of the general class of phenomenon to which it belongs. However, any given instance is likely to be particular and unique. Thus, for example, any given classroom is like all classrooms, but no classroom is the same.

For these reasons, many postpositivist, constructionist, and critical theory qualitative researchers employ theoretical or purposive, and not random, sampling models. They seek out groups, settings, and individuals where (and for whom) the processes being studied are most likely to occur. At the same time, a process of constant comparison between groups, concepts, and observations is necessary, as the researcher seeks to develop an understanding that encompasses all instances of the process, or case, under investigation. A focus on negative cases is a key feature of this process.

These sampling and selection issues would be addressed differently by a postmodern ethnographer in the cultural studies tradition. This investigator would be likely to place greater stress on the intensive analysis of a small body of empirical materials (cases and processes), arguing, after Jean-Paul Sartre (1981, p. ix), that no individual or case is ever just an individual or a case. He or she must be studied as a single instance of more universal social experiences and social processes. The individual, Sartre (1981, p. ix) states, is "summed up and for this reason universalized by his [her] epoch, he [she] in turn resumes it by reproducing him- [her-]self in it as a singularity." Thus to study the particular is to study the general. For this reason, any case will necessarily bear the traces of the universal, and, consequently, there is less interest in the traditional positivist and postpositivist concerns with negative cases, generalizations, and case selection. The researcher assumes that the reader will be able, as Robert Stake (2005) argues, to generalize subjectively from the case in question to his or her own personal experiences.

An expansion on this strategy is given in the method of instances (see Denzin, 1999; Psathas, 1995). Following George Psathas (1995, p. 50), the "method of instances" takes each instance of a phenomenon as an occurrence that evidences the operation of a set of cultural understandings currently available for use by cultural members.

An analogy may be useful. In discourse analysis, "no utterance is representative of other utterances, though of course it shares structural features with them; a discourse analyst studies utterances in order to understand how the potential of the linguistic system can be activated when it intersects at its moment of use with a social system" (Fiske, 1994, p. 195). This is the argument for the method of instances. The analyst examines those moments when an utterance intersects with another utterance, giving rise to an instance of the system in action.

Psathas clarifies the meaning of an instance: "An instance of something is an occurrence . . . an event whose features and structures can be examined to discover how it is organized" (1995, p. 50). An occurrence is evidence that "the machinery for its production is culturally available . . . [for example,] the machinery of turn-taking in conversation" (pp. 50–51).

The analyst's task is to understand how this instance and its intersections work, to show what rules of interpretation are operating, to map and illuminate the structure of the interpretive event itself. The analyst inspects the actual course of the interaction "by observing what happens first, second, next, etc., by noticing what preceded it; and by examining what is actually done and said by the participants" (Psathas, 1995, p. 51). Questions of meaning are referred back to the actual course of interaction, where it can be shown how a given utterance is acted upon and hence given meaning. The pragmatic maxim obtains here (Peirce, 1905). The meaning of an action is given in the consequences that are produced by it, including the ability to explain past experience, and predict future consequences.

Whether the particular utterance occurs again is irrelevant. The question of sampling from a population is also not an issue, for it is never possible to say in advance what an instance is a sample of (Psathas, 1995, p. 50). Indeed, collections of instances "cannot be assembled in advance of an analysis of at least one, because it cannot be known in advance what features delineate each case as a 'next one like the last'" (Psathas, 1995, p. 50).

This means there is little concern for empirical generalization. Psathas is clear on this point. The goal is not an abstract, or empirical, generalization; rather the aim is "concerned with providing analyses that meet the criteria of unique adequacy" (1995, p. 50). Each analysis must be fitted to the case at hand, each "must be studied to provide an analysis *uniquely adequate* for that particular phenomenon" (p. 51, italics in original).

STRATEGIES OF INQUIRY

A strategy of inquiry describes the skills, assumptions, enactments, and material practices that researchers-as-methodological-bricoleurs use when they move from a paradigm and a research design to the collection of empirical materials. Strategies of inquiry connect researchers to specific approaches and methods for collecting and analyzing empirical materials. The case study, for example, relies on interviewing, observing, and document analysis. Research strategies locate researchers and paradigms in specific empirical, material sites, and in specific methodological practices, for example, making a case an object of study (see Bent Flyvbjerg, Chapter 5).

We turn now to a brief review of the strategies of inquiry discussed in this volume. Each is connected to a complex literature with its own history, its own exemplary works, and its own set of preferred ways for putting the strategy into motion. Each strategy also has its own set of problems involving the positivist, postpositivist, and postmodern legacies.

MIXED METHODS RESEARCH

John W. Creswell (Chapter 3) and Charles Teddlie and Abbas Tashakkori (Chapter 4) examine controversies and issues in mixed methods research (MMR), or the third methodological moment. Although there is considerable debate over what constitutes mixed methods research, Creswell and Teddlie and Tashakkori suggest that it is inquiry that focuses on collecting, analyzing, and mixing both quantitative and qualitative empirical materials in a single study, or a series of studies. Creswell identifies 11 key controversies and questions being raised about mixed methods research. These issues include disagreements over definitions; just what is a mixed methods study; paradigm debates—that is, are there incommensurable and incompatible (and irresolvable) differences between paradigms?; how does the current conversation privilege postpositivism?; and what value is added by mixed methods? In giving voice to these controversies, Creswell creates the space for a reassessment of the mixed methods movement and where it is taking the interpretive community.

Teddlie and Tashakkori (and Creswell) offer a history of this field, noting overlaps with recent developments in emergent methods (Hess-Biber & Leavy, 2008), parallels with earlier arguments for triangulation (Denzin, 1970),[2] as well as discourse in the fields of evaluation, nursing, education, disability studies, and sociology. For these researchers, MMR is characterized by eclecticism, paradigm pluralism, a celebration of diversity, a rejection of dichotomies, an iterative approach to inquiry, an emphasis on the research question, and a focus on signature MMR design and analysis strategies (QUAL/QUAN): parallel, sequential, multilevel, sequential mixed, and so on. A typology of designs is reviewed.

Three dominant paradigms—pragmatism, transformative, and dialectical—are also reviewed, even as these authors discuss the arguments against a continued focus on paradigms. Some contend the term paradigm is outmoded. We disagree. Criticisms of MMR include the incompatibility thesis, a pervasive postpositivist bias, the tendency to subordinate QUAL to QUAN, cost, superficial methodological bilingualism, and an entanglement in superficial philosophical debate (e.g., forms of pragmatism). Teddlie and Tashakkori believe many of these issues will be resolved in the next decade.

A Pragmatic Aside

As pragmatists trained in, or sympathetic to, the Chicago School, we are not so certain (Denzin, 2010; Lincoln, 2010). So we respectfully demur.

The MMR links to the pragmatism of John Dewey, William James, Margaret Mead, and Charles Peirce are problematic for us. Classic pragmatism is not a methodology per se. It is a doctrine of meaning, a theory of truth. It rests on the argument that the meaning of an event cannot be given in advance of experience. The focus is on the consequences and meanings of an action or event in a social situation. This concern goes beyond any given methodology—that is, the interpreter examines and inspects, and reflects upon an action and its consequences. Nor are they revealed by a given methodology. The MMR community does not seem to have a method for ascertaining meaning at this level.

Neopragmatists Richard Rorty, Jürgen Habermas, and Cornel West extend the classic doctrine. They endorse a thoroughly interpretive, hermeneutic pragmatism that is explicitly antipositivist, antifoundational, and radically contextual. Basing an argument for mixed methods on this version of pragmatism seems misplaced.

The compatibility thesis for the MMR community asserts that combining qualitative and quantitative methods is a good thing; that is, there is no incompatibility between QUAN and QUAL at the practical or epistemological levels. Under this reading, pragmatism rejects paradigm conflicts between QUAN and QUAL epistemologies. Pragmatism is thus read as a practical and applied research philosophy that supports mixed or multiple methods of social science inquiry (Maxcy, 2003, p. 85). An additional warrant for this is given by K. R. Howe (1988), who appeals to a "what works," or practical consequences, version of pragmatism. This is cash register pragmatism, not classic pragmatism. But this version of what works is not the point. The pragmatist focus is on the consequences of action, not on combining methodologies. And here, the MMR is of little help.

It is one thing to endorse pluralism, or multiple frameworks (Schwandt, 2007, p. 197), but it is quite another to build a social science on a cash register pragmatism. What works means two things, or has two consequences. First, it is a mistake to forget about paradigmatic, epistemological, or methodological differences between and within QUAN/QUAL frameworks. These are differences that matter, but they must not distract us from the second problem. As currently formulated, MMR offers few strategies for assessing the interpretive, contextual level of experience where meaning is created.

THE CASE STUDY

Bent Flyvbjerg (Chapter 5) employs a commonsense definition of the case study as the intensive analysis of an individual unit. He examines, and then refutes, five misunderstandings about this strategy of inquiry: (1) general rather than case knowledge is more valuable; (2) one cannot generalize from an individual case; (3) the case study is not suited to theory building; (4) the case study has a tendency to confirm the researcher's biases; and (5) it is difficult to develop generalizations based on specific case studies.

He demonstrates that concrete case knowledge is more valuable than the vain search for predictive theories and universals. It is possible to generalize from a single case (Charles Darwin, Isaac Newton, Albert Einstein), and it is useful for generating and testing hypotheses. It contains no greater bias toward verification of the researcher's preconceived notions than any other method of inquiry. Often it is not desirable to generalize from case studies. Flyvbjerg clarifies the methodological value of the case study and goes some distance in establishing its importance to the social sciences.

Robert Stake (2005) contends that the case study is not a methodological choice, but a choice of object to be studied, for example, a child, or a classroom. Ultimately, the researcher is interested in a process, or a population of cases, not an individual case per se. Stake identifies several types of case studies (intrinsic, instrumental, collective). Each case is a complex historical and contextual entity. Case studies have unique conceptual structures, uses, and problems (bias, theory, triangulation, telling the story, case selection, ethics). Researchers routinely provide information on such topics as the nature of the case, its historical background, its relation to its contexts and other cases, as well as to the informants who have provided information. In order to avoid ethical problems, the case study researcher needs constant input from conscience, from stakeholders, and from the research community.

PERFORMANCE ETHNOGRAPHY

Judith Hamera (Chapter 6) offers a nuanced, and detailed, discussion of the complex relationship between performance studies, ethnography (and autoethnography), and critical pedagogy. She connects these formations to critical pedagogy theory. Performance ethnography is a way of inciting culture, a way of bringing culture alive, a way of fusing the pedagogical with the performative, with the political. Hamera's chapter addresses the key terms (reflexivity, performance, ethnography, performativity, aesthetics), the philosophical contingencies, the procedural pragmatics, and the pedagogical and political possibilities that exist in the spaces and practices of performance ethnography. Her arguments complement the Tedlock and Spry chapters (7 and 7, volume 3, respectively) in this handbook.

Performance is an embodied act of interpretation, a way of knowing, a form of moral discourse. A politics of possibility organizes the project. Performance ethnography can be used politically, to incite others to moral action. Performance ethnography strengthens a commitment to a civic-minded discourse, a kind of performative citizenship advocated by Zora Neale Hurston, Dwight Conquergood, Soyini Madison, Bella Pollock, and others. Performance ethnography is a way for critical scholars to make sense of this historical movement, a form of action that helps us imagine radically free utopian spaces.

NARRATIVE ETHNOGRAPHY

Barbara Tedlock (Chapter 7) reminds us that ethnography "involves an ongoing attempt to place specific encounters, events, and understandings into a fuller, more meaningful context." Tedlock shows how participant observation has become the observation of participation. As a consequence, the doing, framing, representation, and reading of ethnography have been dramatically changed in the last two decades. The fields of passionate, narrative, evocative, gonzo ethnography and autoethnography have emerged out of this discourse.

Tedlock observes that early anthropology in the United States included a tradition of social criticism and public engagement. Franz Boas, Ruth Benedict, and Margaret Mead shaped public opinion through their social criticisms and their calls for public and political action. By the mid 1960s, the term critical anthropology gained force in the context of the civil rights movement and growing opposition to the Vietnam War. Critical theory in anthropology was put into practice through the production of plays. An indigenous political theater based on the works of Bertolt Brecht, Augusto Boal, Paulo Freire, and others gained force in Latin America, Africa, and elsewhere.

Victor and Edith Turner, and Edward Bruner, developed performance ethnography in the 1980s. Culture was seen as a performance, and interpretation was performative. Ethnodrama and public ethnography emerged as vehicles for addressing social issues. Public ethnography is a discourse that engages with critical issues of the time. It is an extension of critical anthropology. In the late 1990s, under the editorship of Barbara and Dennis Tedlock, the *American Anthropologist* began to publish politically engaged essays. Tedlock observes that "within this politically engaged environment, social science projects serve the communities in which they are carried out, rather than serving external communities of educators, policymakers, military personnel and financiers." Thus does public ethnography take up issues of social justice.

Today, we inhabit a space of braided narrative, double consciousness, performance, creative nonfiction, history, drama, and magical realism, memories forgotten, recaptured, "overtake us as spiders weaving the dreamcatchers of our lives." Amen.

ANALYZING INTERPRETIVE PRACTICE

In Chapter 8, James Holstein and Jaber Gubrium extend their more than two-decade-long constructivist project offering a new language of qualitative research that builds on ethnomethodology, conversational analysis, institutional studies of local culture, and Foucault's critical approach to history and discourse analysis. Their chapter masterfully captures a developing consensus in the interpretive community. This consensus seeks to show how social constructionist approaches can be profitably combined with poststructuralist discourse analysis (Foucault), and the situated study of meaning and order as local, social accomplishments.

Holstein and Gubrium draw attention to the interpretive narrative procedures and practices that give structure and meaning to everyday life. These reflexive practices are both the topic of, and the resources for, qualitative inquiry. Knowledge is always local, situated in a local culture, and embedded in organizational and interactional sites. Everyday stereotypes and ideologies, including understandings about race, class, and gender, are enacted in these sites. The systems of power, what Dorothy Smith (1993) calls the ruling apparatuses, and relations of ruling in society, are played out in these sites. Holstein and Gubrium build on Smith's project, elaborating a critical theory of discourse and social structure. Holstein and Gubrium then show how reflexive discourse and discursive practices transform the processes of analytic and critical bracketing. Such practices make the foundations of local social order visible. This emphasis on constructivist analytics, interpretive resources, and local resources enlivens and dramatically extends the reflexive turn in qualitative research. With this apparatus, we can move to dismantle and contest oppressive realities that threaten to derail social justice initiatives.

GROUNDED THEORY

Kathy Charmaz (Chapter 9) is a leading exponent of the constructivist approach to grounded theory. Grounded theory is a method of qualitative inquiry "in which data collection and analysis reciprocally inform each other through an emergent iterative process." The term "grounded theory" refers to a theory developed from successive conceptual analyses of empirical materials.

Charmaz shows how grounded theory methods offer rich possibilities for advancing qualitative justice research in the 21st century. Grounded theorists have the tools to describe and go beyond situations of social justice. They can offer interpretations and analyses about the conditions under which injustice develops, changes, or is maintained. They can enact an explicit value stance and agenda for change. Some focus on a social justice issue because it illuminates a theoretical problem. Those who explicitly identify as social justice researchers use words like should and ought.

Charmaz suggests that grounded theory, in its essential form, consists of systematic inductive guidelines for collecting and analyzing empirical materials to build middle-range theoretical frameworks that explain collected empirical materials. Her chapter outlines the history of this approach, from the early work of Glaser and Strauss, to its transformations in more recent statements by Glaser, Strauss, and Corbin. She contrasts the positivist-objectivist positions of Glaser, Strauss, and Corbin with her own more interpretive constructivist approach, which stakes out a middle ground between postmodernism and positivism. Grounded theory may be the most widely employed interpretive strategy in the social sciences today. It gives the researcher a specific set of steps to follow that are closely aligned with the canons of "good science." But on this point Charmaz is clear: It is possible to use grounded theory without embracing earlier proponents' positivist leanings (a position long adopted by Guba and Lincoln [see Chapter 6 in volume 1, and Lincoln & Guba, 1985]). She notes that grounded theory mixed methods projects are increasing in fields such as education and health.

Charmaz reviews the basic strategies used by grounded theorists. She moves these strategies into the space of social justice inquiry. She offers key criteria, basic questions that can be asked of any grounded theory study of social justice. Does a study exhibit credibility, and originality? Does it have resonance—is it connected to the worlds of lived experience? Is it useful? Can it be used by people in their everyday worlds? Does it contribute to a better society? With these criteria, she reclaims the social justice tradition of the early Chicago School, while moving grounded theory firmly into this new century. Her constructivist grounded theory is consistent with a symbolic interactionist pragmatism. Constructive grounded theory will be a method for the 21st century.

In the Name of Human Rights

Leading South Afrikaner scholar and poet Antjie Krog (Chapter 10) conducted two years of radio interviews and reportage for the South African Truth and Reconciliation Commission (TRC). Her essay—humorous, autobiographical, painful—opens with a 100-year-old account of a young widow's family story constructed on the basis of human footprints around a water hole. There are several voices in the story: She asks who is the scholar here? Who is raw material? Is it Bleek, the recorder of the original narration? Is it Liebenberg, the scholar of the tracking? Is it Krog, the author of this chapter? Is it the Bushman narrator? Is it the woman in the story? Who has the right to tell this story? Who has the right to enter into this discourse? How does the subaltern speak?

Krog playfully recounts her experience with an academic administrator who told she was raw material, not a scholar. She then discusses the story of Mrs. Konile, whose TRC testimony was first read as incoherent raw material. It is not that the subaltern cannot speak. They cannot be heard by the privileged of either the first or third worlds. We have a duty to listen and to act, to hear *testimonios* as cries to be heard.

RIFFS ON PARTICIPATORY ACTION RESEARCH

Mary Brydon-Miller, Michael Kral, Patricia Maguire, Susan Noffke, and Anu Sabhlok (Chapter 11) contend that participatory action research (PAR) combines theory and practice in a participatory way. It presumes that knowledge generation is a collaborative process. "Each participant's diverse experiences and skills are critical to the outcome of the work" (p. 387).The goal of PAR is to solve concrete community problems by engaging community participants in the inquiry process. PAR is like jazz improvisation—seemingly effortless and spontaneous, but in actuality the result of "rigorous training" (p. 387). PAR is also like the banyan tree—a gathering place of common people, a place of community discussion and decision making. PAR, like the banyan tree, provides a space and place where community members can come together, a place for discussion, dialogue.

Brydon-Miller and colleagues review the several different traditions and histories of PAR, noting that much of the early development of PAR took place outside of traditional academic settings in the "south," or third world. The history is dense, ranging from Paulo Freire's critical pedagogy project in Brazil, to Fals Borda's initiatives in Latin America, the Scandinavian folkschool movement, participatory action networks in Asia, and Australia (Stephen Kemmis and Robin McTaggart), the global young people's initiatives of Michele Fine and associates, to the struggles of feminist, literacy, social justice, labor, civil rights, and academic advocates. Traditionally, PAR challenges the distinction between theory and method. Strategies for collecting, analyzing, understanding, and distributing empirical materials cannot be separated from epistemology, social theory, or ethical stances.

The authors ground their reading of PAR in three sites: Sabhlok's dissertation research with the Self Employed Women's Association in Gujarat, a state in India; Alicia Fitzpatrick's work with American Indian nation youth in the southwestern United States; and Michael Kral's Inuit suicide prevention and reclamation project in Nunavut, Canada. Each case study demonstrates the power of PAR to "challenge and unsettle existing structures of power and privilege, to provide opportunities for those least often heard to share their knowledge and wisdom, and for people to work together to bring about positive social change and to create more just and equitable political and social systems" (p. 396).

QUALITATIVE HEALTH RESEARCH

Janice Morse (Chapter 12) observes that because of its subject matter qualitative health care research is distinct from other forms of qualitative inquiry. Qualitative health researchers deal with serious quality-of-life issues, as well as life-and-death situations. Morse considers the origins, history, content, and scope of qualitative health research. She offers a content analysis of all articles published in 2009 in *Qualitative Health Research*. She shows how qualitative methods can be adapted for use in clinical settings, and ends by making the case that qualitative health research is an important disciplinary subfield in its own right. The classics in the field—*Boys in White; Asylums; Awareness of Dying; Good Days, Bad Days*—are foundational. Their influence extends far beyond the field of health care research.

In 1997, Morse established the International Institute of Qualitative Methodology (IIQM) and *Qualitative Health Research*, a Sage monthly international journal. IIQM soon established links to 115 universities, through hubs in eight international sites. Today, there is a global network of mentors, sponsor journals, and congresses supporting qualitative health research.

Morse examines the many quandaries involved in health care inquiry, ranging from issues with IRBs, to problems with informed consent, studying ill, dying, and diseased persons, and medical staff fears of evaluation. She proposes some research strategies that work to make clinical research possible, ranging from retrospective interviews, to involving caregivers as coinvestigators. She concludes, "Qualitative health research is a specialized form of qualitative research . . . [with] its own needs for education, training, methods, and dissemination of knowledge." We agree.

Conclusion

Together, the chapters in Part III show how qualitative research can be used as a tool to create social change and advance social justice initiatives. Once the previously silenced are heard, they can then speak for themselves as agents of social change. Research is connected to political action, systems of language and meaning are changed, and paradigms are challenged. How to interpret these voices is the topic of Part IV of the *Handbook*. In the meantime, listen to the voices in Part III; these are calls to action.

Notes

1. Mitch Allen's comments have significantly shaped our treatment of the relationship between paradigms and research designs.

2. Denzin's call for triangulation involved combining multiple qualitative methodologies—life story, case study, interviewing, participant observation, ethnography. It did not include combining qualitative and quantitative methodologies.

References

Denzin, N. K. (1970). *The research act in sociology.* London: Butterworths.

Denzin, N. K. (1993). *The alcoholic society: Addiction and recovery of self.* New Brunswick, NJ: Transaction.

Denzin, N. K. (1999). Cybertalk and the method of instances. In S. Jones (Ed.), *Doing Internet research: Critical issues and methods for examining the net* (pp. 107–126). Thousand Oaks, CA: Sage.

Denzin, N. K. (2010). *The qualitative manifesto.* Walnut Creek, CA: Left Coast Press.

Fiske, J. (1994). Audiencing: Cultural practice and cultural studies. In N. K. Denzin & Y. S. Lincoln (Eds.), *Handbook of qualitative research* (pp. 189–198). Thousand Oaks, CA: Sage.

Hess-Biber, S. N., & Leavy, P. (Eds.). (2008). *Handbook of emergent methods.* New York: Guilford.

Howe, K. R. (1988). Against the quantitative-qualitative incompatibility thesis, or dogmas die hard. *Educational Researcher, 17*(8), 10–16.

Janesick, V. J. (2000). The choreography of qualitative research design. In N. K. Denzin & Y. S. Lincoln (Eds.), *Handbook of qualitative research* (2nd ed., pp. 379–399). Thousand Oaks, CA: Sage.

Janesick, V. J. (2010). *"Stretching" exercises for qualitative researchers* (3rd ed.). Thousand Oaks, CA: Sage.

Lincoln, Y. (2010). What a long, strange trip it's been . . . : Twenty-five years of qualitative and new paradigm research. *Qualitative Inquiry, 16*(1), 3–9.

Lincoln, Y. S., & Guba, E. G. (1985). *Naturalistic inquiry.* Beverly Hills, CA: Sage.

Maxcy, S. J. (2003). Pragmatic threads in mixed methods research in the social sciences: The search for multiple modes of inquiry and the end of the philosophy of formalism. In A. Tashakkori & C. Teddlie (Eds.), *Handbook of mixed methods in social & behavioral research* (pp. 51–90). Thousand Oaks, CA: Sage.

Mills, C. W. (1959). *The sociological imagination.* New York: Oxford University Press.

Peirce, C. S. (1905). What pragmatism is. *The Monist, 15*(2), 161–181.

Psathas, G. (1995). *Conversation analysis.* Thousand Oaks, CA: Sage.

Sartre, J.-P. (1981). *The family idiot: Gustave Flaubert, 1821–1857* (Vol. 1).Chicago: University of Chicago Press.

Schwandt, T. A. (2007). *The SAGE dictionary of qualitative inquiry* (3rd ed.). Thousand Oaks, CA: Sage.

Smith, D. E. (1993). High noon in textland: A critique of Clough. *Sociological Quarterly, 34,* 183–192.

Stake, R. E. (2005). Qualitative case studies. In N. K. Denzin & Y. S. Lincoln (Eds.), *The SAGE handbook of qualitative research* (3rd ed., pp. 443–466). Thousand Oaks, CA: Sage.

2

The Politics and Practices of Funding Qualitative Inquiry

Messages About Messages About Messages . . .

Julianne Cheek

Dear Reader,

This chapter is a series of reflections about how it is, and might be, possible to fund qualitative inquiry. Put another way, it is about how to sell our research ideas and research expertise in order to gain the resources we need to be able to do our research. For, no matter what type of qualitative inquiry we do, we are all selling, be it selling our time and/or our labor or/and our research projects. While speaking to issues that in some way touch and affect all qualitative inquirers, the discussion is primarily directed to readers who are perhaps a little unsure of how to begin funding their qualitative inquiry and/or navigate the research marketplace. My hope is that the chapter will provide this group of readers with both practical information that they can use to help them gain funding, as well the impetus to continue the ongoing intellectual work and reflection that thinking about the politics and practices of funding qualitative inquiry demands of us all.

At this point, some readers may be thinking that a discussion about funding qualitative inquiry is not relevant to them. If you are one of these readers, then perhaps you are thinking that the type of research you are interested in does not need large amounts of funding or interaction with funders, it really only needs your time. My response to this is that implicit within this type of thought is the assumption that funding for qualitative research is synonymous with, or limited to, support from sources removed from researchers themselves, most often thought of in terms of monetary support. Also implicit is the assumption that the researcher's time is somehow not funding for research. This overlooks the fact that funding for research comes in many different forms.

For example, funding can be in the form of money for salaries to employ research staff, bring on research students, or even release chief investigators from other duties in order to be able to conduct the research. Support can also come in the form of money for the purchase of equipment such as data recorders and computers, or it can involve in-kind (nonmonetary) support where the equipment is either supplied or loaned for the duration of the project. Monetary, or in some cases in-kind, funding can also be gained to enable necessary travel or access to specialist skills and services such as translation expertise. Other forms of funding for qualitative inquiry can come either directly or indirectly from institutional incentive schemes to "reward" researchers who attract research income for that institution through their grants, publications, and successful research student completions. Such rewards can take the form of, for example, infrastructure grants to establish research centers within that institution, an increased percentage of workload allocation for research, and/or allocation of modest discretionary funds for approved research-related purposes such as conference attendance or research assistant hours.

Morse (2002) points out that it is a myth that qualitative research is cheap, or cheaper than other types of research, to do. It seems to me that this myth has arisen and flourished throughout much of qualitative research's history both without, and also interestingly within, the qualitative research community because of limited notions of funding and what constitutes funding for research. All researchers, regardless of their methodological or substantive interests, require some way of funding their research. This is true of any study, even those qualitative studies largely done by researchers working in their "own time" and not requiring large pieces of equipment, specialized workplaces/laboratories, and/or expensive consumables such as chemicals. It is this allocation of paid work time and/or donation of discretionary private or unpaid time to the study that is in effect funding the research. Thus, I think that funding our qualitative inquiry is a question that concerns all of us.

There were many forms that a chapter about funding and qualitative inquiry could take. For example, one possibility was to focus attention on "how to write a winning proposal" for funding. But this runs the risk of limiting the discussion to one about writing for funders, and often very specific types of funders running large research-granting programs. Funding, as we have seen, can take many forms. It also runs the risk of reducing the discussion to an instrumental "how to" one. Another possibility was to focus on the political dimensions affecting funding for qualitative inquiry, looking, for example, at how we can position our research in relation to a politics of evidence that has been so pervasive for the past decade. But this has already been written about, and written about well, in ongoing and vigorous calls for qualitative inquiry to resist the excesses of a politics of evidence with normalizing, exclusionary, and positivist tendencies (Denzin & Giardina, 2008; Holmes, Murray, Perron, & Rail, 2006). Further, a possible danger of such a focus is limiting the discussion of funding and qualitative inquiry to one that is always in reaction or relation to this politics, a politics imposed on qualitative inquiry from without. This may actually have the effect of sustaining the centrality of that politics in defining the parameters of the discussions we both do have, and importantly might have, about funding and qualitative inquiry. In this way, the politics of evidence can become a distractor displacing qualitative inquiry, funding, and even evidence as the focus (Long, 2010; Morse, 2006a).

Given this, how have I decided to structure the discussion? The explorations and reflections to follow about how it is, and might be, possible to fund qualitative inquiry, focus on two different, yet interconnected areas. The first area is what I have decided to call the *practices* involved in the seeking, gaining, and accepting of funding. It is about the practicalities of funding qualitative inquiry such as where funding might come from, the forms that funding might take, and strategies in locating appropriate funding for a particular piece of research. It is also about crafting a proposal for funding, and what it involves. This includes decisions about whom and what will be studied, as well as when and how and why. But equally, the discussion to follow is about how these decisions can be affected by the politics of funding and the politics of research. It is this *politics* that is the second area of focus in the chapter. It has been my experience that practices associated with locating and obtaining funding for qualitative inquiry cannot be seen apart from the politics that affects them at every point in both the research and funding process. Where a qualitative inquirer chooses to seek funding from, how they go about locating and applying for funding, and what they do when they receive funding, is as much a political discussion as it is a practical one.

What is this politics that I am talking about? The form of political thought that has dominated the thinking of many Western governments and administrators in the past decades, is one derived from neoliberal understandings. This is a politics promoting competition, efficiency, quality, notions of the marketplace, and audit-derived understandings of accountability (Cheek, 2005; Kvale, 2008; Torres, 2002). It is a politics in which one type of research evidence is privileged over another. Implicit within it are "contested notions of evidence. It is both about the way we do our research (the methods or procedures used to produce the evidence) and concomitant ways of thinking about what form(s) evidence must take in order for it to be considered valid, acceptable and therefore of use" (Cheek, 2008, p. 20). For as Denzin (2009, p. 142), drawing on Morse (2006a), points out, it "is not a question of evidence or no evidence." Instead, it is about who can say that something is evidence and something else is not. This shifts the emphasis from evidence per se to the *politics* of evidence, which is about the power that enables one type of research finding to be deemed as evidence and another not. This is a politics that has percolated down to the level of many funders of research, affecting the way that funding for qualitative inquiry is thought about and allocated (Cheek, 2005, 2006; Hammersley, 2005; Morse, 2006b; Stronach, 2006).

Thinking about it, few researchers have remained immune from the effects of the infiltration of this politics into the research arena. For example, at a macro political level qualitative researchers have seen the proliferation of endless forms of government-driven reviews and audits in the quest to ensure, and provide "evidence" of, research efficiency, output, and quality (Cannella & Lincoln, 2004; Denzin, 2009). At a more micro level of research practices, limited understandings of research and research evidence have, and continue to, affect the types of methods used, able to be used, and/or even called methods (Atkinson & Delamont, 2006; Morse, 2006b; Torrance, 2006). As a result, over the past decade, there has been ongoing tension, collision, and at times rupture, at the interfaces of qualitative inquiry and a politics of evidence (Denzin & Giardina, 2006, 2007a, 2008, 2009). These tensions, collisions, and ruptures have spilled over to, and impacted, ways we think about, and do, fund our qualitative inquiry. Given all this, I believe that exploring the interfaces between the politics and practices of funding our qualitative inquiry is absolutely crucial, not only for trying to better understand how best to fund our inquiry, but also because this interface has the potential to shape the form that our inquiry does, and even can, take.

How can this be? How can the interfaces between the politics and practices of funding qualitative inquiry shape the form that our inquiry takes, or might take? An example of what I am thinking about is if we were to choose a particular substantive area for study due to a perception that this will make it more likely to get funded. So, if, for example, a funder has a priority area to which funding will be allocated, then it may be that substantive area we tailor our research to and not another. Or, thinking about methodology, if a funder prefers one type of research approach over another, then we write our research design to fit that preferred approach. Of course, writing within and to the parameters set by funders may not necessarily be a "bad" thing. Indeed, some might call it just common sense. However, it does raise questions about what is driving what—is the funding driving the research, or the research the funding, or something in between? To some extent, this has the potential to turn the original intent of funding, which was as an enabler or support for research, on its head. The means of support (the funding) becomes as much, or even more, the goal as the research to be supported (the research problem). What the researcher might in fact be doing is buying the funding as much as they are selling the research project.

All of the above raises a number of complex issues for qualitative researchers to think about, and at times difficult choices to make, related to the practices and politics affecting the way they fund their qualitative inquiry. For me, chief among these is constantly reflecting on what is my prime motivation—enabling the research or gaining the funding? Am I selling research or buying funding or something in between? How far am I prepared to modify my research in order to get funding for it and, importantly, what is the reason for my decision making in this regard? How is it possible to find ways to fit the politics and funding to qualitative inquiry, and not qualitative inquiry to the politics and funding? What am I prepared to give up, change, or adapt in terms of my qualitative inquiry and what am I not? Many qualitative inquirers have had to make a number of tradeoffs in relation to funding their qualitative inquiry when faced with questions such as these. Talking about such tradeoffs can be confronting and difficult. Perhaps this is why there is not much writing about them. Yet what we *don't* say about what we do can be just as, if not more, instructive and important to consider as what we actually *do* say about what we do (Cheek, 2010a).

Thinking about all this, I came to the conclusion that what I wanted to explore was how it might be possible to be pragmatic and realistic about funding qualitative inquiry in a world where there are demands on most of us to produce research "products," yet at the same time feel like we have some control over what those products are and what they might be. It seemed crucial to me that this discussion must speak, and relate directly, to the everyday reality we live and work in. How can we as qualitative inquirers both thrive and survive (in that order) in this reality? This is a particularly important question for less experienced and beginning researchers, especially those who are seeking their first research or academic post, or who are yet to gain tenure. How do you grapple with, and even accommodate, demands of administrators, tenure and search committees, research agencies, and the research marketplace without the feeling of selling out either in terms of oneself or the type of qualitative inquiry one employs? All of these questions are central and important dimensions of exploring the ideas about ideas about ideas, and messages about messages about messages (Bochner, 2009), related to funding qualitative research. A starting point for unpacking and exposing this cascade of ideas and messages pertains to locating funding for qualitative inquiry, and it is to this that our discussion now turns.

Locating Funding: Where to Begin and Some Hard Questions to Ask Yourself When Doing So

How and where do you begin when trying to locate funding for your qualitative research? Of course, the answer to this depends to a large extent on the research problem you wish to investigate, the type of research you want to do, and what type of funding you need. But in all of this there is a key, immutable point. This point is that, regardless of what strategies you may employ when thinking about how to fund your qualitative inquiry, the first step toward attracting that funding is the development of a well-thought-out research problem and concomitant research design. You must have a very clear idea of what you want to gain funding for, or put another way, what you want to research, why, and how. There are already excellent discussions published pertaining to qualitative research design, one of which is the next chapter in this handbook (Creswell, Chapter 3, this volume). I will not repeat those discussions here. Instead, I want to emphasize that it is only after you are sure that you have spent the time and energy required on the plain hard thinking that Morse (2008) reminds us sits behind the deceptive simplicity of the design of an elegant qualitative inquiry, that you are ready to take the next step in locating funding for that research.

This next step involves not only ascertaining what types of funding are available, but also the way those funding sources understand and think about research. Are they going to be interested in qualitative projects? Do they have particular emphases or priorities in terms of the substantive issues or areas that they will fund? One problem faced by qualitative inquirers in trying to find out this type of information about potential funders and funding schemes is that qualitative inquiry has not been particularly active in, or good at, building up collective knowledge about either funding sources or the experience of interacting with them. There is no collective list of potential funders, for example, nor is there systematic collection of information about the experiences of qualitative researchers who either have attracted funding from a particular source, or who sit on review panels of funding agencies. As a result, much collective wisdom is lost. Nevertheless, strategies do exist that can be employed in the quest to locate possible funding sources for qualitative inquiry.

A beginning strategy might be to use formal networks, such as meetings like the Congress of Qualitative Inquiry held annually at the University of Illinois, and/or informal networks of qualitative inquirers to find out from where funding has been gained for qualitative inquiry, in what form, and for what type of research project. Just as important, also try to find out where funding has not been awarded to qualitative inquiries and the reasons why. This will give you a clue as to possible "unfriendly" funders for qualitative inquiry and may save you much time and energy from the outset. Another strategy might be to access and use databases and/or publications that list potential funding sources, the frequency of their call for applications seeking funding, and the success rates of applications in the respective schemes. These are often country-specific such as the GrantSearch electronic database in Australia that is published in hard copy every two years as the GrantSearch Register of Australian Funding. It advertises that it has over 3,000 entries identifying funding sources for study, travel, research, business and professional development, the arts, sport and recreation, and community groups offered by all levels of government, universities, foundations, the private sector, and overseas sources specifying Australian applicants (GrantSearch Register of Australian Funding, 2010). Of course, the relative importance of, and opportunities for, funding for qualitative inquiry afforded by each of the above categories of potential funding sources will vary from country to country and even within countries.

It is most important to bear in mind when trying to locate funding for qualitative inquiry that accepting funding from a sponsor "links the researcher and research inexorably with the values of that funder" (Cheek, 2005, p. 400). Consequently, in the search for potential funders, at some point it will be necessary to reflect on whether or not funding should be sought from a particular funding source. For example, most researchers will hesitate if offered funding from tobacco companies. For some qualitative researchers working in health-related areas, whether to seek part of the large sums of funds often available from pharmaceutical drug companies is a vexing question creating fine lines to be traversed. And what of seeking support from companies whose profits are derived in some way from outsourcing labor offshore in developing countries where people work for very little and barely enough to survive? Does a funder's environmental record matter? In considering such questions, the politics of funding affecting qualitative inquirers comes from another position—the politics that comes with the funder. Taking up a position in respect to this politics is something that all qualitative inquirers will have to reflect on when working out their strategy to locate funding. Further, some places where qualitative inquirers are employed may have policies about where funding cannot be accepted from. It is important to find this out.

Once potential funding sources have been identified, the search for funding can be refined further with respect to the chances of having a particular qualitative inquiry supported by a particular funder. Sometimes funders have specific substantive areas that they will fund, or priority areas for funding that may change annually. Your project will have a much better chance of being funded if it is in keeping with these areas of interest identified by the funder. Thus, it is important to find out if a funder has priority or interest areas, and if they do, what these areas are. Of course, this can raise dilemmas for you as well in terms of what you are prepared to trade off with respect to your research problem and design in order to "fit" a priority area. You will have to make your own decisions about this. If I am completely honest, at times some of my research has been "fitted" to a particular funder's requirements as seeking and gaining the funding has been my prime motivation. Thinking about it, this has been for a number of reasons. One is the constant pressure that I have experienced over the course of my career, like many other researchers, to attract funding for my research. Another reason is the harsh reality that funds for research are not easy to get and there are not a lot of them. Given this, I have grappled with whether I needed to be pragmatic about all this, and if so how pragmatic was I prepared to be? Was it better to try to fund exactly the project I wanted to do, or could I live with researching something else because the funding was available to do that project and not the one I had originally intended to do? Was it better to be doing some research in an area or none at all, which may have been the outcome if I did not shape my research to fit with the funding call or the funder's agenda? There are no easy answers to these questions. Nor is it a matter of right or wrong. However, each potential position that can be adopted in this regard has a cost of some kind. How much modification we are prepared to make to our research problem and why we would do that are questions each of us as qualitative inquirers will need to think about.

Finding out what a particular funder has previously funded is another way of refining the search for potential funding and funders for qualitative inquiry. Have there been any qualitative projects funded and if so what type of qualitative inquiry has been supported? Try to get hold of any funding guidelines, application forms, or other relevant documents such as annual reports detailing funding or research activities published by the funder. This is because "shaping all application forms or guidelines provided by funders are assumptions, often unwritten and unspoken, about research and the way that research is under-stood" (Cheek, 2005, p. 394). If it is a struggle to fit the qualitative inquiry around, or into, the sections and headings that are required as part of the fund-ing application and/or there is no record of funding qualitative inquiries, then this strongly suggests that qualitative inquiry may not be something that has been part of the thinking of the funder when constructing the funding scheme. At the very least, this indicates that more needs to be found out about this funder's position with respect to qualitative inquiry.

The composition of the panel that will review the applications and the process that they will follow can provide further useful information in this regard. Is there anyone on the review panel with expertise and experience in qualitative inquiry? And if the answer to this is a "yes," then what exactly does that mean? For "yes" can mean qualitative inquirers with extensive experience, or it might mean those with an "acquaintance" with qualitative research, having "attended a short session on qualitative methods at a conference—and they use these iso-lated 'facts' as gold standards" (Morse, 2003a, p. 740). If, on the other hand, the answer is a "no," then is there the possibility for the panel to seek advice from external reviewers for applications outside of the panel's collective expertise? For if there are no persons on the review board with qualitative expertise, and the standard procedure is either not to, or not be able to, seek and/or take into account opinion from outside the panel, then this does not augur well for the likely success of the proposal. If expert external opinion is sought, then how that expert advice is sought is equally important to consider. The way this expertise is sought can often be very ad hoc (Morse 2003a).

Being entirely honest about something that maybe we often do not say about what we do, I have at times weighed in my mind whether having external expert opinion, even if it is positive about the proposed research, really changes any-thing anyway. For example, I have sat on granting and review panels where 0.5 or less of a point in a score out of a possible 100 points has separated those applications that will be funded from those that will not. Every panel member's score awarded to a grant is therefore crucial. Even if only one member has con-cerns, spoken or unspoken, about supporting qualitative inquiry, that member's score can in effect make an application uncompetitive in the funding competi-tion where success rates may be lower than 20%. Thus, the traditional practice of averaging the scores from panel members for a particular application often works against the chances of a qualitative inquiry being funded.

If, after considering the above facets of the practices and processes followed by a funder, it seems as though there is a real opportunity for qualitative inquiry to be funded, then a next step in locating funding can be to approach the funding agency in person. This can be done in different ways and for different purposes depending on a particular sponsor's way of organizing the allocation of funding. If the allocation of funding is organized on the basis of annual granting rounds, then there is little point to meet to ask for funding outside of those funding rounds. In addition, to do so may give the impression that you have not done your homework with respect to this funder's way of operating. In this instance, you may seek to talk to the office and/or manager with responsibility for the oversight of the funding rounds. This is not only to acquire information about that process, but also to introduce both the researcher(s) and the idea for the research to the people who will be dealing with the application on an administrative basis. This enables them to put a face to a name and demonstrates that you are serious both about your idea, and having a working partnership with them with respect to this research. If a potential sponsor has no set dates for funding rounds but applications can be made at any time for funding, or it is not entirely clear how to apply for funding, then it is important to find the appropriate person in the organization to talk to about your research idea and you as a researcher. This can be difficult, so it is important to persist politely when trying to gain entry to the organization and navigate the various levels of contact that are usually gone through before eventually finding the right person to talk to.

If you are successful in getting a meeting time with that person, make sure that you are very well prepared thereby respecting the time that they have given you, as well as making the most of it in terms of putting across your research idea. Try to think about the research from their point of view. Why should they fund this? What do you offer them? The key is to be clear and precise in the message that you are trying to convey and the research that you are trying to sell. Offer to send a one-page concept paper to them before the meeting that outlines the research idea, the type of support being sought, and any preliminary work that has been done. The concept paper should also have information about you and any other researchers that constitute the research team for the project. This is because track record is an important consideration in a potential funder's mind. Avoid submitting a standard format, multipage, and multipurpose curriculum vitae (CV) that may or may not be read by the person. Rather, present a track record in the form of a modified CV with accompanying text that is written in such a way to draw attention to, and highlight, aspects of your research career that demonstrate that, based on your past experience, you have the expertise to do this research, on time, and within budget (Cheek, 2005). If you do not have a lot of research experience, then a starting point can be to join a research team where some members do have this experience. You can then build up your own track record while researching with, and learning from, them as part of the team.

Another strategy for building up a track record is to look for seed funding opportunities directed to less-experienced, early-career researchers. In these schemes, small amounts of funding are made available to less-experienced researchers for research projects, thereby helping them overcome the eternal issue highlighted here: how to get a track record without having a track record!

Locating Funding: Contracting to Do a Piece of Research

A different strategy when trying to locate potential funding for qualitative inquiry is to look for calls or advertisements from government or other organizations seeking to pay researchers to do a specific piece of research. This specificity may pertain to any or all of the substantive focus of the research, the aspects of that substantive focus to be picked up on and how, as well as the time frame in which the research must be done, written up, and the results "delivered." To varying degrees, and not always, there may be some scope for the researcher to develop the focus and methods that will underpin the research. Advertisements for this type of research funding can often be found in the contract/tender section of newspapers. They ask interested researchers and/or organizations to submit a proposal, on a commercial basis, for conducting the specific project. What the funder is looking for in tendering or contracting the research is to buy the expertise and time needed to do the research because they do not have it themselves. For example, tenders may seek researchers able to conduct a specific number of workshops, focus groups, and/or interviews in order to attain certain prespecified research aims. Here, the emphasis is on researchers fitting both themselves and their research to a specific, time-delimited funding opportunity.

An understandable part of the funder's thinking when devising and awarding a tender for research is the question of what is the least amount of money that they need to spend in order to get the expertise they need and the research done. This is not to suggest that the cheapest proposal will necessarily be successful as the expertise and experience of the researchers will be major considerations as will the overall research design. Rather, it is about getting value for money, which "means not only meeting high standards in the research; it also means considering how much, or little, money needs to be allocated to attain those standards" (Cheek, 2005, p. 394). What all of this means is that the budget will play a major part throughout the entire funding application process. It may also mean that the maximum amount of possible funding that has been set aside for this project makes it impossible to conduct a qualitative study that can meet the aims of the research required. It is easy to underestimate the amount of time needed for a qualitative project and associated project costs. It is also easy to fall into the trap of trying to be more competitive in the tender round by undercosting researcher expertise and project costs and/or overcommitting as to what it is possible to "deliver" in the time available to do the research. Help in costing projects and making sure that what is promised is realistic can be obtained from research and/ or business development offices increasingly found in universities and research organizations. These offices also have the remit to source and look out for calls for tendered research.

Tendered research is characterized by short time frames at every part of the research process. There may be only days to prepare an application, and just weeks or a few months to complete the research. Not all qualitative inquiry and approaches are suited to such short time frames. This is compounded if the funder requires interim reports throughout the research in that it is not always easy, or even possible, to "chunk" any interim findings into bits that can be delivered in a piecemeal fashion. Time and energy put into such interim reporting can cause much frustration in that this diverts researcher time and focus from the bigger research picture. A danger of such emphasis on time delimited results is that it can encourage the rise of atheoretical, or at the very least shallow and thin, qualitative research designs and findings. Morse (2003b, p. 846) notes that not having enough time to do and think about our qualitative research "will kill a project or result in a project that has not become all that it could—and should—be." Her observation forces us to think carefully about what the short time frames for the delivery of the research findings might actually mean in practice. Stripped of the theoretical understandings that underpin them, such research designs can become little more than a collection of techniques or a series of steps to be followed.

For some qualitative researchers, gaining funding from contracted research has been part of everyday reality for many years. For other qualitative inquirers, tendered research has only relatively recently become an increasingly important income source as the contemporary research context has continued to see a decline in many countries in the relative amount of monetary and other support given by governments and other funders for researcher-generated projects. Qualitative inquirers thinking about tendering for research need to think deeply about how much of the control of the design they are prepared to give away or can live with giving away. How will they navigate the tensions arising from the entry of "fast capitalist texts" (Brennan, 2002, p. 2) into their qualitative inquiry with, for example, research products being transformed into "deliverables" and research timelines into "milestones"? This is not just a matter of semantics. It is an outworking of messages about messages within messages. One message is that research can be reduced to, or thought of, as a series of tasks. A message that then sits within this message is that once these tasks have been identified, the performance of the research team and the quality of the research can be assessed in relation to whether they have fulfilled these tasks.

For example, I was involved, as part of a team, in doing a contracted piece of research for the Australian government (Cheek et al., 2002). Part of the contract for the research outlined the tasks to be performed by the research team, as well as associated performance criteria that would be used as indicators of success in fulfilling those tasks. One of the tasks stipulated in the Standards and Best Practice section of the contract was to gain "informed consent of all participants." The associated performance indicator identified in the contract was "signed consent forms." Thus, gaining informed consent of all participants was in effect reduced to being synonymous with the production of signed consent forms. Our research team had a far wider view of the contested and complex issues surrounding what both informed consent, and the gaining of that consent, might mean in practice. Yet we signed this contract and attempted to navigate this potential tension by delivering what the funder required in terms of signed consent forms while also ensuring that consent and ethical considerations extended far beyond this. However, we never talked about this tension with the funder. Why was this? Perhaps, looking back, there was a pragmatic edge to what we traded off in terms of meeting the requirements imposed by the funding body while at the same time conducting the research in a way that we felt did not compromise the qualitative inquiry. This research addressed an important substantive area and the results were going to be used by government as part of initiatives being thought about in this area at the time. If we were not doing this research, then perhaps others would be who did not have the same problem with, for example, reducing gaining the informed consent of participants to a task and the production of signed consent forms.

There were, and are, no easy answers to these sorts of issues and tradeoffs. Nor are there right or wrong answers. Rather, it is a matter of thinking deeply about what we are prepared to give up or trade off and what we are not when selling ideas or time to funders. As I have mentioned before, as researchers we are all selling something all of the time. Thus the idea of selling is not an issue for me. However, what is an issue for me, and what I still constantly reflect on, is what I am trying to sell, how I am going about selling it, and most importantly why? Questions that all qualitative inquirers might usefully ask themselves in this regard include the following: Are we selling a research problem, our time, our expertise, or all of the above? How do we feel about selling our time and expertise to do what is, to some extent at least, someone else's research? What are we prepared to trade off in doing that research and what are we not? The importance of reflecting on these types of questions is one of the key messages in this chapter.

Locating Funding: Yet More Considerations *Before* Submitting an Application for Funding

However, even having employed all, or some, of the above strategies in the quest to locate funding for qualitative inquiry, there is yet more homework to do before any application for funding should be made. In the excitement of the possibility of having found a potential funder, or the pressure of a deadline for research proposal or tender submissions, it is easy to overlook the question of what the funder's expectations will be if funding is gained. For example, to what extent will they want to be involved in the research process? What parts of it, if any, will they wish to have control of? Will they expect to have access to the data or parts of it? Will they want representatives on the research team, at team meetings, or to form advisory boards to give input to the form and direction of the research as it unfolds? How will this fit with the research design? How will it affect the researcher/funder/participant relationships in the research and does that matter?

It is just as crucial to consider these matters at the point of applying for funding as it is to focus on trying to write a winning proposal. Before rushing in, or being carried away by the tantalizing possibility of having located a funding source for your research, it is important to remember that applying for and accepting funding from any source is not a neutral activity (Cheek 2005). It involves entering into intellectual and contractual agreements with funding organizations and their agents, such as the manager assigned responsibility for ensuring that the research is completed and on time. Concentrating on winning the funding and worrying later about such details is a poor and dangerous strategy. There is little point in getting the funding if the research cannot proceed as planned because of different expectations on the part of the funder and the researcher as to their respective roles in the research process. All of this is not to paint a picture of doom and gloom. Rather, it is to caution against not thinking through the partnership and agreement you are about to enter into, and making sure that it is one that you want to be in.

The extent and formality of such agreements will vary from funder to funder. Not all funders will have formal expectations about their involvement in, or the way that, the research should be done. Nevertheless, no matter the degree of formality or even informality, it is essential that early on, and absolutely before funding is accepted, researchers and funders discuss, agree upon, and record any assumptions that they have about the research and how it will be done. This includes what can be said about the research and by whom. Not being able to write about and publish part of the research, or any of it at all, because of contractual issues is the uncomfortable place in which some qualitative researchers, including myself (Cheek, 2005), have found themselves. It is thus critical to negotiate how the findings of a study will, and can be, reported, when, and where; the use(s) to which the research data can be put and who owns that data; as well as what can be published in scholarly literature by the researcher(s). Making such agreements is central to building a positive workable relationship with funders built on mutual respect for each other's point of view. It is crucial that this open communication continues throughout the duration of the research project. This is particularly so if something goes wrong or if, for whatever reason, aspects of the research plan, such as the timelines for the research, have to be changed.

It is equally important that these issues have been discussed and negotiated among the research team itself so that there is an agreed position with respect to them *before* they are discussed with the funder. This discussion and negotiation is not always easy, as often there are competing views in the team that need to be navigated. However, one thing is for certain—these competing views will not go away by ignoring them. In addition, the team will need to discuss matters such as what support individual members will have access to; individual responsibilities in contributing to the research especially with respect to time frames and the final report; how often to meet; how disagreements among team members will be resolved; and, very importantly, who in the team will have contact with the funder and on what basis. This is critical to the smooth functioning of the team throughout the project. Having these things thought through, under control, and working well during the research will give the funder confidence in the team. It also makes the life of the funder much easier if they know whom to deal with on the team and the message that they are receiving about the research is clear and consistent.

There should also be agreement between funders and researchers as to what, and by whom, participants in the research will be told about the agreement between the funder and the researcher(s). Qualitative inquiry is built on building trust between participants in the research and those conducting the research.

Central to this trust is being open and honest about who is funding the research and the agreements that have been entered into with that funder with respect to what can, and cannot, be said about that research and any findings. It is also about telling participants exactly who will have access to what data from the research, and how participant anonymity will be ensured. This is particularly important to allay any fears on the part of participants who may be in dependent positions in relation to the funder, such as, for example, the funder's tenants, suppliers, or employees. Such considerations are ethical ones as much as they are practical ones.

Thus, locating any type of funding for qualitative inquiry involves much more than simply locating funding sources. It involves thinking about how the research and researcher will be affected by seeking, and possibly gaining, that funding. In all funding agreements, to a greater or lesser extent, researchers will give away some of their freedom with respect to the project and the way it might be, and actually is, done. Making decisions about how much freedom they are prepared to give up in this regard is one of the fine lines (Cheek, 2008) that qualitative inquirers walk when navigating the funding and research market-places. Thinking about how to navigate these fine lines must be done as part of the search for potential funding sources, well before the research funding is gained, and absolutely before the funding has been accepted and the research is actually underway.

Writing to Attract Funding: Crafting a Proposal for Funding

Having done all this, and having located a potential source or way of funding your research, the next step is crafting a proposal to seek that funding. The discussion that I want to have here is not about qualitative research design and/or how to write a proposal per se for a qualitative inquiry. Good examples of this type of discussion already exist (see, for example, Carey & Swanson, 2003; Morse, 2003b; Penrod, 2003). Rather, the discussion is focused on exposing, in order to be better able to navigate, the tensions inherent in writing a funding proposal for multiple audiences sometimes with multiple understandings of what constitutes "good" research or even research. Or, to put it even more simply, how do you write a proposal for a number of different interested parties and still retain the project you want to do both in terms of intent and approach? Shaping and tailoring a research idea to a particular audience is a crucial part of the craft of writing for funding, a craft built on a set of skills that are largely learned and refined by practice.

When crafting the funding proposal, it will need to be congruent with the guidelines of a funder as well as meeting the requirements of other interested parties such as ethics committees that will need to approve the research before it can proceed. Thus, each application for funding, even for the same project, will vary depending on the characteristics and requirements of the audience being approached. It is not good strategy to work up a generic proposal that is then submitted to a number of funders for two reasons. First, because it may be that individuals serve on more than one review panel and therefore may have seen the proposal before, giving the impression of a nontargeted and recycled funding proposal. Second, when a proposal is written for a potential sponsor's consideration, it is written for a particular audience, whose members have assumptions and expectations of the form a proposal should take and the level of detail that it should contain. These will vary from funding scheme to funding scheme. Thus, as emphasized previously, it is important for researchers to know their audience(s) and its (their) expectations. Sometimes, it may even be possible to have access to research applications that have won funding thereby providing an excellent guide as to how much detail is expected in the proposal and the style of presentation expected by those reviewing the application.

An essential part of crafting the application involves following the guidelines. At the most basic of levels this means conforming to any word or page limits either for individual sections of the application, or the application as a whole. It also means addressing all sections or areas that the guidelines identify. For example, if the guidelines state that an application should comprise a 100-word summary, and then, in no more than 10 pages of text that uses 10-point font or larger, outline the research aims, outcomes, dissemination strategies, significance and novelty value in relation to existing work in the area, methods, ethical considerations, budget and budget justification, and provide a statement about the researcher(s) track record(s), then that is *exactly* what the application should do. A good strategy is to use each of the areas identified in the guidelines as needing to be addressed as headings for the different sections of the text that make up the application. This organizes and gives structure to your writing, as well as making it clear where and how you are addressing these areas. Often, when scoring applications, reviewers will have a sheet where they assign a score to each of these sections, so making it easy to see where and how you have addressed them makes good sense.

A good research proposal is one that is clear and concise. Use accessible language that can be read and understood by panel members who may not be working and/or researching in your exact area of expertise. Writing that is full of jargon will not impress. There must be a clear statement of the question/issue/problem that the research is addressing and everything that is written following that should be in terms of how it is related to addressing the question/issue/problem. Thus, for example, the description of the methods should be explicitly related back to how they enable the aims of the research to be met. Any literature review must move beyond description to be an argument of why the proposed research is needed in relation to both what has preceded it, and is happening currently, in the relevant substantive area. Show how the proposed research fits with the funder's priorities and funding remit. Make these connections throughout the discussion and document. Do not make the reader have to do the work, or expect that they will, as if they are a reviewer with many applications to read it is likely that they will not have the time to do this. Never underestimate the importance of parts of an application that may seem to be more routine or administrative, such as the budget.

It is important to bear in mind that when crafting your proposal, you are selling your research *and* your expertise to this funder. This is why the statement of the researcher's track record is so important. Publications are the hard currency of the track record needed for researchers to be able to compete for funding. Without a strong publishing track record, it will be much more difficult to win funding. Largely for matters of expediency in terms of ease of data collection and manipulation, publication track records are increasingly being assessed using quantitative metrics. The most pervasive of these is impact factor. Although related to impact of a specific journal (Cheek, Garnham, & Quan, 2006), increasingly the term "impact factor" is being used interchangeably with the term "impact" in the commonspeak of funders and university administrators. One effect of this is that in many funding schemes, impact factor is being used when assessing the quality and impact of the work of researchers. Thus, guidelines for applying for funding require the publication track record of researchers to list the impact factor of the journal that a particular journal article was published in. The erroneous assumption is that the higher the impact factor, the higher the scholarship and quality of the applicant's published work. Thus, a supposed measure of the impact of a *journal* is transformed into a measure of the impact and quality of a particular *article*. This in turn is transformed into measures of the impact and quality of a particular *researcher* (Cheek et al., 2006).

This poses considerable challenges for qualitative inquirers and creates messages about messages about messages about where, and why, to publish. Chief among them is, given the increasing emphasis placed on a metric-based, impact-factor-driven publishing track record when assessing applications for funding, should qualitative inquirers seek only to publish in "high-impact" journals? How, when presenting their publishing track record to funding bodies not familiar with qualitative inquiry, do qualitative inquirers demonstrate the impact of publishing in places such as this handbook, for example, which does not have an impact factor? What does opting in or out of trading in the currency developed around metric-based publication measures do to our chances of locating and gaining funding for our research? Where to publish their research and why is another of the fine lines all qualitative inquirers walk.

Writing Our Methods for Funding: Walking Fine Lines and Making Tradeoffs We Can Live With

Part of writing for funding involves making decisions about how we will write our methods for particular audiences. This involves making decisions not only about what methods we might employ but also about what details we might, or might not, give about those methods. I am going to use three examples drawn from my own experience of writing my methods for funding to explore some of the tensions that this writing, and the decisions that underpinned it, created for me. The first of these is about fine lines I walked, and tradeoffs I made, when writing sample size into a qualitative funding proposal in response to needing to have a detailed and justified budget for the proposed project.

EXAMPLE ONE: DECIDING WHAT TO SAY AND/OR NOT TO SAY ABOUT SAMPLE SIZE

The production of a well-thought-out and justified budget is an important part of crafting a research proposal for funding. It is quite reasonable for those who provide funding for research to ask whether or not the proposed project represents appropriate use of the funds for which they have responsibility. It is also reasonable for them to require a justification of the amount of funding being sought. Reasons need to be given for the amount and type of funding sought. Often this means a detailed level of precision and justification in the budget with respect to what exactly funding is being applied for and why. For example, here is a short excerpt from the budget justification section of a grant proposal I was part of developing:

A professional transcriber will be required to transcribe the audio taped interviews. It is estimated that every hour of taped data will take three hours to transcribe. We anticipate 50 interviews of each at least 1 hour, therefore

50 hours minimum of taped interviews plus allowance for 10 hours of extra time as experience has shown some interviews will go for longer. Thus 60 hours of tape x 3 transcribing hours per hour of tape recording = 180 hours of transcription @ $17.50 per hour (quoted by L. . . Supplies, a professional transcribing company). 180 hours × $17.50 = $3,150.

From this justification, it is clear that one of the costs associated with the interview component of the study is that of transcribing the interviews. Thus, this part of the budget is premised on multiplying the number of interviews to be done by the transcription costs associated with one interview to come up with an overall dollar figure.

While on one level this represents very clear crafting of a budget and its justification, on another it raised, and still raises, questions about the tradeoffs that were involved in deriving these numbers.

These questions center on whether it was possible to give precise details about the number of interviews that would be done before the research was underway. In keeping with the inductive approach of qualitative inquiry, we could not be sure of exactly how many participants we would interview in the study. However, costs associated with doing each interview, such as the transcription of the interview, were the major component of the funding being sought. How could we come up with a budget and justify it if a large part of the budget for the project reflected costs related to those interviews but we couldn't say how many we would do? After all, it was not unreasonable for the review committee to expect that we could provide justification for our budget.

After much thought, we decided that we would nominate a specific number of interviews to be conducted in the proposal even though we were not entirely comfortable in so doing. We nominated a sample size of 50 interviews. This number was based on the sample size used in a study reported in the research literature on which, in part, our study drew. We wrote in the proposal that our *anticipated* sample size of a total of 50 interviews (25 older people and 25 family members) was *guided* by that study. We were fortunate enough to gain funding for the project, and after we had completed the research we published the findings. In this article, we specified the sample size we had used (Cheek & Ballantyne, 2001). We then applied for funding for a related study that also involved interviewing older people and their families. When writing this proposal, we were able to refer to our published first study and state that drawing on our previous experience we anticipated that 25 interviews of older people and 25 interviews of family members would meet the needs of the study. We gained funding for this study, carried out the research, and published it. More studies followed and the results were also published (Cheek, Ballantyne, Byers, & Quan, 2007; Cheek, Ballantyne, Gilham, et al., 2006; Cheek, Ballantyne, Roder-Allen, & Jones, 2005). By this stage, we had provided ourselves with a way of overcoming the problem of how it is possible to specify the number of interviews to be conducted when it is not possible to do so with absolute certainty. We could refer to our own work.

Throughout the entire process of doing this, we were employing tradeoffs. If we did not give a number with respect to the number of interviews to be conducted, then it was impossible to apply for funding. This was because we could not stipulate a budget, and also, if I am completely honest, because we knew that without a defined sample size it would be impossible to attract funding from the particular granting scheme we were applying to. Yet, if we did give a number then we may be complicit in giving the impression that it is possible to be certain about aspects of qualitative research design that it is not possible to be certain about. Using words in the proposal such as "it is anticipated" that 25 interviews will meet the needs of the study, and writing in our report of the research about why sometimes we did not end up having 25 interviews of older people and/or their family members but more or less (see Cheek & Ballantyne, 2001), were some of the ways we tried to navigate the tradeoffs we knew we were making. In addition, we found that interviewing 25 people from each group of participants (older people and family members) in these studies provided us with the richness of data and information that we sought. And we are optimistic that our results have influenced practice and attempted to address issues pertaining to social justice and human rights for these groups of people (Cheek, 2010a, 2010b; Cheek, Corlis, & Radoslovich, 2009). Nevertheless, there were very fine lines to walk when making these decisions, and no doubt there may be readers who feel as though we may have sold out a little (or a lot) in what we did.

Morse (2003a) also shares her reflections on the tradeoffs she made when needing to specify a sample size in order to be able to specify a budget. She does this using her experience of having had an application for funding rejected by a review committee. She explains that when crafting this proposal, in keeping with the tenets of qualitative inquiry underpinning her research design, she wrote, "sampling would continue until saturation is reached" (Morse, 2003a, p. 740). However, she then went on to specify an actual number for the sample largely because of the need to have a number in order to be able to develop a budget. The number chosen, and the reasons for providing it, drew on her long experience of doing qualitative inquiry. "Experience has taught me that you must calculate some number as the requested dollar amount; experience has also taught me that it is folly to minimize, rather than maximize, the sample size" (p. 740). However, in this instance, the tradeoff of giving of a number became a problem. Morse puts it this way: "It did not matter what the number was. My sin was to have produced an actual number: 'In qualitative research' they [the review committee] told me, 'the sample size cannot be predicted'" (p. 740). While there may be some merit in such a view, what in effect this did was reduce complex design issues to simplistic "rules" stripped of any theoretical understandings, while effectively dismissing years of experience of conducting qualitative inquiry. Further, in effect it made getting funding for qualitative inquiry nearly impossible, for if there could be no guide to the sample size in the study, then a budget for this research was impossible to develop. If no budget could be developed, then what would be applied for in terms of amount of funding sought?

Both Morse's and my own experiences highlight that when crafting an application qualitative inquirers face the dilemma of negotiating the pragmatics of trying to write a competitive proposal without selling out to expediency. Writing for funding is as much a political as it is a practical activity. Consequently, how and what to write, and equally what to leave out or not write, are much more than decisions about style or following sections in guidelines. Rather, they are decisions about what to defend and what to give up when crafting a proposal. What aspects of qualitative inquiry, both substantively and methodologically, can be/might be/must never be tailored to meet the understandings and requirements of audiences such as funders? These are questions that confront all qualitative inquirers. I wish to continue the conversation about these questions and the fine lines they involve in terms of the decisions made and paths chosen when writing for funding, using the example of writing for ethics committees.

EXAMPLE TWO: WRITING FOR ETHICS OR "GETTING OUR METHODS THROUGH ETHICS" TO GET THE FUNDING?

It may be a bit unusual or unexpected for some readers to think about writing for ethics committees (also referred to as Institutional Review Boards or IRBs in some countries), as part of a discussion about writing our methods for funding. But the fact is that, in some ways, ethics committees are often as much a part of the decision making about if a research project is able to attract funding as are formal research review panels. This is because most funders will require that research is approved by formally constituted ethics committees before funds can be given and/or released. Even if such approval is not a requirement of a particular funder, then, in Australia, for example, university-based researchers must obtain ethics approval from the relevant university ethics committee before their research can proceed. Thus, a critical part of the process of gaining funding for qualitative inquiry is the navigation of, and writing for, the formal review process of the ethics of the research.

On the surface, this seems something that all those committed to qualitative inquiry surely would support. Yet there has been an uneasy tension between the role and function of ethics committees on the one hand, and qualitative inquiry and inquirers on the other. Such tensions increased markedly in the late 1990s and continue as we enter the second decade of the 21st century. Many tensions emanate from disagreements about which parts of the research are ethical issues, and therefore part of the remit of an ethics committee, and which are not. This has particularly pertained to questions of methods against the backdrop of the emergence of a politics of evidence embodying narrow views of what constitutes research evidence (see the opening section of this chapter). Lincoln and Cannella have explored aspects of these tensions with great insight (Cannella & Lincoln, Chapter 5, volume 1; Lincoln & Cannella, 2007). One of their key concerns is whether ethics committees are making what are in fact methodological recommendations rather than ethical ones.

Ethics committees argue that part of their remit is to stop research proceeding that is unethical in terms of it being of poor research design and therefore unable to provide any meaningful or useful results (Lacey, 1998). Thus, the risks of the research far outweigh any possible benefits. While on one level this is a reasonable position for ethics committees to adopt, it is not reasonable if only certain understandings of research and evidence are in play. In the United States (Riesman, 2002), the United Kingdom (Ramcharan & Cutcliffe, 2001), and Australia (Cheek, 2005), ethics committees emerged from the traditions of medicine and medical science, and largely in response to issues that had arisen in relation to questionable medical practices. The methods and traditions of medicine and science are those more in keeping with conventional quantitative methods (Lacey, 1998) and understandings of research as deductively based (van den Hoonaard, 2001). Guidelines drawn up by ethics committees have thus tended to reflect this way of thinking about research.

So what does this mean for how we write our methods? Some qualitative inquirers have experienced having their research blocked by ethics committees, or even dismissed out of hand, on the basis that it is not the experimental, deductively based research that some members of the committee believe that all research should be (Denzin & Giardina, 2007b; Lincoln & Cannella, 2002; Lincoln & Tierney, 2002). The research is thus deemed unethical on the basis of research paradigm. Although, over time, there has been some mellowing of this situation with ethics committees recognizing that qualitative inquiry (or at least some forms of it) is a legitimate form of research, tensions remain. For example, qualitative researchers have found that some of the information ethics commit-tees require is difficult to provide at the outset of an inductively based inquiry. This can pertain to, for example, the requirement to specify the exact wording of every question that participants will be asked during an interview. Or it might be in relation to specifying an exact number in regard to the sample size, thereby once again raising the issues we talked about previously in relation to specifying a sample size when constructing a budget for the research. Further, the practice of some ethics committees of requiring ethics approval every time questions are added in response to emergent themes, or when more participants are needed to be interviewed than first anticipated, creates much frustration for qualitative researchers.

Tensions also arise from the fact that there is sometimes inconsistency between ethics committees. If the qualitative inquiry is to be conducted on sev-eral sites, such as several hospitals, for example, and each site has its own ethics committee that will not accept the approval given by another ethics committee, then qualitative inquirers can find themselves in the position of having gained approval from some committees and not others for the same research. This cre-ates many problems and can even jeopardize the funding received, as the research cannot proceed according to the application that was funded. The time that it can take to navigate the minefield of one or more ethics committees can mitigate against the relatively short time frames of tendered and contract research, thereby in effect making it uncompetitive in winning tenders. As noted previ-ously (Cheek, 2005), what all this potentially means is that ethics committees can be more powerful than any funder in determining what research will and will not get funding or even go ahead. At times, the last and definitive word on method has belonged to ethics committee members, not members of peer-review panels constituted by the funder. And this includes national, so-called "gold star," peer-reviewed funding schemes!

So what to do about all this? Perhaps the key is to ensure the maintenance, in some form, of the two separate discussions that Lincoln and Cannella (2007) noted should be ongoing about ethics and qualitative inquiry. The first of these pertains to the effects of the increasing bureaucratization of ethics and con-comitant tightening regulation of research. It is a conversation about how we might navigate the reality of having to submit our proposed research to ethics committees who may not necessarily be supportive of, or expert in, qualitative inquiry. In the section of this chapter about locating funding, I talked a lot about trying to understand the way that funders think so that we can try to work with, while not necessarily accepting, those understandings. The same applies to ethics committees. Be proactive. Discuss your project with the Chair of the committee.

See if it is possible to get copies of previous applications to the committee to get an idea of their depth and the way they have been written. Do the hard reflective and reflexive work about what you are prepared to give up and what you are not in terms of your research and its methods in order to get it "through ethics."

However, only to focus on "getting ethics" or "getting through" ethics committees is to be complicit in reducing understandings of ethics to a focus on expediency and instrumentality. There is another discussion to be had, as Lincoln and Cannella (2007) remind us. This is a broader discussion. It is about what ethics is, and might be, in terms of research. It involves creating spaces in our teaching, the enactment of our research, and our research training where we model the ethics of our research and research practices (Lincoln & Cannella, 2007; Schwandt, 2007). In this discussion, there is less emphasis on the mechanics of navigating ethics processes and more on the reasons for talking about ethics in the first place. Rather than simply dwelling on the negative effects of the increasing interference of ethics committees in matters pertaining more to methodology than to ethics, this conversation can be a more positive and constructive one to have. For as Hurdley, while reflecting on the bureaucratization of ethics, reminds us, there is still the possibility of "constant active reflection within these confines" in that "limited horizons do not inhibit depth and richness of insight" (Hurdley, 2010, p. 518).

EXAMPLE THREE: MIXED METHODS—WRITING FOR DESIGN OR WRITING FOR FUNDING?

The third example I wish to use to explore tensions around writing our methods for funding shifts the focus to a discussion about choosing what methods to use in our research, and importantly *how* we choose to use those methods. Mixed methods provide an interesting vehicle for this discussion. Recently, there has been an upsurge of interest in, and concomitant writing about, what is termed mixed methods research both without, and significantly within, the folds of qualitative inquiry. There are now whole journals, books (Creswell & Plano Clark, 2007; Greene, 2007; Hesse-Biber, 2010; Morse & Niehaus, 2009; Teddlie & Tashakkori, 2009), and handbooks (Tashakkori & Teddlie, 2003) devoted to it. Advocates of mixed methods argue that this type of research design can add a type of depth and multi-dimensionality to the analysis not otherwise possible. While this may be so, it also seems to me that mixed methods as a research approach is very vulnerable to being reduced to a technique in the way that it is thought about and used, and that writing for funding exacerbates this vulnerability. What do I mean by this and why do I think this? The rest of this section of the chapter unpacks these ideas.

Despite the rise in the popularity and prominence of mixed methods research design, it remains a difficult to define and somewhat contested concept. In large part, this is due to the different emphases given to what is to be mixed, and how, when mixed methods is written about and/or discussed. Most often, mixed methods refers to the use of qualitative and quantitative methods in the same study or program or sequence of studies (Creswell, 2003; Hesse-Biber, 2010; Morse & Niehaus, 2009). However, it can also refer to the use of two methods from the same paradigm, for example, two qualitative methods in the same study, although this way of "mixing" methods has not achieved the same prominence. Responding to the traditional primacy of quantitative approaches over qualitative ones in mixed methods discourses, Hesse-Biber identifies the centering of qualitative approaches to mixed methods research, and providing "researchers with a more detailed understanding of qualitative mixed methods perspectives and practices" (2010, p. 9) as two of her four aims when writing her recent book on mixed methods.

Morse and Niehaus (2009) provide the following definition of mixed methods that attempts to pick up on and incorporate the diversity of emphases in mixed method design. They write, "a mixed method design is a scientifically rigorous *research project,* driven by the inductive or deductive *theoretical drive,* and comprised of a qualitative or quantitative *core component* with qualitative or quantitative *supplementary component(s)*" (2009, p. 14, emphasis in the original). In this definition, the emphasis is on mixed methods in terms of an overall research design that is theoretically informed, rather than on the fact that methods have been "'mixed" in a study and/or the specific mix of methods that will be employed. It stands in stark contrast to a "methods-centric" conception of the field of mixed methods research with a focus "primarily on the construction of mixed methods designs, often to the detriment of how they interact with the research problem" (Hesse-Biber, 2010, p. vi). This is a significant point that we will return to later in this discussion as it has implications for the way that we think about writing an application for funding employing a mixed methods approach.

It is interesting in terms of the recent rise of interest in mixed methods that, in reality, this research approach is not actually new. It has been around in various forms for many years, including in qualitative inquiry. For example, think of ethnography involving observations, interviews, and sometimes other ways of collecting data (Morse & Niehaus, 2009). What is new is the degree of prominence this approach has assumed, especially in the past decade. In part, this is due to renewed scholarship in the area exemplified by the work of Morse and Niehaus (2009), Hesse-Biber (2010), Creswell and Plano Clark (2007), Mertens (2005), and others. But this in itself cannot fully account for the degree of heightened interest in mixed methods and the almost fervent urgency with which students and more experienced researchers take classes and workshops in it. Perhaps the politics and practices of the research marketplace can add another layer to the possible explanations for this elevated interest.

Interviewed in 2004 (the transcript of the interview can be found in Hesse-Biber & Leavy, 2006, p. 335), Morse made an interesting comment when asked about how she saw what was termed "multimethods" evolving. Her response was, "I think it is going to get in a terrible mess but will sort itself out in the end." When asked what she meant by this, part of her response was as follows: "I think that the pressure to do mixed methods, in order to get funding, overwhelms or overrides the goals of qualitative inquiry. I think the funding agencies say they fund qualitative inquiry, meaning that they really do fund mixed methods. This still places qualitative inquiry in an inferior position" (p. 335). Here, Morse points to the way that writing for funding can affect the methods chosen *and* the way we choose to write our methods. An example of this was when I was approached to be part of a large quantitatively focused funding bid on the basis that a (small) qualitative component would give an edge to the competitiveness of the grant in question. This perception arose from the fact that in the previous funding round more studies that had a mix of qualitative and quantitative methods were successful. The assumption was that it was the fact that there were different methods mixed that gave the successful proposals their competitive edge, rather than the theoretical drive of the design and the congruity of the mixing of methods with that drive.

How to respond to approaches such as this creates dilemmas for qualitative inquirers. On the one hand, it may be that, even if for questionable reasons, the qualitative "bit" was added as an afterthought to a quantitatively driven project, doing that qualitative component of the research may enhance the findings of the research. Participating in the research as part of the team may offer the opportunity to heighten that team's understandings of qualitative inquiry. Joining a strong research team may also help build track record for the individual qualitative researcher. On the other hand, to accept such invitations runs the risk that methods that have been stripped of their theoretical underpinnings are considered to constitute qualitative inquiry. Similarly, perpetuating an instrumental use of mixed methods design puts the emphasis when thinking about that design on the use of different methods per se, rather than the use of different methods in an overall coherent and theoretically driven design. In so doing, it reduces mixed methods design *itself* to a technique rather than a theoretically grounded research approach. As Morse and Niehaus (2009) and Hesse-Biber (2010) emphasize, mixed methods is a theoretically driven study design, not simply the insertion of a mix of methods into a study.

All of this raises important points for qualitative inquirers to reflect on with respect to their motives in writing their methods in particular ways for funding. One starting point for such reflection is a somewhat unsettling and provocative question. When we write our application for funding, is the reason for choosing a mixed method design (or any other design for that matter) that the question will be better answered by this approach, or is it that by using this approach as opposed to a wholly qualitative design the chances of funding will be increased? Another starting point might be to reflect upon why qualitative inquiry within a mixed methods frame is seemingly more acceptable to some funders than research that is wholly qualitative. Perhaps this is because in some funder's minds mixed methods fits "well with the global economic imperative of the 1990s to do more with less and with the rising evidence-based practice movement" (Giddings, 2006, p. 196).

Perhaps, too, it is because descriptions of mixed methods read superficially might seem familiar to many funders and members of grant review panels. The QUAN → qual, QUAN + qual, QUAL → quan, and QUAL + quan symbols developed by Morse (1991) appear reassuringly similar to what science "should" look like. So does the language in the following excerpt from a description of some of the strategies within mixed methods: "The sample selection for the qualitative and quantitative components of sequential (QUAL → quan) or simultaneous (QUAL + quan) triangulation must be independent" (Morse, 1991, p. 122). Morse's incorporation of notations, symbols, and arrows into complicated figures that visually represent the mixed method strategy bears an uncanny resemblance to traditional ways of representing science and scientific "speak." While this in itself is not a problem, what is a problem is if that resemblance is what reassures funders and others that the research is sound and the methods reliable, rather than what those symbols are representing and conveying. Yet the tradeoff is that without this type of conceptualization and notation, the risk is that understandings of this approach will become muddled and unclear.

None of this is to suggest that mixed methods are not a valuable and important part of qualitative inquiry. Nor should it give the impression that a mixed methods research design is necessarily more inherently problematic than any other research approach with respect to the tensions and potential ruptures that exist at the interface of qualitative inquiry and funding. Rather, what it is to suggest is that mixed methods provides an excellent example of the fine lines we walk between selling and not selling out when we write our methods for funding. Achieving prominence in the repertoire of methods and study designs looked upon favorably by funders may not necessarily work in the interests of mixed methods design. As Hesse-Biber and Leavy point out, "more is not necessarily better" (2006, p. 334) with respect to methods; but it can be if, and it is *if* that is the crucial word here, it is the right design used for the right reasons to explore the problem or question that the research seeks to address.

Funding: Wheeling and Dealing in a Research Marketplace

Our conversation about the politics and practices of funding qualitative inquiry has ranged widely across issues such as how to locate funding, what that funding might be, how we might think about writing for that funding, and what this might mean in practice. At various points throughout this conversation, we have touched on the notion of a research marketplace where research is bought and sold. In this research marketplace, funding for qualitative inquiry is about much more than supporting a specific research project. Funding is a commodity, a unit of exchange. For example, individual researchers can trade their research for jobs, promotion, and tenure based on their research "performance." Institutions also trade in this marketplace, trading institutional research performance for rewards such as research infrastructure funding from governments, as well as a competitive ranking in the marketplace. The discussion to follow explores these ideas further using the metaphor of "wheeling and dealing" in a research marketplace as the organizing construct. As such, it is the most politically overt section of the chapter, shifting the focus of our discussion about the politics and practice of funding qualitative inquiry from the more micro level of specific projects, funders, or methods to a more macro, wider societal context.

Arising in the late 1990s, continuing throughout the first decade of the 2000s, and exacerbated by the global financial crisis of 2008 and 2009, there has been a period of economic restraint and funding cuts by governments in most Western countries. As a result, most universities and other research-intensive organizations are forced to run "mixed economies," where part of their funding comes from government operating grants and the other part is reliant on the generation of income from staff activities. This has created an imperative, and increasingly an expectation, for individual staff members to generate income for cash-strapped institutions. Gaining research funding is one way staff can do this, as funding for research can generate income for institutions in several ways. The first is from profit arising directly from the research undertaken. This is when contracted and tendered research can become very interesting and attractive. Normally, in this type of research funding it is possible to charge consultancy market rates both for the research team's time as well as research costs and overheads. This is in contrast to funding schemes that have a set limit on the amount of costs and overheads that they will pay, and which may not pay at all for the researchers' time if they are already employed by a university, for example. Given all this, it might seem that universities, research organizations, and researchers alike would focus more and more on contracted and tendered research funding. However, it is not this simple. There are messages about the messages.

These messages about messages are related to the fact that research income is also one of the variables in the schemes developed and used by governments to assess the research performance of higher education and research-oriented institutions. In many countries, a complex array of ever-changing formulas have been used in the quest to transform the individual research problems and projects of researchers employed in institutions into measures of collective institutional research performance (Cheek, 2006; Torrance, 2006). In Australia, for example, over the course of the last decade there have been several versions of proposed ways of measuring and ensuring quality and excellence in research. All have been premised on audit-driven notions of accountability designed to give government, industry, business, and the wider community assurance of the excellence of research conducted in Australia's higher education institutions. The current scheme in play at the time of writing this chapter is called Excellence in Research for Australia (ERA). ERA is a complex scheme that, like so many of its predecessors, as it unfolds becomes even more complex. There are 12 key 2010 documents alone listed on the Excellence in Research for Australia website (July 2010) including a 53-page booklet of evaluation guidelines and an 89-page booklet detailing submission guidelines! "Rewards" will flow from the Australian government to higher education institutions based on their research performance as calculated by the formulas embedded in the ERA scheme. Those institutions ranked highest will receive the largest share of the pool of dollars allocated for distribution.

However, that is not the end of the story. The results of the ERA assessment exercise will be publicly released and published at both institutional and national levels. This will enable comparisons to be made with respect to research performance not only between institutions, but also within institutions at the departmental level. League tables can be drawn up and published where the rankings of institutions in terms of this formulaic-determined research performance are displayed. Universities ranked highly in these tables can, and do, market themselves in the research marketplace as being "the top," a "top," or in the "top eight," and so on research universities in Australia. This marketing can then be used to attract sponsors of funding wishing to be associated with highly ranked and therefore prestigious research universities. It can also be used as part of the marketing to attract more research students. In turn, this generates more research outputs in the form of completed research student projects and publications, which in turn generates more income through assessment exercises that use research income, numbers of research student completions, and publications as part of their formula. In this way, not only do schemes such as ERA generate "rewards" for research performance, they also contribute to the possibility of this cycle of "rewards" continuing. Thus, layer upon complicated layer is deposited in a landscape known as the research marketplace.

But there are still more messages about the messages. In this landscape, not all research income is necessarily equal. In these assessment exercises, schemes, and/ or formulas, often it is *where* the money comes from, not just the absolute amount of it, that matters. One effect of this has been to create a complicated system of classifying funding. For example, in Australia at the time of writing this chapter, funding received is divided into various categories depending on its source. Highly sought after and prized are grants that appear on the Australian Competitive Grant Register (2010). The number of Australian Competitive Grants (ACG), as well as the amount of dollars attached to them, held by a particular university or individual researcher have been, and are, used as a measure of quality and research activity for institutions and individual researchers alike.

Yet there are even more messages about these messages to unpack. For, in Australia, among all grants, National Health and Medical Research Council (NH&MRC) and Australian Research Council (ARC) grants are prized the most. Historically, these funding schemes have attracted more "rewards" from government both monetarily and prestige-wise. Indeed, institutions will sometimes draw up tables of their relative national ranking with respect to number of grants, and amount of dollars, received from the NH&MRC and ARC alone. This is particularly the case when doing so presents them in a better light than their relative ranking on the league table of national research performance. This selective reporting of performance is part of wheeling and dealing in national and, increasingly, international research marketplaces. At the time of writing this chapter, the website of the University of Sydney (2010) proudly boasts that "Sydney researchers scored the 'research double' topping both the National Health and Medical Research Council (NH&MRC) and the Australian Research Council (ARC) for the number and dollar value of new, peer-reviewed, researcher driven research projects commencing in 2009." It goes on to state that "Sydney not only leads the Nation, it achieved a personal best by attracting record amounts of funding from both the ARC and NH&MRC for research projects starting in 2009." Here, the language of a competitive marketplace such as "research double," "topping," and "personal best" is overt. In this research marketplace, it is the amount and type of funding that both counts and is counted!

The effect of such wheeling and dealing, and the translation of research funding into other forms of funding, cascades down to the level of the individual researcher. The amount of dollars received by that researcher, and where they come from, are used as indicators of individual research performance and impact. What those dollars are used for, or even if they are really needed, is not the point. For example, in some types and fields of research the grant might be for large pieces of equipment. In such cases, the amount of the funding is actually as much a measure of the expense of the equipment as it is of the quality or the intensity of the research in a given institution. Another effect at the level of the individual researcher of this increasing emphasis on funding as being able to provide additional income for institutions, is that researchers and/or areas without this research income are increasingly viewed as not being as research-productive or research-intensive as those researchers or departments attracting large amounts of dollars. Writing on one's CV that one has funded research by working on it for some 30 hours a week above paid workload allocation does not have the same currency in a market-driven research context as does writing that one has attracted some hundreds of thousands of dollars of funding in the past two years, even if that funding has been to buy an expensive piece of equipment or equip a laboratory. This works against many qualitative inquirers whose major form of support or funding for their research is their own time either as a percentage of their paid workload, or the time they use on weekends or evenings to do research over and above any such allocated percentage.

An effect of differentially rewarding types of funding for research is that the gaining of specific categories of funding has become an end in itself, rather than that funding being a means to support a specific piece of research. The danger in this is that the research design becomes subverted and shaped by the demands and expectations of highly prized funding sources. For example, if a so called "gold star" research scheme has historically been adverse to funding qualitative research in general, or some types of qualitative research specifically, how do qualitative researchers position themselves in relation to this? Does this mean we abandon this source of funding, or do we abandon our qualitative inquiry and put up approaches and techniques that we think the funder will support? If we choose not to abandon our qualitative inquiry altogether, do we try to make our qualitative inquiry look more like the type of research that these funders and their decision-making panels will expect and/or understand? How far are we prepared to go in terms of shaping our research to fit these schemes? Is it better to opt out of, or opt to be in, this research marketplace and the spaces it creates?

But it is not as simple as that. There is ambivalence in these categories of opting out and opting in and their possible effects. Opting in, and thereby gaining currency in this marketplace, may paradoxically provide opportunities to promote and advance qualitative inquiry. Perhaps there is the possibility that external funding can be used as a currency to gain institutional power and positions on panels awarding funds in granting schemes where qualitative inquirers can work from within to try to change practices that work against qualitative inquiry. Furthermore, in many institutions, attracting this type of "prized" funding is "rewarded" with infrastructure monies and in-kind support to build critical masses of researchers and develop research centers. In turn, this may provide the opportunity to fund forms of qualitative inquiry that may not otherwise be able to attract monetary or other forms of support, thereby helping resist the potential reduction and homogenization of qualitative inquiry into forms acceptable to external funding agencies. Thus, paradoxically, although participating in a research marketplace does not necessarily advance qualitative inquiry, it might. Yet even given this possibility, a question that lingers in my mind is whether this is an example of a way to resist the excesses of the research marketplace by turning it against itself, or a case of selling out—at least in part. Is there a danger in this that inadvertently a two-tiered structure of qualitative researcher is created, a new binary where those with the currency highly prized in the research marketplace, the "haves," are the primary and dominant category, with their poor cousins, the marketplace "have nots" dependent on them?

Denzin and Lincoln remind us that all of us are "stuck in the present working against the past as we move into a politically charged and challenging future" (2005, p. xv). At times, this sense of being stuck in a present working against the past has resulted in feelings of fatigue and frustration on my part. For example, I wonder about where the next research productivity reform or audit will come from and what form it will take. I think about how much time I have used, and will again use, to respond to relentless demands for demonstrating delimited forms of evidence about the impact/quality/products (or some other form of research marketspeak) of my research only to find that with a change of government it has all changed anyway. Thinking about the past decade, these audits and reviews congeal and blur into each other. They are new versions of the same old rhetoric, ideas about ideas about ideas, depositing layer upon layer on bedrock of positivistic-influenced assumptions about research and evidence.

In all of this, it has not always been easy or comfortable for me to navigate the tension between critiquing the spaces I research in, and surviving in the spaces of the research marketplace of which, whether I like it or not, my research has been part (Cheek, 2007). At times, I have questioned my motives in applying for certain types of external funding for my research. Was my motive to obtain the external funding to do a project I was burning to do, or was it that I needed the external funding to score points on some form of research marketplace scorecard? If the answer is both of the above, then which mattered most to me? In wheeling and dealing in this market, and enjoying the privileges and trappings that this can "buy," such as tenure, promotion, and research infrastructure, have I had to do things that I would rather not talk about—the "yes but" thinking? Have I been part of what Stronach and Torrance (1995) referred to close to two decades ago as preserving little private spaces to be radical in, while doing something else in various dimensions of my professional life? And, if so, could I be accused of saying a lot about what I do in this chapter and not enough about what I do not say about what I do (Cheek, 2010a)?

Like so many other qualitative inquirers, I am still searching for some sort of middle ground in all of this. I cannot tell you exactly what this middle ground might look like, as I suspect it will vary for each of us. However, I can tell you that the middle ground that I am looking for is a place from which to engage the politics and practices of funding qualitative inquiry and the research marketplace on my terms, not someone else's. It is a place from which any engagement with those politics and practices is because I choose to engage with them not because I have to, or because they constantly engage my time and energy destructively (Cheek, 2008). In this middle ground, I can choose how to engage with a politics not of my own making.

Signing Off for Now: The Politics and Practice of Funding as an Ongoing Conversation

So reader, how to conclude? It is customary to call the final section of an extended discussion such as the one in this chapter a conclusion. However, somehow at this point the word "conclusion" does not seem right or an easy fit with what has been, and remains to be, said. It seems too final, too much like having the last word when there is no last word to be had. At best, this chapter could only ever hope to be "a comment within an ongoing discussion" (Maxey, 1999, p. 206). This ongoing discussion is about moving away from reactionary positions be they in terms of a funder's requirements, or a politics of evidence, or a critique of qualitative inquiry from within qualitative inquiry itself. It is an ongoing discussion about being in places that are of our own making as qualitative inquirers and places that we choose to be in. From such places, we can apply for funding and take the hard decisions that this involves with respect to what is negotiable and what is not, and know that we and not others have made those decisions. From such places, we can be confident that the thinking and reflection that sits behind taking up such positions will contribute to the ongoing development and strength of qualitative inquiry. This is because when we are forced to try to articulate on what basis we have made these decisions we develop further our understandings about what enables something to be called both "qualitative" and "inquiry." And, importantly, such development comes out of qualitative inquiry itself rather than being imposed on it. Put another way, it enables us to choose the messages about the messages about the messages that we will take on board, and those that we will ignore.

References

Atkinson, P., & Delamont, S. (2006). In the roiling smoke: Qualitative inquiry and contested fields. *International Journal of Qualitative Studies in Education, 19*(6), 747–755.

Australian Competitive Grants Register (ACGR). (2010). Available at http://www.inno vation.gov.au/Section/Research/Pages/AustralianCompetitiveGrantsRegister (ACGR).aspx

Bochner, A. P. (2009). Warm ideas and chilling consequences. *International Review of Qualitative Research, 2*(3), 357–370.

Brennan, M. (2002). *The politics and practicalities of grassroots research in education.* Available at http://www.staff.vu.edu.au/alnarc/forum/marie_brennan.html

Cannella, G. S., & Lincoln, Y. S. (2004). Dangerous discourses II: Comprehending and countering the redeployment of discourses (and resources) in the generation of liberatory inquiry. *Qualitative Inquiry, 10*(2), 165–174.

Carey, M. A., & Swanson, J. (2003). Pearls, pith, and provocation: Funding for qualitative research. *Qualitative Health Research, 13*(6), 852–856.

Cheek, J. (2005). The practice and politics of funded qualitative research. In N. K. Denzin & Y. S. Lincoln (Eds.), *The SAGE handbook of qualitative research* (3rd ed., pp. 387–409). Thousand Oaks, CA: Sage.

Cheek, J. (2006). The challenge of tailor-made research quality: The RQF in Australia. In N. K. Denzin & M. D. Giardina (Eds.), *Qualitative inquiry and the conservative challenge* (pp. 109–126). Walnut Creek, CA: Left Coast Press.

Cheek, J. (2007). Qualitative inquiry, ethics, and the politics of evidence: Working within these spaces rather than being worked over by them. In N. K. Denzin & M. D. Giardina (Eds.), *Ethical futures in qualitative research: Decolonizing the politics of knowledge* (pp. 9–43). Walnut Creek, CA: Left Coast Press.

Cheek, J. (2008). A fine line: Positioning qualitative inquiry in the wake of the politics of evidence. *International Review of Qualitative Research, 1*(1). Walnut Creek, CA: Left Coast Press.

Cheek, J. (2010a). Human rights, social justice, and qualitative research: Questions and hesitations about what we say about what we do. In N. K. Denzin & M. D. Giardina (Eds.), *Qualitative inquiry and human rights* (pp. 100–111). Walnut Creek, CA: Left Coast Press.

Cheek, J. (2010b). A potent mix: Older people, transitions, practice development and research. *Journal of Research in Nursing, 15,* 2.

Cheek, J., & Ballantyne, A. (2001). Moving them on and in: The process of searching for and selecting an aged care facility. *Qualitative Health Research, 11*(2), 221–237.

Cheek, J., Ballantyne, A., Byers, L., & Quan, J. (2007). From retirement village to residential aged care: What older people and their families say. *Health and Social Care in the Community, 15*(1), 8–17.

Cheek, J., Ballantyne, A., Gilham, D., Mussared, J., Flett, P., Lewin, G., et al. (2006). Improving care transitions of older people: Challenges for today and tomorrow. *Quality in Aging, 7*(4), 18–25.

Cheek, J., Ballantyne, A., Roder-Allen, G., & Jones, J. (2005). Making choices: How older people living in independent living units decide to enter the acute care system. *International Journal of Nursing Practice, 11*(2), 52–57.

Cheek, J., Corlis, M., & Radoslovich, H. (2009). Connecting what we do with what we know: Building a community of research and practice. *International Journal of Older People Nursing, 4*(3), 233–238.

Cheek, J., Garnham, B., & Quan, J. (2006). "What's in a number": Issues in providing evidence of impact and quality of research(ers). *Qualitative Health Research, 16*(3), 423–435.

Cheek, J., Price, K., Dawson, A., Mott, K., Beilby, J., & Wilkinson, D. (2002). *Consumer perceptions of nursing and nurses in general practice.* Available at http://www.health .gov.au/internet/main/publishing.nsf/Content/work-pr-nigp-res-cons-rept

Creswell, J. W. (2003). *Research design: Qualitative, quantitative and mixed methods approaches* (2nd ed.). Thousand Oaks, CA: Sage.

Creswell, J. W., & Plano Clark, V. L. (2007). *Designing and conducting mixed methods research.* Thousand Oaks, CA: Sage.

Denzin, N. K. (2009). The elephant in the living room: Or extending the conversation about the politics of evidence. *Qualitative Research, 9,* 139–160.

Denzin, N. K., & Giardina, M. D. (2006). *Qualitative inquiry and the conservative challenge.* Walnut Creek, CA: Left Coast Press.

Denzin, N. K., & Giardina, M. D. (2007a). *Ethical futures in qualitative research: Decolonizing the politics of knowledge.* Walnut Creek, CA: Left Coast Press.

Denzin, N. K., & Giardina, M. D. (2007b). Introduction. In N. K. Denzin & M. D. Giardina (Eds.), *Ethical futures in qualitative research: Decolonizing the politics of knowledge* (pp. 9–43). Walnut Creek, CA: Left Coast Press.

Denzin, N. K., & Giardina, M. D. (2008). *Qualitative inquiry and the politics of evidence.* Walnut Creek, CA: Left Coast Press.

Denzin, N. K., & Giardina, M. D. (2009). *Qualitative inquiry and social justice.* Walnut Creek, CA: Left Coast Press.

Denzin, N. K., & Lincoln, Y. S. (2005). Preface. In N. K. Denzin &Y. S. Lincoln (Eds.), *The SAGE handbook of qualitative research* (3rd ed., pp. ix–xix). Thousand Oaks, CA: Sage.

Excellence in Research for Australia. (2010). *Key 2010 documents.* Available at http://www.arc.gov.au/era/key_docs10.htm

Giddings, L. S. (2006). Mixed-methods research: Positivism dressed in drag? *Journal of Research in Nursing, 11*(3), 195–203.

GrantSearch Register of Australian Funding. (2010). *Funding at your fingertips.* Available at http://www.grantsearch.com.au/

Greene, J. C. (2007). *Mixed methods in social inquiry.* San Francisco: Jossey-Bass.

Hammersley, M. (2005). Close encounters of a political kind: The threat from the evidence-based policy-making and practice movement. *Qualitative Researcher, 1*, 2–4.

Hesse-Biber, S. N. (2010). *Mixed methods research: Merging theory with practice.* New York: Guilford.

Hesse-Biber, S. N., & Leavy, P. (2006). *The practice of qualitative research.* Thousand Oaks, CA: Sage.

Holmes, D., Murray, S. J., Perron, A., & Rail, G. (2006). Deconstructing the evidence-based discourse in health sciences: Truth, power, and fascism. *International Journal of Evidence-Based Healthcare, 4*(3), 180–186.

Hurdley, R. (2010). In the picture or off the wall? Ethical regulation, research habitus, and unpeopled ethnography. *Qualitative Inquiry, 16*(6), 517–528.

Kvale, S. (2008). Qualitative inquiry between scientistic evidentialism, ethical subjectivism and the free market. *International Review of Qualitative Research, 1*(1), 5–18.

Lacey, E. A. (1998). Social and medical research ethics: Is there a difference? *Social Sciences in Health, 4*(4), 211–217.

Lincoln, Y. S., & Cannella, G. S. (2002, April). *Qualitative research and the radical right: Cats and dogs and other natural enemies.* Paper presented at the 66th annual meeting of the American Educational Research Association, New Orleans, LA.

Lincoln, Y. S., & Cannella, G. S. (2007). Ethics and the broader rethinking/reconceptualization of research as construct. In N. K. Denzin & M. D. Giardina (Eds.), *Ethical futures in qualitative research: Decolonizing the politics of knowledge* (pp. 67–84). Walnut Creek, CA: Left Coast Press.

Lincoln, Y. S., & Tierney, W. G. (2002, April). *"What we have here is a failure to commu-nicate . . .": Qualitative research and institutional review boards (IRBs).* Paper presented at the 66th annual meeting of the American Educational Research Association, New Orleans, LA.

Long, B. (2010). [Review of the book *Qualitative inquiry and the politics of evidence*]. *Qualitative Health Research, 20*(3), 432–434.

Maxey, I. (1999). Beyond boundaries? Activism, academia, reflexivity and research. *Area, 31*(3), 199–208.

Mertens, D. (2005). *Research and evaluation in education and psychology: Integrating diversity with quantitative, qualitative, and mixed methods.* Thousand Oaks, CA: Sage.

Morse, J. M. (1991). Approaches to qualitative-quantitative methodological triangulation. *Methodology Corner, 40*(2), 120–123.

Morse, J. M. (2002). Myth #53: Qualitative research is cheap. *Qualitative Health Research, 12*(10), 1307–1308.

Morse, J. M. (2003a). The adjudication of qualitative proposals. *Qualitative Health Research, 13*(6), 739–742.

Morse, J. M. (2003b). A review committee's guide for evaluating qualitative proposals. *Qualitative Health Research, 13*(6), 833–851.

Morse, J. M. (2006a). The politics of evidence. *Qualitative Health Research, 16*(3), 395–404.

Morse, J. M. (2006b). Reconceptualizing qualitative inquiry. *Qualitative Health Research, 16*(3), 415–422.

Morse, J. M. (2008). Deceptive simplicity. *Qualitative Health Research, 18*(10), 1311.

Morse, J. M., & Niehaus, L. (2009). *Mixed method design: Principles and procedures.* Walnut Creek, CA: Left Coast Press.

Penrod, J. (2003). Getting funded: Writing a successful qualitative small-project proposal. *Qualitative Health Research, 13*(6), 821–832.

Ramcharan, P., & Cutcliffe, J. R. (2001). Judging the ethics of qualitative research: Considering the "ethics as process" model. *Health and Social Care in the Community, 9*(6), 358–366.

Riesman, D. (2002, November/December). Reviewing social research. *Change,* 9–10.

Schwandt, T. (2007). The pressing need for ethical education: A commentary on the growing IRB controversy. In N. K. Denzin & M. D. Giardina (Eds.), *Ethical futures in qualitative research: Decolonizing the politics of knowledge* (pp. 85–98). Walnut Creek, CA: Left Coast Press.

Stronach, I. (2006). Enlightenment and the "heart of darkness": (Neo)imperialism in the Congo, and elsewhere. *International Journal of Qualitative Studies in Education, 19*(6), 757–768.

Stronach, I., & Torrance, H. (1995). The future of evaluation: A retrospective. *Cambridge Journal of Education, 25*(3), 283–300.

Tashakkori, A., & Teddlie, C. (Eds.). (2003). *Handbook of mixed methods in social and behavioral research.* Thousand Oaks, CA: Sage.

Teddlie, C., & Tashakkori, A. (2009). *Foundations of mixed methods research: Integrating quantitative and qualitative approaches in the behavioral and social sciences.* Thousand Oaks, CA: Sage.

Torrance, H. (2006). Research quality and research governance in the United Kingdom. In N. K. Denzin & M. D. Giardina (Eds.), *Qualitative inquiry and the conservative challenge* (pp. 127–148). Walnut Creek, CA: Left Coast Press.

Torres, C. A. (2002). The state, privatization and educational policy: A critique of neo-liberalism in Latin America and some ethical and political implications. *Comparative Education, 38*(4), 365–385.

University of Sydney. (2010). *Research achievements.* Available at http://www.usyd.edu.au/research/about/major_achievements.shtml

van den Hoonaard, W. C. (2001). Is research-ethics review a moral panic? *Canadian Review of Sociology and Anthropology, 38*(1), 19–36.

3

Controversies in Mixed Methods Research

John W. Creswell

Mixed methods has emerged in the last few years as a research approach popular in many disciplines and countries, and supported through diverse funding agencies. With such growth, it is not surprising that critical commentaries have surfaced through papers presented at conferences and in published journal articles. These critics have come from both within (e.g., Greene, 2008; Morse, 2005; Creswell, Plano Clark, & Garrett, 2008) and outside (Denzin & Lincoln, 2005; Howe, 2004) the mixed methods community. Although concerns have mounted, they have been largely ignored by social scientists and the mixed methods community.

This chapter gives voice and focus to these controversies. I discuss 11 far-ranging controversies from basic concerns about defining and describing mixed methods, to philosophical debates, and on into the procedures for conducting a study.

For each controversy, I present critical questions, diverse stances, and lingering questions. At the end of this chapter, I reflect on the implications of these controversies. I hope this discussion will help mixed methods researchers, students, and policy makers appreciate the still-unanswered questions, view the multiple perspectives that have emerged, and reflect on new commitments that the mixed methods field needs to make. For qualitative researchers, I hope that this reflection will encourage the continued discussion of the strong vital role that qualitative research has and continues to play in mixed methods research.

The thoughts to follow will reflect my own writings of the last 20 years and will include, at times, a self-reflective critique. My methodological development consisted of formal training as a postpositivist in the 1970s, self-education as a constructivist through teaching qualitative courses in the 1980s, and advocacy for mixed methods through my writings and teachings from the 1990s to the present. As one spokesperson for mixed methods, many controversies have come to my attention through scholarly papers presented at conferences, articles published in the *Journal of Mixed Methods Research* (JMMR) while I served as founding coeditor for the last five years, and papers sent to me by authors who wanted me to keep abreast of emerging issues. As I look across these diverse materials, I hope to foster the ongoing conversation about the controversies and the many possible answers that scholars have offered to them.

Some Recent Questions

Some of the controversies that I will present figured prominently in a discussion in March 2009. I was attending and presenting at the University of Aberdeen in Scotland (Creswell, 2009d) at the Economic & Social Research Council (ESRC) Seminar Series sponsored by the Health Services Research Unit at the University of Aberdeen. I had finished my overview of mixed methods research to a gathering of 50 scholars primarily from the health sciences. They had assembled in historic Elphinstone Hall, an ancient venue with a high, vaulted, hammer-beam roof, banners hanging from the rafters, and oak-paneled walls lined with pictures of distinguished scholars dating back centuries. Much to my surprise, the conference organizer suddenly asked small groups to form and record their questions about both the advantages and the challenges of using mixed methods research. Not wanting to miss a key opportunity to capture their challenges and critical thoughts, I hastily began taking notes. They spoke about claims being made about the value of mixed methods research ("Is mixed methods seen as the answer to everything?" "Are there undue expectations raised by mixed methods that cannot be fulfilled?"), about philosophical and theoretical issues ("Is there opposition to mixed methods from those who hold strong worldview positions?" "Does a dominant paradigm prevail in mixed methods?" "Is qualitative research working on an even playing field with quantitative in mixed methods?"), and about the procedures and processes of research ("Is there a good fit between the research question and mixed methods?" "Do researchers have expertise and competence in both areas?").

The irony of "new" voices of concern about mixed methods arising in the "old," historic setting of Elphinstone Hall did not escape my attention. But, in retrospect, hearing the issues was not surprising. Concerns have been voiced in recent respected journal articles (Giddings, 2006; Howe, 2004), in the third edition of this handbook (Denzin & Lincoln, 2005), in conference presentations (Holmes, 2006), and in articles published in the *Journal of Mixed Methods Research.* In 2006, I had presented my views about unresolved issues in a journal article on the role of qualitative research in mixed methods (Creswell, Shope, Plano Clark, & Green, 2006), and at a panel presentation made at the 2007 International Qualitative Inquiry Congress (Creswell, 2007). In light of these discussions, it is timely to address these controversies. In this chapter, I address 11 controversies and raise several questions, as outlined in Table 3.1. The controversies, as a group, reflect what Kuhn (1970) said years ago about the transition period in research:

> The proliferation of competing articulations, the willingness to try anything, the expression of explicit discontent, the recourse to philosophy, and to debate over fundamentals, all these are symptoms of a transition from normal to extraordinary research. (p. 91)

Table 3.1 Eleven Key Controversies and Questions Being Raised in Mixed Methods Research

Controversies	Questions Being Raised
1. The changing and expanding definitions of mixed methods research	What is mixed methods research? How should it be defined? What shifts are being seen in its definition?
2. The questionable use of qualitative and quantitative descriptors	Are the terms "qualitative" and "quantitative" useful descriptors? What inferences are made when these terms are used? Is there a binary distinction being made that does not hold in practice?
3. Is mixed methods a "new" approach to research?	When did the conceptualization of mixed methods begin? Does mixed methods predate the period often associated with its beginning? What initiatives began prior to the late 1980s?
4. What drives the interest in mixed methods?	How has interest grown in mixed methods? What is the role of funding agencies in its development?

(Continued)

Table 3.1 (Continued)

5. Is the paradigm debate still being discussed?	Can paradigms be mixed? What stances on paradigm use in mixed methods have developed? Should the paradigm for mixed methods be based on scholarly communities?
6. Does mixed methods privilege postpositivism?	In the privileging of postpositivism in mixed methods, does it marginalize qualitative, interpretive approaches and relegate them to secondary status?
7. Is there a fixed discourse in mixed methods?	Who controls the discourse about mixed methods? Is mixed methods nearing a "metanarrative?"
8. Should mixed methods adopt a bilingual language for its terms?	What is the language of mixed methods research? Should the language be bilingual or reflect quantitative and qualitative terms?
9. Are there too many confusing design possibilities for mixed methods procedures?	What designs should mixed methods researchers use? Are the present designs complex enough to reflect practice? Should entirely new ways of thinking about designs be adopted?
10. Is mixed methods research misappropriating designs and procedures from other approaches to research?	Are the claims of mixed methods overstated (because of misappropriation of other approaches to research)? Can mixed methods be seen as an approach lodged within a larger framework (e.g., ethnography)?
11. What value is added by mixed methods beyond the value gained through quantitative or qualitative research?	Does mixed methods provide a better understanding of a research problem than either quantitative or qualitative research alone? How can the value of mixed methods research be substantiated through scholarly inquiry?

Changing and Expanding Definitions

Heading the list of controversies would certainly be the fundamental question: What is mixed methods research? How should it be defined? To answer these questions requires a brief historical review of shifts in the definition of mixed methods over the years. For example, an early definition of mixed methods came from writers in the field of evaluation, Greene, Caracelli, and Graham (1989). They emphasized the mixing of *methods* and the disentanglement of methods and paradigms when they said,

> In this study, we defined mixed-method designs as those that include at least one quantitative method (designed to collect numbers) and one qualitative method (designed to collect words), where neither type of method is inherently linked to any particular inquiry paradigm. (p. 256)

Ten years later, the definition had shifted from mixing two methods to mixing in all phases of the research process, and mixed methods was being seen as a *methodology* (Tashakkori & Teddlie, 1998). Included within this process would be mixing from philosophical (i.e., worldview) positions, to final inferences, and to the interpretations of results. Thus, Tashakkori and Teddlie (1998) defined mixed methods as the combination of "qualitative and quantitative approaches in the methodology of a study" (p. ix). These authors reinforced this methodological orientation in their preface to the *Handbook of Mixed Methods in Social & Behavioral Research* by writing, "mixed methods research has evolved to the point where it is a separate methodological orientation with its own worldview, vocabulary, and techniques" (Tashakkori & Teddlie, 2003, p. x).

A few years later, when Plano Clark and I (Creswell & Plano Clark, 2007) wrote a definition for mixed methods into our introductory book, we blended *both* a methods and a methodological orientation along with a central assumption being made with this type of research. We said,

> Mixed methods research is a research design with philosophical assumptions as well as methods of inquiry. As a methodology, it involves philosophical assumptions that guide the direction of the collection and analysis and the mixture of qualitative and quantitative approaches in many phases of the research process. As a method, it focuses on collecting, analyzing, and mixing both quantitative and qualitative data in a single study or series of studies. Its central premise is that the use of quantitative and qualitative approaches, in combination, provides a better understanding of research problems than either approach alone. (p. 5)

This definition was patterned on describing an approach using multiple meanings, such as found in Stake's (1995) definition of a case study. Our definition of mixed methods had both a philosophy and a method orientation, and it conveyed components of the *core characteristics* of mixed methods that I advance today in workshops and presentations (e.g., see Creswell, 2009a). In mixed methods, the researcher

- collects and analyzes persuasively and rigorously both qualitative and quantitative data (based on research questions);
- mixes (or integrates or links) the two forms of data concurrently by combining them (or merging them), or sequentially by having one build on the other, and in a way that gives priority to one or to both;
- uses these procedures in a single study or in multiple phases of a program of study;
- frames these procedures within philosophical worldviews and a theoretical lens; and
- combines the procedures into specific research designs that direct the plan for conducting the study.

These core characteristics have provided some common features for describing mixed methods research. They evolved from many years of reviewing mixed methods articles and determining how researchers use both qualitative and quantitative methods in their studies.

I am not alone in proposing some common features. In a highly cited JMMR article, Johnson, Onwuegbuzie, and Turner (2007) suggested a composite definition for mixed methods based on 19 definitions provided by 21 highly published mixed methods researchers. After sharing these definitions, they noted the variations in definitions, from what was being mixed (e.g., methods, methodologies, or types of research), the place in the research process in which mixing occurred (e.g., data collection, data analysis), the scope of the mixing (e.g., from data to worldviews), the purpose or rationale for mixing (e.g., breadth, corroboration), and the elements driving the research (e.g., bottom-up, top-down, the core component). Incorporating these diverse perspectives, the authors end with a composite definition:

Mixed methods research is the type of research in which a researcher or team of researchers combines elements of qualitative and quantitative research approaches (e.g., use of qualitative and quantitative viewpoints, data collection, analysis, inference techniques) for the purposes of breadth and depth of understanding and corroboration. (p. 123)

In this definition, the authors do not view mixed methods simply as methods, but more as a methodology that spans from viewpoints to inferences. They do not view mixed methods as only data collection, but rather as the more general combination of qualitative and quantitative research. They incorporate diverse viewpoints, but do not specifically mention paradigms (as in the Greene et al., 1989, definition) or philosophy (as in the Creswell & Plano Clark, 2007, definition). Their purposes for mixed methods—breadth and depth of understanding and corroboration—do not speak to how the research question may suggest mixed methods rather than force-fitting a line of inquiry into either a quantitative or qualitative approach. Perhaps most important, they suggest that there is a common definition that should be used.

Another definition has been advanced by Greene (2007), who stated that mixed methods was an orientation toward looking at the social world

> that actively invites us to participate in dialogue about multiple ways of seeing and hearing, multiple ways of making sense of the social world, and multiple standpoints on what is important and to be valued and cherished. (p. 20)

This definition has moved mixed methods into an entirely new realm of conceptualization, and perhaps a useful one. Defining mixed methods as "multiple ways of seeing" opens up broad applications beyond using it as only a research method. It can be used, for example, as an approach to think about designing documentaries (Creswell & McCoy, in press), or a means for "seeing" participatory approaches to HIV-infected populations in the Eastern Cape of South Africa (Olivier, de Lange, Creswell, & Wood, 2009). Lately, I have begun my workshops on mixed methods by indicating that we have many instances of mixed methods in our social world. I start with Al Gore's film-documentary, *An Inconvenient Truth,* about global warming and Gore's combined use of mixed method-like statistical trends and personal stories (David, Bender, Burns, & Guggenheim, 2006). Defining mixed methods as a way of seeing opens up applications for it in many aspects of social life.

However, I still have unresolved concerns after reviewing these diverse definitions. Do we need a common definition or common set of core characteristics? Will such common features limit what we see as mixed methods? Do we need multiple definitions? For those individuals new to mixed methods, do they need a commonly accepted definition to convey the purpose of their research and to convince others of the legitimacy of their approach?

The Questionable Use of Qualitative and Quantitative Descriptors

Researchers talk about mixed methods using descriptors such as "qualitative" and "quantitative." The use of statistics and stories in Gore's film reinforces a binary distinction between qualitative and quantitative research. Are the terms "qualitative" and "quantitative" useful descriptors to use? What are the inferences being made when these terms are used? This controversy has brought forward one group of writers who have found the terms "qualitative" and "quantitative" intermingled with designs and paradigms, rather than referring to methods of data collection and analysis. It also has brought forward another group of writers who feel that the use of these terms fosters an unacceptable binary or dichotomy that minimizes the diversity in methods.

Giddings (2006) felt that the terms "qualitative" and "quantitative" became normative descriptors for research paradigms in the 1970s and 1980s, and that the term "qualitative" gave nonpositivist researchers "a place to stand" (p. 199). When writers have used the term "qualitative paradigm," it has often been in the context of the qualitative-quantitative debates in evaluation and the social sciences (Greene, 2007). Greene pointed out that it was helpful to separate the research methods of "qualitative" and "quantitative" from broader philosophical issues, and to refrain from intermingling methods and philosophy. Another intermingling occurs at the design level. Vogt (2008) took the strong position: "To think in terms of quantitative and qualitative *designs* is a category mistake" (p. 1, emphasis added). He felt that all research designs—such as surveys, document analysis, experiments, and quasi-experiments—could accommodate data coded as numbers and words.

The use of "qualitative" and "quantitative" has been further discouraged because it creates a binary distinction that does not hold in practice. Often writers equate "qualitative" to text data and "quantitative" to numbers data. In a recent *JMMR* article, Sandelowski, Voils, and Knafl (2009) countered this binary thinking by pointing out that counting often involved qualitative judgments, and that numbers often related to context. Further, qualitative data are sometimes transformed in data analysis into categorical data, and a binary configuration overlooked both within-group (e.g., qualitative) and between-group similarities (e.g., qualitative and quantitative). Resonating with this thought, Giddings (2006) stated that binary positioning made methodological diversity invisible.

Adding confusion to the meaning of "qualitative" and "quantitative" have been those who felt that mixed methods should mean collecting mono-methods—*multiple* qualitative sources of data or quantitative sources of data

(Shank, 2007; Vogt, 2008) instead of collecting *both* qualitative and quantitative data (mixed methods). Some writers have been clear that multiple sources of one kind of data (i.e., qualitative or quantitative data) should be called "multiple methods" (Morse & Niehaus, 2009, Appendix 1), not mixed methods. Again, regardless as to how mixed methods is viewed, both perspectives rely on a normative, binary distinction between "qualitative" and quantitative" to reinforce their positions.

A strong case can be made that "qualitative" and "quantitative" should refer to methods. A useful diagram is advanced by Crotty (1998), who provided a conceptual framework for sorting out these layers of research into epistemology, theoretical perspectives (e.g., feminist theory), methodology, and methods. But to throw out the terms "quantitative" and "qualitative" seems to disrupt a long-established pattern of communication that has been used in the social, behavior, and health sciences. Until we have replacement terms, a means of discourse across fields is helpful, but we need to be careful how we use the terms. On the issue of the binary distinction, writers in the mixed methods field have tended to dismiss the dichotomy in favor of a continuum for presenting qualitative and quantitative differences (Creswell, 2008; Tashakkori & Teddlie, 2003). Writers in mixed methods are also careful to distinguish "multi-method studies" in which multiple types of *qualitative* or *quantitative* data are collected (see Creswell & Plano Clark, 2007) from "mixed methods studies" that incorporate collecting *both* qualitative and quantitative data. In the health sciences, the term "multi-method" is typically used to convey studies in which both forms of data are gathered (e.g., see Stange, Crabtree, & Miller, 2006), although in a study of National Institutes of Health–funded projects, Plano Clark (2009) found that "multimethod" meant multiple methods of quantitative *or* qualitative data 64% of the time, and "mixed methods" 36% of the time.

In light of these discussions about intermingling and the binary distinction, should we refrain from using the terms "qualitative" and "quantitative?" Why do mixed methods writers not clearly distinguish among methods, designs, and paradigms? Should mixed methods involve multiple qualitative or quantitative methods or some combine of both?

The New Versus the Old

Historically, researchers have used both forms of methods in these studies. This leads to another controversy: Is mixed methods a "new" approach or is it simply pouring new ideas into old packaging? Emphasizing the "new," recent writers have called mixed methods the third methodological "movement" (following quantitative and qualitative) (Tashakkori & Teddlie, 2003, p. 5), the "third research paradigm" (Johnson & Onwuegbuzie, 2004, p. 15), and "a new star in the social science sky" (Mayring, 2007, p. 1). Claims such as these have left some critics to wonder "exactly what the new mixed methods movement is claiming. The major proponents insist that what they developed is a new way of doing research" (Holmes, 2006, p. 2).

I often date the beginnings of mixed methods back to the late 1980s and early 1990s with the coming together of several publications all focused on describing and defining what is now known as mixed methods. These writers worked independently and they came from sociology in the United States (Brewer & Hunter, 1989) and in the United Kingdom (Fielding & Fielding, 1986), from evaluation in the United States (Greene et al., 1989), from management in the United Kingdom (Bryman, 1988), from nursing in Canada (Morse, 1991), and from education in the United States (Creswell, 1994). A critical mass of writings came together within a short space of time, and all of these individuals were writing books, chapters, and articles on an approach to research that moved from simply using quantitative and qualitative approaches as distinct, separate strands in a study to research that actually linked or combined them. At this time, qualitative inquiry had become largely accepted as a legitimate methodology in the social sciences and was moving into the "blurred genres" stage (Denzin & Lincoln, 2005). Philosophical debates between quantitative and qualitative researchers were still underway (Reichardt & Rallis, 1994) but beginning to soften, and new methodologies to address the complex problems of society were being encouraged.

In retrospect, I now wonder if these writers were truly the first individuals to talk about combining quantitative and qualitative data. Individuals in my workshops have for some time been saying that mixed methods is not "new." Holmes (2006) raised this question when he commented,

> The major proponents insist that what they have developed is a new way of doing research—an alternative to qualitative and quantitative research, but what's new about that? . . . ethnographers and other social researchers have been gathering data using mixed methods at least since the 1920s, and case study researchers and anyone using triangulation have also been using mixed methods. (p. 2)

To probe whether or not it is a "new" idea requires returning to historical documents in fields such as sociology, evaluation, and action research. How does the pre-late-1980s discussion fit with what is known about mixed methods today? Three threads of thinking prior to the late 1980s can give us insight: the use of multiple methods, the discussions about using qualitative research within a research world largely dominated by quantitative research, and the informal initiatives to combine methods.

In terms of multiple methods, in 1959 Campbell and Fiske advanced the use of multiple methods in convergent and discriminant validation of psychological traits using a multitrait-multimethod matrix. They felt that more than one trait as well as more than one method must be employed in the validation process. Their discussion, however, was limited to multiple *quantitative* sources of data. During the 1970s, Denzin (1978) identified several types of combinations of methodologies in the study of the same phenomena or programs through his idea of *data triangulation*—the use of various data sources in a study. He said, "I now offer as a final methodological rule the principle that multiple methods should be used in every investigation" (Denzin, 1978, p. 28).

Throughout the 1970s and on into the 1980s, several noted authors were calling for the use of qualitative research on equal footing with more quantitative-experimental methods (Patton, 1980). Campbell (1974) gave a noted presentation at the American Psychological Association meeting on "Qualitative Knowing in Action Research" for the Kurt Lewin Award address. He suggested that a true scientific approach was to eliminate the question of the position of ultimate authority between quantitative and qualitative research and to reestablish the importance of qualitative research. Cronbach (1975), in his well-known article "Beyond the Two Disciplines of Scientific Psychology," cast doubt on the idea that the social sciences could be modeled only on the natural sciences. Both Campbell and Cronbach started out as quantitative researchers and then embraced qualitative or naturalistic research through their writing.

Other authors began combining methods informally, and these writers were clearly the pioneers of mixed methods thinking today. In sociology, Sieber (1973) discussed the "interplay" of fieldwork and survey methods, and identified procedures for combining the two methods. Lamenting the fact that there were "too few examples to adduce general principles" (p. 1358), Sieber suggested the need for a "new style of research" (p. 1337). He further discussed the sequence of both methods with "concurrent scheduling" and "interweaving" the two methods (p. 1357). Equally important, he cited a number of studies that incorporated both interviews and surveys, and he discussed his own projects that included these forms of data collection (Sieber & Lazersfeld, 1966).

Another example of early mixed methods thinking comes from the field of evaluation in which Patton advanced "methodological mixes" (Patton, 1980, p. 108). He advocated for the use of anthropological naturalistic research in evaluation based on the "holistic-inductive paradigm" to complement the more traditional "hypothetical-deductive" approach. He recommended several models for program evaluation built on this combination. A design could be the pure hypothetical-deductive approach with an experimental design, quantitative data, and a statistical analysis, or a pure qualitative approach with naturalistic inquiry, qualitative measurement, and a content analysis. Then he suggested four "mixed form" models (p. 112) that varied from using experimental or naturalistic designs, qualitative or quantitative measurements, and often the transformation of qualitative data into counts. The diagram he sketched for the four models was remarkably similar to diagrams of mixed methods designs presented by recent authors (e.g., Johnson & Onwuegbuzie, 2004; Tashakkori & Teddlie, 1998).

Taking these readings as a whole, a good case can be made that mixed methods was underway much earlier than the late 1980s. These early writers focused on gathering multiple methods, including both quantitative (e.g., surveys) and qualitative (e.g., interviews) data. They initiated a language for mixed methods through such terms as the more general word "interplay" and more specific terms, such as "concurrent scheduling" (Sieber, 1973, pp. 1353, 1358). They provided examples of studies that employed multiple methods, and they took a process approach of thinking about the "interplay" through design, data collection, and data analysis. They conceptualized different types of mixed methods designs, such as those involving data transformation (Patton, 1980), and those including one form of method building on the other (Sieber, 1973).

On the other hand, although these early writers were interested in the "interplay" of quantitative and qualitative data, they did not specifically discuss how they would integrate the two data sources, or the reasons for integration as mixed methods is described today (e.g., see Bryman, 2006). They did not explicate the vast array of design possibilities in response to different purposes that is seen today (Creswell & Plano Clark, 2007, 2011). Although they started the discussion about names for the designs, they had a limited repertoire for designs (e.g., concurrent scheduling) as compared to the extensive list of design possibilities discussed recently (see Creswell & Plano Clark, 2011). They did not have a notation system (e.g., pluses and arrows) for providing a shorthand description of designs that would begin to emerge in 1991 (see Morse, 1991). Some of the detailed discussions about procedures (e.g., developing an instrument based on qualitative data), the use of mixed methods questions (Creswell & Plano Clark, 2011), or the larger philosophical issues (see Greene, 2007) were not present in their discussions.

The pre-late-1980s writers did, however, lay a foundation for mixed methods. As Tashakkori and Teddlie (2003) commented, these early writers "were mostly unaware that they were doing anything out of the ordinary" (p. 5). They used informal, commonsense ways of conducting research. A colleague recently remarked, "What is most amazing about mixed methods is that all of these (current) writers have taken ideas that have been around for a long time and spun them into a way of research, a methodology!" (Duane Shell, personal communication, August 17, 2009). Today, we have systematic, detailed, and defined ways of thinking about mixed methods research. But is a systematic approach better than the more intuitive early approach? Why do current mixed methods researchers (including myself) not give more credit to the early researchers who had the initial ideas that have now been embraced today as mixed methods?

What Really Drives Mixed Methods?

The ideas of a "new movement" or a "new star" suggest that some trends in methodology are building. What has promoted the escalation of interest in mixed methods? As suggested at the Aberdeen, Scotland, seminar, is it simply a response to funding initiatives?

Interest in mixed methods has grown since the *Handbook of Mixed Methods in Social & Behavioral Research* (Tashakkori & Teddlie, 2003) was published eight years ago (Creswell, 2009b). This handbook, consisting of four sections covering 759 pages, addressed current and future issues, methodological issues, and analytical issues. Using the base year of 2003 as a rough benchmark, it has been documented how interest has developed in the use of the term "mixed methods," as reported in funded projects at the National Institutes of Health (Plano Clark, 2010). Journals exclusively devoted to reporting mixed methods empirical studies and methodological discussions have also been initiated, such as in 2007, the *Journal of Mixed Methods Research* (Sage); in 2008, the *International Journal of Multiple Research Approaches* (eContent Management Pty); and in 2009, the *International Journal of Mixed Methods in Applied Business & Policy Research* (Academic Global). To these journals, I can also add journals started much earlier, such as *Quality and Quantity* (1967, Springer), *Field Methods* (1989, Sage), and the *International Journal of Social Research Methodology* (1998, Routledge). In addition, a number of recent journals have published special issues focusing exclusively or largely on mixed methods, such as *Research in Schools* (2006), *Annals of Family Medicine* (2004), and the *Journal of Counseling Psychology* (2005). At least 16 major books have been written about mixed methods, including recent books by Creswell and Plano Clark (2011), Greene (2007), Plano Clark and Creswell (2008), Teddlie and Tashakkori (2009), and Morse and Niehaus (2009). Mixed methods books are being published that have a distinct discipline focus, such as for nursing and health researchers (Andrew & Halcomb, 2009) and psychologists (Mayring, Huber, Gurtler, & Kiegelmann, 2007; Todd, Nerlich, McKeown, & Clarke, 2004). Chapters can be found in methods books in discipline fields such as social work (Engel & Schutt, 2005) and family research (Greenstein, 2006). An international conference on mixed methods has been offered in the United Kingdom for the last five years, along with international publications on mixed methods around the globe: in psychology from Europe (Mayring et al., 2007), in nursing from Australia (Andrew & Halcomb, 2009), in linguistics from Japan (Heigham & Croker, 2009), in the social sciences from Switzerland (Bergman, 2008), and in education from South Africa (Creswell & Garrett, 2008).

In light of these developments, I must ask what has given impetus to this interest? It may well be that funding sources have encouraged mixed methods research with the global economic imperative—starting in the 1990s—to do more with less (Giddings, 2006). In a mixed methods study of family adoption practices, Miall and March (2005) wrote about how their funders forced them to change their questions and design from their initial plan of starting with quantitative questions that would be intentionally followed by qualitative questions. Holmes (2006) alleged that mixed methods reduced researchers to "depersonalized technicians," which tacitly supported funding agencies to seek projects with convergence on a single answer rather than differences in opinions and beliefs.

On the other side, certainly the legitimacy of qualitative research has encouraged researchers to think in a pluralistic way. Interdisciplinary research problems now call for addressing complex issues using skilled methodologists from both quantitative and qualitative research who bring diverse approaches to studies (Mayring et al., 2007). Still, questions linger about whether mixed methods is simply a response to funding interests and whether the research questions addressed by mixed methods researchers truly merit a "mixed" methodology. Those coming from a philosophical, postmodern perspective have suggested that researchers are "accepting uncritically and undigested" mixed methods (Freshwater, 2007, p. 145).

The Paradigm Debate Continues

Philosophically oriented writers for years have debated whether mixed methods research is possible because it mixes worldviews or paradigms. They ask: Can paradigms (ontologies or realities) be mixed? Some writers adhere to the idea that paradigms or worldviews have rigid boundaries and cannot be mixed. Holmes (2006) asked: "Can we really have one part of the research which takes a certain view about reality nested alongside another which takes a contradictory view? How would we reconcile, or even work with, competing discourses within a single project?" (p. 5). The logic being used here was that mixed methods was untenable because methods were linked to paradigms, and therefore the researcher, in using mixed methods research, was mixing paradigms. This stance has been described as the purist stance (see Rossman & Wilson, 1985), and it has been called the "incompatibility thesis" (Howe, 2004) and discussed in the mixed methods literature as mixing viewpoints (Johnson et al., 2007, p. 123). Individuals that hold this position view paradigms as having discrete and impermeable boundaries, an idea reinforced by the clear-cut boxes and lines around the alternative inquiry paradigms in the literature (e.g., see Guba & Lincoln's tables, 2005; or Creswell's table of worldviews, 2009c). Granted, by 2005, Guba and Lincoln had taken down these artificial boundaries by declaring cautiously that elements of paradigms might be blended together in a study. Contributing to this perspective was certainly a "delinking" of paradigms and methods, such as conveying that many different research methods would be linked to certain paradigms, and that a paradigm justification did not dictate specific data collection and analysis methods (Johnson & Onwuegbuzie, 2004).

With the gate now opened to thinking about use of multiple paradigms, mixed methods writers have now taken varied stances on incorporating paradigms into mixed methods. For example, a dialectic stance by Greene and Caracelli (1997) suggested that multiple paradigms might be used in mixed methods studies, but that each paradigm needed to be honored and that their combined use contributed to healthy tensions and new insights. In my writings, I took a similar stance, but suggested that multiple paradigms related to different phases of a research design (Creswell & Plano Clark, 2007, 2011), thus linking paradigms to research designs. For example, a mixed methods study that begins with a quantitative survey phase reflects an initial postpositivist leaning, but, in the next qualitative phase of focus groups, the researcher shifts to a constructivist paradigm. Relinking paradigms and designs makes sense.

Still others advocated for one underlying paradigm that fits mixed methods, and some found their paradigm in pragmatism with historical roots back to Charles Peirce, William James, John Dewey, Richard Rorty, and others (Johnson & Onwuegbuzie, 2004; Tashakkori & Teddlie, 2003). Pragmatism emphasizes the importance of the research questions, the value of experiences, and practical consequences, action, and understanding of real-world phenomena. Advocates said that it is a "philosophical partner for mixed methods research" (Johnson & Onwuegbuzie, 2004, p. 16). A different paradigmatic stance, suggested by Mertens (2003, 2009), is found in the transformative-emancipatory framework that made explicit the goal for research to "serve the ends of creating a more just and democratic society that permeates the entire research process" (Mertens, 2003, p. 159). Mertens thus creatively relates this goal to different phases in designing a mixed methods study.

Whether the paradigm for mixed methods involves a single paradigm, multiple paradigms, or phased-in paradigms, Morgan (2007) recently reminded the mixed methods community of the importance of Kuhn's (1970) original description of a paradigm. Using the definition of a paradigm as "shared belief systems that influence the kinds of knowledge researchers seek and how they interpret the evidence they collect" (Morgan, 2007, p. 50), Morgan found paradigms to be (1) worldviews, an all-encompassing perspective on the world; (2) epistemologies, incorporating ideas from the philosophy of science such as ontology, methodology, and epistemology; (3) "best" or "typical" solutions to problems; and (4) shared beliefs of a "community of scholars" in a research field. It is this last perspective (embraced by Kuhn, 1970) that Morgan strongly endorses, and he discussed how researchers share a consensus in specialty areas about what questions are most meaningful and which procedures are most appropriate for answering their questions.

Another mixed methods writer, Denscombe (2008), agreed with this perspective and took it one step further. Denscombe outlined how "communities" may work using such ideas as sharing identity, researching common problems, forming networks, collaborating in pursuing knowledge, and developing informal groupings. This line of thinking has focused attention on the emerging fragmentation of the mixed methods field in which various disciplines adopt mixed methods in different ways, create unique practices, and cultivate their own specialized literatures. For example, at the Veterans Administration Research Center in Ann Arbor, Michigan, in the health sciences, colleagues have conceptualized mixed methods as formative and summative evaluation procedures (Forman & Damschroder, 2007). This conceptualization adapts mixed methods to the Veterans Administration health services context of intervention research. The rise of discipline-oriented mixed methods books is another instance of adapting mixed methods to scholarly communities. Still, I wonder if discipline fragmentation of mixed methods will lead to further philosophical differences among scholars in mixed methods. Will the scholarly community line of thinking continue or will the conversation return to the difficulty of mixing realities? Is the idea of mixing realities actually all about whether one paradigm takes precedence over another in mixed methods research?

Mixed Methods Privileges Postpositivism

Critics make the allegation that mixed methods favors postpositivist thinking over more interpretive approaches. Does mixed methods privilege postpositivist thinking and marginalize interpretive approaches? Several authors have taken this position. The context for many of these concerns resides in what is seen as a conservative challenge to qualitative inquiry (Denzin & Giardina, 2006). Denzin and Giardina believe that conservative regimes enforce scientifically based models of research (SBR). For example, the 2001 No Child Left Behind Act (NCLB) in education emphasized accountability, high-stakes testing, and performance scores for students. The model for research being advanced was to "apply rigorous, systematic, and objective methodology to obtain reliable and valid knowledge" (Ryan & Hood, 2006, p. 58). Within this context, qualitative research is marginalized, and it minimizes complex and dynamic contexts, subtle social differences produced by gender, race, ethnicity, linguistics status, and class, and multiple kinds of knowledge (Lincoln & Canella, 2004). In 2002, one year after the No Child Left Behind Act was implemented, the National Research Council established guidelines in their report, *Scientific Research in Education,* that called for a quantitative approach to research through guiding principles asking for significant questions that could be empirically studied, relevant theory, methods closely tied to the research questions, explanations of findings using a logical chain of reasoning, replicated studies and generalizations, and disseminated research for critique by the professional scientific community (Ryan & Hood, 2006; Shavelson & Towne, 2002). Howe (2004) called the National Research Council's perspective "mixed-methods experimentalism" (p. 48) and felt that it assigned a prominent role to quantitative experimental research and a lesser role to qualitative, interpretive research. Further, this approach "elevates quantitative-experimental methods to the top of the methodological hierarchy and constrains qualitative methods to a largely auxiliary role in pursuit of the *technocratic* aim of accumulating knowledge of 'what works'" (Howe, 2004, pp. 53–54). He also stated, "It is not that qualitative methods can never be fruitfully and appropriately used in this way, but their natural home is within an interpretivist framework with the democractic aim of seeking to understand and give voice to the insider's perspective" (p. 54). This interpretivist aim values outcomes assessed by various stakeholders, includes all relevant voices in the dialogue, and engages in qualitative data collection procedures to promote dialogue, such as participant observation, interviews, and focus groups. This dialogue also needs to be *critical* with the views of participants subjected to rational scrutiny.

Howe's theme was echoed again in the following years' publication of the third edition of this handbook (Denzin & Lincoln, 2005). Denzin and Lincoln talked directly about the "mixed-methods movement" as taking qualitative methods out of their natural home, which is in the "critical, interpretive framework" (p. 9). Finally, in a provocative article by Giddings (2006), titled, "Mixed-methods Research: Positivism Dressed in Drag?" the issue of the hegemony of positivism and the marginalization of nonpositivist research methodologies in mixed methods was addressed. She conveyed the idea that certain "thinking" went on in research that was reflected in methodologies and "the 'thinking' of positivism continues in the 'thinking' of mixed methods" (p. 200). Giddings felt that this mixed methods "thinking" was expressed through analysis and prescriptive styles, structured approaches to research design and data collection, and the use qualitative aspects "fitted in" (p. 200).

There is little doubt that a good case can be made that, in certain approaches, mixed methods researchers have relegated qualitative inquiry to a secondary role. A good example would be the embedded research design (Creswell & Plano Clark, 2007), in which qualitative methods often provide a supportive role in experimental, intervention studies. Our feeling has long been that the use of qualitative approaches *whatever their role* in traditional quantitative experiments elevates qualitative research to a new status and opens the door for seeing qualitative research as a legitimate form of inquiry. Whether this will materialize can certainly be debated. The structured ways of designing mixed methods projects that we embrace in our text (Creswell & Plano Clark, 2007) also reinforces Giddings' idea of the structured "thinking" in our approach to mixed methods. In mixed methods data analysis, the use of "manifest effect sizes" by Onwuegbuzie and Teddlie (2003, p. 356) reinforces a postpositivist leaning of mixed methods.

On the other hand, many studies in mixed methods can be found that give priority to qualitative methods. Some designs subordinate quantitative methods to qualitative methods (see the exploratory sequential design mentioned by Creswell & Plano Clark, 2007). Also, the writings on applying the transformative-emancipatory framework to mixed methods emphasize qualitative research (Mertens, 2009). A close reading of the National Research Council's report on scientific research in education shows that the types of questions recommended for scholarly educational research were both quantitative (descriptive, experimental) as well as qualitative (exploratory), a point that Howe (2004) concedes. Although more critical, interpretivist articles are needed in the mixed methods field, some evidence exists that the number of articles is growing. A recent paper (Sweetman, Badiee, & Creswell, 2010) has identified mixed methods studies that honor the inclusion and dialogue of communities of action within Mertens's transformative-emancipatory framework. This paper examined several mixed methods studies that addressed disability, ethnic, feminism, and social class as theoretical standpoints and advanced ways that researchers might incorporate these standpoints into their mixed methods projects. Further evidence of standpoint epistemology—typically found in qualitative research—is found in recently published articles in *JMMR* addressing women's social capital (Hodgkin, 2008) and African American women's interest in science (Buck, Cook, Quigley, Eastwood, & Lucas, 2009). Despite these studies, what is the evidence that mixed methods research marginalizes interpretive approaches? Do we need more mixed methods research that incorporates an interpretive perspective? Is the use of qualitative research in a supportive role in intervention studies marginalizing qualitative inquiry, or is it advancing it within fields that traditionally honored experimental methods? Do we need more articles that embrace "mixed methods interpretivism," in which quantitative research is relegated to a secondary role within qualitative research, as Howe (2004) would recommend?

A Fixed Discourse in Mixed Methods

Unquestionably, more interpretive, theoretical studies in mixed methods would broaden the audience and discourse of it. This raises another controversy about the discourse of mixed methods. Some critics are asking: Is there a dominant discourse in mixed methods? Is messiness allowed in? These questions speak to the issue of mixed methods privileging postpositivist thinking—a postmodern concern about the discourse in mixed methods. Who controls this discourse and the language that is being used in mixed methods research? Several authors have weighed in on this issue.

A recent important article takes up these concerns (Freshwater, 2007). Freshwater is an editor and leading researcher in nursing as well as a postmodernist. She was concerned about how mixed methods was being "read" and the discourse that followed. Discourse was defined as a set of rules or assumptions for organizing and interpreting the subject matter of an academic discipline or field of study in mixed methods. The uncritical acceptance of mixed methods as an emerging dominant discourse ("is nearing becoming a metanarrative" [Freshwater, 2007, p. 139]) impacts how it is located, positioned, presented, and perpetuated. She called on mixed methods writers to make explicit the internal power struggle between the mixed methods text as created by the researcher and the text as seen by the reader/audience. Mixed methods, she felt, was too "focused on fixing meaning" (p. 137). Expanding on this, she stated that mixed methods was mainly about doing away with "indeterminancy and moving toward incontestability"

(p. 137), citing as key examples the objective third-person style of writing, the flatness, and the disallowance for competing interpretations to coexist. She requested that mixed methods researchers adopt a "sense of incompleteness" (p. 138) and recommended that reforms required the

> need to explore the possibility of hybridization in which a radical intertextuality of mixing forms, genres, conventions, and media is encouraged, where there are no clear rules of representation and where the researcher, who is in reality working with radical undecidability and circumscribed indeterminacy, is able to make this experience freely available to readers and writers. (p. 144)

These ideas were a positive criticism, and a call for mixed methods writers to insert questions into their discourses, to acknowledge the messiness of mixed methods, and to recognize that it is a field still in "adolescence" (Tashakkori & Teddlie, 2003, p. x).

Still, by providing a visual of the mixed methods research process that follows linear development, Johnson and Onwuegbuzie (2004) erase the "messiness." A certain tidiness is given when specific names are assigned to research designs (e.g., explanatory sequential designs—Creswell & Plano Clark, 2007), when researchers do not attend to the "messiness" in conducting the designs (e.g., see Creswell et al., 2008), and when writers look for a consensus in definitions (Johnson et al., 2007). These examples all point toward "fixing" or the field "being fixed." But these points open up further questions, such as how should mixed methods writers discuss its messiness, its blurred borders, and its problems? Will unstructured mixed methods serve well the beginning researcher as well as the more experienced researcher?

To Be Bilingual or Not

A related issue is whether any one ideological camp dominates the language of mixed methods research. Is there a dominant language or set of terms for mixed methods? Vygotsky and Cole (1978) propose that the sociocultural perspective of language shapes how individuals make sense of the world, and that the learning process consists of a gradual internalization of this language. What is the language of mixed methods? One issue being discussed is whether we need a "bilingual" language for mixed methods research so that it does not favor quantitative or qualitative research. Raising this question is reminiscent of concerns in qualitative research in the early 1980s around the topic of qualitative validity, and how terms such as trustworthiness and authenticity created a "new," distinct language to discuss validity (Lincoln & Guba, 1985).

As the language of mixed methods develops, a confusing picture has emerged about the nomenclature to use. For example, in writing about validity, Onwuegbuzie and Johnson (2006) intentionally called validity "legitimation" and thereby created a new word in the mixed methods lexicon. In our specification of types of research designs, we created new names, such as the "exploratory sequential design," to provide a descriptive label signifying that the design would first fulfill the intent of exploring using qualitative data followed by explanation using quantitative data (Creswell & Plano Clark, 2007). Illustrating an example of a made-up bilingual term, writers in a recent psychology text used the term "qualiquantology" to express their discomforting hybridity of mixing qualitative and quantitative methods (Stenner & Rogers, 2004).

Other writers in the mixed methods field use a less bilingual vocabulary. Leaning toward a more quantitative language, Teddlie and Tashakkori (2009) use the term "inferences," or "meta-inferences," to denote when the results are incorporated into a coherent conceptual framework to provide an answer to the research question. Although "inferences" may relate to either qualitative or quantitative research, it seems to be employed frequently in drawing conclusions from a sample to a population in a quantitative study. Another example is the use of the term "construct validity" by Leech, Dellinger, Brannagan, and Tanaka (2010) as an overarching validity concept for mixed methods research. This term is drawn from quantitative measurement ideas. On the qualitative side, the idea of personal transformation advanced by Mertens (2009) clearly has qualitative roots. Unquestionably, the language that has emerged is both bilingual and oriented toward one form of inquiry (quantitative or qualitative). The use of glossaries in recent mixed methods books suggests the need for a common vocabulary (see Morse & Niehaus, 2009; Teddlie & Tashakkori, 2009). These examples, however, raise difficult questions about who controls the language of mixed methods, how it is conveyed, and what the language should be. It also introduces questions about how the writing up of mixed methods proposals and projects influences what gets approved, funded, and published.

A Baffling (and Complex) Array of Designs

It is not only the language that introduces confusion and controversy into the mixed methods discourse. In research designs—a topic that has filled the pages of mixed methods writings—researchers are confronted by a baffling array of names and types of ways to conduct mixed methods research. How might a mixed methods researcher conduct a mixed methods study? When my colleague, Vicki Plano Clark, and I wrote an introduction to the field for beginning mixed methods researchers (Creswell & Plano Clark, 2007), we presented 12 different classification systems of designs drawn from diverse fields of evaluation, nursing, public health, and education.

Not wanting to add to the confusion, we suggested a parsimonious set of designs. Triangulation (or now called convergent) designs involved one phase of qualitative and quantitative data collection gathered concurrently. Explanatory or exploratory designs required two phases of data collection, quantitative data collection followed sequentially by qualitative data collection (or vice versa). Embedded designs, in which one form of data was embedded within another, may be either a single- or a double-phase design with concurrent or sequential approaches. In all of these designs, we focused on the weight given to qualitative and quantitative data, the timing of both forms of data, and the mixing of the data in the research process. To present these designs, we used a modified notation system first developed by Morse (1991), and we sketched diagrams of procedures and advanced guidelines for constructing these diagrams found in the literature (Ivankova, Creswell, & Stick, 2006).

We now know that these designs are not complex enough to mirror actual practice, although our thinking at the time was to advance designs for the first-time mixed methods researcher. Also, we are more aware of the complex designs being used and reported in the literature. For example, Nastasi and colleagues wrote about a complex evaluation design with multiple stages and the combination of both sequential and concurrent phases (Nastasi et al., 2007). The designs reported in journals have incorporated "unusual blends" of methods, such as combinations of quantitative and qualitative longitudinal data, discourse analysis with survey data, secondary data sets with qualitative follow-ups, and the combination of qualitative themes with survey data to produce new variables (Creswell, 2011). The representation of designs has also advanced joint matrices for arraying both quantitative and qualitative data in the same table, an approach encouraged by the matrix feature of qualitative software products (see Kuckartz, 2009).

Our designs and the many classifications bring a typology approach to mixed methods design. Arguing that we need an alternative to typologies, Maxwell and Loomis (2003) conceptualized a systems approach of five interactive dimensions of the research process consisting of the purpose, the conceptual framework, the questions, the methods, and the issue of validity. With this approach, they provided a fuller, more expansive view of the way to conceptualize mixed methods designs. Another approach comes from the creative thinking of Hall and Howard (2008). They suggested a synergistic approach in which two or more options interacted so that their combined effect was greater than the sum of the individual parts. Instead of looking at mixed methods as a priority of one approach over the other, or a weighting of one approach, the researcher considered their value and representations equal. The researcher also viewed the two as equal from an ideology of multiple points of view, balancing objectivity with subjectivity. Collaboration consisted of the equal skill expertise about qualitative and quantitative methodologies on a research team.

The synergistic approach, along with other challenges to typological perspectives has contributed to a softening of the differences between qualitative and quantitative research, provided answers to questions about dominance of one method over the other (e.g., Denzin & Lincoln, 2005), and honored the formation of research teams with diverse expertise. In light of these discussions, are typologies of research designs outdated? Are newer, more free-flowing designs an improved way to think about designing a mixed methods study?

Misappropriating Designs

Another procedural question about designs is whether mixed methods is misappropriating designs from other fields. As mixed methods continues to grow in popularity and use, is the field misappropriating traditional designs and calling them "mixed methods" (thereby overstating the value and claims of mixed methods)? Several examples stand out. Scale development (DeVellis, 1991) has been available to the researcher for many years in quantitative research. Early phases of scale development often call for an initial exploration, even though this may consist of reviewing the literature rather than conducting an extensive qualitative data collection procedure, such as the use of focus groups (Vogt, King, & King, 2004). One might argue that scale development should be a distinct procedure from mixed methods research, and yet, mixed methods designs with the purpose of developing an instrument are available in the journal literature (e.g., Myers & Oetzel, 2003).

Another example would be content analysis, a quantitative procedure involving the collection of qualitative data and its transformation and analysis by quantitative counts. In this approach, *both* qualitative and quantitative are not collected, but both qualitative research (in data collection) and quantitative research (in data analysis) are employed. If one views mixed methods as collecting both quantitative and qualitative data, then content analysis does not qualify as mixed methods research. Is content analysis a separate approach or is data transformation also a part of mixed methods designs as suggested by Sandelowski et al. (2009)? What are appropriate boundaries for mixed methods research?

Perhaps mixed methods is actually a subordinated set of procedures used within a large number of designs. I call this approach using a "framework" for conducting mixed methods procedures. It is basically the idea that some larger framework becomes a placeholder within which the researcher gathers quantitative and qualitative data (or conducts mixed methods procedures). This idea first surfaced when a participant at a workshop asked, "Is ethnography mixed methods research?" The sense of this question was that ethnographers have traditionally collected both quantitative and qualitative data and used both in their description and analysis of culture-sharing groups. Morse and Niehaus (2009) discussed this question, and concluded that many ethnographers do see their methodology as a distinct approach, and that ethnography needs to be viewed as independent of mixed methods.

But I wonder if seeing mixed methods as a subordinate procedure within ethnography is the most appropriate stance. Researchers seem to use mixed methods within larger frameworks of many types. Evidence for these frameworks comes from using mixed methods procedures within narrative studies (Elliot, 2005), experiments (Sandelowski, 1996), and case studies (Luck, Jackson, & Usher, 2006). Other frameworks can be seen as well, such as using mixed methods within a social network analysis (Quinlin, 2010), an overarching research question (Yin, 2006), a feminist lens (Hesse-Biber & Leavy, 2007), or in action research (Christ, 2009). If the mixed methods designs can be stretched to include these different frameworks, then the potential for extending use of mixed methods in many ways is possible. But where is the boundary between mixed methods and other designs? Is a boundary needed? If mixed methods researchers are claiming other designs for their own, can their claims be justified?

Value Added?

Regardless of the design and whether it is appropriate, the utility of mixed methods research—from a pragmatic approach—is tied to whether it is a valuable approach. In our earlier definition (Creswell & Plano Clark, 2007), we end with the assumption that the combination of methods provides a better understanding than either quantitative method or qualitative method alone. Can this assumption be substantiated? In tracing the recent history of mixed methods, I referred to a question asked by the president of Sage Publications during a luncheon meeting. He asked me, "Does mixed methods provide a better understanding of a research question than either quantitative or qualitative research alone?" (Creswell, 2009b, p. 22). This difficult question is central to justifying mixed methods and giving it legitimacy. Unfortunately, it remains unanswered in the mixed methods community.

I can provide a hypothetical series of studies on how it *might* be addressed. One approach is to turn to research procedures used in early studies that compared participant observation with survey results (Vidich & Shapiro, 1955) or interviews with surveys (Sieber, 1973) and examine if the two databases converge or diverge in understanding a research problem. A second approach is to proceed with an experiment in which groups of readers examine a study divided into a qualitative, a quantitative, and a mixed methods part. In this experiment, outcomes are specified such as the quality of interpretation, the inclusion of more evidence, the rigor of the study, or the persuasiveness of the study, and the three groups could be compared experimentally. A third approach is to examine some outcomes suggested by authors of published mixed methods studies. One such outcome might be "yield," such as that advanced by O'Cathain, Murphy, and Nicholl (2007), in which they assess it by the number of publications and whether the authors of a mixed methods study actually integrate the data. Other outcomes could be analyzed using qualitative document analysis approaches, and themes developed from statements of value posed by authors of mixed methods empirical articles and methodological studies. For example, authors from the field of communication studies suggested that the value of mixed methods lies in addressing limitations in the results learned from one method:

> To address more thoroughly this question, and account for some of the possible limitations of study-one, a broader based assessment of students' involvement in intercultural communication courses was pursued. (Corrigan, Pennington, & McCroskey, 2006, pp. 15–16)

Other options may also exist. The mixed methods community does not have an adequate answer to this controversy, and so I ask: When and how can we begin to answer this question? Does a mixed method better address the core research question being asked in a study than either quantitative or qualitative alone? What criteria should be used in assessing it? Why have mixed methods researchers not pursued this issue more vigorously?

Conclusion

Striking at the heart of its existence, critical comments about mixed methods are being made about its meaning and definition (raising concerns about expectations, as I learned at Aberdeen). The form of this conversation has been to debate whether mixed methods is a "method," a "methodology," some combination, or a way of seeing. Related to this larger issue is whether it is a "new" way of researching, reinforces a slanted use of terms, and creates a false binary distinction between quantitative and qualitative data (and research).

Assuming that mixed methods researchers take paradigms (i.e., worldviews, beliefs, values) seriously (an assumption that several writers have questioned; see Holmes, 2006, and Sale, Lohfeld, & Brazil, 2002), I see the paradigm discussion as an important discussion in the mixed methods literature. Diverse stances have emerged from a single paradigm perspective, such as pragmatism or the transformational-emancipatory perspective, to multiple paradigm use in a dialectic approach, and to relating the paradigm to the design. Some discussion has moved away from which one paradigm, or how many to use, to a focus on paradigm use within communities of scholars. Still, critics are concerned about whether the current approaches to mixed methods privilege postpositivist thinking and create discourses that "fix" the otherwise messy content of mixed methods.

No subject has been so widely discussed in the mixed methods literature as its designs and its methods. This emphasis places importance on the methods, sometimes at the expense of minimizing the importance of the research question in directing scholarly inquiry (Gurtler, Huber, & Kiegelmann, 2007). At other times, critics of the mixed methods literature see a baffling list of different types of designs with unusual names, the potential of mixed methods claiming many more designs than it deserves, and having questionable outcomes.

The implications of these controversies are that many of them are interrelated and my sorting them out here is contrived—a heuristic. When authors talk about the controversies, I have found their discussion to cover many topics rather than an in-depth analysis of any one controversy. Also, the range of controversies is quite extensive, stretching from basic issues of the legitimacy and meaning of mixed methods to its philosophical underpinnings, and on to the pragmatics of conducting a mixed methods study. Fundamentally, my position is that the mixed methods community needs to squarely place these controversies on the table for discussion and honor their presence.

Some readers will say that I have overlooked critical controversies such as the relationship of research problems to methods, validity, and evaluation of mixed methods, the writing of a mixed methods study, and the common question of "who cares about methods?" Other readers will undoubtedly see my views as deliberately "transgressive" (Richardson, 1997): a turn to challenging mixed methods rather than advocating for it. Others will see my remarks as an attempt to open up the discourse about mixed methods, much like I have advocated in authored and coauthored editorials for the *Journal of Mixed Methods Research.* Still others might consider my justifications both for and against the issues as evidence of postpositivist leanings (or even worse the creation of new metanarratives). All of these renderings may be both right and wrong. As a pragmatist, I can confidently say that I am interested in the consequences of this discussion of controversies, the seeds of which were sprouted at Aberdeen. Perhaps rather than finding irony in the space of Elphinstone Hall in Scotland, I should have seen instead the long shadows that the walls were casting. In the end, I advise those interested in mixed methods to reassess their commitment to controversies now being raised. As Kuhn (1970) said, "A revolution is for me a special sort of change involving a certain sort of reconstruction of group commitments" (p. 181).

References

Andrew, S., & Halcomb, E. J. (Eds.). (2009). *Mixed methods research for nursing and the health sciences.* Chichester, UK: Blackwell.

Bergman, M. M. (2008). *Advances in mixed methods research.* London: Sage.

Brewer, J., & Hunter, A. (1989). *Multimethod research: A synthesis of styles.* Newbury Park, CA: Sage.

Bryman, A. (1988). *Quantity and quality in social research.* London and New York: Routledge.

Bryman, A. (2006). Integrating quantitative and qualitative research: How is it done? *Qualitative Research, 6*(1), 97–113.

Buck, G., Cook, K., Quigley, C., Eastwood, J., & Lucas, Y. (2009). Profiles of urban, low SES, African-American girls' attitudes toward science: A sequential explanatory mixed methods study. *Journal of Mixed Methods Research, 3*(4), 386–410.

Campbell, D. T. (1974). *Qualitative knowing in action research.* Paper presented at the annual meeting of the American Psychological Association, New Orleans, LA.

Campbell, D. T., & Fiske, D. W. (1959). Convergent and discriminant validation by the multitrait-multimethod matrix. *Psychological Bulletin, 56,* 81–105.

Christ, T. (2009). Designing, teaching, and evaluating two complementary mixed methods research courses. *Journal of Mixed Methods Research, 3*(4), 292–325.

Corrigan, M. W., Pennington, B., & McCroskey, J. C. (2006). Are we making a difference? A mixed methods assessment of the impact of intercultural communication instruction on American students. *Ohio Communication Journal, 44,* 1–32.

Creswell, J. W. (1994). *Research design: Qualitative, quantitative, and mixed methods approaches.* Thousand Oaks, CA: Sage.

Creswell, J. W. (2007, May). *Concerns voiced about mixed methods research.* Paper presented at the International Qualitative Inquiry Congress, University of Illinois, Champaign.

Creswell, J. W. (2008). *Educational research: Planning, conducting, and evaluating quantitative and qualitative research* (3rd ed.). Upper Saddle River, NJ: Pearson Education.

Creswell, J. W. (2009a, October). *The design of mixed methods research in occupational therapy.* Presentation to the Society for the Study of Occupation, New Haven, CT.

Creswell, J. W. (2009b). *How SAGE has shaped research methods: A 40-year history.* London: Sage.

Creswell, J. W. (2009c). *Research design: Qualitative, quantitative, and mixed methods approaches* (3rd ed.). Thousand Oaks, CA: Sage.

Creswell, J. W. (2009d, March). *What qualitative evidence means for mixed methods intervention trials in the health sciences.* Paper presented at the Economic & Social Research Council (ESRC) Research Seminar hosted by the Health Services Research Unit, Kings College, University of Aberdeen, Scotland.

Creswell, J. W. (2010). Mapping the developing landscape of mixed methods research. In A. Tashakkori & C. Teddlie (Eds.), *SAGE handbook of mixed methods in social & behavioral research* (2nd ed., pp. 45–68). Thousand Oaks, CA: Sage.

Creswell, J. W., & Garrett, A. L. (2008). The "movement" of mixed methods research and the role of educators. *South African Journal of Education, 28,* 321–333.

Creswell, J. W., & McCoy, B. R. (in press). The use of mixed methods thinking in documentary development. In S. N. Hesse-Biber (Ed.), *The handbook of emergent technologies in social research.* Oxford, UK: Oxford University Press.

Creswell, J. W., & Plano Clark, V. L. (2007). *Designing and conducting mixed methods research.* Thousand Oaks, CA: Sage.

Creswell, J. W., & Plano Clark, V. L. (2011). *Designing and conducting mixed methods research* (2nd ed.). Thousand Oaks, CA: Sage.

Creswell, J. W., Plano Clark, V. L., & Garrett, A. L. (2008). Methodological issues in conducting mixed methods research designs. In M. M. Bergman (Ed.), *Advances in mixed methods research* (pp. 66–83). London: Sage.

Creswell, J. W., Shope, R., Plano Clark, V. L., & Green, D. O. (2006). How interpretive qualitative research extends mixed methods research. *Research in the Schools, 13,* 1–11.

Cronbach, L. J. (1975). Beyond the two disciplines of scientific psychology. *American Psychologist, 30,* 116–127.

Crotty, M. (1998). *The foundations of social research: Meaning and perspective in the research process.* London: Sage.

David, L., Bender, L., Burns, S. (Producers), & Guggenheim, D. (Director). (2006). *An inconvenient truth* [Motion picture]. United States: Paramount Classics.

Denscombe, M. (2008). Communities of practice: A research paradigm for the mixed methods approach. *Journal of Mixed Methods Research, 2,* 270–283.

Denzin, N. K. (1978). *The research act: A theoretical introduction to sociological methods.* New York: McGraw-Hill.

Denzin, N. K., & Giardina, M. D. (2006). Introduction: Qualitative inquiry and the conservative challenge. In N. K. Denzin & M. D. Giardina (Eds.), *Qualitative inquiry and the conservative challenges* (pp. ix–xxxi). Walnut Creek, CA: Left Coast Press.

Denzin, N. K., & Lincoln, Y. S. (Eds.). (2005). *The SAGE handbook of qualitative research* (3rd ed.). Thousand Oaks, CA: Sage.

DeVellis, R. F. (1991). *Scale development: Theory and application.* Newbury Park, CA: Sage.

Elliot, J. (2005). *Using narrative in social research: Qualitative and quantitative approaches.* London: Sage.

Engel, R. J., & Schutt, R. K. (2005). *The practice of research in social work.* Thousand Oaks, CA: Sage.

Fielding, N. G., & Fielding, J. L. (1986). *Linking data.* Beverly Hills, CA: Sage.

Forman, J., & Damschroder, L. (2007, February). *Using mixed methods in evaluating intervention studies.* Presentation at the Mixed Methodology Workshop at the national meeting of the Veterans Administration Health Services Research & Development, Arlington, VA.

Freshwater, D. (2007). Reading mixed methods research: Contexts for criticism. *Journal of Mixed Methods Research, 1*(2), 134–145.

Giddings, L. S. (2006). Mixed-methods research: Positivism dressed in drag? *Journal of Research in Nursing, 11*(3), 195–203.

Greene, J. C. (2007). *Mixed methods in social inquiry.* San Francisco, CA: John Wiley.

Greene, J. C. (2008). Is mixed methods social inquiry a distinctive methodology? *Journal of Mixed Methods Research, 2*(1), 7–22.

Greene, J. C., & Caracelli, V. J. (Eds.). (1997). Advances in mixed-method evaluation: The challenges and benefits of integrating diverse paradigms. *New Directions for Evaluation, 74.* San Francisco: Jossey-Bass.

Greene, J. C., Caracelli, V. J., & Graham, W. F. (1989). Toward a conceptual framework for mixed-method evaluation designs. *Educational Evaluation and Policy Analysis, 11*(3), 255–274.

Greenstein, T. N. (2006). *Methods of family research* (2nd ed.). Thousand Oaks, CA: Sage.

Guba, E. G., & Lincoln, Y. S. (2005). Paradigmatic controversies, contradictions, and emerging confluences. In N. K. Denzin & Y. S. Lincoln (Eds.), *The SAGE handbook of qualitative research* (3rd ed., pp. 191–215). Thousand Oaks, CA: Sage.

Gurtler, L., Huber, L., & Kiegelmann, M. (2007). Conclusions: The reflective use of combined methods—a vision of mixed methodology. In P. Mayring, G. L. Huber, L. Gurtler, & M. Kiegelmann (Eds.), *Mixed methodology in psychological research* (pp. 243–245). Rotterdam/Taipei: Sense Publishers.

Hall, B., & Howard, K. (2008). A synergistic approach: Conducting mixed methods research with typological and systemic design considerations. *Journal of Mixed Methods Research, 2*(3), 248–269.

Heigham, J., & Croker, R. A. (2009). *Qualitative research in applied linguistics: A practical introduction.* London: Palgrave Macmillan.

Hesse-Biber, S. N., & Leavy, P. L. (2007). *Feminist research practice: A primer.* Thousand Oaks, CA: Sage.

Hodgkin, S. (2008). Telling it all: A story of women's social capital using a mixed methods approach. *Journal of Mixed Methods Research, 2*(4), 296–316.

Holmes, C. A. (2006, July). Mixed (up) methods, methodology and interpretive frameworks. Paper presented at the Mixed Methods Conference, Cambridge, UK.

Howe, K. R. (2004). A critique of experimentalism. *Qualitative Inquiry, 10,* 42–61.

Ivankova, N. V., Creswell, J. W., & Stick, S. L. (2006). Using mixed methods sequential explanatory design: From theory to practice. *Field Methods, 18*(1), 3–20.

Johnson, R. B., & Onwuegbuzie, A. J. (2004). Mixed methods research: A research paradigm whose time has come. *Educational Researcher, 33,* 14–26.

Johnson, R. B., Onwuegbuzie, A. J., & Turner, L. A. (2007). Toward a definition of mixed methods research. *Journal of Mixed Methods Research, 1*(2), 112–133.

Kuckartz, U. (2009). *Realizing mixed-methods approaches with MAXQDA.* Unpublished manuscript, Department of Education, Phillipps-Universitaet, Marburg, Germany. Available at http://maxqda.com/download/MixMethMAXQDA-Nov01-2010.pdf

Kuhn, T. S. (1970). *The structure of scientific revolutions* (2nd ed.). Chicago: University of Chicago Press.

Leech, N. L, Dellinger, A. B., Brannagan, K. B., & Tanaka, H. (2010). Evaluating mixed research studies: A mixed methods approach. *Journal of Mixed Methods Research, 4*(1), 17–31.

Lincoln, Y. S., & Cannella, G. S. (2004). Qualitative research, power, and the radical right. *Qualitative Inquiry, 10*(2), 175–201.

Lincoln, Y. S., & Guba, E. G. (1985). *Naturalistic inquiry.* Beverly Hills, CA: Sage.

Luck, L., Jackson, D., & Usher, K. (2006). Case study: A bridge across the paradigms. *Nursing Inquiry, 13*(2), 103–109.

Maxwell, J., & Loomis, D. (2003). Mixed methods design: An alternative approach. In A. Tashakkori & C. Teddlie (Eds.), *Handbook of mixed methods in social & behavioral research* (pp. 241–272). Thousand Oaks, CA: Sage.

Mayring, P. (2007). Introduction: Arguments for mixed methodology. In P. Mayring, G. L. Huber, L. Gurtler, & M. Kiegelmann (Eds.), *Mixed methodology in psychological research* (pp. 1–4). Rotterdam/Taipei: Sense Publishers.

Mayring, P., Huber, G. L., Gurtler, L., & Kiegelmann, M. (Eds.). (2007). *Mixed methodology in psychological research.* Rotterdam/Taipei: Sense Publishers.

Mertens, D. M. (2003). Mixed methods and the politics of human research: The transformative-emancipatory perspective. In A. Tashakkori & C. Teddlie (Eds.), *Handbook of mixed methods in social & behavioral research* (pp. 135–164). Thousand Oaks, CA: Sage.

Mertens, D. M. (2009). *Transformative research and evaluation.* New York: Guilford.

Miall, C. E., & March, K. (2005). Community attitudes toward birth fathers' motives for adoption placement and single parenting. *Journal of Family Issues, 26,* 380–410.

Morgan, D. L. (2007). Paradigms lost and pragmatism regained: Methodological implications of combining qualitative and quantitative methods. *Journal of Mixed Methods Research, 1*(1), 48–76.

Morse, J. M. (1991). Approaches to qualitative-quantitative methodological triangulation. *Nursing Research, 40,* 120–123.

Morse, J. M. (2005). Evolving trends in qualitative research: Advances in mixed methods designs. *Qualitative Health Research, 15,* 583–585.

Morse, J. M., & Niehaus, L. (2009). *Mixed method design: Principles and procedures.* Walnut Creek, CA: Left Coast Press.

Myers, K. K., & Oetzel, J. G. (2003). Exploring the dimensions of organizational assimilation: Creating and validating a measure. *Communication Quarterly, 51*(4), 438–457.

Nastasi, B. K., Hitchcock, J., Sarkar, S., Burkholder, G., Varjas, K., & Jayasena, A. (2007). Mixed methods in intervention research: Theory to adaptation. *Journal of Mixed Methods Research, 1*(2), 164–182.

No Child Left Behind Act of 2001, Pub. L. No. 107–110, 115 Stat. 1425 (2002).

O'Cathain, A., Murphy, E., & Nicholl, J. (2007). Integration and publications as indicators of "yield" from mixed methods studies. *Journal of Mixed Methods Research, 1*(2), 147–163.

Olivier, T., de Lange, N., Creswell, J. W., & Wood, L. (2009, July). *Teachers as video producers and agents of change: A transformative mixed methods approach.* Paper presented at the fifth annual Mixed Methods Conference, Harrogate, UK.

Onwuegbuzie, A. J., & Johnson, R. B. (2006). Types of legitimation (validity) in mixed methods research. *Research in the Schools, 13*(1), 48–63.

Onwuegbuzie, A. J., & Teddlie, C. (2003). A framework for analyzing data in mixed methods research. In A. Tashakkori & C. Teddlie (Eds.), *Handbook of mixed methods in social & behavioral research* (pp. 351–383). Thousand Oaks, CA: Sage.

Patton, M. Q. (1980). *Qualitative evaluation methods.* Beverly Hills, CA: Sage.

Plano Clark, V. L. (2010). The adoption and practice of mixed methods: U.S. trends in federally funded health-related research. *Qualitative Inquiry, 16*(6), 428–440.

Plano Clark, V. L., & Creswell, J. W. (2008). *The mixed methods reader.* Thousand Oaks, CA: Sage.

Quinlin, E. (2010). Representations of rape: Transcending methodological divides. *Journal of Mixed Methods Research, 4*(2), 127–143.

Reichardt, C. S., & Rallis, S. F. (Eds.). (1994). *The qualitative-quantitative debate: New perspectives.* San Francisco: Jossey-Bass.

Richardson, L. (1997). *Fields of play: Constructing an academic life.* New Brunswick, NJ: Rutgers University Press.

Rossman, G. B., & Wilson, B. L. (1985). Numbers and words: Combining quantitative and qualitative methods in a single large-scale evaluation study. *Evaluation Review, 9*(5), 627–643.

Ryan, K. E., & Hood, L. K. (2006). Guarding the castle and opening the gates. In N. K. Denzin & M. D. Giardina (Eds.), *Qualitative inquiry and the conservative challenge* (pp. 57–77). Walnut Creek, CA: Left Coast Press.

Sale, J. E. M., Lohfeld, L. H., & Brazil, K. (2002). Revisiting the quantitative-qualitative debate: Implications for mixed-methods research. *Quality and Quantity, 36*, 43–53.

Sandelowski, M. (1996). Using qualitative methods in intervention studies. *Research in Nursing & Health, 19*(4), 359–364.

Sandelowski, M., Voils, C. I., & Knafl, G. (2009). On quantitizing. *Journal of Mixed Methods Research, 3*(3), 208–222.

Shank, G. (2007). How to tap the full potential of qualitative research by applying qualitative methods. In P. Mayring, G. L. Huber, L. Gurtler, & M. Kiegelmann (Eds.), *Mixed methodology in psychological research* (pp. 7–13). Rotterdam/Taipei: Sense Publishers.

Shavelson, R. J., & Towne, L. (Eds.) (2002). *Scientific research in education*. Washington, DC: National Research Council, National Academy Press.

Sieber, S. D. (1973). The integration of fieldwork and survey methods. *American Journal of Sociology, 78*, 1335–1359.

Sieber, S. D., & Lazarsfeld, P. F. (1966). *The organization of educational research* (USOE Cooperative Research Project No. 1974). New York: Columbia University, Bureau of Applied Social Research.

Stake, R. (1995). *The art of case study research*. Thousand Oaks, CA: Sage.

Stange, K. C., Crabtree, B. F., & Miller, W. L. (2006). Publishing multimethod research. *Annals of Family Medicine, 4*, 292–294.

Stenner, P., & Rogers, R. S. (2004). Q methodology and qualiquantology. In Z. Todd, B. Nerlich, S. McKeown, & D. D. Clarke (Eds.), *Mixing methods in psychology: The integration of qualitative and quantitative methods in theory and practice* (pp. 101–120). Hove and New York: Psychology Press.

Sweetman, D., Badiee, M., & Creswell, J. W. (2010). Use of the transformative framework in mixed methods studies. *Qualitative Inquiry, 16*(6), 441–454.

Tashakkori, A., & Teddlie, C. (1998). *Mixed methodology: Combining qualitative and quantitative approaches*. Thousand Oaks, CA: Sage.

Tashakkori, A., & Teddlie, C. (Eds.). (2003). *Handbook of mixed methods in social & behavioral research*. Thousand Oaks, CA: Sage.

Tashakkori, A., & Teddlie, C. (2003). The past and future of mixed methods research: From data triangulation to mixed model designs. In A. Tashakkori & C. Teddlie (Eds.), *Handbook of mixed methods in social & behavioral research* (pp. 671–701). Thousand Oaks, CA: Sage.

Teddlie, C., & Tashakkori, A. (2009). *Foundations of mixed methods research: Integrating quantitative and qualitative approaches in the social and behavioral sciences*. Thousand Oaks, CA: Sage.

Todd, Z., Nerlich, B., McKeown, S., & Clarke, D. D. (2004). *Mixing methods in psychology: The integration of qualitative and quantitative methods in theory and practice*. Hove and New York: Psychology Press.

Vidich, A. J., & Shapiro, G. (1955). A comparison of participant observation and survey data. *American Sociological Review, 20*(1), 28–33.

Vogt, D. S., King, D. W., & King, L. A. (2004). Focus groups in psychological assessment: Enhancing content validity by consulting members of the target population. *Psychological Assessment, 16,* 231–243.

Vogt, P. W. (2008). Quantitative versus qualitative is a distraction: Variations on a theme by Brewer & Hunter (2006). *Methodological Innovations Online, 3,* 1–10.

Vygotsky, L. S., & Cole, M. (1978). *Mind in society the development of higher psychological processes.* Cambridge, MA: Harvard University Press.

Yin, R. K. (2006). Mixed methods research: Are the methods genuinely integrated or merely parallel? *Research in the Schools, 13*(1), 41–47.

Mixed Methods Research

Contemporary Issues in an Emerging Field

Charles Teddlie and Abbas Tashakkori[1]

The field of mixed methods research (MMR), which we have called the "third methodological movement," has evolved as a result of discussions about methods and paradigms in the social and behavioral sciences that have been ongoing for at least three decades. The "paradigm debate" between quantitatively oriented and qualitatively oriented researchers was based on sets of interlocking epistemological, ontological, and methodological assumptions. MMR offers a third alternative based on pragmatism, which argues that the two methodological approaches are compatible and can be fruitfully used in conjunction with one another (e.g., Howe, 1988; Tashakkori & Teddlie, 1998).

This chapter briefly presents several important issues in contemporary MMR, including a definition of MMR, theoretical and conceptual issues, issues in conducting MMR, and criticisms of the third methodological movement. We advise the reader to consider this to be a "sampler" of some of the contemporary issues relevant to MMR and, if you are interested, to continue your exploration of the field by reading some of the numerous cited references.

Definitions and Origins of Mixed Methods Research

DEFINITION OF MIXED METHODS RESEARCH

As writing in the field of MMR has become more sophisticated, several authors have labored to identify and define exactly *what mixed methods research is* (e.g., Creswell, 2010; Greene, 2007, 2008; Johnson, Onwuegbuzie, & Turner, 2007; Tashakkori & Teddlie, 1998, 2003a). There is even continued debate over what the field should be called with variants including, but certainly not limited to, MMR, multimethod research, mixed methods, mixed methodology, mixed research, integrated research, and so forth.

Fortunately, there appears to be some consensus around "mixed methods research" as the de facto term due to common usage (e.g., the names of the leading journal in the field and of a handbook now in its second edition). We suspect that this term will endure, since it now has the trappings of a "brand name" that has been widely disseminated throughout the social and behavioral sciences.

As for the definition of MMR, Johnson et al. (2007) presented 19 alternative meanings from leaders in the field. While these meanings had varying levels of specificity, the authors of this analysis settled upon the following "composite" definition:

> Mixed methods research is the type of research in which a researcher or team of researchers combines elements of qualitative and quantitative research approaches (e.g., use of qualitative and quantitative viewpoints, data collection, analysis, inference techniques) for the broad purposes of breadth and depth of understanding and corroboration. (Johnson et al., 2007, p. 123)

From our perspective, this definition works because it includes what we believe is an essential characteristic of MMR: *methodological eclecticism,* a term that has only occasionally been used (e.g., Hammersley, 1996; Yanchar & Williams, 2006). Hammersley originally described this characteristic as follows:

> What is being implied here is a form of methodological eclecticism; indeed, the *combination* of quantitative and qualitative methods is often proposed, on the ground that this promises to cancel out the respective weaknesses of each method. (Hammersley, 1996, p. 167, italics in original)

Our definition of methodological eclecticism goes beyond simply combining qualitative (QUAL) and quantitative (QUAN) methods to cancel out respective weaknesses. *Eclectic,* the root word of eclecticism, means "choosing what appears to be the best from diverse sources, systems, or styles."[2] For us, *methodological eclecticism involves selecting and then synergistically integrating the most appropriate techniques from a myriad of QUAL, QUAN, and mixed methods* in order to more thoroughly investigate a phenomenon of interest. A researcher employing methodological eclecticism is a *connoisseur*[3] *of methods* who knowledgeably (and often intuitively) selects the best techniques available to answer research questions that frequently evolve during the course of an investigation.[4]

ORIGINS OF MIXED METHODS RESEARCH, WITH AN EMPHASIS ON QUALITATIVE METHODS

MMR emerged as a distinct orientation in the late 1970s from applied fields in the social and behavioral sciences, such as evaluation, nursing, and education (e.g., Greene, Caracelli, & Graham, 1989; Miles & Huberman, 1984, 1994; Morse, 1991; Patton, 1980, 1990, 2002; Reichardt & Cook, 1979; Rossman & Wilson, 1985). Its origin in the applied, rather than pure, human sciences was not coincidental, since those disciplines often require a pragmatic, wide-angle lens utilizing all data sources available to answer practical questions.

Numerous studies from this early MMR involved researchers adding a QUAL component to a study that was initially a QUAN-only project in order to make greater sense out of the numerical findings. In evaluation research, this involved adding a formative component (how or why did the program succeed or fail) to the summative component (did the program work). In the human sciences, this distinction relates to causal effects (i.e., *whether* X causes Y) as opposed to causal mechanisms (i.e., *how* did X cause Y) (e.g., Shadish, Cook, & Campbell, 2002).[5]

In our own research, we have found that information gleaned from narratives generated by participants and investigators often proves to be the most valuable source in understanding complex phenomena. For example, qualitatively oriented case studies of differentially effective schools express the complexity of evolving contextual and behavioral patterns in those institutions much more thoroughly than statistical summaries of numeric indicators (Teddlie & Stringfield, 1993). A simple way of saying this is that narratives (stories) are intrinsically more interesting (and often more enlightening) than numbers to many researchers, the participants in their studies, and their audiences. It is no coincidence that several MMR pioneers (e.g., Creswell, Miles and Huberman, Morse, Patton) have also written QUAL methods texts.

We want to unambiguously express our regard for the powerful contributions of QUAL methods in this fourth edition of *The SAGE Handbook of Qualitative Research* due to the concern that some scholars have expressed about MMR subordinating QUAL methods to a secondary role behind QUAN methods (e.g., Denzin & Lincoln, 2005; Howe, 2004). This is not how we interpret the MMR literature we have reviewed from the past 30-plus years. In fact, QUAL + quan studies emphasizing the detailed, impressionistic perceptions of human "data-gathering instruments" and their interpretations of their outcomes are among the most valuable of all the extant MMR literature.

We also believe that MMR can add an important dimension to QUAN research. There has been much discussion (e.g., Mosteller & Boruch, 2002; Shavelson & Towne, 2002) about the importance of randomized controlled trials (RCTs) in the social and behavioral sciences. While RCTs may represent the "gold standard" for the identification of causal effects, the addition of a QUAL component (e.g., case studies) to the design allows researchers to discuss causal mechanisms as well. There are several examples of this in the MMR literature, including (1) the mixed methods intervention program of research in the health sciences (Song, Sandelowski, & Happ, 2010) and (2) the group-case method (also known as experimental ethnography) in several disciplines (e.g., Teddlie, Tashakkori, & Johnson, 2008). MMR enables researchers to examine issues in those fields in ways that traditional QUAN methods cannot alone.

Some Contemporary Characteristics of Mixed Methods Research

We begin this section by acknowledging that there are others writing in the MMR field who will disagree with the inclusion of some or all of the characteristics described below, or with our interpretation of certain of those characteristics. Such is the nature of most emerging fields in academia, as new ideas are put forth and contested by those highly interested in the topic. This is especially the case with regard to MMR, whose development has been enhanced greatly by the juxtaposition of diverse perspectives. (Table 4.1 presents eight contemporary characteristics of MMR.)

We described the first contemporary characteristic of MMR in the previous section of this chapter: *methodological eclecticism*. This characteristic stems from rejection of the incompatibility (of methods) thesis, which stated that it is inappropriate to mix QUAL and QUAN methods in the same study due to epistemological differences between the paradigms that are purportedly related to them. Howe (1988) countered this point of view with his *compatibility thesis*, which contends that "combining quantitative and qualitative methods is a good thing" and "denies that such a wedding of methods is epistemologically incoherent" (p. 10). Howe proposed pragmatism as an alternative paradigm, a suggestion that has been endorsed by many others (e.g., Biesta, 2010; Johnson & Onwuegbuzie, 2004; Maxcy, 2003; Tashakkori & Teddlie, 1998).

Table 4.1 Eight Contemporary Characteristics of Mixed Methods Research

	Description of Characteristic
1.	Methodological eclecticism
2.	Paradigm pluralism
3.	Emphasis on diversity at all levels of the research enterprise
4.	Emphasis on continua rather than a set of dichotomies
5.	Iterative, cyclical approach to research
6.	Focus on the research question (or research problem) in determining the methods employed within any given study
7.	Set of basic "signature" research designs and analytical processes
8.	Tendency toward balance and compromise that is implicit within the "third methodological community"

Methodological eclecticism not only means that we are free to combine methods, but that we do so by choosing what we believe to be the best tools for answering our questions. We have called this choice of "best" methods for answering research questions, "design quality"[6] and have included it as an essential part of our framework for determining the inference quality of MMR (Tashakkori & Teddlie, 2008). Furthermore, we believe that the best method for any given study in the human sciences may be purely QUAL, purely QUAN, or (in many cases) mixed.

Schulenberg (2007) presented a complex example of methodological eclecticism in a mixed methods study of the processes that occur in police decision making. Her data sources included interviews administered to individual officers, documents provided by the interviewees, QUAL data gathered from police department websites, documents obtained from provincial governments, census data, and tabulations of statistical data on the proportion of apprehended youth actually charged with crimes. The interview data gathered from police officers were originally QUAL in nature (from semistructured protocols), but were also converted into numbers (quantitized).

Schulenberg (2007) used these diverse data sources to generate five separate databases that addressed her research questions and hypotheses. She employed eight types of QUAL techniques and six types of statistical QUAN techniques including *t* tests, chi-squares, multiple regression, analysis of variance, manifest and latent content analysis, the constant comparative method, and grounded theory techniques. The *methodological eclecticism (connoisseurship)* of this criminologist/sociologist is apparent.

The second contemporary characteristic of MMR is *paradigm pluralism,* or the belief that a variety of paradigms may serve as the underlying philosophy for the use of mixed methods. This characteristic is, of course, a function of the rejection of the incommensurability (of paradigms) thesis, which is widely accepted within the MMR community.

We believe that contemporary MMR is a kind of "big tent" in that researchers who currently use mixed methods come from a variety of philosophical orientations (e.g., pragmatism, critical theory, the dialectic stance). We believe that it is both unwise, and unnecessary, at this time to exclude individuals from the MMR community because their conceptual frameworks are different. We agree with Denzin's (2008, p. 322) paraphrase of a theme originally stated by Guba (1990): "A change in paradigmatic postures involves a personal odyssey; that is we each have a personal history with our preferred paradigm and this needs to be honored."

While paradigm pluralism is widely endorsed by many mixed methods scholars, theoretical and conceptual dialogues related to MMR have been, and will continue to be, of great importance. Recent developments and controversies in this area are summarized later.

The third characteristic of contemporary MMR is *a celebration of diversity at all levels of the research enterprise* from the broader more conceptual dimensions to the narrower more empirical ones. This is demonstrated in methodological eclecticism and paradigm pluralism, but also extends to other issues. For example, MMR can simultaneously address a diverse range of confirmatory and exploratory questions,[7] while single approach studies often address only one or the other. Additionally, MMR provides the opportunity for an assortment of divergent views in conclusions and inferences due to the complexity of the data sources and analyses.

MMR emerged partially out of the literature on triangulation (e.g., Campbell & Fiske, 1959; Denzin, 1978; Patton, 2002) and has commonly been associated with the *convergence* of results from different sources. Nevertheless, there is a growing awareness (e.g., Erzberger & Kelle, 2003; Greene, 2007; Johnson & Onwuegbuzie, 2004; Tashakkori & Teddlie, 2008) that an equally important result of combining information from different sources is divergence or dissimilarity, which can then provide greater insight into complex aspects of the same phenomenon and/or to the design of a new study or phase for further investigation.

The fourth characteristic of contemporary MMR is *an emphasis on continua rather than a set of dichotomies.* A hallmark of MMR is its replacement of the "either-or" with continua that describe a range of options (e.g., Newman, Ridenour, Newman, & DeMarco, 2003; Patton, 1980, 1990, 2002; Ridenour & Newman, 2008; Tashakkori & Teddlie, 2003c). For example, we have applied what we called the QUAL-MIXED-QUAN multidimensional continuum to a variety of research issues including statement of purpose, research questions, designs, sampling, data collection and analysis, and validity or inference quality (Teddlie & Tashakkori, 2009). The either-or dichotomies (e.g., explanatory or exploratory questions, statistical or thematic analyses) have been replaced with a range of options (including integrated questions and innovative methods for mixed data analysis).

The fifth characteristic of contemporary MMR *is an iterative, cyclical approach to research.* MMR is characterized by the cycle of research, which includes both deductive and inductive logic[8] in the same study (e.g., Krathwohl, 2004; Tashakkori & Teddlie, 1998). The cycle may be seen as moving from grounded results (facts, observations) through inductive logic to general inferences (abstract generalizations or theory), then from those general inferences (or theory) through deductive logic to tentative hypotheses or predictions of particular events/outcomes. Research may start at any point in the cycle: Some researchers start from theories or abstract generalizations, while others start from observations or other data points. This cycle may be repeated iteratively as researchers seek deeper levels of a phenomenon. We believe that all research projects go through a full cycle at least once, regardless of their starting point (e.g., Teddlie & Tashakkori, 2009).

This cyclical approach to research may also be conceptualized in terms of the distinction between

- the *context or logic of justification*—the process associated with the testing of predictions, theories, and hypotheses, and

- the *context or logic of discovery*—the process associated with understanding a phenomenon in more depth, the generation of theories and hypotheses.

While several authors writing in MMR acknowledge the logic of justification as a key part of their research, they also emphasize the importance of the *context of discovery,* which involves creative insight possibly leading to new knowledge (e.g., Hesse-Biber, 2010; Johnson & Gray, 2010; Teddlie & Johnson, 2009). This discovery component of MMR often, but not always, comes from the emergent themes associated with QUAL data analysis.

We also conceptualize the cyclical nature of research as a kind of "ebb and flow" that characterizes some of the *signature MMR processes,* such as sequential research designs. More details on these signature MMR processes are presented later in this section.

The sixth characteristic endorsed by many writing in MMR is *a focus on the research question (or research problem) in determining the methods/approaches employed within any given study* (e.g., Bryman, 2006; Johnson & Onwuegbuzie, 2004; Tashakkori & Teddlie, 1998). This *centrality of the research question* was initially intended to move researchers (particularly novice researchers) beyond intractable philosophical issues associated with the paradigms debate and toward the selection of methods that were best suited for their investigations.

Much has been written about the starting point for research; that is, do researchers start with a worldview or conceptual problem, a general purpose for conducting research, a research question, or some combination thereof? Newman et al. (2003) have argued convincingly that during the past four decades the research purpose has gained in importance relative to the research question. We maintain, however, that once a researcher has decided what she is interested in studying (e.g., what motivates the study, purpose, personal/political agenda, etc.), the specifics of her research questions will determine the choice of the best tools to use and how to use them. Experienced researchers are well aware of the fact that research questions undergo (often small) modifications and refocusing during the course of a study. Nevertheless, research questions generally direct the path of a research project.

MMR questions are usually broad, calling for both in-depth, emergent QUAL data *and* focused and preplanned QUAN data. These broad "umbrella" questions are often followed by more specific subquestions. In some (sequential) MMR projects, however, mixed questions emerge after the data are collected and analyzed, rather than being stated as initial "umbrella" questions. For example, a broad and emergent question may be asked and answered by collecting and analyzing QUAL data, followed by a question regarding the pervasiveness of the findings in a broader context or with regard to generaliziblity to a population. Despite the emergent (or sometimes preplanned) sequence in these MMR studies, both groups of findings must be incorporated toward broader understandings (i.e., meta-inferences).

The seventh characteristic of contemporary MMR is a *set of basic research designs and analytical processes,* most of which are agreed upon, although they go by different names and diagrammatic illustrations. For example, we refer to *parallel mixed designs* (Teddlie & Tashakkori, 2009, p. 341, italics in original) as,

a family of MM designs in which mixing occurs in an independent manner either simultaneously or with some time lapse. The QUAL and QUAN *strands* are planned and implemented in order to answer related aspects of the same questions.

These designs have also been referred to as concurrent, simultaneous, and *triangulation designs* (Creswell & Plano Clark, 2007, p. 85), but there is much commonality across their definitions.

Earlier in this section, we referred to *signature MMR design and analysis processes,* such as sequential mixed designs or conversion procedures. We call these design and analysis processes "signature" terms because they help to define MMR in relation to QUAN or QUAL methods; that is, they are unique to MMR and help set this approach apart from the other two. These signature design and analysis processes include the following:

- *Sequential mixed designs* "are a family of MM designs in which mixing occurs across chronological phases (QUAL, QUAN) of the study; questions or procedures of one *strand* emerge from or are dependent on the previous strand; *research question*s are built upon one another and may evolve as the study unfolds" (Teddlie & Tashakkori, 2009, p. 345, italics in original).

- *Quantitizing* refers to the process of converting qualitative data to numerical codes that can be statistically analyzed (e.g., Miles & Huberman, 1994; Sandelowski, Voils, & Knafl, 2009).

- *Qualitizing*[9] refers to the process by which quantitative data are transformed into data that can be analyzed qualitatively (e.g., Tashakkori & Teddlie, 1998).

More signature designs and analytical procedures indigenous to MMR are discussed later. While there is general agreement about the existence of these unique MMR design and analytical processes, there is considerable disagreement about terminology and definitions, and these disagreements widen as more complex typologies are generated. For example, many believe that a complete typology of MMR designs is not possible due to the emergent nature of the QUAL component of the research and the ability of MMR designs to mutate, while others seek agreement on a set number of basic designs for the sake of simplicity and pedagogy.

The eighth contemporary characteristic of MMR is *a tendency toward balance and compromise that is implicit within the "third methodological community."* MMR is based on rejecting the either-or of the incompatibility thesis; therefore, we as a community are inclined toward generating a balance between the excesses of both the QUAL and QUAN orientations, while forging a unique

MMR identity. This balance is in keeping with Johnson and Onwuegbuzie's (2004) depiction of pragmatism as seeking a middle ground between philosophical dualisms and finding workable solutions for seemingly insoluble conceptual disputes.

In this context, we refer again to Denzin's (2008) paraphrase of three of Guba's (1990) themes regarding paradigms:

- "There needs to be decline in confrontationalism by alternative paradigm proponents."

- "Paths for fruitful dialog between and across paradigms need to be explored."

- "The three main interpretive communities . . . must learn how to cooperate and work with one another" (Denzin, 2008, p. 322).

We believe that most mixed methods researchers are in agreement with these themes that call for compromise in dialogues among the three methodological communities.

Theoretical and Conceptual Issues in Mixed Methods Research

While there is agreement on some broad characteristics of MMR, there are several ongoing dialogues regarding basic theoretical and conceptual issues within MMR. We concentrate on two: (1) issues related to the paradigms, which are also referred to by several other terms such as stances, approaches, frameworks, perspectives, mental models, and so forth and (2) issues related to the language of MMR.

ISSUES RELATED TO THE USE OF PARADIGMS (OR CONCEPTUAL FRAMEWORKS OR MENTAL MODELS)

In this section, we first provide more details on the concept of paradigm pluralism. Then we present three alternative paradigmatic positions for MMR, followed by a discussion of some arguments against the continued focus on paradigm issues.

We presented paradigm pluralism as one of the contemporary characteristics of MMR earlier. The belief that multiple paradigms may serve as the underlying conceptual framework for MMR is a practical solution to some thorny philosophical and conceptual issues: Researchers simply use the philosophical framework that best fits their particular "intellectual odyssey."

Most MMR scholars can agree with paradigm pluralism as a starting point, but then they have to (1) consider the alternative paradigmatic positions and (2) *ascertain which of those positions is most closely related to their own perspective.* The following three paradigmatic positions[10] are the most widely accepted in contemporary MMR:

- pragmatism and its interpretations,
- frameworks associated with the axiological assumption (Mertens, 2007), and
- the dialectical stance, which involves using multiple assumptive frameworks within the same study (e.g., Greene, 2007; Greene & Caracelli, 2003).

Before examining these positions further, we need to briefly reconsider the ramifications of paradigm pluralism, which was posited in opposition to the single paradigm-single method thesis (e.g., postpositivism and QUAN methods; constructivism and QUAL methods). Denzin (2008, p. 317) considers the rejection of the single paradigm-single method thesis to be historical:

> When the field went from one to multiple epistemological paradigms, many asserted that there was incompatibility between and across paradigms, not just incompatibility between positivism and its major critic, constructivism. . . . Ironically, as this discourse evolved, the complementary strengths thesis emerged, and is now accepted by many in the mixed-methods community. Here is where history starts to be rewritten. That is multiple paradigms can be used in the same mixed-methods inquiry. . . . Thus the demise of the single theoretical and/or methodological paradigm was celebrated.

It is important to realize that Denzin's analysis emphasizes not only paradigm pluralism, but also that researchers *may use multiple frameworks in the same study,* which is supported by only one of the contemporary positions noted above (the dialectical stance). Researchers who prescribe to pragmatism or a framework based on the axiological assumption typically use only that perspective in their research.

PRAGMATISM AND ITS INTERPRETATIONS

There is an affinity for pragmatism as the paradigm of choice for many mixed methodologists (e.g., Tashakkori & Teddlie, 1998). This affinity is a historical one going back to Howe's (1988) postulation of the compatibility thesis based on pragmatism. The pragmatic approach to philosophical issues is appealing to many applied scientists who utilize a kind of "everyday pragmatism" (Biesta, 2010) in their solution of research and evaluation problems.

A more *philosophically nuanced pragmatism* has emerged recently (e.g., Biesta, 2010; Greene & Hall, 2010; Johnson & Onwuegbuzie, 2004; Maxcy, 2003; Teddlie & Tashakkori, 2009). This pragmatism asks, "Apart from the rejection of the either-or, what does pragmatism mean for MMR?" We briefly describe three recent interpretations of pragmatism (Johnson and colleagues; Biesta, 2010; Greene, 2007) that have advanced the conversation.

Johnson and colleagues have ventured into a kind of "paradigm or systems building" with regard to *philosophical pragmatism.* Johnson and Onwuegbuzie (2004) presented 21 characteristics of pragmatism in an effort to more completely delineate the tenets of this philosophy and how they relate to MMR.

Johnson et al. (2007) defined three pragmatisms: of the right, of the left, and of the center (*classical pragmatism*). Johnson (2009, p. 456) further defined *dialectical pragmatism* as a "supportive philosophy for mixed methods research" that combines classical pragmatism with Greene's (2007) dialectical approach. The cumulative contribution of Johnson and colleagues' work is that we now have a clearly articulated and detailed account of pragmatism as it relates to MMR.

In contrast, Biesta (2010, p. 97) contends that "pragmatism should not be understood as a philosophical position among others, but rather as a set of philosophical tools that can be used to address problems." Biesta emphasizes that John Dewey warned against philosophical system building. Biesta concludes that Deweyan pragmatism contributes to the dismantling of the epistemological dualism of objectivity/subjectivity:

> The major contribution of Dewey is that he engages with this discussion from a different starting point so that the either/or of objectivism and subjectivism loses its meaning. . . . This is tremendously important for the field of mixed methods research as it does away with alleged hierarchies between different approaches and rather helps to make the case that different approaches generate *different* outcomes, *different* connections between doing and undergoing, between actions and consequences, so that we always need to judge our knowledge claims pragmatically, that is in relation

to the processes and procedures through which the knowledge has been generated. (Biesta, 2010, p. 113, italics in original)

Biesta concludes that philosophical pragmatism leads us to understand that no methodological approach is intrinsically better than another in knowledge generation. We have to evaluate the results from our research studies in terms of how good a job we did in selecting, utilizing, and integrating all the available methodological tools. Did we succeed in our efforts at *methodological eclecticism?*

Greene (2007) referred to pragmatism as the *alternative paradigm* (to the dominant traditional ones) that promotes the active mixing of methods and integration of research findings. Greene and Hall (2010) further described how thinking pragmatically affects the manner in which mixed researchers conduct their research. For Greene and Hall and others (e.g., Biesta, 2010; Johnson & Onwuegbuzie, 2004), pragmatism results in a problem-solving, action-oriented inquiry process based on a commitment to democratic values and progress.

FRAMEWORKS ASSOCIATED WITH THE AXIOLOGICAL ASSUMPTION

Mertens (2007) identified four basic assumptions associated with paradigms that were previously delineated by Guba and Lincoln (2005): axiological, epistemological, ontological, and methodological. Mertens, Bledsoe, Sullivan, & Wilson (2010, p. 195) further described the *axiological assumption* that "takes precedence and serves as a basis for articulating the other three belief systems because the transformative paradigm emerged from the need to be more explicit about how researchers can address issues of social justice." The axiological assumption is based on "power differences and ethical implications that derive from those differences" between marginalized and other groups (Mertens et al., p. 195).

In discussions of pragmatism, the philosophical issues that are emphasized are epistemological in nature concerning issues such as what is knowledge, how is it acquired, and the relationship between the knower and "known." On the other hand, scholars working within transformative or critical frameworks (e.g., feminism) give precedence to axiological considerations, which center on the nature of value judgments. This *axiological assumption* means that scholars working within transformative/critical frameworks have a different perspective on research methods. For these scholars, mixed methods are tools that are used in the service of value systems that are always foremost.

THE DIALECTIC STANCE OR WAY OF THINKING

The dialectic stance assumes that all paradigms have something to offer, and that employing multiple paradigms contributes to greater understanding of phenomena under study. Pragmatism and axiologically oriented frameworks utilize one perspective exclusively, while the dialectical stance calls for the juxtaposition of multiple assumptive frameworks within the same study. Greene (2007, p. 114) expresses it thus:

> I have adopted the stance that method cannot be divorced from the inquirer's assumptions about the world and about knowledge, the inquirer's theoretical predispositions, professional experience, and so forth. . . . So when one mixes methods, one may also mix paradigmatic and mental model assumptions as well as broad features of inquiry methodology.

Greene's dialectical stance directs attention away from the so-called incommensurable attributes of paradigms and toward different and distinctive (but not inherently incompatible) attributes such as distance-closeness, outside-insider, emic and etic, particularity and generality, and so forth. Greene and Hall's (2010) dialectical stance agrees with Biesta's (2010) pragmatism in that these philosophical systems are *not* "paradigm packages" with interlocking philosophical assumptions or beliefs.

ARGUMENTS AGAINST THE CONTINUED FOCUS ON "PARADIGMS"

The term "paradigm" has played a crucial role in the development of the three methodological communities since the initial publication of Kuhn's (1962) *The Structure of Scientific Revolutions.* Recently, authors have expressed increasing doubt about the utility of the continued focus on paradigm issues in MMR. For instance, Bazeley (2009, p. 203) concluded that "Although the epistemological arguments of the 'paradigm wars' sharpened our thinking about issues related to mixed methodology, their lingering legacy has been to slow the progress of integration of methods."

Morgan (2007) deconstructed the term "paradigm" into four possible (and not mutually exclusive) positions:

- paradigms as worldviews (ways of perceiving and experiencing the world),
- paradigms as epistemological stances (which Morgan called the *metaphysical paradigm*),

- paradigms as model examples (i.e., "exemplars" demonstrating how research is conducted), and

- paradigms as shared beliefs about types of questions, methods of study (and so on) among a community of scholars or within a field of study.

Morgan argued that Guba and Lincoln (e.g., Lincoln & Guba, 1985; Guba & Lincoln, 1994, 2005) used the metaphysical paradigm to draw attention to QUAL research as an alternative to QUAN research. This metaphysical version focused on the basic assumptions or beliefs noted above, with a special emphasis on epistemological considerations, drawing essential, incommensurable differences between the QUAL and QUAN perspectives thereby leading to the paradigm wars.

Morgan further argued that now is the time to move from what he considers the outmoded concept of *metaphysical paradigms*[11] to paradigms as *shared beliefs in a research field* due to conceptual problems with the former position (e.g., a *strong* stand on incommensurability) and to the fact that the latter position is a more accurate interpretation of Kuhn's use of the term.[12] Morgan's focus on shared beliefs in a research field has contributed to an increasing emphasis on the *community of scholars* perspective (e.g., Creswell, 2010; Tashakkori & Creswell, 2008), which is a position that has been reinforced by Denscombe's (2008) discussion of the nature that such a community might take.

THE LANGUAGE OF MIXED METHODS RESEARCH

We previously identified the language of mixed methods as one of the major issues in MMR (Teddlie & Tashakkori, 2003). At that time, we distinguished between MMR using a *bilingual language* that combined QUAL and QUAN terms or generating a *new language* with terms unique to the field itself. Since that time, we have seen manifestations of both tendencies.

For instance, we recently (Teddlie & Tashakkori, 2009, p. 282) generated a list of common analytical processes used in both QUAL and QUAN research that are examples of a bilingual language. These processes are cognitively interchangeable, although one uses numbers and the other employs words as data. For example, a bilingual mixed methods researcher knows that cluster analysis employs the same *modus operandi* as the categorizing process of the constant comparative method: that is, maximizing between-group variation and minimizing within-group variation. Other examples include comparing analyses from one part of a sample with analyses from another part of the sample; comparison of actual results with expected results; and contrasting components of research design or elements to find differences.

Recognition of these common processes is a step in the direction of developing a language that crosses methodological lines. On the other hand, Box 4.1 presents a partial list of unique terms related to mixed methods data analysis that have emerged since the 1990s. The emergence of new analytical processes constitutes one of the most creative areas in MMR and often comes from researchers working on practical solutions for answering their research questions using available QUAL and QUAN data. Using mixed data analysis as an example, it appears that the language used in MMR will involve both bilingual terms and unique mixed terms (e.g., Box 4.1).

Box 4.1   Partial List of Data Analysis
Terms Indigenous to Mixed Methods Research

A partial list of MMR data analysis terms includes

- crossover track analysis
- data conversion or transformation
- data importation
- fully integrated mixed data analysis
- fused data analysis
- inherently mixed data analysis
- integrated data display
- integrated data reduction
- iterative sequential mixed analysis
- morphed data analysis
- multilevel mixed data analysis
- narrative profile formation
- parallel mixed data analysis
- parallel track analysis
- qualitizing
- quantitizing
- sequential mixed data analysis
- single track analysis
- typology development
- warranted assertion analysis

These terms were generated or employed by several authors, including Bazeley, 2003; Caracelli & Greene, 1993; Greene, 2007; Greene, Caracelli, & Graham, 1989; Li, Marquart, & Zercher, 2000; Onwuegbuzie & Combs, 2010; Onwuegbuzie, Johnson, & Collins, 2007; Onwuegbuzie & Teddlie, 2003; Tashakkori & Teddlie, 1998; Teddlie & Tashakkori, 2003, 2009.

Issues in Conducting Mixed Methods Research

Issues related to how to conduct MMR appear to have gained in importance relative to discussions of theoretical and conceptual issues recently. This trend is probably a reflection of the growing acceptance of MMR as a distinct methodological orientation and increased curiosity regarding the specifics of exactly how such research is conducted, disseminated, and utilized.

Chapters in the second edition of the *SAGE Handbook of Mixed Methods in Social & Behavioral Research* not only describe how to do MMR, but also illustrate how researchers' worldviews affect the manner in which they conduct their research. Box 4.2 presents information on how the different paradigmatic orientations summarized in the previous section of this chapter affect MMR praxis.

Box 4.2 How Worldviews Affect MMR Praxis

There is general agreement that a researcher's worldview affects the manner in which that person conducts his or her research, yet there have been few explicit discussions of how that occurs in MMR. Several of the chapters in the recently published second edition of the *SAGE Handbook of Mixed Methods in Social & Behavioral Research* presented detailed versions of actual or hypothetical researchers and how they conducted MMR within a particular worldview (or assumptive framework or mental mode). These chapters included

- Greene and Hall (2010) described Michelle (a hypothetical researcher), who is conducting research on the interactions among middle school children as they go through their daily routines. Michelle's perspective is that of the *dialectic inquirer* who is attuned to the values underlying the multiple philosophical frameworks (constructivist epistemology, feminist ideology) that guide her research.
- Greene and Hall (2010) described Juan (another hypothetical researcher), whose perspective is that of a *pragmatic inquirer* who is studying schools that are struggling to simultaneously serve the needs of their diverse study bodies and to meet the accountability mandates of NCLB (No Child Left Behind).
- Hesse-Biber's (2010) description of research conducted within the *feminist tradition,* including studies as diverse as forestland usage in Nepal and sex work in Tijuana.
- Mertens and colleagues' (2010) description of research conducted within the *transformative paradigm tradition,* including studies on inclusive education for disabled people in New Zealand and poverty reduction in Rwanda.

While there are several broad issues in conducting MMR (from generating research questions through making inferences from integrated data analyses), we can only discuss a couple here. We have selected research design, because there has been substantial work done in this area, and data analysis, because this is an area where considerable creative energy is currently being expended.

THE DESIGN OF MIXED METHODS STUDIES: A DIVERSITY OF OPTIONS

Design typologies have long been an important feature of MMR starting with Greene et al. (1989) writing in the field of evaluation and Morse (1991) in nursing. The reasons for the importance of MMR design typologies include their role in establishing a common language for the field, providing possible blueprints for researchers who want to employ MMR designs, legitimizing MMR by introducing designs that are clearly distinct from those in QUAN or QUAL research, and providing useful tools for pedagogical purposes.

Recently, some authors have contended that there is an overemphasis on research design typologies (e.g., Adamson, 2004; Bazeley, 2009), arguing that other areas (e.g., data analysis) should be stressed more. While such design typologies may not be featured as extensively in future writing in the field, they will continue to be an essential element of MMR. This is partly due to the fact that many of the proposed data analysis procedures in MMR are actually design-bound; that is, they are related to a specific type (or family) of designs (e.g., sequential data analysis in sequential mixed methods designs).

While some authors argue for a set number of prespecified designs, others contend that MMR design typologies can never be exhaustive, due to the iterative nature of MMR research projects (i.e., new components or strands might be added during the course of a project). This is an important point, since many inexperienced researchers want a design "menu" from which to select the "correct" one, similar to those provided in QUAN research (e.g., Shadish et al., 2002). In contrast, researchers using mixed methods are encouraged to continuously reexamine the results from one strand of a study compared to the results from another, and make changes both in the design and data collection procedures accordingly.

Researchers seeking their own *MMR design family* have a variety of viable options in the current "marketplace" (e.g., Creswell & Plano Clark, 2007; Greene, 2007; Leech & Onwuegbuzie, 2009; Maxwell & Loomis, 2003; Morse, 1991, 2003; Teddlie & Tashakkori, 2009). Nastasi, Hitchcock, and Brown (2010) recently examined various design typologies,[13] divided them into basic and complex categories, and determined that they differed with regard to nine distinct criteria or dimensions.

While some find the lack of consensus regarding the specific number and types of designs disconcerting, we believe that this is a healthy sign and that the most useful of the typologies will survive. The ultimate value of these typologies lies in their ability to provide researchers with viable design options to choose from and build upon (i.e., modify, expand, combine) when they are planning or implementing their MMR studies. The diversity in design typologies can be best exemplified by briefly examining two points of view that are distinct and have continued to evolve since first introduced: those of Jennifer Greene and our own. Other perspectives are equally valuable, but we chose these two because they make particularly interesting contrasts.

Greene contends that researchers cannot divorce method from "assumptive frameworks" when designing MMR studies; therefore, she encourages mixing those frameworks in single research studies. Her designs are anchored in mixing methods for five basic purposes that emerged from Greene et al. (1989): triangulation, complementarity, development, initiation, and expansion. Caracelli and Greene (1993) distinguished between *component designs* in which the methods are connected or mixed only at the level of inference and *integrated designs* in which the methods are integrated throughout the course of the study.

Greene (2007) presented two examples of component designs (convergence, extension) and four examples of integrated designs (iteration, blending, nesting or embedding, mixing for reasons of substance or values). These six examples of MMR designs map onto the five basic purposes for mixing with each example aligned with one or two of the original purposes. Greene (2007, p. 129) concludes that designing a MMR study does *not* involve following a formula or set of prescriptions, but rather is "an artful crafting of the kind of mix that will best fulfill the intended purposes for mixing within the practical resources and contexts at hand."

In our approach to MMR, we have always treated design as separable from research purpose. That is not to deny the importance of purpose; obviously, if you did not have a purpose for doing a study, you would not be doing it. We think purpose is a complex, psycho-socio-political concept and we believe each individual has a multiplicity of purposes for doing research ranging from "advancing your career" to "understanding complex phenomena" to "improving society." These purposes are intertwined and often change over time.

Our design typology has evolved as MMR has developed over the past decade (Tashakkori & Teddlie, 1998, 2003c; Teddlie & Tashakkori, 2009). The base of our system is a three-stage model of the research process that evolved from Patton's (2002, p. 252) "pure and mixed strategies" for conducting research. These three stages are conceptualization (formulation of questions specific to the research study), experiential (methodological operations, data generation, analysis, and so forth), and inferential (emerging theories, explanations, inferences, and so forth). Mixed designs are those in which the QUAL and QUAN approaches are integrated across the three stages. There are (currently) four families of mixed methods designs in our typology: parallel, sequential, conversion, and fully integrated. These families are based on what we call "type of implementation process"; that is, how does the integration of the QUAL and QUAN strands actually occur when conducting a study. Increasingly, MMR studies seem to use a combination of the basic configurations, often leading to fully integrated designs with multiple types/sources of data.

Similar to Greene's perspective, we distinguish between whether integration occurs at only one stage of the process (for us, the experiential stage) or throughout the study. Our latest solution to this thorny issue is the distinction between mixed and *quasi-mixed designs;* the former was defined in the previous paragraph, while we define the latter as designs in which two types of data are collected, but there is little or no integration of findings and *inferences* from the study.

Both of these perspectives regarding MMR designs

- reflect coherent and internally consistent perspectives,
- are currently viable as they continue to evolve in interesting ways related to changes in the field,
- are heuristic in terms of informing MMR dissertations and other projects, and
- have advanced the MMR designs literature over time (and have, themselves, evolved as a result).

In comparing our position regarding MMR design with hers, Greene (2007, p. 117) concluded,

my own thinking about mixed methods design shares considerable intellectual space with those of Tashakkori and Teddlie, but also contains some differences. . . . There is certainly ample space in the contemporary mixed methods conversation for these complementary yet distinct sets of ideas.

MIXED METHODS DATA ANALYSIS

Mixed methods data analyses are the processes whereby QUAN and QUAL data analysis strategies are combined, connected, or integrated in research studies (Teddlie & Tashakkori, 2009). Much creative energy is currently being expended on topics related to MMR data analysis, especially that involving integrated computer-generated applications (e.g., Bazeley, 2010). Bazeley (2009, p. 206) recently concluded that an indicator of the maturation of MMR would come when it moves from "a literature dominated by foundations and design typologies" toward a field "in which there are advances in conceptualization and breakthroughs derived from analytical techniques that support integration."

We limit our discussion of analysis issues to two topics foreshadowed in the previous section on the language of mixed methods: (1) the identification of analogous analytical processes in QUAL and QUAN research, and (2) the generation of a unique lexicon of MMR analysis procedures indigenous to the area. The analogous processes represent what Greene (2007, p. 155) called, "using aspects of the analytic framework of one methodological tradition within the analysis of data from another tradition."

In an early demonstration of this process, Miles and Huberman (1984/1994) took matrices from the QUAN tradition (e.g., contingency tables filled with numbers or percentages generated from chi-square analysis) and applied that framework to the QUAL tradition by crossing two dimensions and then completing the cells with narrative information. In one example, Miles and Huberman (1994) illustrated the implementation of a longitudinal school improvement project by using columns that represented years and rows that represented levels of intervention. Cross-case comparisons between schools demonstrated where there were differences in reform implementation between more and less successful schools.

Similarly, Onwuegbuzie (2003) applied the QUAN concept of effect sizes to generate an analogous QUAL typology including three broad categories (manifest, adjusted, and latent QUAL effect sizes). Effect sizes in QUAN research refer to the strength of the relationship between two numeric variables calculated by statistical indices. The generation of effect sizes in QUAL research is an analytical process in which the strength of the relationship between narrative variables is calculated after these variables have been quantitized.

In the future, we believe that MMR researchers will increasingly apply the analytical frameworks used in either the QUAL or QUAN tradition in developing analogous techniques within the other tradition. This requires both appropriate training in the QUAN and QUAL approaches and the ability to creatively see analogous processes from the mixed methods perspective.

Similarly, creative insight on the part of a variety of researchers has resulted in the lengthy list of data analysis terms indigenous to MMR in Box 4.1. These terms refer to general analytical processes (e.g., data conversion); specific techniques within more general analytical processes (e.g., crossover track analysis within parallel mixed data analysis); and complex iterative mixed data analyses utilizing multiple computer programs. Bazeley (2003, p. 385, italics added) has called the latter process *fused data analysis,* which she describes as follows:

> Software programs . . . offer . . . the capacity of qualitative data analysis (QDA) software to incorporate quantitative data into a qualitative analysis, and to transform qualitative coding and matrices developed from qualitative coding into a format which allows statistical analysis. . . . *The "fusing" of analysis then takes the researcher beyond blending of different sources to the place where the same sources are used in different but interdependent ways in order to more fully understand the topic at hand.*

Another noteworthy trend in mixed methods data analysis was discussed in the section on the third characteristic of contemporary MMR: the celebration of diversity at all levels of the research enterprise. This characteristic is exemplified in mixed methods data analysis by the growing awareness that divergence of findings and inferences across the QUAL and QUAN strands is equally as informative as convergence (or even more so), because that divergence leads researchers to more complex understandings and toward further research studies.

Critiques of Mixed Methods Research

Several criticisms of MMR have been voiced, especially as the field has become more visible since the turn of the 21st century. In this section, we briefly review some of the most salient of those criticisms.

From a historical perspective, the most common criticism of MMR is the incompatibility thesis, which stated that it is inappropriate to mix QUAL and QUAN methods in the same study due to epistemological differences between the paradigms that are purportedly related to them (e.g., Howe, 1988). This issue was addressed in the discussion regarding the first contemporary characteristic of MMR, *methodological eclecticism,* which contends that we are free to combine the best methodological tools in answering our research questions. While the philosophical justification for methodological eclecticism is important, the historical argument against the incompatibility thesis is probably more compelling: Researchers have been fruitfully combining QUAL and QUAN methods throughout the history of the social and behavioral sciences resulting in multi-layered research that is distinct from either QUAL or QUAN research alone.

Criticisms of MMR from the QUAL research and postmodern communities (e.g., Denzin & Lincoln, 2005; Howe, 2004; Sale, Lohfeld, & Brazil, 2002) have involved several issues, which have in turn been addressed by the MMR community (e.g., Creswell, Shope, Plano-Clark, & Green, 2006; Teddlie et al., 2008). Perhaps the most salient of these issues is the concern that MMR subordinates QUAL methods to a secondary position to QUAN methods. As noted in the first section of this chapter, we unequivocally express our regard for the powerful contributions of QUAL methods and interpret the overwhelming majority of truly mixed research as involving a thorough integration of both methods. Fortunately, recent literature (e.g., Creswell et al., 2006; Denzin, 2008) indicates that the QUAL and MMR communities can be involved in a productive discourse respectful of diverse viewpoints and cognizant of our many points of agreement.

Valuable criticisms of MMR include logistical ones (i.e., its implementation in actual research studies), including concerns about the costs of such research and about who does the research (e.g., teams of researchers, solo investigators). We believe that the employment of QUAL, QUAN, or MMR approaches in any given study depends on the research questions that are being addressed and that many issues are best and most efficiently answered using either the QUAL-only or QUAN-only approach. MMR techniques should be used only when necessary to adequately answer the research questions, because the mixed approach is inherently more expensive than the QUAL or QUAN alone orientations. Mixed studies take longer to conduct, which is a major issue for doctoral students, as well as researchers operating under stringent timelines to complete contracted work. Researchers bidding for contracts using MMR should be especially careful to provide accurate budgets for what it would take to do the work comprehensively, especially the QUAL component, which may involve time-consuming ethnographies. MMR projects that underestimate the time and money required to complete all components of the design will likely result in "QUAL-light" research that does not deliver what was promised.

As for who does the research, there is concern that a "minimal competence model or methodological" bilingualism is "superficial, perhaps even unworkable" (Denzin, 2008, p. 322). Issues of mixed methods pedagogy are beyond the scope of this chapter, but there is an active literature developing in this area (e.g., Christ, 2009, 2010; Creswell, Tashakkori, Jensen, & Shapley, 2003; Tashakkori & Teddlie, 2003b) that includes details on current MMR courses being taught and how they have evolved over time (Christ, 2010). The collaborative approach to MMR has been described by Shulha and Wilson (2003) and successful examples of it are found in the literature (e.g., Day, Sammons, & Qu, 2008).

In our discussion of "methodological connoisseurship," we indicated that mixed methodologists knowledgeably (and often intuitively) select the best techniques available to answer research questions that may evolve during the course of a research project. The question arises: How is such experience and judgment developed across diverse methods, especially in the QUAL area? There is no simple answer to this question, but we believe that a combination of coursework and field experiences is necessary to begin the journey toward "methodological connoisseurship." The field experiences are crucial and we advocate an active mentorship between professors who are mixed methodologists and their graduate students. Preferably, this mentorship would include field experiences in research projects where the professor is the principal investigator and/or dissertations in which the student is required to conduct extensive QUAL and QUAN research to answer different parts of the research questions being investigated. We have served on several dissertation committees where students have completed successful MMR projects and have begun their journey toward becoming "methodological connoisseurs." (See Schulenburg [2007] and Ivankova, Creswell, & Stick [2007], for examples of research articles based on mixed methods dissertations.)

Another criticism of MMR concerns the quality of the writing of many articles and chapters in the field. Leech (2010) conducted interviews with early developers of the field who concluded that authors need to do a better job of (1) expressing where their research fits within the current MMR literature; (2) presenting their own definition of MMR; (3) explaining where and how the mixing of methods occurred in their research; and (4) explicitly describing their philosophical orientation. Creswell (2009) has recently presented a preliminary "map" delineating subareas of MMR that should help authors in "locating" themselves within the field. The multiple definitions of MMR presented by Johnson et al. (2007) should help authors in describing their own perspectives, while the various design typologies offer options with regard to how authors can describe the mixing of methods in their research projects. Furthermore, the explicit delineation of at least three philosophical orientations in the field (pragmatism, frameworks associated with the axiological assumption, the dialectic stance) with other emerging alternatives (e.g., critical realism) provides authors with alternative philosophical orientations from which to choose and then make explicit in their writings.

Finally, Freshwater (2007), Greene (2007), Greene and Hall (2010), and others have expressed a concern that MMR is prematurely headed toward some "fixed" unity or consensus for social inquiry that will preclude the consideration of and respect for multiple approaches. For example, Freshwater (2007, p. 141) criticizes the "idolatry of integration and coherence," which she sees as "rife throughout nursing and the healthcare literature." This concern is akin to the apprehension that Smith and Heshusius (1986) voiced about "closing down the conversation" with regard to the quantitative-qualitative debate. We can understand this concern intellectually, since one of the characteristics of MMR is a "tendency toward balance and compromise," but we do not see MMR as becoming a static unified approach toward social inquiry that will stifle diverse viewpoints.

Perhaps our confidence that MMR leads toward a "celebration of diversity at all levels of the research enterprise" comes from our experiences in editing two volumes of the *SAGE Handbook of Mixed Methods in Social & Behavioral Research,* which have presented

- a wide variety of philosophical and conceptual models for MMR,

- an increasingly diverse set of methodological tools that can be employed in all aspects of conducting integrated research, especially those related to data analysis and the inferential process, and

- a diversity of applications of MMR across disciplinary boundaries and within specific lines of research.

Closely linked to this perspective regarding the inherent diversity of MMR is our perception of it as an extension of everyday sense making. Everyday problem solvers (naïve researchers) use multiple approaches concurrently or in sequence, examine a variety of evidence in decision making (or even in forming impressions), and question the credibility of their impressions, conclusions, and decisions. Although using a different type of data, more sophisticated methods of analysis, and more stringent standards of evidence and inference, a mixed methods researcher (the *methodological connoisseur* described earlier) follows the same general path that is characterized by a reliance on diverse sources of evidence.

Where Will We Be in 10 Years?

It is always difficult to predict the future, especially for a field that has only formally emerged in the past 15 to 20 years. The following comments are, therefore, our best guesses based on what we see as the trajectory of the field and are presented with the acknowledgment that future historic events could radically change the course of MMR.

1. There will be a gradual acceptance of pragmatism as the primary philosophical orientation associated with MMR, just as constructivism is associated with QUAL research and postpositivism with QUAN methods. Philosophical pragmatism as it relates to MMR will be defined more precisely. Other philosophical points of view will exist along with pragmatism as a basis for MMR, and this will be acceptable due to the belief of most mixed methodologists in paradigm pluralism. There will be relatively less emphasis on discussion of theoretical and conceptual issues.

2. A generic set of MMR designs will emerge over time and will be popularized in textbooks. These designs will include "signature" designs plus others that will emerge. Debates about which typology (among the half dozen or so most well-known ones) will subside as this generic set of prototypical designs is popularized. There will be relatively less emphasis on discussion of design issues in MMR.

3. Analysis issues will become more important, fueled by advances in the computer analysis of mixed methods data (e.g., Bazeley, 2009, 2010). Within MMR, data will be conceptualized "less in terms of words or numbers and more in terms of transferable units of information" (Teddlie & Tashakkori, 2009, p. 283). Mixed methodologists will develop widely accepted principles of mixed methods data analysis that will supersede the typologies that currently exist. The development of these principles of mixed methods data analysis is crucial to the continuation of MMR as a separate methodological movement.

4. MMR will continue to be adopted throughout the social and behavioral sciences. The form that it takes within any particular discipline will depend on the existing conceptual and methodological orientations within those fields. A challenge for mixed methodologists will be to develop and maintain a "core identity" (e.g., a set of commonly understood methodological principles) that cuts across disciplinary lines.

5. An alternative future is for MMR to continue to pave the way for human sciences research to be more inclusive (eclectic) and research question oriented. This will result in fewer projects being identified as purely QUAL or QUAN, and more that are simply called "research projects" (not labeled specifically as MMR). Unless mixed methodologists develop a core identity of commonly understood

methodological principles, it may simply be absorbed into this eclectic blend of research methodologies.

Notes

1. We wish to express our gratitude to Norman Denzin, Yvonna Lincoln, and Harry Torrance for their very helpful comments and suggestions on earlier versions of this chapter.

2. This definition was taken from *The American Heritage Dictionary of the English Language* (1969, p. 412).

3. Denzin and Lincoln (2005, p. 4) similarly refer to QUAL researchers as *bricoleurs,* who creatively use a variety of QUAL methodological practices.

4. We do not want readers to confuse our use of the term "connoisseur of methods" with the well-known "educational connoisseurship" of Eisner (1998), which involves the art of appreciation and is a "qualitative, artistically grounded approach to educational evaluation" (Eisner, 1979, p. 11).

5. We are not implying that causal effects are examined exclusively by QUAN research or causal mechanisms solely by QUAL research. There are many examples of QUAN results being used descriptively and of QUAL results employed in examining the causes of phenomena (e.g., Maxwell, 2004; Yin, 2003).

6. *Design quality* is the degree to which the investigator has utilized the most appropriate procedures for answering the research question(s) and implemented them effectively. It consists of *design suitability, fidelity, within-design consistency, and analytic adequacy* (Tashakkori & Teddlie, 2008).

7. We do not believe in the dichotomy of QUAL and QUAN approaches on the basis of type of questions. Both exploratory and confirmatory questions may be found in QUAN and in QUAL research.

8. Abductive logic is a third type of logic that occurs when a researcher observes a surprising event and then tries to determine what might have caused it (e.g., Erzberger & Kelle, 2003; Peirce, 1974). It is the process whereby a hypothesis is generated, so that the surprising event may be explained.

9. Quantitizing and qualitizing refer to techniques that convert a QUAN-only or QUAL-only into a MMR study. Some researchers within the QUAL community (e.g., poststructuralists) are unlikely to utilize these techniques.

10. Critical realism (Maxwell & Mittapalli, 2010) has recently been proposed as another framework for the use of mixed methods, but its inclusion is beyond the scope of this chapter.

11. In his critique of the metaphysical paradigm, Morgan (2007, p. 68) acknowledged the valuable contribution that it had made in shifting discussions from mechanical concerns about methods only to larger philosophical and conceptual issues.

12. These arguments then lead Morgan (2007, p. 68) to an alternative position, which he called the *pragmatic approach* that concentrates on "methodology as an area that connects issues at the abstract level of epistemology and the mechanical level of actual methods." Morgan's approach emphasizes issues such as abduction, intersubjectivity, and transferability that supersede the traditional dichotomies (e.g., induction/deduction).

13. Maxwell and Loomis (2003) presented a systemic perspective on research design in MMR that was *non-typological* in nature: the interactive model of design, which consisted of five components (i.e., purposes, conceptual framework, research questions, methods, validity).

References

Adamson, J. (2004). [Review of the book *Handbook of mixed methods in social & behavioral research*]. *International Journal of Epidemiology, 33*(6), 1414–1415.

Bazeley, P. (2003). Computerized data analysis for mixed methods research. In A. Tashakkori & C. Teddlie (Eds.), *Handbook of mixed methods in social & behavioral research* (pp. 385–422). Thousand Oaks, CA: Sage.

Bazeley, P. (2009). Integrating data analyses in mixed methods research. *Journal of Mixed Methods Research, 3*(3), 203–207.

Bazeley, P. (2010). Computer assisted integration of mixed methods data sources and analysis. In A. Tashakkori & C. Teddlie (Eds.), *SAGE handbook of mixed methods in social & behavioral research* (2nd ed., pp. 431–467). Thousand Oaks, CA: Sage.

Biesta, G. (2010). Pragmatism and the philosophical foundations of mixed methods research. In A. Tashakkori & C. Teddlie (Eds.), *SAGE handbook of mixed methods in social & behavioral research* (2nd ed., pp. 95–117). Thousand Oaks, CA: Sage.

Bryman, A. (2006). Paradigm peace and the implications for quality. *International Journal of Social Research Methodology Theory and Practice, 9*(2), 111–126.

Campbell, D. T., & Fiske, D. W. (1959). Convergent and discriminant validation by the multitrait-multimethod matrix. *Psychological Bulletin, 56*, 81–105.

Caracelli, V. J., & Greene, J. C. (1993). Data analysis strategies for mixed-method evaluation designs. *Educational Evaluation and Policy Analysis, 15*(2), 195–207.

Christ, T. W. (2009). Designing, teaching, and evaluating two complementary mixed methods research courses. *Journal of Mixed Methods Research, 3*(4), 292–325.

Christ, T. W. (2010). Teaching mixed methods and action research: Pedagogical, practical, and evaluative considerations. In A. Tashakkori & C. Teddlie (Eds.), *SAGE handbook of mixed methods in social & behavioral research* (2nd ed., pp. 643–676). Thousand Oaks, CA: Sage.

Creswell, J. W. (2009). Mapping the field of mixed methods research. *Journal of Mixed Methods Research, 3*(2), 95–108.

Creswell, J. W. (2010). Mapping the developing landscape of mixed methods research. In A. Tashakkori & C. Teddlie (Eds.), *SAGE handbook of mixed methods in social & behavioral research* (2nd ed., pp. 45–68). Thousand Oaks, CA: Sage.

Creswell, J. W., & Plano Clark, V. L. (2007). *Designing and conducting mixed methods research.* Thousand Oaks, CA: Sage.

Creswell, J., Shope, R., Plano-Clark, V., & Green, D. (2006). How interpretive qualitative research extends mixed methods research. *Research in the Schools, 13*(1), 1–11.

Creswell, J., Tashakkori, A., Jensen, K., & Shapley, K. (2003). Teaching mixed methods research: Practice, dilemmas and challenges. In A. Tashakkori & C. Teddlie (Eds.), *Handbook of mixed methods in social & behavioral research* (pp. 619–638). Thousand Oaks, CA: Sage.

Day, C., Sammons, P., & Qu, Q. (2008). Combining qualitative and quantitative methodologies in research on teachers' lives, work, and effectiveness: From integration to synergy. *Educational Researcher, 37*(6), 330–342.

Denscombe, M. (2008). Communities of practice: A research paradigm for the mixed methods approach. *Journal of Mixed Methods Research, 2,* 270–283.

Denzin, N. K. (1978). *The research act: A theoretical introduction to sociological method* (2nd ed.). New York: McGraw-Hill.

Denzin, N. K. (2008). The new paradigm dialogs and qualitative inquiry. *International Journal of Qualitative Studies in Education, 21,* 315–325.

Denzin, N. K., & Lincoln, Y. S. (2005). Introduction: The discipline and practice of qualitative research. In N. K. Denzin & Y. S. Lincoln (Eds.), *The SAGE handbook of qualitative research* (3rd ed., pp. 1–32). Thousand Oaks, CA: Sage.

Eisner, E. W. (1979). The use of qualitative forms of evaluation for improving educational practice. *Educational Evaluation and Policy Analysis, 1*(6), 11–19.

Eisner, E. W. (1998). *The enlightened eye: Qualitative inquiry and the enhancement of educational practice.* Upper Saddle River, NJ: Merrill.

Erzberger, C., & Kelle, U. (2003). Making inferences in mixed methods: The rules of integration. In A. Tashakkori & C. Teddlie (Eds.), *Handbook of mixed methods in social & behavioral research* (pp. 457–490). Thousand Oaks, CA: Sage.

Freshwater, D. (2007). Reading mixed methods research: Contexts for criticism. *Journal of Mixed Methods Research, 1*(2), 134–146.

Greene, J. C. (2007). *Mixing methods in social inquiry.* San Francisco: Jossey-Bass.

Greene, J. C. (2008). Is mixed methods social inquiry a distinctive methodology? *Journal of Mixed Methods Research, 2*(1), 7–22.

Greene, J. C., & Caracelli, V. J. (2003). Making paradigmatic sense of mixed-method practice. In A. Tashakkori & C. Teddlie (Eds.), *Handbook of mixed methods in social & behavioral research* (pp. 91–110). Thousand Oaks, CA: Sage.

Greene, J. C., Caracelli, V. J., & Graham, W. F. (1989). Toward a conceptual framework for mixed-method evaluation designs. *Educational Evaluation and Policy Analysis, 11,* 255–274.

Greene, J. C., & Hall, J. (2010). Dialectics and pragmatism: Being of consequence. In A. Tashakkori & C. Teddlie (Eds.), *SAGE handbook of mixed methods in social & behavioral research* (2nd ed., pp. 119–143). Thousand Oaks, CA: Sage.

Guba, E. G. (1990). Carrying on the dialog. In E. G. Guba (Ed.), *The paradigm dialog* (pp. 368–378). Thousand Oaks, CA: Sage.

Guba, E. G., & Lincoln, Y. S. (1994). Competing paradigms in qualitative research. In N. K. Denzin & Y. S. Lincoln (Eds.), *Handbook of qualitative research* (pp. 105–117). Thousand Oaks, CA: Sage.

Guba, E. G., & Lincoln, Y. S. (2005). Paradigmatic controversies, contradictions, and emerging confluences. In N. K. Denzin & Y. S. Lincoln (Eds.), *The SAGE handbook of qualitative research* (3rd ed., pp. 191–215). Thousand Oaks, CA: Sage.

Hammersley, M. (1996). The relationship between qualitative and quantitative research: Paradigm loyalty versus methodological eclecticism. In J. T. E. Richardson (Ed.), *Handbook of qualitative research methods for psychology and the social sciences* (pp. 159–174). Leicester, UK: BPS Books.

Hesse-Biber, S. (2010). Feminist approaches to mixed methods research: Linking theory and praxis. In A. Tashakkori & C. Teddlie (Eds.), *SAGE handbook of mixed methods in social & behavioral research* (2nd ed., pp. 169–192). Thousand Oaks, CA: Sage.

Howe, K. R. (1988). Against the quantitative-qualitative incompatibility thesis or dogmas die hard. *Educational Researcher, 17,* 10–16.

Howe, K. R. (2004). A critique of experimentalism. *Qualitative Inquiry, 10*(1), 42–61.

Ivankova, N. V., Creswell, J. W., & Stick, S. (2006). Using mixed methods sequential explanatory design: From theory to practice. *Field Methods, 18*(1), 3–20.

Johnson, R. B. (2009). Comments on Howe: Toward a more inclusive "Scientific Research in Education." *Educational Researcher, 38,* 449–457.

Johnson, R. B., & Gray, R. (2010). A history of philosophical and theoretical issues for mixed methods research. In A. Tashakkori & C. Teddlie (Eds.), *SAGE handbook of mixed methods in social & behavioral research* (2nd ed., pp. 69–94). Thousand Oaks, CA: Sage.

Johnson, R. B., & Onwuegbuzie, A. (2004). Mixed methods research: A research paradigm whose time has come. *Educational Researcher, 33*(7), 14–26.

Johnson, R. B., Onwuegbuzie, A. J., & Turner, L. A. (2007). Toward a definition of mixed methods research. *Journal of Mixed Methods Research, 1*(2), 112–133.

Krathwohl, D. R. (2004). *Methods of educational and social science research: An integrated approach* (2nd ed.). Long Grove, IL: Waveland Press.

Kuhn, T. S. (1962). *The structure of scientific revolutions.* Chicago: University of Chicago Press.

Leech, N. L. (2010). Interviews with the early developers of mixed methods research. In A. Tashakkori & C. Teddlie (Eds.), *SAGE handbook of mixed methods in social & behavioral research* (2nd ed., pp. 253–272). Thousand Oaks, CA: Sage.

Leech, N. L., & Onwuegbuzie, A. J. (2009). A typology of mixed methods research designs. *Quality and Quantity, 43,* 265–275.

Li, S., Marquart, J. M., & Zercher, C. (2000). Conceptual issues and analytic strategies in mixed-method studies of preschool inclusion. *Journal of Early Intervention, 23,* 116–132.

Lincoln, Y. S., & Guba, E. G. (1985). *Naturalistic inquiry.* Beverly Hills, CA: Sage.

Maxcy, S. (2003). Pragmatic threads in mixed methods research in the social sciences: The search for multiple modes of inquiry and the end of the philosophy of formalism. In A. Tashakkori & C. Teddlie (Eds.), *Handbook of mixed methods in social & behavioral research* (pp. 51–90). Thousand Oaks, CA: Sage.

Maxwell, J. A. (2004). Causal explanation, qualitative research, and scientific inquiry in education. *Educational Researcher, 33*(2), 3–11.

Maxwell, J. A., & Loomis, D. (2003). Mixed methods design: An alternative approach. In A. Tashakkori & C. Teddlie (Eds.), *Handbook of mixed methods in social & behavioral research* (pp. 241–272). Thousand Oaks, CA: Sage.

Maxwell, J. A., & Mittapalli, K. (2010). Realism as a stance for mixed method research. In A. Tashakkori & C. Teddlie (Eds.), *SAGE handbook of mixed methods in social & behavioral research* (2nd ed., pp. 145–167). Thousand Oaks, CA: Sage.

Mertens, D. M. (2007). Transformative paradigm: Mixed methods and social justice. *Journal of Mixed Methods Research, (1)*3, 212–225.

Mertens, D. M., Bledsoe, K. L., Sullivan, M., & Wilson, A. (2010). Utilization of mixed methods for transformative purposes. In A. Tashakkori & C. Teddlie (Eds.), *SAGE handbook of mixed methods in social & behavioral research* (2nd ed., pp. 193–214). Thousand Oaks, CA: Sage.

Miles, M. B., & Huberman, M. A. (1984). *Qualitative data analysis: A sourcebook for new methods.* Thousand Oaks, CA: Sage.

Miles, M. B., & Huberman, M. A. (1994). *Qualitative data analysis: An expanded sourcebook.* (2nd ed.). Thousand Oaks, CA: Sage.

Morgan, D. (2007). Paradigms lost and pragmatism regained: Methodological implications of combining qualitative and quantitative methods. *Journal of Mixed Methods Research, (1)*1, 48–76.

Morse, J. M. (1991). Approaches to qualitative-quantitative methodological triangulation. *Nursing Research, 40*(2), 120–123.

Morse, J. M. (2003). Principles of mixed methods and multimethod research design. In A. Tashakkori & C. Teddlie (Eds.), *Handbook of mixed methods in social & behavioral research* (pp. 189–208). Thousand Oaks, CA: Sage.

Mosteller, F., & Boruch, R. (Eds.). (2002). *Evidence matters: Randomized trials in education research.* Washington, DC: Brookings Institution Press.

Nastasi, B. K., Hitchcock, J. H., & Brown, L. (2010). An inclusive framework for conceptualizing mixed methods design typologies: Moving toward fully integrated synergistic research models. In A. Tashakkori & C. Teddlie (Eds.), *SAGE handbook of mixed methods in social & behavioral research* (2nd ed., pp. 305–338). Thousand Oaks, CA: Sage.

Newman, I., Ridenour, C., Newman, C., & DeMarco, G. M. P., Jr. (2003). A typology of research purposes and its relationship to mixed methods research. In A. Tashakkori & C. Teddlie (Eds.), *Handbook of mixed methods in social & behavioral research* (pp. 167–188). Thousand Oaks, CA: Sage.

Onwuegbuzie, A. J. (2003). Effect sizes in qualitative research: A prolegomenon. *Quality & Quantity: International Journal of Methodology, 37,* 393–409.

Onwuegbuzie, A., & Combs, J. (2010). Emergent data analysis techniques in mixed methods research: A synthesis. In A. Tashakkori & C. Teddlie (Eds.), *SAGE handbook of mixed methods in social & behavioral research* (2nd ed., pp. 397–430). Thousand Oaks, CA: Sage.

Onwuegbuzie, A. J., Johnson, R. B., & Collins, K. M. T. (2007). Conducting mixed analysis: A general typology. *International Journal of Multiple Research Approaches, 1*(1), 4–17.

Onwuegbuzie, A. J., & Teddlie, C. (2003). A framework for analyzing data in mixed methods research. In A. Tashakkori & C. Teddlie (Eds.), *Handbook of mixed methods in social & behavioral research* (pp. 351–384). Thousand Oaks, CA: Sage.

Patton, M. Q. (1980). *Qualitative evaluation methods.* Thousand Oaks, CA: Sage.

Patton, M. Q. (1990). *Qualitative research and evaluation methods* (2nd ed.). Thousand Oaks, CA: Sage.

Patton, M. Q. (2002). *Qualitative research and evaluation methods* (3rd ed.). Thousand Oaks, CA: Sage.

Peirce, C. S. (1974). *Collected papers* (C. Hartshore, P. Weiss, & A. Burks, Eds.). Cambridge, MA: Harvard University Press.

Reichardt, C. S., & Cook, T. D. (1979). Beyond qualitative *versus* quantitative methods. In T. D. Cook & C. S. Reichardt (Eds.), *Qualitative and quantitative methods in program evaluation* (pp. 7–32). Thousand Oaks CA: Sage.

Ridenour, C. S., & Newman, I. (2008). *Mixed methods research: Exploring the interactive continuum.* Carbondale: Southern Illinois University Press.

Rossman, G., & Wilson, B. (1985). Numbers and words: Combining quantitative and qualitative methods in a single large scale evaluation study. *Evaluation Review, 9,* 627–643.

Sale, J., Lohfeld, L., & Brazil, K. (2002). Revisiting the qualitative-quantitative debate: Implications for mixed-methods research. *Quality and Quantity, 36,* 43–53.

Sandelowski, M., Voils, C. I., & Knafl, G. (2009). On quantitizing. *Journal of Mixed Methods Research, 3*(3), 208–222.

Schulenberg, J. L. (2007). Analyzing police decision-making: Assessing the application of a mixed-method/mixed-model research design. *International Journal of Social Research Methodology, 10,* 99–119.

Shadish, W., Cook, T., & Campbell, D. (2002). *Experimental and quasi-experimental designs for general causal inference.* Boston: Houghton Mifflin.

Shavelson, R. J., & Towne, L. (Eds.). (2002). *Scientific research in education.* Washington, DC: National Research Council, National Academy Press.

Shulha, L., & Wilson, R. (2003). Collaborative mixed methods research. In A. Tashakkori & C. Teddlie (Eds.), *Handbook of mixed methods in social & behavioral research* (pp. 639–670). Thousand Oaks, CA: Sage.

Smith, J. K., & Heshusius, L. (1986). Closing down the conversation: The end of the quantitative-qualitative debate among educational researchers. *Educational Researcher, 15,* 4–12.

Song, M., Sandelowski, M., & Happ, M. B. (2010). Current practices and emerging trends in conducting mixed methods intervention studies. In A. Tashakkori & C. Teddlie (Eds.), *SAGE handbook of mixed methods in social & behavioral research* (2nd ed., pp. 725–747). Thousand Oaks, CA: Sage.

Tashakkori, A., & Creswell, J. (2008). Envisioning the future stewards of the social-behavioral research enterprise. *Journal of Mixed Methods Research, 2*(4), 291–295.

Tashakkori, A., & Teddlie, C. (1998). *Mixed methodology: Combining the qualitative and quantitative approaches.* Thousand Oaks, CA: Sage.

Tashakkori, A., & Teddlie, C. (Eds.). (2003a). *Handbook of mixed methods in social & behavioral research.* Thousand Oaks, CA: Sage.

Tashakkori, A., & Teddlie, C. (2003b). Issues and dilemmas in teaching research methods courses in social and behavioral sciences: US perspective. *International Journal of Social Research Methodology, 6,* 61–77.

Tashakkori, A., & Teddlie, C. (2003c). The past and future of mixed methods research: From data triangulation to mixed model designs. In A. Tashakkori & C. Teddlie (Eds.), *Handbook of mixed methods in social & behavioral research* (pp. 671–702). Thousand Oaks, CA: Sage.

Tashakkori, A., & Teddlie, C. (2008). Quality of inference in mixed methods research: Calling for an integrative framework. In M. M. Bergman (Ed.), *Advances in mixed methods research: Theories and applications* (pp. 101–119). London: Sage.

Teddlie, C., & Johnson, B. (2009). Methodological thought before the twentieth century. In C. Teddlie & A. Tashakkori (Eds.), *The foundations of mixed methods research: Integrating quantitative and qualitative techniques in the social and behavioral sciences* (pp. 40–61). Thousand Oaks, CA: Sage.

Teddlie, C., & Stringfield, S. (1993). *Schools make a difference: Lessons learned from a 10-year study of school effects.* New York: Teachers College Press.

Teddlie, C., & Tashakkori, A. (2003). Major issues and controversies in the use of mixed methods in the social and behavioral sciences. In A. Tashakkori & C. Teddlie (Eds.), *Handbook of mixed methods in social & behavioral research* (pp. 3–50). Thousand Oaks, CA: Sage.

Teddlie, C., & Tashakkori, A. (2009). *The foundations of mixed methods research: Integrating quantitative and qualitative techniques in the social and behavioral sciences.* Thousand Oaks, CA: Sage.

Teddlie, C., Tashakkori, A., & Johnson, B. (2008). Emergent techniques in the gathering and analysis of mixed methods data. In S. Hesse-Biber & P. Leavy (Eds.), *Handbook of emergent methods in social research* (pp. 389–413). New York: Guilford.

Yanchar, S. C., & Williams, D. D. (2006). Reconsidering the compatibility thesis and eclecticism: Five proposed guidelines for method use. *Educational Researcher, 35*(9), 3–12.

Yin, R. K. (2003). *Case study research: Design and methods* (3rd ed.). Thousand Oaks, CA: Sage.

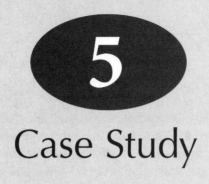

Case Study

Bent Flyvbjerg[1]

> *[C]onduct has its sphere in particular circumstances. That is why some people who do not possess theoretical knowledge are more effective in action (especially if they are experienced) than others who do possess it. For example, suppose that someone knows that light flesh foods are digestible and wholesome, but does not know what kinds are light; he will be less likely to produce health than one who knows that chicken is wholesome.*
>
> —Aristotle

What Is a Case Study?

Definitions of "case study" abound. Some are useful, others not. Merriam-Webster's dictionary (2009) defines a case study straightforwardly as follows:

> *Case Study.* An intensive analysis of an individual unit (as a person or community) stressing developmental factors in relation to environment.

According to this definition, case studies focus on an "individual unit," what Robert Stake (2008, pp. 119–120) calls a "functioning specific" or "bounded system." The decisive factor in defining a study as a case study is the choice of the individual unit of study and the setting of its boundaries, its "casing" to use Charles Ragin's (1992, p. 217) felicitous term. If you choose to do a case study, you are therefore not so much making a methodological choice as a choice of what is to be studied. The individual unit may be studied in a number of ways, for instance qualitatively or quantitatively, analytically or hermeneutically, or by mixed methods. This is not decisive for whether it is a case study or not; the demarcation of the unit's boundaries is. Second, the definition stipulates that case studies are "intensive." Thus, case studies comprise more detail, richness, completeness, and variance—that is, depth—for the unit of study than does cross-unit analysis. Third, case studies stress "developmental factors," meaning that a case typically evolves in time, often as a string of concrete and interrelated events that occur "at such a time, in such a place" and that constitute the case when seen as a whole. Finally, case studies focus on "relation to environment," that is, context. The drawing of boundaries for the individual unit of study decides what gets to count as case and what becomes context to the case.

Against Webster's commonsensical definition of case study, the Penguin *Dictionary of Sociology* (Abercrombie, Hill, & Turner, 1984, p. 34; and verbatim in the 1994 and 2006 editions) has for decades contained the following highly problematic, but unfortunately quite common, definition of case study:

> *Case Study.* The detailed examination of a single example of a class of phe-nomena, a case study cannot provide reliable information about the broader class, but it may be useful in the preliminary stages of an investiga-tion since it provides hypotheses, which may be tested systematically with a larger number of cases.

This definition is indicative of much conventional wisdom about case study research, which, if not directly wrong, is so oversimplified as to be grossly mislead-ing. The definition promotes the mistaken view that the case study is hardly a methodology in its own right, but is best seen as subordinate to investigations of larger samples. Whereas it is correct that the case study is a "detailed examination of a single example," it is wrong that a case study "cannot provide reliable informa-tion about the broader class." It is also correct that a case study *can* be used "in the preliminary stages of an investigation" to generate hypotheses, but it is wrong to see the case study as a pilot method to be used only in preparing the real study's larger surveys, systematic hypotheses testing, and theory building. The Penguin definition juxtaposes case studies with large-sample, statistical research in an unfortunate manner that blocks, instead of brings out, the productive comple-mentarity that exists between the two types of methodology, as we will see below.

John Gerring (2004, p. 342) has correctly pointed out that the many academic attempts to clarify what "case study" means has resulted in a definitional morass, and each time someone attempts to clear up the mess of definitions it just gets worse. If we need a definition of what a case study is, we are therefore better off staying with commonsensical definitions like that from Webster's above than with more loaded academic definitions like that from the Penguin *Dictionary of Sociology.*

The Case Study Paradox

Case studies have been around as long as recorded history and today they account for a large proportion of books and articles in psychology, anthropology, sociology, history, political science, education, economics, management, biology, and medical science. For instance, in recent years roughly half of all articles in the top political science journals have used case studies, according to Alexander George and Andrew Bennett (2005, pp. 4–5). Much of what we know about the empirical world has been produced by case study research, and many of the most treasured classics in each discipline are case studies.

But there is a paradox here. At the same time that case studies are widely used and have produced canonical texts, it may be observed that the case study as a methodology is generally held in low regard, or is simply ignored, within the academy. For example, only 2 of the 30 top-ranked U.S. graduate programs in political science require a dedicated graduate course in case study or qualitative methods, and a full third of these programs do not even offer such a course. In contrast, all of the top 30 programs offer courses in quantitative methods and almost all of them require training in such methods, often several courses (George & Bennett, 2005, p. 10). In identifying this paradox of the case study's wide use and low regard, Gerring (2004, p. 341) rightly remarks that the case study survives in a "curious methodological limbo," and that the reason is that the method is poorly understood.

In what follows, we will try to resolve Gerring's paradox and help case study research gain wider use and acceptance by identifying five misunderstandings about the case study that systematically undermine the credibility and use of the method. The five misunderstandings can be summarized as follows:

Misunderstanding No. 1	General, theoretical knowledge is more valuable than concrete case knowledge.
Misunderstanding No. 2	One cannot generalize on the basis of an individual case; therefore, the case study cannot contribute to scientific development.

(Continued)

(Continued)

Misunderstanding No. 3	The case study is most useful for generating hypotheses; that is, in the first stage of a total research process, while other methods are more suitable for hypotheses testing and theory building.
Misunderstanding No. 4	The case study contains a bias toward verification, that is, a tendency to confirm the researcher's preconceived notions.
Misunderstanding No. 5	It is often difficult to summarize and develop general propositions and theories on the basis of specific case studies.

The five misunderstandings may be said to constitute the conventional view, or orthodoxy, of the case study. We see that theory, reliability, and validity are at issue; in other words, the very status of the case study as a scientific method. In what follows, we will correct the five misunderstandings one by one and thereby clear the ground for a use of case study research in the social sciences that is based on understanding instead of misunderstanding.

Misunderstanding No. 1

> General, theoretical knowledge is more valuable than concrete case knowledge.

In order to understand why the conventional view of case study research is problematic, we need to grasp the role of cases and theory in human learning. Here, two points can be made. First, the case study produces the type of concrete, context-dependent knowledge that research on learning shows to be necessary to allow people to develop from rule-based beginners to virtuoso experts. Second, in the study of human affairs, there appears to exist only context-dependent knowledge, which thus presently rules out the possibility for social science to emulate natural science in developing epistemic theory, that is, theory that is explanatory and predictive. The full argument behind these two points can be found in Flyvbjerg (2001, Chaps. 2–4). For reasons of space, I can only give an outline of the argument here. At the outset, however, we can assert that if the two points are correct, it will have radical consequences for the conventional view of the case study in research and teaching. This view would then be problematic.

Phenomenological studies of human learning indicate that for adults there exists a qualitative leap in their learning process from the rule-governed use of analytical rationality in beginners to the fluid performance of tacit skills in what Pierre Bourdieu (1977) calls virtuosos and Hubert and Stuart Dreyfus (1986), true human experts. Here we may note that most people are experts in a number of everyday social, technical, and intellectual skills like giving a gift, riding a bicycle, or interpreting images on a television screen, while only few reach the level of true expertise for more specialized skills like playing chess, composing a symphony, or flying an airplane.

Common to all experts, however, is that they operate on the basis of intimate knowledge of several thousand concrete cases in their areas of expertise. Context-dependent knowledge and experience are at the very heart of expert activity. Such knowledge and expertise also lie at the center of the case study as a research and teaching method; or to put it more generally yet—as a method of learning. Phenomenological studies of the learning process therefore emphasize the importance of this and similar methods; it is only because of experience with cases that one can at all move from being a beginner to being an expert. If people were exclusively trained in context-independent knowledge and rules, that is, the kind of knowledge that forms the basis of textbooks, they would remain at the beginner's level in the learning process. This is the limitation of analytical rationality; it is inadequate for the best results in the exercise of a profession, as student, researcher, or practitioner.

In teaching situations, well-chosen case studies can help students achieve competence, while context-independent facts and rules will bring students just to the beginner's level. Only few institutions of higher learning have taken the consequence of this. Harvard University is one of them. Here both teaching and research in the professional schools are modeled to a wide extent on the understanding that case knowledge is central to human learning (Christensen & Hansen, 1987; Cragg, 1940).

It is not that rule-based knowledge should be discounted; such knowledge is important in every area and especially to novices. But to make rule-based knowledge the highest goal of learning is topsy-turvy. There is a need for both approaches. The highest levels in the learning process, that is, virtuosity and true expertise, are reached only via a person's own experiences as practitioner of the relevant skills. Therefore, beyond using the case method and other experiential methods for teaching, the best that teachers can do for students in professional programs is to help them achieve real practical experience, for example, via placement arrangements, internships, summer jobs, and the like.

For researchers, the closeness of the case study to real-life situations and its multiple wealth of details are important in two respects. First, it is important for the development of a nuanced view of reality, including the view that human behavior cannot be meaningfully understood as simply the rule-governed acts found at the lowest levels of the learning process, and in much theory. Second, cases are important for researchers' own learning processes in developing the skills needed to do good research. If researchers wish to develop their own skills to a high level, then concrete, context-dependent experience is just as central for them as to professionals learning any other specific skills. Concrete experiences can be achieved via continued proximity to the studied reality and via feedback from those under study. Great distance from the object of study and lack of feedback easily lead to a stultified learning process, which in research can lead to ritual academic blind alleys, where the effect and usefulness of research becomes unclear and untested. As a research method, the case study can be an effective remedy against this tendency.

The second main point in connection with the learning process is that there does not and probably cannot exist predictive theory in social science. Social science has not succeeded in producing general, context-independent theory and has thus in the final instance nothing else to offer than concrete, context-dependent knowledge. And the case study is especially well suited to produce this knowledge. In his later work, Donald Campbell (1975, p. 179) arrives at a similar conclusion. Earlier, he (Campbell and Stanley, 1966, pp. 6–7) had been a fierce critic of the case study, stating that "such studies have such a total absence of control as to be of almost no scientific value." Now he explained that his work had undergone "an extreme oscillation away from my earlier dogmatic disparagement of case studies." Using logic that in many ways resembles that of the phenomenology of human learning, Campbell explains,

> After all, man is, in his ordinary way, a very competent knower, and qualitative common-sense knowing is not replaced by quantitative knowing. . . . This is not to say that such common sense naturalistic observation is objective, dependable, or unbiased. But it is all that we have. It is the only route to knowledge—noisy, fallible, and biased though it be. (1975, pp. 179, 191)

Campbell is not the only example of a researcher who has altered his views about the value of the case study. Hans Eysenck (1976, p. 9), who originally saw the case study as nothing more than a method of producing anecdotes, later realized that "sometimes we simply have to keep our eyes open and look carefully at individual cases—not in the hope of proving anything, but rather in the hope of learning something!" Final proof is hard to come by in social science because of the absence of "hard" theory, whereas learning is certainly possible. More recently, similar views have been expressed by Charles Ragin, Howard Becker, and their colleagues in explorations of what the case study is and can be in social inquiry (Ragin & Becker, 1992).

As for predictive theory, universals, and scientism, so far social science has failed to deliver. In essence, we have only specific cases and context-dependent knowledge in social science. The first of the five misunderstandings about the case study—that general theoretical (context-independent) knowledge is more valuable than concrete (context-dependent) case knowledge—can therefore be revised as follows:

Predictive theories and universals cannot be found in the study of human affairs. Concrete case knowledge is therefore more valuable than the vain search for predictive theories and universals.

Misunderstanding No. 2

One cannot generalize on the basis of an individual case; therefore, the case study cannot contribute to scientific development.

The view that one cannot generalize on the basis of a single case is usually considered to be devastating to the case study as a scientific method. This second misunderstanding about the case study is typical among proponents of the natural science ideal within the social sciences. Yet even researchers who are not normally associated with this ideal may be found to have this viewpoint. According to Anthony Giddens, for example,

Research which is geared primarily to hermeneutic problems may be of generalized importance in so far as it serves to elucidate the nature of agents' knowledgeability, and thereby their reasons for action, across a wide range of action-contexts. Pieces of ethnographic research like . . . say, the traditional small-scale community research of fieldwork anthropology—are not in themselves generalizing studies. But they can easily become so if carried out in some numbers, so that judgements of their typicality can justifiably be made. (1984, p. 328)

It is correct that one can generalize in the ways Giddens describes, and that often this is both appropriate and valuable. But it would be incorrect to assert that this is the only way to work, just as it is incorrect to conclude that one cannot generalize from a single case. It depends upon the case one is speaking of, and how it is chosen. This applies to the natural sciences as well as to the study of human affairs (Platt, 1992; Ragin & Becker, 1992).

For example, Galileo's rejection of Aristotle's law of gravity was not based upon observations "across a wide range," and the observations were not "carried out in some numbers." The rejection consisted primarily of a conceptual experiment and later of a practical one. These experiments, with the benefit of hindsight, are self-evident. Nevertheless, Aristotle's view of gravity dominated scientific inquiry for nearly 2,000 years before it was falsified. In his experimental thinking, Galileo reasoned as follows: If two objects with the same weight are released from the same height at the same time, they will hit the ground simultaneously, having fallen at the same speed. If the two objects are then stuck together into one, this object will have double the weight and will according to the Aristotelian view therefore fall faster than the two individual objects. This conclusion ran counter to common sense, Galileo found. The only way to avoid the contradiction was to eliminate weight as a determinant factor for acceleration in free fall. And that was what Galileo did. Historians of science continue to discuss whether Galileo actually conducted the famous experiment from the leaning tower of Pisa, or whether this experiment is a myth. In any event, Galileo's experimentalism did not involve a large random sample of trials of objects falling from a wide range of randomly selected heights under varying wind conditions, and so on, as would be demanded by the thinking of the early Campbell and Giddens. Rather, it was a matter of a single experiment, that is, a case study, if any experiment was conducted at all. (On the relation between case studies, experiments, and generalization, see Bailey, 1992; Griffin, Botsko, Wahl, & Isaac, 1991; Lee, 1989; Wilson, 1987.) Galileo's view continued to be subjected to doubt, however, and the Aristotelian view was not finally rejected until half a century later, with the invention of the air pump. The air pump made it possible to conduct the ultimate experiment, known by every pupil, whereby a coin or a piece of lead inside a vacuum tube falls with the same speed as a feather. After this experiment, Aristotle's view could be maintained no longer. What is especially worth noting in our discussion, however, is that the matter was settled by an individual case due to the clever choice of the extremes of metal and feather. One might call it a critical case: For if Galileo's thesis held for these materials, it could be expected to be valid for all or a large range of materials. Random and large samples were at no time part of the picture. Most creative scientists simply do not work this way with this type of problem.

Carefully chosen experiments, cases, and experience were also critical to the development of the physics of Isaac Newton, Albert Einstein, and Niels Bohr, just as the case study occupied a central place in the works of Charles Darwin. In social science, too, the strategic choice of case may greatly add to the generalizability of a case study. In their classical study of the "affluent worker," John Goldthorpe, David Lockwood, Frank Beckhofer, and Jennifer Platt (1968–1969) deliberately looked for a case that was as favorable as possible to the thesis that the working class, having reached middle-class status, was dissolving into a society without class identity and related conflict (see also Wieviorka, 1992). If the thesis could be proved false in the favorable case, then it would most likely be false for intermediate cases. Luton, then a prosperous industrial center outside of London with companies known for high wages and social stability—fertile ground for middle-class identity—was selected as a case, and through intensive fieldwork the researchers discovered that even here an autonomous working-class culture prevailed, lending general credence to the thesis of the persistence of class identity. Below we will discuss more systematically this type of strategic sampling.

As regards the relationship between case studies, large samples, and discoveries, William Beveridge (1951; here quoted from Kuper & Kuper, 1985) observed immediately prior to the breakthrough of the quantitative revolution in the social sciences, "[M]ore discoveries have arisen from intense observation [of individual cases] than from statistics applied to large groups." This does not mean that the case study is always appropriate or relevant as a research method, or that large random samples are without value. The choice of method should clearly depend on the problem under study and its circumstances.

Finally, it should be mentioned that formal generalization, be it on the basis of large samples or single cases, is considerably overrated as the main source of scientific progress. Economist Mark Blaug (1980)—a self-declared adherent to the hypothetico-deductive model of science—has demonstrated that while economists typically pay lip service to the hypothetico-deductive model and to generalization, they rarely practice what they preach in actual research. More generally, Thomas Kuhn has shown that the most important precondition for science is that researchers possess a wide range of practical skills for carrying out scientific work. Generalization is just one of these. In Germanic languages, the term "science" (*Wissenschaft*) means literally "to gain knowledge." And formal generalization is only one of many ways by which people gain and accumulate knowledge. That knowledge cannot be formally generalized does not mean that it cannot enter into the collective process of knowledge accumulation in a given field or in a society. Knowledge may be transferable even where it is not formally generalizable. A purely descriptive, phenomenological case study without any attempt to generalize can certainly be of value in this process and has often helped cut a path toward scientific innovation. This is not to criticize attempts at formal generalization, for such attempts are essential and effective means of scientific development. It is only to emphasize the limitations, which follows when formal generalization becomes the only legitimate method of scientific inquiry.

The balanced view of the role of the case study in attempting to generalize by testing hypotheses has been formulated by Harry Eckstein:

> *[C]omparative and case studies are alternative means to the end of testing theories, choices between which must be largely governed by arbitrary or practical, rather than logical, considerations* ... [I]t is impossible to take seriously the position that case study is suspect because problem-prone and comparative study deserving of benefit of doubt because problem-free. (1975, pp. 116, 131, emphasis in original; see also Barzelay, 1993)

Eckstein here uses the term "theory" in its "hard" sense, that is, comprising explanation and prediction. This makes Eckstein's dismissal of the view that case studies cannot be used for testing theories or for generalization stronger than my own view, which is here restricted to the testing of "theory" in the "soft" sense, that is, testing propositions or hypotheses. Eckstein shows that if predictive theories would exist in social science, then the case study could be used to test these theories just as well as other methods.

More recently, George and Bennett (2005) have demonstrated the strong links between case studies and theory development, especially through the study of deviant cases, and John Walton (1992, p. 129) has similarly observed that "case studies are likely to produce the best theory." Already, Eckstein noted, however, the striking lack of genuine theories within his own field, political science, but apparently failed to see why this is so:

> Aiming at the disciplined application of theories to cases forces one to state theories more rigorously than might otherwise be done—provided that the application is truly "disciplined," i.e., designed to show that valid theory compels a particular case interpretation and rules out others. As already stated, this, unfortunately, is rare (if it occurs at all) in political study. One reason is the lack of compelling theories. (1975, pp. 103–104)

The case study is ideal for generalizing using the type of test that Karl Popper called "falsification," which in social science forms part of critical reflexivity. Falsification is one of the most rigorous tests to which a scientific proposition can be subjected: If just one observation does not fit with the proposition, it is considered not valid generally and must therefore be either revised or rejected.

Popper himself used the now famous example of "All swans are white," and proposed that just one observation of a single black swan, that is, one deviant case, would falsify this proposition and in this way have general significance and stimulate further investigations and theory building. The case study is well suited for identifying "black swans" because of its in-depth approach: What appears to be "white" often turns out on closer examination to be "black." Deviant cases and the falsifications they entail are main sources of theory development, because they point to the development of new concepts, variables, and causal mechanisms, necessary in order to account for the deviant case and other cases like it.

We will return to falsification in discussing the fourth misunderstanding of the case study below. For the present, however, we can correct the second misunderstanding—that one cannot generalize on the basis of a single case and that the case study cannot contribute to scientific development—so that it now reads:

One can often generalize on the basis of a single case, and the case study may be central to scientific development via generalization as supplement or alternative to other methods. But formal generalization is overvalued as a source of scientific development, whereas "the force of example" and transferability are underestimated.

Misunderstanding No. 3

The case study is most useful for generating hypotheses, while other methods are more suitable for hypotheses testing and theory building.

The third misunderstanding about the case study is that the case method is claimed to be most useful for generating hypotheses in the first steps of a total research process, while hypothesis-testing and theory-building is best carried out by other methods later in the process, as stipulated by the Penguin definition of case study at the beginning of this chapter. This misunderstanding derives from the previous misunderstanding that one cannot generalize on the basis of individual cases. And since this misunderstanding has been revised as above, we can now correct the third misunderstanding as follows:

The case study is useful for both generating and testing of hypotheses but is not limited to these research activities alone.

Eckstein—contravening the conventional wisdom in this area—goes so far as to argue that case studies are better for testing hypotheses than for producing them. Case studies, Eckstein (1975, p. 80) asserts, "are valuable at all stages of the theory-building process, but most valuable at that stage of theory-building where least value is generally attached to them: the stage at which candidate theories are tested." George and Bennett (2005, pp. 6–9) later confirmed and expanded Eckstein's position, when they found that case studies are especially well suited for theory development because they tackle the following tasks in the research process better than other methods:

- Process tracing that links causes and outcomes (see Box 5.1)
- Detailed exploration of hypothesized causal mechanisms
- Development and testing of historical explanations
- Understanding the sensitivity of concepts to context
- Formation of new hypotheses and new questions to study, sparked by deviant cases

Even rational choice theorists have begun to use case study methods to test their theories and hypotheses, which, if anything, should help deflate the decades-old antagonism between quants and qualts over case study research (Bates, Greif, Levi, Rosenthal, & Weingast, 1998; Flyvbjerg, 2006).

Box 5.1   Falsifying Nobel Prize Theories Through Process Tracing

Some years ago, the editor of *Harvard Business Review* contacted me and asked for a comment on an article he was printing by Princeton psychologist Daniel Kahneman. The editor was puzzled by the fact that Kahneman's Nobel Prize–winning theories on decision making under uncertainty explained failure in executive decisions in terms of inherent optimism (Lovallo & Kahneman, 2003), whereas my group and I explained similar phenomena in terms of strategic misrepresentation, that is, lying as part of principal-agent behavior (Flyvbjerg, Holm, & Buhl, 2002). Who was right, the editor asked? Optimism is unintentional self-deception, whereas lying is intentional deception of others. The question therefore boiled down to whether deception, which caused failure—that much we agreed upon—was intentional or not. The statistical methods that both Kahneman and I had relied upon in our studies of deception could not answer this question. It was now necessary to process trace all the way into people's heads in order to understand whether intention was present or not. Through a number of case studies and interviews, my group and I established that deception is in fact often intentional, especially for very large and expensive decisions taken under political and organizational pressure. We thus falsified optimism as a global explanation of executive failure and developed a new and more nuanced theory that combines optimism and strategic misrepresentation in accounting for failure (Flyvbjerg, 2007).

Testing of hypotheses relates directly to the question of "generalizability," and this in turn relates to the question of case selection. Here, generalizability of case studies can be increased by the strategic selection of cases (for more on the selection of cases, see Ragin, 1992; Rosch, 1978). When the objective is to achieve the greatest possible amount of information on a given problem or phenomenon, a representative case or a random sample may not be the most appropriate strategy. This is because the typical or average case is often not the richest in information. Atypical or extreme cases often reveal more information because they activate more actors and more basic mechanisms in the situation studied. In addition, from both an understanding-oriented and an action-oriented perspective, it is often more important to clarify the deeper causes behind a given problem and its consequences than to describe the symptoms of the problem and how frequently they occur. Random samples emphasizing representativeness will seldom be able to produce this kind of insight; it is more appropriate to select some few cases chosen for their validity.

Table 5.1 summarizes various forms of sampling. The *extreme,* or *deviant, case* can be well suited for getting a point across in an especially dramatic way, which often occurs for well-known case studies such as Sigmund Freud's "Wolf-Man" and Michel Foucault's "Panopticon." The deviant case is also particularly well suited for theory development, because it helps researchers understand the limits of existing theories and to develop the new concepts, variables, and theories that will be able to account for what were previously considered outliers.

In contrast, a *critical case* can be defined as having strategic importance in relation to the general problem. The above-mentioned strategic selection of lead and feather for the test of whether different objects fall with equal velocity is an example of critical case selection. This particular selection of materials provided the possibility to formulate a type of generalization that is characteristic of critical cases, a generalization of the sort, "If it is valid for this case, it is

Table 5.1 Strategies for the Selection of Samples and Cases

Type of Selection	Purpose
A. Random selection	To avoid systematic biases in the sample. The sample's size is decisive for generalization.
1. Random sample	To achieve a representative sample that allows for generalization for the entire population.
2. Stratified sample	To generalize for specially selected subgroups within the population.
B. Information-oriented selection	To maximize the utility of information from small samples and single cases. Cases are selected on the basis of expectations about their information content.
1. Extreme/deviant cases	To obtain information on unusual cases, which can be especially problematic or especially good in a more closely defined sense. To understand the limits of existing theories and to develop new concepts, variables, and theories that are able to account for deviant cases.
2. Maximum variation cases	To obtain information about the significance of various circumstances for case process and outcome; e.g., three to four cases that are very different on one dimension: size, form of organization, location, budget, etc.
3. Critical cases	To achieve information that permits logical deductions of the type, "If this is (not) valid for this case, then it applies to all (no) cases."
4. Paradigmatic cases	To develop a metaphor or establish a school for the domain that the case concerns.

valid for all (or many) cases." In its negative form, the generalization would be, "If it is not valid for this case, then it is not valid for any (or only few) cases" (see also Box 5.2).

Box 5.2   Critical Case for Brain Damage

An occupational medicine clinic wanted to investigate whether people working with organic solvents suffered brain damage. Instead of choosing a representative sample among all those enterprises in the clinic's area that used organic solvents, the clinic strategically located a single workplace where all safety regulations on cleanliness, air quality, and the like, had been fulfilled. This model enterprise became a critical case: If brain damage related to organic solvents could be found at this particular facility, then it was likely that the same problem would exist at other enterprises that were less careful with safety regulations for organic solvents. Via this type of strategic choice, one can save both time and money in researching a given problem, and one may generalize in the following manner from a critical case: "If it is valid for this case, it is valid for all (or many) cases." In its negative form, the generalization would be, "If it is not valid for this case, then it is not valid for any (or only few) cases." In this instance, the occupational medicine clinic found brain damage related to organic solvents in the model enterprise and concluded that the problem needed to be dealt with in all enterprises in its jurisdiction.

How does one identify critical cases? This question is more difficult to answer than the question of what constitutes a critical case. Locating a critical case requires experience, and no universal methodological principles exist by which one can with certainty identify a critical case. The only general advice that can be given is that when looking for critical cases, it is a good idea to look for either "most likely" or "least likely" cases, that is, cases that are likely to either clearly confirm or irrefutably falsify propositions and hypotheses. A model example of a "least likely" case is Robert Michels's (1962) classic study of oligarchy in organizations. By choosing a horizontally structured grassroots organization with strong democratic ideals—that is, a type of organization with an especially low probability of being oligarchic—Michels could test the universality of the oligarchy thesis, that is, "If this organization is oligarchic, so are most others." A corresponding model example of a "most likely" case is W. F. Whyte's (1943) study of a Boston slum neighborhood, which according to existing theory should have exhibited social disorganization, but in fact showed quite the opposite (see also the articles on Whyte's study in the April 1992 issue of the *Journal of Contemporary Ethnography*).

Cases of the "most likely" type are especially well suited to falsification of propositions, while "least likely" cases are most appropriate for tests of verification. It should be remarked that a most likely case for one proposition is the least likely for its negation. For example, Whyte's slum neighborhood could be seen as a least likely case for a hypothesis concerning the universality of social organization. Hence, the identification of a case as most or least likely is linked to the design of the study, as well as to the specific properties of the actual case.

A final strategy for the selection of cases is choice of the *paradigmatic case.* Thomas Kuhn has shown that the basic skills, or background practices, of natural scientists are organized in terms of "exemplars," the role of which can be studied by historians of science. Similarly, scholars like Clifford Geertz and Michel Foucault have often organized their research around specific cultural paradigms: A paradigm for Geertz lay for instance in the "deep play" of the Balinese cockfight, while for Foucault, European prisons and the "Panopticon" are examples. Both instances are examples of paradigmatic cases, that is, cases that highlight more general characteristics of the societies in question. Kuhn has shown that scientific paradigms cannot be expressed as rules or theories. There exists no predictive theory for how predictive theory comes about. A scientific activity is acknowledged or rejected as good science by how close it is to one or more exemplars, that is, practical prototypes of good scientific work. A paradigmatic case of how scientists do science is precisely such a prototype. It operates as a reference point and may function as a focus for the founding of schools of thought.

As with the critical case, we may ask, "How does one identify a paradigmatic case?" How does one determine whether a given case has metaphorical and prototypical value? These questions are even more difficult to answer than for the critical case, precisely because the paradigmatic case transcends any sort of rule-based criteria. No standard exists for the paradigmatic case because it sets the standard. Hubert and Stuart Dreyfus see paradigmatic cases and case studies as central to human learning. In an interview with Hubert Dreyfus (author's files), I therefore asked what constitutes a paradigmatic case and how it can be identified. Dreyfus replied,

Heidegger says, you recognize a paradigm case because it shines, but I'm afraid that is not much help. You just have to be intuitive. We all can tell what is a better or worse case—of a Cézanne painting, for instance. But I can't think there could be any rules for deciding what makes Cézanne a paradigmatic modern painter. . . . [I]t is a big problem in a democratic society where people are supposed to justify what their intuitions are. In fact, nobody really can justify what their intuition is. So you have to make up reasons, but it won't be the real reasons.

One may agree with Dreyfus that intuition is central to identifying paradigmatic cases, but one may disagree it is a problem to have to justify one's intuitions. Ethnomethodological studies of scientific practice have demonstrated that all variety of such practice relies on taken-for-granted procedures that feel largely intuitive. However, those intuitive decisions are accountable, in the sense of being sensible to other practitioners or often explicable if not immediately sensible. That would frequently seem to be the case with the selection of paradigmatic cases. We may select such a case on the basis of taken-for-granted, intuitive procedures but are often called upon to account for that selection. That account must be sensible to other members of the scholarly communities of which we are part. This may even be argued to be a general characteristic of scholarship, scientific or otherwise, and not unique to the selection of paradigmatic social scientific case studies. For instance, it is usually insufficient to justify an application for research funds by stating that one's intuition says that a particular research should be carried out. A research council ideally operates as society's test of whether the researcher can account, in collectively acceptable ways, for his or her intuitive choice, even though intuition may be the real, or most important, reason why the researcher wants to execute the project.

It is not possible consistently, or even frequently, to determine in advance whether or not a given case—Geertz's cockfights in Bali, for instance—is paradigmatic. Besides the strategic choice of case, the execution of the case study will certainly play a role, as will the reactions to the study by the research community, the group studied, and, possibly, a broader public. The value of the case study will depend on the validity claims that researchers can place on their study, and the status these claims obtain in dialogue with other validity claims in the discourse to which the study is a contribution. Like other good craftspeople, all that researchers can do is use their experience and intuition to assess whether they believe a given case is interesting in a paradigmatic context, and whether they can provide collectively acceptable reasons for the choice of case.

Concerning considerations of strategy in the choice of cases, it should also be mentioned that the various strategies of selection are not necessarily mutually exclusive. For example, a case can be simultaneously extreme, critical, and paradigmatic. The interpretation of such a case can provide a unique wealth of information, because one obtains various perspectives on and conclusions about the case according to whether it is viewed and interpreted as one or another type of case. Finally, a case that the researcher initially thought was one type may turn out to be another, upon closer study (see Box 5.3).

Box 5.3   From Critical Case to Extreme Case, Unwittingly

When I was planning a case study of rationality and power in urban policy and planning in Aalborg, Denmark, reported in Flyvbjerg (1998a), I tried to design the study as a "most likely" critical case in the following manner: If rationality in urban policy and planning were weak in the face of power in Aalborg, then, most likely, they would be weak anywhere, at least in Denmark, because in Aalborg the rational paradigm of policy and planning stood stronger than anywhere else. Eventually, I realized that this logic was flawed, because my research of local relations of power showed that one of the most influential "faces of power" in Aalborg, the Chamber of Industry and Commerce, was substantially stronger than its equivalents elsewhere. This had not been clear at the outset because much less research existed on local power relations than research on local planning. Therefore, instead of a critical case, unwittingly I ended up with an extreme case in the sense that both rationality and power were unusually strong in Aalborg. My study thus became one of what happens when strong rationality meets strong power in the arena of urban policy and planning. But this selection of Aalborg as an extreme case happened to me; I did not deliberately choose it. It was a frustrating experience, especially during those several months after I realized I did not have a critical case until it became clear that all was not lost because I had something else. As a case researcher charting new terrain, one must be prepared for such incidents, I believe.

Misunderstanding No. 4

> The case study contains a bias toward verification, that is, a tendency to confirm the researcher's preconceived notions.

The fourth of the five misunderstandings about case study research is that the method maintains a bias toward verification, understood as a tendency to confirm the researcher's preconceived notions, so that the study therefore becomes of doubtful scientific value. Jared Diamond (1996, p. 6), for example, holds this view. He observes that the case study suffers from what he calls a "crippling drawback," because it does not apply "scientific methods," which Diamond understands as methods useful for "curbing one's tendencies to stamp one's pre-existing interpretations on data as they accumulate."

Francis Bacon (1853, p. xlvi) saw this bias toward verification not simply as a phenomenon related to the case study in particular, but as a fundamental human characteristic. Bacon expressed it like this:

> The human understanding from its peculiar nature, easily supposes a greater degree of order and equality in things than it really finds. When any proposition has been laid down, the human understanding forces every-thing else to add fresh support and confirmation. It is the peculiar and perpetual error of the human understanding to be more moved and excited by affirmatives than negatives.

Bacon certainly touches upon a fundamental problem here, a problem that all researchers must deal with in some way. Charles Darwin (Barlow, 1958, p. 123), in his autobiography, describes the method he developed in order to avoid the bias toward verification:

> I had . . . during many years followed a golden rule, namely, that whenever a published fact, a new observation or thought came across me, which was opposed to my general results, to make a memorandum of it without fail and at once; for I had found by experience that such facts and thoughts were far more apt to escape from the memory than favorable ones. Owing to this habit, very few objections were raised against my views, which I had not at least noticed and attempted to answer.

The bias toward verification is general, but the alleged deficiency of the case study and other qualitative methods is that they ostensibly allow more room for the researcher's subjective and arbitrary judgment than other methods: They are often seen as less rigorous than are quantitative, hypothetico-deductive methods. Even if such criticism is useful, because it sensitizes us to an important issue, experienced case researchers cannot help but see the critique as demonstrating a lack of knowledge of what is involved in case study research. Donald Campbell and others have shown that the critique is fallacious, because the case study has its own rigor, different to be sure, but no less strict than the rigor of quantitative methods. The advantage of the case study is that it can "close in" on real-life situations and test views directly in relation to phenomena as they unfold in practice.

According to Campbell, Ragin, Geertz, Wieviorka, Flyvbjerg, and others, researchers who have conducted intensive, in-depth case studies, typically report that their preconceived views, assumptions, concepts, and hypotheses were wrong and that the case material has compelled them to revise their hypotheses on essential points. The case study forces upon the researcher the type of falsifications described above. Ragin (1992, p. 225) calls this a "special feature of small-N research," and goes on to explain that criticizing single case studies for being inferior to multiple case studies is misguided, since even single case studies "are multiple in most research efforts because ideas and evidence may be linked in many different ways."

Geertz (1995, p. 119) says about the fieldwork involved in most in-depth case studies that "The Field" itself is a "powerful disciplinary force: assertive, demanding, even coercive." Like any such force, it can be underestimated, but it cannot be evaded. "It is too insistent for that," says Geertz. That he is speaking of a general phenomenon can be seen by simply examining case studies, such as those by Eckstein (1975), Campbell (1975), and Wieviorka (1992). Campbell (1975, pp. 181–182) discusses the causes of this phenomenon in the following passage:

> In a case study done by an alert social scientist who has thorough local acquaintance, the theory he uses to explain the focal difference also generates prediction or expectations on dozens of other aspects of the culture, and he does not retain the theory unless most of these are also confirmed. . . . Experiences of social scientists confirm this. Even in a single qualitative case study, the conscientious social scientist often finds no explanation that seems satisfactory. Such an outcome would be impossible if the caricature of the single case study . . . were correct—there would instead be a surfeit of subjectively compelling explanations.

According to the experiences cited above, it is falsification and not verification that characterizes the case study. Moreover, the question of subjectivism and bias toward verification applies to all methods, not just to the case study and other qualitative methods. For example, the element of arbitrary subjectivism will be significant in the choice of categories and variables for a quantitative or structural investigation, such as a structured questionnaire to be used across a large sample of cases. And the probability is high that (1) this subjectivism survives without being thoroughly corrected during the study, and (2) that it may affect the results, quite simply because the quantitative/structural researcher does not get as close to those under study as does the case study researcher and therefore is less likely to be corrected by the study objects "talking back." George and

Bennett (2005, p. 20) describe this all-important feature of case study research like this:

> When a case study researcher asks a participant "were you thinking X when you did Y," and gets the answer, "No, I was thinking Z," then if the researcher had not thought of Z as a causally relevant variable, she may have a new variable demanding to be heard.

Statistical methods may identify deviant cases that can lead to new hypotheses, but in isolation these methods lack any clear means of actually identifying new hypotheses. This is true of all studies that use existing databases or that collect survey data based on questionnaires with predefined standard questions. Unless statistical researchers do their own archival work, interviews, or face-to-face surveys with open-ended questions—like case study researchers—they have no means of identifying left-out variables (George & Bennett, 2005, p. 21). According to Ragin (1992, p. 225; see also Ragin, 1987, pp. 164–171):

> This feature explains why small-N qualitative research is most often at the forefront of theoretical development. When N's are large, there are few opportunities for revising a casing [that is, the delimitation of a case]. At the start of the analysis, cases are decomposed into variables, and almost the entire dialogue of ideas and evidence occurs through variables. One implication of this discussion is that to the extent that large-N research can be sensitized to the diversity and potential heterogeneity of the cases included in an analysis, large-N research may play a more important part in the advancement of social science theory.

Here, too, this difference between large samples and single cases can be understood in terms of the phenomenology for human learning discussed above. If one thus assumes that the goal of the researcher's work is to understand and learn about the phenomena being studied, then research is simply a form of learning. If one assumes that research, like other learning processes, can be described by the phenomenology for human learning, it then becomes clear that the most advanced form of understanding is achieved when researchers place themselves within the context being studied. Only in this way can researchers understand the viewpoints and the behavior that characterizes social actors. Relevant to this point, Giddens states that valid descriptions of social activities presume that researchers possess those skills necessary to participate in the activities described:

> I have accepted that it is right to say that the condition of generating descriptions of social activity is being able in principle to participate in it. It involves "mutual knowledge," shared by observer and participants whose action constitutes and reconstitutes the social world. (1982, p. 15)

From this point of view, the proximity to reality, which the case study entails, and the learning process that it generates for the researcher will often constitute a prerequisite for advanced understanding. In this context, one begins to understand Beveridge's conclusion that there are more discoveries stemming from intense observation of individual cases than from statistics applied to large groups. With the point of departure in the learning process, we understand why the researcher who conducts a case study often ends up by casting off preconceived notions and theories. Such activity is quite simply a central element in learning and in the achievement of new insight. More simple forms of understanding must yield to more complex ones as one moves from beginner to expert.

On this basis, the fourth misunderstanding—that the case study supposedly contains a bias toward verification, understood as a tendency to confirm the researcher's preconceived ideas—is revised as follows:

> *The case study contains no greater bias toward verification of the researcher's preconceived notions than other methods of inquiry. On the contrary, experience indicates that the case study contains a greater bias toward falsification of preconceived notions than toward verification.*

Misunderstanding No. 5

> It is often difficult to summarize and develop general propositions and theories on the basis of specific case studies.

Case studies often contain a substantial element of narrative and one can get into a terrible quicksand today talking about the matter of narrative in social science (for a good overview of narrative inquiry, see Chapter 2 in volume 3 by Susan

Chase; Todd Landman, in press). After certain strands of discourse theory have defined any text as narrative and everything as text, it seems that narrative is everything. But if something is everything, maybe it is nothing, and we are back to square one. It is difficult to avoid the subject of narrative completely, however, when considering the case study and qualitative research. In my own work, when I think about narrative, I do not think of discourse theory but of Miles Davis, the jazz icon. When asked how he kept writing classics through a four-decades-long career, he answered, "I first write a beginning, then a middle, and finally the ending." Narrative suggests questions about plot, that is, a sequence of events and how they are related, and Davis set out the naked minimum. Obviously, plots and narratives may be hatched in many ways. But if you write the kind of classic narrative that Davis talks about, with a beginning, a middle, and an end, you typically first try to get the attention of the reader, often by means of a hook, that is, a particularly captivating event or problematic that leads into the main story. You then present the issues and who are involved, including their relationships. Gradually, you reel in the reader to a point of no return, from where the main character— who in a case study need not be a person but could be, say, a community, a program, or a company—has no choice but to deal with the issues at hand, and in this sense is tested. At this stage, typically, there is conflict and the conflict escalates. Finally, harmony is restored by the conflict being resolved, or at least explained, as may be the appropriate achievement in a social science narrative.

To Alasdair MacIntyre (1984, pp. 214, 216), the human being is a "story-telling animal," and the notion of a history is as fundamental a human notion as the notion of an action. Other observers have noted that narrative seems to exist in all human societies, modern and ancient, and that it is perhaps our most fundamental form for making sense of experience (Mattingly, 1991, p. 237; Novak, 1975, p. 175; see also Abbott, 1992; Arendt, 1958; Bal, 1997; Carr, 1986; Fehn, Hoestery, & Tatar, 1992; Rasmussen, 1995; Ricoeur, 1984). Narrative thus seems not only to be the creation of the storyteller, but seems also to be an expression of innate relationships in the human mind, which we use to make sense of the world by constructing it as narrative.

The human propensity for narrative involves a danger, however, of what has been called the narrative fallacy. The fallacy consists of a human inclination to simplify data and information through overinterpretation and through a preference for compact stories over complex data sets (Taleb, 2010, p. 63). It is easier to remember and make decisions on the basis of "meaningful" stories than to remember strings of "meaningless" data. Thus, we read meaning into data and make up stories, even where this is unwarranted. As a case in point, consider the inspirational accounts of how the Internet led to a "new economy" where productivity had been disconnected from share prices; or the fairy tale that increasing real estate prices are enough to sustain economic growth in a nation. Such stories are easy to understand and act on—for citizens, policy makers, and scholars—but they are fallacies and as such they are treacherous. In social science, the means to avoid the narrative fallacy is no different from the means to avoid other error: the usual systematic checks for validity and reliability in how data are collected and used.

Dense narratives based on thick description will provide some protection against the narrative fallacy. Such narratives typically approach the complexities and contradictions of real life. Accordingly, they may be difficult or impossible to summarize into neat formulas, general propositions, and theories (Benhabib, 1990; Mitchell & Charmaz, 1996; Roth, 1989; Rouse, 1990; White, 1990). This tends to be seen by critics of the case study as a drawback. To the case study researcher, however, a particularly "thick" and hard-to-summarize narrative is not a problem. Rather, it is often a sign that the study has uncovered a particularly rich problematic. The question, therefore, is whether the summarizing and generalization, which the critics see as an ideal, is always desirable. Friedrich Nietzsche (1974, p. 335, para. 373) is clear in his answer to this question. "Above all," he says about doing science, "one should not wish to divest existence of its *rich ambiguity*" (emphasis in original).

Lisa Peattie (2001, p. 260) explicitly warns against summarizing dense case studies: "It is simply that the very value of the case study, the contextual and interpenetrating nature of forces, is lost when one tries to sum up in large and mutually exclusive concepts." The dense case study, according to Peattie, is more useful for the practitioner and more interesting for social theory than either factual "findings" or the high-level generalizations of theory.

The opposite of summing up and "closing" a case study is to keep it open. Two strategies work particularly well in ensuring openness. First, when writing up their case studies, authors may demur from the role of omniscient narrator and summarizer. Instead, they may choose to tell the story in its diversity, allowing the story to unfold from the many-sided, complex, and sometimes-conflicting stories that the actors in the case have told researchers. Second, authors of case studies may avoid linking their study with the theories of any one academic specialization. Instead, they may choose to relate the case to broader philosophical positions that cut across specializations. In this way, authors leave scope for readers of different backgrounds to make different interpretations and draw diverse conclusions regarding the question of what the case is a case of. The goal is not to make the case study be all things to all people. The goal is to allow the study to be different things to different people. Here it is useful to describe the case with so many facets—like life itself—that different readers may be attracted, or repelled, by different things in the case. Readers are not pointed down any one theoretical path or given the impression that truth might lie at the end of such a path. Readers will have to discover their own path and truth inside the case. Thus, in addition to the interpretations of case actors and case narrators, readers are invited to decide the meaning of the case and to interrogate actors' and narrators' interpretations in order to answer that categorical question of any case study: "What is this case a case of?"

Case stories written like this can neither be briefly recounted nor summarized in a few main results. The case story is itself the result. It is a "virtual reality," so to speak. For the reader willing to enter this reality and explore it inside and out, the payback is meant to be a sensitivity to the issues at hand that cannot be obtained from theory. Students can safely be let loose in this kind of reality, which provides a useful training ground with insights into real-life practices that academic teaching often does not provide.

If we return again briefly to the phenomenology for human learning, we may understand why summarizing case studies is not always useful and may sometimes be counterproductive. Knowledge at the beginner's level consists precisely in the reduced formulas that characterize theories, while true expertise is based on intimate experience with thousands of individual cases and on the ability to discriminate between situations, with all their nuances of difference, without distilling them into formulas or standard cases. The problem is analogous to the inability of heuristic, computer-based expert systems to approach the level of virtuoso human experts, even when the systems are compared with the experts who have conceived the rules upon which these systems operate. This is because the experts do not use rules but operate on the basis of detailed case experience. This is *real* expertise. The rules for expert systems are formulated only because the systems require it; rules are characteristic of expert *systems,* but not of real human *experts.*

In the same way, one might say that the rule formulation that takes place when researchers summarize their work into theories is characteristic of the culture of research, of researchers, and of theoretical activity, but such rules are not necessarily part of the studied reality constituted by Bourdieu's (1977, pp. 8, 15) "virtuoso social actors." Something essential may be lost by this summarizing—namely the possibility to understand virtuoso social acting, which, as Bourdieu has shown, cannot be distilled into theoretical formulas—and it is precisely their fear of losing this "something" that makes case researchers cautious about summarizing their studies. Case researchers thus tend to be skeptical about erasing phenomenological detail in favor of conceptual closure.

Ludwig Wittgenstein shared this skepticism. According to Gasking and Jackson, Wittgenstein used the following metaphor when he described his use of the case study approach in philosophy:

> In teaching you philosophy I'm like a guide showing you how to find your way round London. I have to take you through the city from north to south, from east to west, from Euston to the embankment and from Piccadilly to the Marble Arch. After I have taken you many journeys through the city, in all sorts of directions, we shall have passed through any given street a number of times—each time traversing the street as part of a different journey. At the end of this you will know London; you will be able to find your way about like a born Londoner. Of course, a good guide will take you through the more important streets more often than he takes you down side streets; a bad guide will do the opposite. In philosophy I'm a rather bad guide. (1967, p. 51)

This approach implies exploring phenomena firsthand instead of reading maps of them. Actual practices are studied before their rules, and one is not satisfied by learning only about those parts of practices that are open to public scrutiny; what Erving Goffman (1963) calls the "backstage" of social phenomena must be investigated, too, like the side streets that Wittgenstein talks about.

With respect to intervention in social and political affairs, Andrew Abbott (1992, p. 79) has rightly observed that a social science expressed in terms of typical case narratives would provide "far better access for policy intervention than the present social science of variables." Alasdair MacIntyre (1984, p. 216) similarly says, "I can only answer the question 'What am I to do?' if I can answer the prior question 'Of what story or stories do I find myself a part?'" In a similar vein, Cheryl Mattingly (1991, p. 237) points out that narratives not only give meaningful form to experiences we have already lived through, they also provide us a forward glance, helping us to anticipate situations even before we encounter them, allowing us to envision alternative futures. Narrative inquiries do not—indeed, cannot—start from explicit theoretical assumptions. Instead, they begin with an interest in a particular phenomenon that is best understood narratively. Narrative inquiries then develop descriptions and interpretations of the phenomenon from the perspective of participants, researchers, and others.

William Labov and Joshua Waletzky (1966, pp. 37–39) write that when a good narrative is over, "it should be unthinkable for a bystander to say, 'So what?'" Every good narrator is continually warding off this question. A narrative that lacks a moral that can be independently and briefly stated, is not necessarily pointless. And a narrative is not successful just because it allows a brief moral. A successful narrative does not allow the question to be raised at all. The narrative has already supplied the answer before the question is asked. The narrative itself is the answer (Nehamas, 1985, pp. 163–164).

A reformulation of the fifth misunderstanding, which states that it is often difficult to summarize specific case studies into general propositions and theories, thus reads as follows:

> *It is correct that summarizing case studies is often difficult, especially as concerns case process. It is less correct as regards case outcomes. The problems in summarizing case studies, however, are due more often to the properties of the reality studied than to the case study as a research method. Often it is not desirable to summarize and generalize case studies. Good studies should be read as narratives in their entirety.*

It must again be emphasized that despite the difficulty or undesirability in summarizing certain case studies, the case study as such can certainly contribute to the cumulative development of knowledge, for example, in using the principles to test propositions described above under the second and third misunderstandings.

Current Trends in Case Study Research

This chapter began by pointing out a paradox in case study research, namely, that even as case studies are widely used in social science and have produced many of the classic texts here, it may be observed that the case study as a methodology is generally held in low regard, or is simply ignored, within large and dominant parts of the academy. This state of affairs has proved remarkably long-lived.

However, as pointed out by George and Bennett (2005, pp. 4–5), recently a certain loosening of positions has taken place. A more collaborative approach is gaining ground, where scholars begin to see that different methodological approaches have different strengths and weaknesses and are essentially complementary. The old and often antagonistic division between quants and qualts is losing ground as a new generation of scholars trained in both quantitative and qualitative methods is emerging. For these scholars, research is problem-driven and not methodology-driven, meaning that those methods are employed that for a given problematic best help answer the research questions at hand. More often than not, a combination of qualitative and quantitative methods will do the task best. Finally, some of the most ambitious claims regarding how the quantitative revolution would make possible a social science on a par with natural science in its ability to explain and predict have been scaled back, making room for the emergence of a more realistic and balanced attitude to what social science can and cannot do. The chapters in this volume on mixed methods, by John Creswell (Chapter 3), and Charles Teddlie and Abbas Tashakkori (Chapter 4), are good examples of this loosening of positions and more balanced attitude.

If the moment of the quantitative revolution in social science is called positivistic, as is often the case, then today we are in a postpositivist and possibly postparadigmatic moment (Schram, 2006). My own efforts at developing a social science suited for this particular moment have been concentrated on what I call "phronetic social science," named after the ancient Greek term for practical wisdom, or common sense, *phronesis* (Flyvbjerg, 2001; Schram & Caterino, 2006). And this is what the new social science is: commonsensical. It is common sense to give up wars that cannot be won, like the methods war over quantitative versus qualitative methods, or the science wars, which pit social science against natural science. It is also common sense to finally acknowledge that case studies and statistical methods are not conflicting but complementary (see Box 5.4).

Box 5.4   Complementarity in Action:
From Case Studies to Statistical Methods, and Back

My current research on megaprojects was originally sparked by events at the Channel tunnel, which links the United Kingdom and France, and the Danish Great Belt tunnel, linking Scandinavia with continental Europe. These are the two longest underwater rail tunnels in Europe, each costing several billion dollars. Soon after construction of the Channel tunnel began, costs started escalating, and at the opening of the tunnel, in 1994, costs had doubled in real terms leaving the project in serious financial trouble. But maybe the British and French had just been unlucky? Perhaps the Danes would do better on the Great Belt tunnel? Not so. Here the cost overrun was larger still, at 120% in real terms, and the tunnel proved financially nonviable even before it opened to traffic in 1997, several years behind schedule. I did a case study of these two hugely expensive projects in order to document and understand the apparent incompetence in their planning and execution (Flyvbjerg, Bruzelius, & Rothengatter, 2003). The study raised the inevitable question of whether the Channel and Great Belt tunnels were outliers regarding cost overrun and viability or whether such extreme lack of ability to build on budget was common for large-scale infrastructure projects. Searching the world's libraries and asking colleagues, I found that no study existed that answered these questions in a statistically valid manner. I therefore decided to do such a study and my group and I now turned from case studies to statistical methods. To our amazement, our studies showed, with a very high level of statistical significance, that the Channel and Great Belt projects were not outliers, they were normal; nine out of ten projects have cost overrun. Even more surprisingly, when we extended our data back in time we found that for the 70 years for which we were able to find data there had been no improvement in performance regarding getting cost estimates right and staying on budget. The same apparent error of cost underestimation and overrun was being repeated decade after decade. We now began debating among ourselves whether an error that is being repeated over and over by highly trained professionals is really an error, or whether something else was going on. To answer this question, we went back to case studies and process tracing (see Box 5.1). We found that cost overrun and lack of viability were not best explained by simple error but by something more sinister and Machiavellian, namely strategic misrepresentation of costs and benefits by promoters during appraisal in order to get projects funded and built. From my initial case-based curiosity with the outcomes at the Channel and Great Belt tunnels—and by going from case studies to statistical methods and back—my group and I had uncovered a deep-rooted culture of deception in the planning and management of large-scale infrastructure projects (Flyvbjerg, 2007). As a recent spin-off from this research, my group and I are now investigating whether the success of one in ten projects in staying on budget—documented in our statistical studies—may be replicated or is due to luck. Here, again, we are back to case study research, now studying success as a deviant case.

The complementarity between case studies and statistical methods may be summarized as in Table 5.2. The main strength of the case study is depth—detail, richness, completeness, and within-case variance—whereas for statistical methods it is breadth. If you want to understand a phenomenon in any degree of thoroughness—say, child neglect in the family or cost overrun in urban regeneration—what causes it, how to prevent it, and so on, you need to do case

Table 5.2   Complementarity of Case Studies and Statistical Methods

	Case Studies	Statistical Methods
Strengths	• Depth	• Breadth
	• High conceptual validity	• Understanding how widespread a phenomenon is across a population
	• Understanding of context and process	• Measures of correlation for populations of cases
	• Understanding of what causes a phenomenon, linking causes and outcomes	• Establishment of probabilistic levels of confidence
	• Fostering new hypotheses and new research questions	
Weaknesses	• Selection bias may overstate or understate relationships	• Conceptual stretching, by grouping together dissimilar cases to get larger samples
	• Weak understanding of occurrence in population of phenomena under study	• Weak understanding of context, process, and causal mechanisms
	• Statistical significance often unknown or unclear	• Correlation does not imply causation
		• Weak mechanisms for fostering new hypotheses

studies. If you want to understand how widespread the phenomenon is, how it correlates with other phenomena and varies across different populations, and at what level of statistical significance, then you have to do statistical studies. If you want to understand both, which is advisable if you would like to speak with weight about the phenomenon at hand, then you need to do both case studies and statistical analyses. The complementarity of the two methods is that simple, and that beautiful.

When you think about it, it is amazing that the separation and antagonism between qualitative and quantitative methods often seen in the literature, and in university departments, have lasted as long as they have. This is what happens when tribalism and power, instead of reason, rules the halls of academia. As such, it is testimony to the fact that academics, too, are all too human, and not testimony to much else. The separation is not a logical consequence of what graduates and scholars need to know in order to do their studies and do them well; quite the opposite. Good social science is opposed to an either/or and stands for a both/and on the question of qualitative versus quantitative methods. The *International Encyclopedia of the Social & Behavioral Sciences* (Smelser & Baltes, 2001, p. 1513) is certainly right when it points out that the case study and statistical methods can "achieve far more scientific progress together than either could alone."

This being said, it should nevertheless be added that the balance between case studies and statistical methods is still biased in favor of the latter in social science, so much so that it puts case studies at a disadvantage within most disciplines. For the time being, it is therefore necessary to continue to work on clarifying methodologically the case study and its relations to other social science methods in order to dispel the methodological limbo in which the method has existed for too long. This chapter is intended as such clarification.

Note

1. The author wishes to thank Maria Flyvbjerg Bo for her help in improving an earlier version of this chapter.

References

Abbott, A. (1992). What do cases do? Some notes on activity in sociological analysis. In C. C. Ragin & H. S. Becker (Eds.), *What is a case? Exploring the foundations of social inquiry* (pp. 53–82). Cambridge, UK: Cambridge University Press.

Abercrombie, N., Hill, S., & Turner, B. S. (1984). *Dictionary of sociology.* Harmondsworth, UK: Penguin.

Arendt, H. (1958). *The human condition.* Chicago: University of Chicago Press.

Bacon, F. (1853). Novum organum. In *Physical and metaphysical works of Lord Bacon* (Vol. 1). London: H. G. Bohn.

Bailey, M. T. (1992). Do physicists use case studies? Thoughts on public administration research. *Public Administration Review, 52*(1), 47–54.

Bal, M. (1997). *Narratology: Introduction to the theory of narrative* (2nd ed.). Toronto: University of Toronto Press.

Barlow, N. (Ed.). (1958). *The autobiography of Charles Darwin.* New York: Norton.

Barzelay, M. (1993). The single case study as intellectually ambitious inquiry. *Journal of Public Administration Research and Theory, 3*(3), 305–318.

Bates, R., Greif, A., Levi, M., Rosenthal, J.-L., & Weingast, B. (1998). *Analytic narratives.* Princeton, NJ: Princeton University Press.

Benhabib, S. (1990). Hannah Arendt and the redemptive power of narrative. *Social Research, 57*(1), 167–196.

Beveridge, W. I. B. (1951). *The art of scientific investigation.* London: Heinemann.

Blaug, M. (1980). *The methodology of economics: Or how economists explain.* Cambridge, UK: Cambridge University Press.

Bourdieu, P. (1977). *Outline of a theory of practice.* Cambridge, UK: Cambridge University Press.

Campbell, D. T. (1975). Degrees of freedom and the case study. *Comparative Political Studies, 8*(1), 178–191.

Campbell, D. T., & Stanley, J. C. (1966). *Experimental and quasi-experimental designs for research.* Chicago: Rand McNally.

Carr, D. (1986). *Time, narrative, and history.* Bloomington: Indiana University Press.

Christensen, C. R., & Hansen, A. J. (Eds.). (1987). *Teaching and the case method.* Boston, MA: Harvard Business School Press.

Cragg, C. I. (1940). Because wisdom can't be told (Harvard Business School Reprint 451–005). *Harvard Alumni Bulletin,* 1–6.

Diamond, J. (1996, November 14). The roots of radicalism. *The New York Review of Books,* pp. 4–6.

Dreyfus, H., & Dreyfus, S. (with Athanasiou, T.). (1986). *Mind over machine: The power of human intuition and expertise in the era of the computer.* New York: Free Press.

Eckstein, H. (1975). Case study and theory in political science. In F. J. Greenstein & N. W. Polsby (Eds.), *Handbook of political science* (Vol. 7, pp. 79–137). Reading, MA: Addison-Wesley.

Eysenck, H. J. (1976). Introduction. In H. J. Eysenck (Ed.), *Case studies in behaviour therapy.* London: Routledge and Kegan Paul.

Fehn, A., Hoestery, I., & Tatar, M. (Eds.). (1992). *Neverending stories: Toward a critical narratology.* Princeton, NJ: Princeton University Press.

Flyvbjerg, B. (2001). *Making social science matter: Why social inquiry fails and how it can succeed again.* Cambridge, UK: Cambridge University Press.

Flyvbjerg, B. (2006). A perestroikan straw man answers back: David Laitin and phronetic political science. In S. F. Schram & B. Caterino (Eds.), *Making political science matter: Debating knowledge, research, and method* (pp. 56–85). New York and London: New York University Press.

Flyvbjerg, B. (2007). Policy and planning for large-infrastructure projects: Problems, causes, cures. *Environment and Planning B: Planning and Design, 34*(4), 578–597.

Flyvbjerg, B., Bruzelius, N., & Rothengatter, W. (2003). *Megaprojects and risk: An anatomy of ambition.* Cambridge, UK: Cambridge University Press.

Flyvbjerg, B., Holm, M. K. S., & Buhl, S. L. (2002). Underestimating costs in public works projects: Error or lie? *Journal of the American Planning Association, 68*(3), 279–295.

Gasking, D. A. T., & Jackson, A. C. (1967). Wittgenstein as a teacher. In K. T. Fann (Ed.), *Ludwig Wittgenstein: The man and his philosophy* (pp. 49–55). Sussex, UK: Harvester Press.

Geertz, C. (1995). *After the fact: Two countries, four decades, one anthropologist.* Cambridge, MA: Harvard University Press.

George, A. L., & Bennett, A. (2005). *Case studies and theory development in the social sciences.* Cambridge, MA: MIT Press.

Gerring, J. (2004). What is a case study and what is it good for? *The American Political Science Review, 98*(2), 341–354.

Giddens, A. (1982). *Profiles and critiques in social theory.* Berkeley: University of California Press.

Giddens, A. (1984). *The constitution of society: Outline of the theory of structuration.* Cambridge, UK: Polity Press.

Goffman, E. (1963). *Behavior in public places: Notes on the social organization of gatherings.* New York: Free Press.

Goldthorpe, J. H., Lockwood, D., Beckhofer, F., & Platt, J. (1968–1969). *The affluent worker* (Vols. 1–3). Cambridge, UK: Cambridge University Press.

Griffin, L. J., Botsko, C., Wahl, A.-M., & Isaac, L. W. (1991). Theoretical generality, case particularity: Qualitative comparative analysis of trade union growth and decline. In C. C. Ragin (Ed.), *Issues and alternatives in comparative social research* (pp. 110–136). Leiden, The Netherlands: E. J. Brill.

Kuper, A., & Kuper, J. (Eds.). (1985). *The social science encyclopedia.* London: Routledge and Kegan Paul.

Labov, W., & Waletzky, J. (1966). Narrative analysis: Oral versions of personal experience. In *Essays on the verbal and visual arts: Proceedings of the American Ethnological Society* (pp. 12–44). Seattle, WA: American Ethnological Society.

Landman, T. (in press). Phronesis and narrative analysis. In B. Flyvbjerg, T. Landman, & S. Schram (Eds.), *Real social science: Applied phronesis.* Cambridge, UK: Cambridge University Press.

Lee, A. S. (1989). Case studies as natural experiments. *Human Relations, 42*(2), 117–137.

Lovallo, D., & Kahneman, D. (2003, July). Delusions of success: How optimism undermines executives' decisions. *Harvard Business Review,* 56–63.

MacIntyre, A. (1984). *After virtue: A study in moral theory* (2nd ed.). Notre Dame, IN: University of Notre Dame Press.

Mattingly, C. (1991). Narrative reflections on practical actions: Two learning experiments in reflective storytelling. In D. A. Schön (Ed.), *The reflective turn: Case studies in and on educational practice* (pp. 235–257). New York: Teachers College Press.

Merriam-Webster Online Dictionary. (2009). *Case study.* Available at http://www.merriam-webster.com/dictionary/case%20study

Michels, R. (1962). *Political parties: A study of the oligarchical tendencies of modern democracy.* New York: Collier.

Mitchell, R. G., Jr., & Charmaz, K. (1996). Telling tales, writing stories: Postmodernist visions and realist images in ethnographic writing. *Journal of Contemporary Ethnography, 25*(1), 144–166.

Nehamas, A. (1985). *Nietzsche: Life as literature.* Cambridge, MA: Harvard University Press.

Nietzsche, F. (1974). *The gay science.* New York: Vintage.

Novak, M. (1975). "Story" and experience. In J. B. Wiggins (Ed.), *Religion as story.* Lanham, MD: University Press of America.

Peattie, L. (2001). Theorizing planning: Some comments on Flyvbjerg's *Rationality and power. International Planning Studies, 6*(3), 257–262.

Platt, F. (1992). "Case study" in American methodological thought. *Current Sociology, 40*(1), 17–48.

Ragin, C. C. (1987). *The comparative method: Moving beyond qualitative and quantitative strategies.* Berkeley: University of California Press.

Ragin, C. C. (1992). "Casing" and the process of social inquiry. In C. C. Ragin & H. S. Becker (Eds.), *What is a case? Exploring the foundations of social inquiry* (pp. 217–226). Cambridge, UK: Cambridge University Press.

Ragin, C. C., & Becker, H. S. (Eds.). (1992). *What is a case? Exploring the foundations of social inquiry.* Cambridge, UK: Cambridge University Press.

Rasmussen, D. (1995). Rethinking subjectivity: Narrative identity and the self. *Philosophy and Social Criticism, 21*(5–6), 159–172.

Ricoeur, P. (1984). *Time and narrative.* Chicago: University of Chicago Press.

Rosch, E. (1978). Principles of categorization. In E. Rosch & B. B. Lloyd (Eds.), *Cognition and categorization* (pp. 27–48). Hillsdale, NJ: Lawrence Erlbaum.

Roth, P. A. (1989). How narratives explain. *Social Research, 56*(2), 449–478.

Rouse, J. (1990). The narrative reconstruction of science. *Inquiry, 33*(2), 179–196.

Schram, S. F. (2006). Return to politics: Perestroika, phronesis, and post-paradigmatic political science. In S. F. Schram & B. Caterino (Eds.), *Making political science matter: Debating knowledge, research, and method* (pp. 17–32). New York and London: New York University Press.

Schram, S. F., & Caterino, B. (Eds.). (2006). *Making political science matter: Debating knowledge, research, and method.* New York and London: New York University Press.

Smelser, N. J., & Baltes, P. B. (Eds.). (2001). *International encyclopedia of social & behavioral sciences.* Elmsford, NY: Pergamon.

Stake, R. E. (2008). Qualitative case studies. In N. K. Denzin & Y. S. Lincoln (Eds.), *Strategies of qualitative inquiry* (3rd ed., pp. 119–150). Thousand Oaks, CA: Sage.

Taleb, N. N. (2007). *The black swan: The impact of the highly improbable* (2nd ed.). London and New York: Penguin.

Walton, J. (1992). Making the theoretical case. In C. C. Ragin & H. S. Becker (Eds.), *What is a case? Exploring the foundations of social inquiry* (pp. 121–137). Cambridge, UK: Cambridge University Press.

White, H. (1990). *The content of the form: Narrative discourse and historical representation.* Baltimore: Johns Hopkins University Press.

Whyte, W. F. (1943). *Street corner society: The social structure of an Italian slum.* Chicago: University of Chicago Press.

Wieviorka, M. (1992). Case studies: History or sociology? In C. C. Ragin & H. S. Becker (Eds.), *What is a case? Exploring the foundations of social inquiry* (pp. 159–172). Cambridge, UK: Cambridge University Press.

Wilson, B. (1987). Single-case experimental designs in neuro-psychological rehabilitation. *Journal of Clinical and Experimental Neuropsychology, 9*(5), 527–544.

6

Performance Ethnography

Judith Hamera

My students did not understand "Sandy Sem's"[1] response to her parents' traumatic negotiation of their survivor status, and the relationship between that status and a class assignment she was given by her teacher. "Sandy's" mother and father were victims and survivors of the Khmer Rouge autohomeo-genocide in Cambodia between 1975 and 1979, and their experiences of these atrocities haunted them in their new lives as refugees in Long Beach, California. As I observe in my analysis of the family's use of Khmer classical dance (Hamera, 2007, pp. 138–171), her parents would not share details of their ordeal, or even much about their lives, and "Sandy" did not press them. Raised in a cultural moment celebrating memoir and self-disclosure; with understandable pride in their own cultures of origin and family traditions; and deeply, if perhaps unreflectively, inheritors to the idea of testimony as both personally and socially redemptive, my class could not easily assimilate her logic, articulated in a field-note of mine that I shared with them:

> "Sandy Sem": We had some project for school, to talk about our culture and our families—like grandmothers and grandfathers and stuff. But you can't ask them [her parents] about that, him [her father] especially because he gets mad and the teacher—right—she's going to believe that. And I'm going to go in, okay, and say: "My family's from Cambodia and everybody's dead from the war or over here somewhere but nobody says," okay? So I just made it up.

How could she just "make it up"? How could she not want to push her parents to "tell the truth"? Don't they, and didn't she, have an obligation to know and share everything about where she came from? How could others learn from what was "just made up," and enabling others to learn was important, right? Why was

I, their professor, who proclaimed commitment to rigorous inquiry, not pushing back at the family to "speak the truth to power"? Isn't that what good critical scholars do?

Try as we might, we couldn't come to a collective understanding of why "Sandy's" response might be useful, or necessary, or "right." What if we translate her situation into space, I asked? Where would she sit? Would she look at her audience? Who is her audience? Does she have one? Where are her parents? Who else is around—and where are they? Desks were moved and space, literal and conceptual, opened up. "Sandy's" position was embodied by, not one, but two students. One was sitting facing the audience, looking down at a blank page in an open notebook. "The ethnographer" stood on one side with her own note-book and "the teacher," holding a grade book, stood on other. Another "Sandy" sat with her back to the first, looking in the opposite direction. From that direction, receding in a diagonal as if toward a vanishing point, were "the parents," silent except for occasional sounds (sighs of exhaustion, sharp intakes of breath as if in pain), their backs to one another, and further still were "the others" and "the ancestors." The "others" and "the ancestors" were moving, sometimes in tight circles around one another, sometimes randomly across the space. They murmured, barely audible.

Here, between the murmurs, the paralinguistic articulations of pain and resignation, the inadequacy of notebooks and grade book: Here was the logic of "Sandy's" response. The "others" and "ancestors" were too far away to hear, the "ethnographer" and "teacher" too removed in other ways to understand. "Sandy's" logic was born of a nuanced reading of context—verbal and even more important, extra-verbal: the circulation of affective energy in her home, in her parents' lives, and in their histories. She had negotiated the collapse of time and space ("here and now," "there and then") in her personal, familial, and cultural pasts, and made a decision that my students could only grasp by engaging and embodying that circulation in a charged environment in the best way they knew how.

They also came to understand her tactical resistance to the teacher's imperative to narrate her family for a "show and tell," however well intended, within a larger politics and commerce of testimony. "Truths," particularly those of the disenfranchised, could and were so easily co-opted by an all-pervasive corporate media culture pedaling disclosure as a commodity: whether simple sensationalism, "ethnic color" as discursive décor, or alibi for an easy sentimental but apolitical empathy. This was a form of what Jon McKenzie (2001b) has so aptly identified as the imperative to "perform or else." In this context, silence and subterfuge were personally prudent and socially productive, useful, even empowering for "Sandy" in ways that demanded respect: a respect generated by a critical performance intervention that was both hers and theirs, one that was, in some important way, shared, however imperfectly and asymmetrically. They understood the simplicity of their own earlier interpretations. Oh, one student observed, *this* is what Victor Turner meant by performance as making, not faking.

Performance Ethnography as a Strategy of Inquiry

This example demonstrates the utility of performance ethnography as pedagogy, but the method is more than a pedagogical technique. In fact, performance ethnography is vitally important as a pedagogical tool for precisely the same reasons it is a potent conceptual and methodological one (see also Alexander, 2006; Denzin, 2003, 2006). It exposes the dynamic interactions between "power, politics, and poetics" (Madison, 2008, p. 392), and challenges researchers to represent these interactions to make meaningful interventions: those that produce new understanding and insist that this understanding generate more just circumstances.[2]

Performance ethnography offers the researcher a vocabulary for exploring the expressive elements of culture, a focus on embodiment as a crucial component of cultural analysis and a tool for representing scholarly engagement, and a critical, interventionist commitment to theory in/as practice. In some cases, performance ethnography takes performance *per se* as an object of study. In others, it uses the idea of performance to tease apart phenomena not normally thought of in these terms. Some performance ethnographers stage their research as a form of interpretation and/or publication, as my class did with "Sandy Sem." Some use performative writing techniques to enact research dynamics on the page. These options are mutually reinforcing, not mutually exclusive, as illustrated by the examples in this discussion, and particularly the case study: D. Soyini Madison's *Water Rites* (2006c).

This chapter offers some of the basic epistemological, historical, and methodological infrastructure of performance ethnography and examines provocative new possibilities. It is inevitably selective and partial. The method itself is suspicious of the putatively "finished," preferring instead the Bakhtinian (1984) notion of the "unfinalizeable": the idea that there can never be a last definitive word, only penultimate ones. In addition to this theoretical commitment, the sheer number of intellectual turns contributing to performance ethnography speaks to its institutional unfinalizability as well as its vitality. This orientation to research is both interdisciplinary and polydisciplinary: interdisciplinary because it relies on and forges connections between a variety of fields—communication and theater studies, for example, or music and folklore. It is polydisciplinary because so many areas claim and contribute to it: anthropology, communication, dance, ethnomusicology, folklore, performance studies, theater studies. A definitive list would include nearly every academic formation in the humanities and qualitative social sciences, and many of these are themselves interdisciplinary. Performance ethnography is inter- and polydisciplinary because performance itself demands it. Plato considered this one of performance's great weaknesses: that it could not enclose a discrete field of knowledge to claim as its own private preserve. Theater and performance artists, on the other hand, appreciate that *poiesis* requires integrating knowledge from multiple areas of expertise (specialized knowledge), the full scope of the senses (embodied knowledge), critique (politically engaged conceptual knowledge), and pragmatic knowledge (know-how).

The institutional situation of performance ethnography is relational—betwixt and between the disciplines—as are its practices; the idea of relationality binds method and metamethodology together. The relationality of performance ethnography also requires teasing out complex exchanges between specific practices and the larger context, which must be construed broadly. It includes the standard "when, where, and how" of a field site, as well as the power and privilege differentials that permeate it, the historical relationships that organize it, and the tropes that emerge to shape what can and cannot be said, enacted, and understood about it. The performance ethnographer explores the interanimating relationships that produce context: precisely the oscillation between "here/now" and "there/then" that so permeated the "Sems'" lives. There is no "now" innocent of history, and no "local" fully exempt from global flows of people, resources, and capital (see, for example, Alexander, 2008).

In keeping with Dwight Conquergood's (2006b) call for rhetorical reflexivity, performance ethnography generally, and my perspective here, are explicitly critical. That is, performance ethnography is inherently committed to what D. Soyini Madison calls "the doing or 'performance' of critical theory" (2005, p. 15) as its strategy of inquiry.[3] First, it assumes congruence, not division, between theory and method. Methodology is infused with theoretical commitments and theory is incarnated through methodology. Madison's emphasis on "doing" critical theory underscores the action-oriented nature of critical theory in practice. "Doing" makes a move and, coupled with "critical," that move is one of activation and activism, of unsettling and challenging conventional meaning and advocating for change (see Denzin, 2003, 2006; Madison, 2008). Framing performance ethnography as the "doing of critical theory" honors the tradition of, and ongoing commitments to, "intellectual rebellion" that define this research: investments in interrogating what often passes for the conventional wisdom

(Madison, 2005, p. 13). "Doing" critical theory means investigating our research sites, our own methods and motives, our tactics of scholarly representation, and the structures of our own privilege. It means repeatedly and explicitly asking, Who benefits? Who decides? Who decides who decides? Does it have to be this way? What are the alternatives? As Jill Dolan (2005), Raymond Williams (1981), and others have observed, there is a utopian element to performance, one shared by performance ethnography's critical project: not proscriptive, not "pie in the sky," but "processual, as an index to the possible, to the 'what if.'" (Dolan, p. 13). The subjunctive dimension of performance enables ethnographers to investigate what is, and imagine, inspire, and initiate what could be: justice, engaged citizenship, generative public discourse, and transformative political *poiesis*.

Methodological Infrastructure

We typically think of infrastructure as the nearly invisible but indispensable support that makes viable communities possible: roads, phone and data networks, utilities. These are basic public goods. When infrastructure crumbles through neglect, or when it is privatized for the profit of the few, possibilities for social exchange diminish. Performance ethnography has intellectual infrastructure: keywords, formative figures, and key questions that also make community possible.[4] Scholars may draw upon some of them or all of them, entering and exiting at different points depending on their research trajectories. In inter- and polydisciplinary practices like performance ethnography, conceptual infrastructure provides a pluralist, contested, yet shared terrain: continually in flux but nevertheless a common intellectual inheritance on which we depend and to which we contribute as we define or refine our own research.

KEYWORDS

Raymond Williams (1983) famously used the idea of "keywords" to examine shifting social, historical, and political values adhering to terms like "culture," "industry," and "democracy." These "historical semantics" (p. 23) expose the mutability and political utility of such words, as well as attempts to arrest their meaning. Performance ethnography has its own set of keywords; "critical," discussed above, is certainly one of them. Boundaries between definitions and ethics blur in performance ethnography; definitions point to necessary ethical clarification and ethics shape definitions. Definitions of keywords enable the researcher to operationalize responsibilities for ethical and rigorous engagement. A complete survey of all important keywords in performance ethnography is beyond the scope of this chapter, but four in particular are essential to understanding the method's conceptual infrastructure and the interpretive criteria that characterize ethical, generative research: performance, ethnography, performativity, and aesthetics.

Performance is a productively elastic term "on the move" (Conquergood, 1995). In *Opening Acts* (Hamera, 1991b, 2006b), I define it as both an event and a heuristic tool that illuminates presentational and representational elements of culture (p. 5). Performance makes and does things: materially, affectively, imaginatively. To use performance as a method of inquiry, the researcher gives focused attention to the denotative, sensory elements of the event: how it looks, sounds, smells, shifts over time. This also includes accounting for the event's affective dynamics: which emotions seem "authorized" and encouraged, which silenced, how they can be expressed and contained, how emotions and behaviors intersect to produce meaning. Performance as a strategy of inquiry also demands that the researcher place her site of inquiry within larger sets of ongoing historical, political, intellectual, and aesthetic conversations. It requires approaching cultural work—both that of the researcher and that of the researched—as imaginative in its most precise sense: as co-created within and between communities, as expressive and meaningful, and as embedded in the specifics of time and place, even as it may create its own unique visions of both.

Performance ethnographers view "performance" expansively by focusing on the expressive dimensions of culture, and then tracing the social, rhetorical force of particular expressions, including those characterizing the research act itself. From this perspective, both live and mediated events are performances. Both theatrical expressions that "key" audiences by signaling acts to be regarded with heightened awareness, and banal, nearly invisible practices of everyday life are performances (Bauman, 1977; Berger & del Negro, 2004; Hamera, 2006b, pp. 12–21; Hamera, 2007). Silence is a performance, as "Sandy Sem" illustrated. Rituals of state power—executions, civil defense drills, deployments of folk practices—and resistance to that power—urban rebellions—are performances (Afary, 2009; Alexander Craft, 2008; Conquergood, 2002a; Davis, 2007). Interpersonal conversations are performances (Hawes, 2006).

Ethnography, "participant observation," meets "performance" on the terrain of expression. Where traditional ethnography asks, "How and why do my research interlocutors express what they do?" performance ethnography takes a more layered and critical approach, examining expression *about* the site as well as *within* it. It demands explicit attention to the politics of representing that expression, not just to conventions of accurately recording and interpreting it. Performance ethnography lifts up the "graph," the always already taken-for-grantedness of writing. As the braided genealogy below demonstrates, this is far more complex than an imagined dichotomy between text and performance. Rather, "performance" reminds "ethnography" that embodiment and the politics of positionality are as central to representing the fieldwork encounter as they are to participating in it. "Performance" makes a claim on ethnography, as do other modifiers like "critical," "feminist," and "indigenous." This claim concerns both the *subject* of inquiry—expressive culture as constitutive of social life—and the *practices* of inquiry on the page, the stage, or both.

Performativity is one way that performance makes and does something. Performative utterances make interventions in the world as they are spoken. Through their repetition, these utterances stabilize the power of words and, by extension, the authorities and conventions undergirding that power. Judith Butler (1993) redeployed J. L. Austin's formulation to describe the apparently stable character of identity. This stability, she argues, does not result from a set of essential, unchanging, innate characteristics. Rather, it is an effect produced through repetition. Performance theorists have used performativity to theorize multiple dimensions of identity, and the material and ideological exigencies that constrain or enable particular kinds of repetitions. Elin Diamond (1996) describes the methodological utility in this move from a theoretical notion of performativity to analysis of a specific enactment: "[a]s soon as performativity comes to rest on *a* performance, questions of embodiment, of social relations, of ideological interpellations, of emotional and political effects, all become discussable" and interruptible (p. 5). Scholars examine and instigate these interruptions as they interrogate the rhetorical force of performatives, along with their roles in forging communal coherence or inserting relational or even intrapersonal instability (see Alexander, 2006; Dolan, 2005; Hamera, 2007; Johnson, 2003; Muñoz, 2006; Pollock, 2006, 2007).

Aesthetics are the criteria and implicit social contracts that shape how performance and performative repetitions are perceived and understood. As the genealogies discussed below demonstrate, performance ethnography's deep roots in the creative arts and criticism mean that aesthetics are a crucial component of its conceptual infrastructure. Aesthetics are never exempt from context. They always require a modifier: "feminist," "Black," "butoh," "White Eurocentric," "queer," "15th-century," and so on.

Commonly reduced to the study of formal properties in the so-called "fine arts," aesthetics are in fact deeply and profoundly communal and political, and by no means only elite matters. The properties and presumptions intrinsic to the production and consumption of culture are expressive currency, binding members of communities together. Politics suffuses aesthetic judgments, including what counts as "beautiful" or "creative," and what institutions are authorized to make and enforce these views. Aesthetics support decision making among our research interlocutors in the field as well as our own on stage, and on the page.

Performance ethnographers do not see aesthetics as the unique property of "the arts." Rather, they are inseparable from lived experience, and the imaginative work of meaning making. The research process itself, whether qualitative or quantitative, is organized by aesthetic conventions. Both physicists and performance ethnographers talk about "beautiful theories," demonstrating that aesthetics are important intellectual criteria, even if what "beautiful" means varies with context. In performance ethnography, it is useful to think of aesthetics as sets of interpretive and expressive strategies to be interrogated, deployed, or resisted. The researcher must be mindful of the history and specific ideological freight each strategy carries. She needs to know the unique conventions, standards of taste, genres, and techniques circulating, however implicitly, within her site. This demands precision and, for this reason, awareness of aesthetics serves as an important interpretive criterion of rigorous performance ethnography. Consider Harris Berger's (1999) study of heavy metal, jazz, and rock musicians in America's so-called "rust belt" cities. He writes,

> Observing that a piece of music is infused with a quality of aggressiveness, for example, is only the starting point of our description of the participant's experience; merely adding contextual and bodily dimensions to the account does not suffice. . . . The righteous rage of an American Christian metal band and the disgusted rage of an English hardcore outfit are not the same . . . (pp. 251–252)

Berger notes the detailed genre distinctions that are deeply meaningful to these musicians, and provides painstaking accounts of their musical syntax. Aesthetics matter deeply here. They frame the communication and perception of communal identity for both musicians and the researcher. Aesthetics drives analysis in this ethnography, and finds expression in extensive thick description of the technical elements in these groups' music, sustained immersion in the field, and multisite comparisons across communities.

Aesthetics also organize how performance ethnographers stage their work. Do they strive for audience empathy with their interlocutors, or for an alienation that activates the audience, turning them into spect-actors.[5] As the analysis of *Water Rites* (Madison, 2006c) below illustrates, careful shaping of research in/as performance is as crucial to its social force as the dynamics, rhythms, and textures of metal, jazz, and rock are to Berger's musicians.

GENEALOGIES

Performance ethnography's strengths and complexities as an orientation to research can be productively examined through select examples from its complex genealogy. In some cases, this means retrospectively reclaiming works that implemented the core commitments and practices of performance ethnography without using a specific disciplinary affiliation. In some cases, it involves recognizing the centripetal pull of performance across multiple disciplines: anthropology, folklore, the oral interpretation of literature, speech communication, and theater, among others. The genealogy below should not be read as strictly linear. It is not a list of who "begat" whom. Anthropologically informed negotiations of performance, ethnography, and aesthetics did not birth oral interpretation and communication scholars' explorations of these same terms. This is a braided genealogy, one in which relationships between keywords and strategies are, and continue to be, in conversation with one another. "From" in the subheadings does not indicate an eventual convergence on a methodological consensus but rather a disciplinary starting point for ongoing conversations.

From Anthropology

Zora Neale Hurston's (1990) *Mules and Men* is one particularly rich example of performance ethnography. In her introduction to the work, Hurston describes Black Southern folk culture that "was fitting me like a tight chemise. I couldn't see for wearing it" (p. 1). She credits the "spy-glass of Anthropology" for giving her the ability to navigate the challenges of participant observation but, in fact, her work stands in contrast to the ocularcentric metaphor with which it begins. Instead, Hurston presents the "telling and the told" (Madison, 1998; Pollock, 1990) through what we now call "orature." As articulated by Ngugi wa Thiong'o (1998, 2007), "orature" describes the interpenetration of speech, writing, music, dance, even the cinematic, so as to resist simplistic dichotomies between text and performance. As a director/choreographer, novelist and playwright as well as an anthropologist, Hurston was keenly attuned to the theatricality of the lore she collected. She focused careful attention on the contexts and exchanges that inspired "breakthroughs into performance" (Hymes, 1981), noting not just the clearly bounded "folk tales" but their elasticity as they stretched to accommodate a wide range of social performances: teasing, joke telling, and "big old lies." Moreover, using literary and dramatic devices from the "fourth wall" to free indirect discourse, she shares the explicit theatricality of her research practice with her readers so they can feel the grains of the voices, the pacing, the overall flow of events. Even her footnotes ventriloquate voices from the field, blurring the positions of researcher/writing and researched/speaking into orature in this most "textual" of devices.[6]

Victor Turner (1982) was also interested in this "both-and" quality of performance ethnography. He described performance itself as a "liminal" experience: betwixt and between consensual reality and fantasy, neither simply here, nor simply there. For Turner, performance is constitutive; in a profound challenge to the antitheatrical bias that has constricted Western epistemology since Plato, Turner asserts that performance makes, not fakes, social life. Working closely with director and performance theorist Richard Schechner (1985), Turner applied the performance paradigm to the ethnographic enterprise. Schechner explicitly positions performance ethnography "between theatre and anthropology." Central to this task was his identification of the shared liminality of the ethnographer and the performer using psychoanalyst D. W. Winnicott's idea of the transitional object. The ethnographer was not a "native" just as a performer was not the character. Yet she was "not-not" the native/character either. This liminality—this threshold status—is intellectually productive; it encourages self-reflexivity with the recognition that identity is not immutable but fluid, social, and contextual. And it opens up conceptual spaces betwixt and between identities for an imaginative, even poetic theorizing of cultural processes.

From Oral Interpretation and Communication

The oral interpretation of literature, rooted in the elocutionary movement, is based on the premise that performance is an embodied hermeneutic tool: a way of "doing" analysis that moves beyond inscription to enactment.[7] Central to this commitment to performance is Wallace Bacon's (1979) "sense of the other," the idea that embodiment in performance constructed through detailed analysis could generate critical insight into multiple dimensions of difference in literary texts. Dwight Conquergood drew from and radicalized oral interpretation to fashion a performance ethnography that demanded "body-to-bodyness" (Olomo/ Jones, 2006, p. 341) beyond the boundaries of the field encounter and the margins on the page.[8] In his classic essay "Rethinking Ethnography," Conquergood (1991/2006b) clearly articulates the importance of a return to the body. His own fieldwork in a Hmong refugee camp (1988), and among Chicago street gangs

(1997), foregrounded the corporeality of culture: its processuality as an ensemble of behaviors, and dances with history and politics. Research methods are not a separate category of experience in this view. They are also enactments. Conquergood made the move from ethnographic inscription to ethnographic enactment, from writing to performing culture. Performance-based research held out the promise of truly "radical research" (2002b). Conquergood (1991/ 2006b) argued for, and skillfully demonstrated, rhetorical reflexivity by asking bracing questions about interrelationships between culture and power, expanding these questions beyond the preserve of "the field" to include genres of academic production. At its most profound, Conquergood's commitment to performance as a tool of knowledge production challenges the scriptocentric academy, and text-based knowledges that often disenfranchise those outside its own economies. He argued for performance-based methods that "revitalize the connection between practical knowledge (knowing how), propositional knowledge (knowing that), and political savvy (knowing who, when, and where)" (Conquergood, 2002b, p. 153). D. Soyini Madison summarizes all of these contributions in her generative recasting of performance ethnography as coperformance:

> Coperformance as dialogical performance means you not only do what subjects do, but you are intellectually and relationally invested in their symbol-making practices as you experience them with a range of yearnings and desires. Coperformance, for Conquergood, . . . is a "doing with" that is a deep commitment. (2005, p. 168)

MORAL MAPS

Conquergood (1982) offered what is, for many, a definitive way to examine the ethical pitfalls of performance ethnography in his essay, "Performing as a Moral Act." The goal of the ethnographer is coperformance, achieved dialogically through the persistent posing of unsettling questions like the "Key Questions" below. These questions; a disciplined grasp and thick description of aesthetics in the field, on the stage, and on the page; self-reflexivity; and the commitment to "doing" critical theory help the researchers avoid four fundamental ethical errors. The *curator's exhibitionism* is an error of aesthetics: confusing a prurient desire to showcase the "exotic" with a rigorous understanding of how expressive behaviors actually work. The "show and tell" impulse "Sandy Sem" subverted with her silence might fall here. The *custodian's rip-off* fails the fundamental relationality of coperformance. Here, field sites and interlocutors are raw materials to be recoded as products of the researcher's putatively autonomous "genius," a form of intellectual piracy. The *enthusiast's infatuation* marks a failure to rigorously "do" critical theory. Where the first two positions see research interlocutors as objects for display or raw materials for self-fashioning and self-promotion, this position absorbs all differences into a romantic celebration of a simple difference from, or similarity to, the self. Irreducible difference is ignored, difficult issues superficially glossed over or excused. The *cynic's cop-out* insists on the unintelligibility of difference and the inability to overcome distances inevitably encountered in ethnographic research. This is an alienated and alienating stand, ultimately impotent, bereft of the utopian sense of performance so crucial to sustained efforts to do critical theory.

Drawing on the anthropological and oral interpretation traditions, performance studies scholars continue to grapple with the ways "performance," "ethnography," "performativity," and "aesthetics" inform one another. They continue to raise questions about how performance works, challenging assumptions that corporeality and textuality are mutually exclusive representational modes in the field or in scholarly inquiry. Dance practices are especially fruitful sites: Limit cases, because they are so often reduced to untranslatable embodiment. In my studies of dancing communities in Los Angeles (Hamera, 2007), I argue that dance is enmeshed in language: in the stories and demonstrations that train the next generation, in the productive imprecision of metaphor that describes how a move looks or feels, in the institutional prose (laws, syllabi, press kits, word of mouth) that enables or circumscribes it. For me, analyzing the ways dance constructs diverse communities means dancing with my interlocutors as much as listening to and writing about them. The commitment to "dance with" as well as "write about" also opens up opportunities for challenging hegemonic assumptions about genres of performance. Ballet and modern dance both carry the imprimatur of elite "high art," at odds with the material circumstances of most of the artists who create it. Training with amateur and professional dancers showed me these techniques' other lives: as homeplaces for a wide range of performers to come together, bound in solidarity and in difference, sometimes briefly, sometimes over decades, by the rigors of their shared rituals.

KEY QUESTIONS

There are no prescriptions for operationalizing performance ethnography. The complexities of each site, each researcher's embodied particularity, each location in place and history demands its own unique negotiations. But this does not mean blind or naïve reinvention of good research practices. A set of key questions for performance ethnographers raised throughout the research process reminds us of our aesthetic, ethical, and intellectual responsibilities. Madison has marked the popularity of performance as a mode of research by wryly observing, "everyone I know and don't know is thinking, speaking, and writing in the language of performance, or trying to" (2006b, p. 243). This plurality of disciplines and discourses enables creative and generative play with epistemological and methodological conventions, but performance ethnography is not a playground without accountability and innocent of history. On the contrary, the productive pliability of performance and its multiple disciplinary locations require the researcher to articulate her own conceptual commitments by answering basic questions about her research design. This is the methodological and ethical equivalent of the site survey: the meticulous accounting for how performance opens up a specific research site in demographic and discursive detail. Like the site survey, these questions orient the researcher, pointing her to ever more nuanced understanding of what it means to "profess performance" from her unique disciplinary or interdisciplinary orientation (Jackson 2004).[9] Answering these questions exposes performance ethnography as relational in yet one more sense: it positions the researcher vis-à-vis other individual methodologists using similar vocabularies.

1. How does performance emerge in my research site? Because the term refers to both events and a heuristic tool, its use in specific contexts of research demands critical reflection and precision. Does it announce itself through its self-conscious theatricality? Is "performance" a term I use to explain expressive force, expressive techniques, both or neither? Do my research interlocutors think of what they are doing as performance, or is this a term I am using to communicate something powerful about their actions to the audiences for my research? What conceptual permissions does "performance" offer me as a researcher? What dangers does it hold? What preconceptions do I bring to the term? Am I assuming performance is inherently creative, derivative, live, resistant, reactionary?

2. Where is my performance located in time and place, and how do these times and places intersect with history, with other places, other institutions? What global matrices construct the "local" in my site? Which historical ones undergird the "here and now"?

3. When I use "performance" and reflect on my own assumptions underlying this use, which scholarly conversations am I participating in, however implicitly? What obligations does participation in these conversations impose? Do I need to understand specific techniques, vocabulary, bibliography? How does my use of "performance" contribute to, challenge, or subvert turns in these conversations?

4. How do I conceptualize the act of research itself as a performance, beyond the simple idea of demonstrating "competent execution": the techno-bureaucratic definition of the term? How have I engaged my interlocutors? As coperformers? As "extras" or props? How do I represent exchanges with my interlocutors, in all of their sensory and social complexities? To what extent am I translating performances, not only in the sense of moving between languages, or between verbal and nonverbal modes of communication, but also between modes of representation, especially corporeality and textual fixity? How do I understand and communicate the entire research endeavor as a set of aesthetic, ethical, political, and rhetorical elements, decisions, and responsibilities?

5. How and where does my research make meaningful interventions? What changes as a result of my work? What good does it do, what is it good for, and what does "good" mean in this research context? Who does it serve? How do I share my research with my interlocutors who are represented in my work? How are they affected? What do I want my audiences to do as a result of exposure to my research?

These five sets of questions capture the processual dynamics at the heart of the method. Further, they serve as interpretive cautions: reminders of our responsibilities to our research communities broadly construed.[10] They invite the researcher to reflect on the ways "performance" circulates in her scholarship.

Water Rites: A Case Study

Water Rites, conceived and directed by D. Soyini Madison (2006c) and realized in performance by students at the University of North Carolina at Chapel Hill, is an exemplary illustration of how a deeply ethical and coperformative representational strategy, a critically engaged commitment to intervene in the politics of privatization, and a disciplined deployment of aesthetics actually work in performance ethnography. This multimedia production relies on fluidity of form as well as content. Like the vision of water as a public good to which it is committed, the work flows between genres: memoir and personal narrative, movement, ethnographic field notes, sound, projections (both the techno-managerial PowerPoint slide and documentary photographs), and *actos:* short, highly politicized and often highly satirical sketches.[11] The result is a model of engaged performance ethnography. It is itself a water rite, turning on the phonic relation of "rite/right": a ritual that reinforces shared humanity and an entitlement arising from this same nonnegotiable status. It demands that its viewers pay attention to the politics of water, pay attention to the human costs and institutional profits, pay attention to their own memories, consumption, and taken-for-grantedness of water, pay attention to what must be different.[12] A full analysis of *Water Rites* exceeds the scope of this essay, but a brief discussion of three key moments demonstrates the aesthetic potency of performance ethnography as a critical method.

Water Rites opens by establishing the intimate coupling of free flow and restriction that characterize the binaries of water politics, casting this coupling as both a personal and global exigency.

RECORDER 1

Dear Journal: October 12, 1998, University of Ghana, Legon—Accra, Ghana, West Africa. There is no water in my house—the pipes are dry. There's no water left in my storage containers. There's no water anywhere here in Legon. I can't find water and it scares me. They warned us about the pipes drying up, but I never thought it would go on this *long*. How could there not be water?

RECORDER 2

Dear Journal: January 2006, London, England. These are the facts: More than 1 billion people lack access to clean and affordable water and about 2 billion lack access to sanitation . . .

RECORDER 1

Kweku, said he will come and we will search for water . . . he told me he knows where we can get enough to fill the containers. I just want him to hurry up and get here. It's just too scary not having water . . . too weird and scary. I worry how the students here are managing?

RECORDER 2

In the urban areas of Ghana, only 40 percent of the population has a water tap that is flowing; 78 percent of the poor in urban areas do not have piped water.

Though the Recorders give voice to Madison's research and experience, they are not simple figures of ethnographic authority. They record the interpenetration of personal affect, demographic context, and the larger realities of global water politics. Note how the Recorders' statements are themselves a flow as discourse moves from medium to medium and place to place. The "Dear Journal" indicator of fixed, written affect, dissolves into speaking, which in turn struggles to stay afloat in a rising tide of near primal anxiety: "How could there not be water?" Ellipses and repetition underscore this anxiety and the failure of language to fully capture it: "It's just too scary not having water . . . too weird and scary." Likewise, speaking dissolves the distance between University of Ghana, Legon—Accra, Ghana, West Africa, and London, England. The first location shows us the consequences of policies forged, in part, in the second; the second, free of the policy-inflicted exigencies of the first, is a source of "facts" to illuminate and enlarge those experiences. Writing and information can flow freely across borders and genres for a privileged Western subject. For much of the world, life-sustaining water does not.

The personal and the factual are interanimating registers of discourse in *Water Rites,* but they are not the only ones. *Water Rites* shows as well as tells. One of the most compelling examples is the use of empty plastic water bottles. Dozens of them form rivers of bottles, moats of bottles: aggregate yet highly individual. They provide visual continuity throughout the performance and/because they continually remind the audience of the social costs of private water. The sounds of the empty bottles hitting the floor, their transparency, the way they roll—all concretize both flow and restriction acoustically, visually, tactilely. One of the dramatic punctums organizing the piece demonstrates the polyvalence of water as it circulates in Madison's ethnographic work, through individual performers' memories of water, and through global networks of privatization and profit.

> Sounds of water rise and the "Donkey and Fetching Water Scene" is projected on both screens. As the Fetching Water scenes are projected, sounds of water rise to a high pitch as actors rise from their islands as if they are moving through water. They leave their boxes on the island—feeling the opposing force of the water—the actors rise and begin to search among the water bottles for the special one that they want—they read the various brands and inspect the size and shape of some of the bottles until they find the one they want. When each actor finds the "right" water bottle, they reach to the floor against the force of the water and lay down holding the bottle in various semi-fetal positions with their backs to the audience.
> *The water sounds fade but they can still be heard.*

This seemingly small nonverbal moment is itself a water rite. The force of water is registered in multiple ways: scenes documenting the unrelenting, body-breaking labor of fetching water; the roar of rushing water; and the performers' kinesthetic struggles against the current. That force is juxtaposed against the triviality of brand choice: a privileged way to "fetch water" where one can afford to have a "special" (clean, safe) kind. Even when reduced to accessories held in all those bottles, the sounds of water can still be heard. What to make of the semi-fetal positions of the performers? Perhaps they are allegories for the way ideologies of privatization and environmental devastation have infantilized consumers who choose not to ask, "Who decides who gets water? Who decides who decides?" Perhaps they remind the audience that we all come from water, that our fetal and evolutionary homes were water worlds. Perhaps they are exhausted, unable to swim any longer against the riptides of global capital and the institutions channeling it.

Water Rites shares narratives of both exhaustion and activation: accounts from West and South Africa, India, and Bolivia. These accounts are affect-ing in a double sense. They are *affective* in Sara Ahmed's (2004) definition: a form of cultural politics that is social and rhetorical rather than individual and interior. They also demand an *effect* from the audience, one activated not by pathos or solely by personal empathy. Local and international water activists and corporate stand-ins affirm what must be done, sometimes by negation. But one particular provocation pushes the audience beyond an instrumental view of performance and change, challenging them to deploy their own privileged access to facts and global mobility, as established in the work's opening moments discussed above.

MADELINE

And every once in a while one of you people . . . will whine or someone will yell at us, WHY WON'T YOU LISTEN? And I reply the same way that I always reply. You're either a beggar or a chooser. And if you have such a problem with it, get out of the street, get out of your hemp clothes and your teeshirts with defiant phrases and your classrooms where you discuss over and over again what's *wrong* with the international system. Stop throwing around your buzzwords and get out of your idea that *you* are going to change anything by being small. *Especially* you, who was born big, was born with privilege and money and the stamp *American* that won't come off no matter how hard you rub it or how many tattoos you put over it. You accomplish nothing by celebrating your smallness. And the only thing I have to say for myself is a piece of advice for you. Become a chooser— maybe you'll be a better listener than me. . . . Maybe you'll rewrite the manual. Until you do, I'm afraid I can't help you.

Who is Madeline? A person of authority at the World Bank or the International Monetary Fund? A generic person of privilege and influence feeling so-called "compassion fatigue"? An internal voice members of the audience hear but would like to disown? Whoever she is, she demands that the audience enact their commitments. This is a call to move beyond Gayatri Spivak's (1990) mandate to "unlearn your privilege" (p. 42). It is a demand to acknowledge our own complicity, look within, deploy it in critical interventions, and be accountable in the attempt (see Alexander Craft, McNeal, Mwangola, & Zabriskie, 2007, p. 56).

Water Rites demonstrates how performance ethnography does more than represent the problematics of water privatization; it intervenes in them. In so doing, it offers tactics, themes, and commitments central to emerging research: novelizing ethnographic discourse, exploring the performative potential of objects, and probing the inextricable links binding the present and the past, the local and the global.

Emerging Paradigms and New Directions in Performance Ethnography

Performance ethnography gives a lot of permission. Its potency as an analytical, political, and representational tool has attracted scholars alert to new opportunities to explore expressive culture, embodiment, and aesthetics and to do critical theory. This innovative work looks both forward and backward. It seeks out new genealogies, new modes of performance and the performative, and new forms of scholarly representation.

One emerging trajectory in performance ethnography is historical and involves intersections of performance and the archive. Scholars interested in this intersection draw on the insights of Diana Taylor (2003), and her useful formulations "the archive" and "the repertoire." The archive "exists as documents, maps, literary texts, letters, archeological remains, bones, videos films, CDs, all those items supposedly resistant to change" (p. 19), while the repertoire "enacts embodied memory: performances, gestures, orality, dance, singing—in short, all those acts usually thought of as ephemeral, nonreproducible knowledge" (p. 20). Taylor is not interested preserving the conventional false binary that separates these two spheres, but instead shows that they thoroughly interpenetrate one another: both are mediated, highly selective, and citational. Both are "mnemonic resources" (Roach, 1996, p. 26). Scholars are actively investigating the interanimation of the archive and the repertoire in/as performance ethnography, and dance studies offers a compelling example.

In *Choreographing the Folk,* Anthea Kraut (2008) examines Zora Neale Hurston's work as director and choreographer, offering close analyses of her concert *The Great Day,* and particularly the Bahamanian fire dance that was a central feature of the production. Kraut discusses Hurston's deployment of folk idioms in performance, and in materials that supported it, including promotional literature and correspondence with patrons and colleagues. Of special interest are the ways Hurston's theories of the folk in motion on stage emerge as distinct from those in her work on the page. Kraut analyzes the sometimes-fraught negotiations between Hurston, her patrons, and collaborators, her attempts to delineate distinct genres of African American vernacular dance, and her own assertions of aesthetic/ethnographic authority. Especially important in this analysis is the highly racialized entertainment market for products of performance ethnography, and particularly those framed as "folk," in the 1930s. Consistent with the inter- and polydisciplinary nature of performance ethnography, Kraut's book contributes to African American and American studies as well as performance and dance studies. Among many other contributions, it recovers dance for the history of performance ethnography and charts the contested, commercial path one ethnographer took to stage the results of her inquiry.

Performance ethnography can also illuminate new sites using the idea of performance in ways that may seem counterintuitive. For example, the process of commodification, the circulation of objects, and the imagined communities constructed by them can be productively viewed as performances. Examining objects and social processes through performance does not dispense with embodiment as a crucial concern. Rather, it expands focus to include the ways embodiment is invoked, ventriloquated, or staged through specific markets and desires. Ngugi wa Thiong'o (1999) observes, "There is a performance to space, to architecture, to sculpture." When spaces and objects are infused with exoticism, difference, and marketability, the idea of performance can illuminate the flows of power and pleasure that define commodity situations.

Genres of Native American art are productive examples. Here, the performance ethnographer examines the circulation of these objects in specific contexts, teasing out the complex pleasures and fantasies undergirding their consumption. I have argued (Hamera, 2006a, 2006c) that, in the case of Navajo folk art, the invisible, putatively "vanishing" native is both brought to life and frozen in forms that could be superficially viewed as naïve, politically innocent, and timeless—products of a homogenous "folk," yet appreciated for their seeming idiosyncrasy. Further, the art object functions as a perpetual performance of inclusion and appreciation for the collector, one that offers absolution from his/her position of relative privilege vis-à-vis the artist; exemption from the often sordid history of non-Indian desires for, and designs on, Indian objects; and recognition for "a good eye" replete with multicultural aesthetic sophistication. At the same time, consuming the objects, especially those that are characterized in terms of "authenticity," offers the collector vicarious immersion in native culture.

Finally, and perhaps most controversially, performance ethnographers may weave performance and aesthetics into "novelized" accounts. "Novelizing" comes from Mikhail Bakhtin's view of the novel's social situation. Michael Bowman (1995) operationalizes novelizing as

> a willingness to engage in a kind of verbal-textual-semiotic "misrule" which carries with it an "indeterminacy," as Bakhtin would say, "a certain semantic open-endedness," which has the *potential* to destabilize canonical notions of performance/text relations, of performance process, as well as of performance/audience relations. Although a novelistic production may have its preferred meanings, values, or political-cultural agenda, it also contains voices and values that contradict the ones it prefers. (p. 15)

As *Water Rites* demonstrates, performance ethnographers novelize the stage by including both multiple, contrary voices (indigenous activists, recorders, "Madeline," dismissive yuppies), and multiple media (image, sound, movement, *actos*, personal narrative). Sometimes these voices and media reinforce each other, but often they contradict and problematize, shifting the interpretive burden to the audience with the hope that they "will be better listeners than me" (see "Madeline" above). They even go beyond to "ethnographize" the process of novelizing the stage, detailing the politics of adaptation and performance itself (see Goldman, 2006).

Novelizing can be applied to the entire ethnographic project itself, challenging norms of solitary authorship as an extension of the historical anthropologist "hero." From this perspective, we can conceptualize novelizing authorship and methodologies as a quilt: not the type that subsumes all difference into a unified whole but one that stitches together sometimes contradictory aesthetics and commitments. As Renee Alexander Craft et al. (2007) observes, collaborative interventions are not always seamless meetings of the minds.

> One of my sister-quilters picks up a piece of cloth to add to her quilt-pattern. I grimace. With so many prettier pieces in her pile, I wonder why she has chosen that one. I look up to ask, when I see her eyes fixed on the fabric in my hand, her eyebrows knitting and un-knitting like mine. We meet each other's gaze, laugh, tease, and continue working. (p. 78)

Alexander Craft's "sister quilters" are performance ethnographers coming together across a wide range of boundaries to offer a manifesto for Black feminist performance ethnography, one committed to novelizing conventional understandings of gender and Blackness in/as cultural practices by examining "modalities of blackness within discourses of Africa, modalities of Africa within discourses of blackness, and all of the messiness in between" (Alexander Craft et al., 2007, p. 62) and by "minding the gaps" (p. 70).

Novelizing can go even further: Fieldwork can be communicated through actual novels. This is not as fraught an operation as it might first appear, as Kamala Visweswaran (1994) reminds us. Fiction and ethnography are never fully discrete discourses; each hinges on devices, tropes, and claims that define the other. Indeed, even my use of "Sandy Sem" here can be read as inserting a fiction into ethnography, with the quotation marks around her name designating the pseudonym—a reminder that "truth" is never simple, or even fully knowable. Yet novelizing the ethnographic text does not propel the researcher out of the realm of politics, ethics, and rigor. She must still address the key questions above, still commit to "doing" critical theory. Perhaps no one meets this burden as well as Martiniquen novelist Patrick Chamoiseau, best known for his prize-winning work *Texaco*. His earlier novel, *Solibo Magnificent* (1997), offers a fully novelized ethnography remarkable for its sensitivity to orature, to what performance can and cannot change, and to the complexities of postcolonial politics on his island nation. This beautiful and poignant novel includes a caution given to the ethnographer/narrator/writer. Chamoiseau, playfully reinscribed by master storyteller Solibo as "Oiseau de Cham," (an allusion to the biblical Shem and, literally, "bird of the field") is reminded of the ultimate limits of the ethnographic enterprise, particularly one committed to "the word," the rich and irreducible corporeality of cultural performance.

> (Solibo Magnificent used to tell me: "Oiseau de Cham, you write. Very nice. I, Solibo, I speak. You see the distance? . . . you want to capture the word in your writing. I see the rhythm you try to put into it, how you want to grab words so they ring in the mouth. You say to me: Am I doing the right thing, Papa? Me, I say: One writes but words, not the word, you should have spoken. To write is to take the conch out of the sea to shout: here's the conch! The word replies: where's the sea? But that's not the most important thing. I'm going and you're staying. I spoke but you, you're writing, announcing that you come from the word. You give me your hand over the distance. It's all very nice, but you just touch the distance") (pp. 28–29)

Chamoiseau reminds us that, as performance ethnographers, we all reach across the distances separating the linearity of language—written or spoken— from the flux of experience. Sometimes just touching that distance by novelizing ethnography is the best we can do, whether we speak, write, dance, or paint the performances we encounter.

These examples of new directions in performance ethnography share common themes that have characterized the method from its inception. They are deeply concerned with the transnational: the interpenetration of locales across nation-state boundaries or within them (the day-to-day politics of neocolonialism; fantasies of engaging native others through Navajo folk art). They examine structures of community formation, whether as an imagined community of "the folk," a sorority of ethnographers, or the solidarity or atomization of the audience-performer relationship (Alexander Craft et al., 2007; Chamoiseau, 1997; Hamera, 2006a, 2006c; Kraut, 2008). Multiple dimensions of difference, and the intersectionality of difference in/as performance are explicit elements of each.

Conclusion

The themes outlined above, particularly difference, connection, and transnationalism, coupled with the critical commitment to interrogate structures of oppression, have taken on new urgency in a post-9/11 context. As Norman Denzin and Michael Giardina (2007) argue, this context impels artists and scholars "to try to make sense of what is happening, to seek nonviolent regimes of truth that honor culture, universal human rights, and the sacred; and to seek critical methodologies that protect, resist, and help us represent and imagine radically free utopian spaces" (p. 10). Performance ethnography is such a method, incarnating critical interventions so they live in the flesh as well as on the page or the screen, though we must continually resist the temptation to conflate all performance with utopian space. As Jon McKenzie (2001a) reminds us, performance itself is an agent of globalization and its discontents. In the spirit of Denzin and Giardina, "Jenny Sem" and Solibo Magnificent challenge us to interpret and represent what can, must, cannot and will not be said in our research sites. We take up the challenge because the power of performance, as paradigm and shared corporeality, gives us the radical hope that acts of poiesis will productively intervene in our understanding of the world, and in the world itself.

Notes

1. Both "Sem" and "Sandy" are pseudonyms. As the example indicates, the Sem family's experiences led them to impose thresholds of secrecy that I was never able to fully cross. For a full discussion of these dynamics, see Hamera (2007).

2. Madison's formulation resonates with Dwight Conquergood's (2002b) characterization of performance studies itself as composed of creativity (artistry), communication (analysis), and citizenship (activism).

3. Critical theory approaches social formations, embedded in their specific histories, with the goal of teasing out the intricate workings of power. In so doing, it seeks a more just and emancipatory order. "Critical theory" in the generic sense includes critical race theory, disability studies, feminism, indigenous knowledges, Marxism, poststructuralism, psychoanalysis, and other methods that interrogate structures and practices of domination. "Critical Theory" as a specific body of literature was defined by members of the Frankfurt School as a more radical hermeneutic form of Marxism. For examples of how critical theory broadly construed enters performance studies, see Madison and Hamera (2006, pp. 1–64).

4. My view of infrastructure here resonates strongly with Shannon Jackson's (2005) "infrastructural memory," a construct that links aesthetics, discussed later in this section, and materiality in productive ways. "Infrastructural memory" is especially useful in understanding emerging relationships between performance and the archive, as noted in the final section of this essay.

5. "Spect-actors" is Augusto Boal's (1979) term for activated spectators: those driven to intervene in the theatrical experience to address injustice rather than simply passively consume the event and, by extension, the status quo. Activating spect-actors is a crucial component in his *Theatre of the Oppressed.*

6. See, for example, Hurston, 1990, p. 94.

7. For a history of oral interpretation within the academic construction of "performance," see Jackson (2004). For a history of the move from elocution to oral interpretation, see Edwards (1999). For a critique of elocution as the performance of whiteness naturalized, see Conquergood (2006a).

8. See Jackson (2009) for a deft theorizing of the relationship between oral interpretation and ethnography.

9. Jackson's book provides a valuable history of the institutionalization of performance, important background for those who want to fully understand its circulation across disciplines, and its disciplinary debts, presumptions, and vocabularies.

10. See Pollock (2006) for a complementary set of qualities to these questions: international, immersive, incorporative, integrative, and interventionist.

11. Luis Valdez developed the *acto* as part of his work with El Teatro Campesino and the United Farm Workers Union. More information on the form is available from his *Actos* (1971), and Eugène van Erven's *Radical People's Theatre* (1988), pp. 43–53.

12. Madison articulates an ethnographic ethic of "paying attention" in her article, "The Dialogic Performative in Performance Ethnography" (2006a).

References

Afary, K. (2009). *Performance and activism: Grassroots discourse after the Los Angeles rebellion of 1992.* Lanham, MD: Lexington Books.

Ahmed, S. (2004). *The cultural politics of emotion.* New York: Routledge.

Alexander, B. K. (2006). *Performing Black masculinity: Race, culture, and queer identity.* Lanham, MD: AltaMira Press.

Alexander, B. K. (2008). Queer(y)ing the postcolonial through the West(ern). In N. K. Denzin, Y. S. Lincoln, & L. T. Smith (Eds.), *Handbook of critical and indigenous methodologies* (pp. 101–131). Thousand Oaks, CA: Sage.

Alexander Craft, R. (2008). "Una raza, dos etnias": The politics of be(com)ing/performing "Afropanameño." *Latin American and Caribbean Ethnic Studies, 3*(2), 123–149.

Alexander Craft, R., McNeal, M., Mwangola, M., & Zabriskie, Q. M. (2007). The quilt: Towards a twenty-first-century Black feminist ethnography. *Performance Research, 12*(3), 54–83.

Bacon, W. (1979). *The art of interpretation* (3rd ed.). New York: Holt, Rinehart & Winston.

Bakhtin, M. (1984). *Problems of Dostoevsky's poetics* (C. Emerson, Ed. & Trans.). Minneapolis: University of Minnesota Press.

Bauman, R. (1977). *Verbal art as performance.* Rowley, MA: Newbury House.

Berger, H. M. (1999). *Metal, rock, and jazz: Perception and the phenomenology of musical experience.* Hanover, NH: Wesleyan University Press.

Berger, H. M., & del Negro, G. (2004). *Identity and everyday life: Essays in the study of folklore, music, and popular culture.* Middletown, CT: Wesleyan University Press.

Boal, A. (1979). *Theatre of the oppressed* (C. A. McBride & M. O. L. McBride, Trans.). New York: Theatre Communications Group.

Bowman, M. S. (1995). "Novelizing" the stage: Chamber theatre after Breen and Bakhtin. *Text and Performance Quarterly, 15*(1), 1–23.

Butler, J. (1993). *Bodies that matter: On the discursive limits of sex.* New York: Routledge.

Chamoiseau, P. (1997). *Solibo magnificent* (R. M. Réjouis & V. Vinkurov, Trans.). New York: Vintage.

Conquergood, D. (1982). Performing as a moral act: Ethical dimensions of the ethnography of performance. *Literature in Performance, 5*(2), 1–13.

Conquergood, D. (1988). Health theatre in a Hmong refugee camp. *TDR: The Drama Review, 32*(3), 174–208.

Conquergood, D. (1995). Of caravans and carnivals: Performance studies in motion. *TDR: The Drama Review, 39*(4), 137–141.

Conquergood, D. (1997). Street literacy. In J. Flood, S. B. Heath, & D. Lapp (Eds.), *Handbook of research on teaching literacy through the communicative and visual arts* (pp. 334–375). New York: Macmillan.

Conquergood, D. (2002a). Lethal theatre: Performance, punishment, and the death penalty. *Theatre Journal, 54*(3), 339–367.

Conquergood, D. (2002b). Performance studies: Interventions and radical research. *TDR: The Drama Review, 46*(2), 145–156.

Conquergood, D. (2006a). Rethinking elocution: The trope of the talking book and other figures of speech. In J. Hamera (Ed.), *Opening acts: Performance in/as communication and cultural studies* (pp. 141–160). Thousand Oaks, CA: Sage.

Conquergood, D. (2006b). Rethinking ethnography. In D. S. Madison & J. Hamera (Eds.), *Handbook of performance studies* (pp. 351–365). Thousand Oaks, CA: Sage. (Original work published 1991)

Davis, T. (2007). *Stages of emergency: Cold war nuclear civil defense.* Durham, NC: Duke University Press.

Denzin, N. K. (2003). *Performance ethnography: Critical pedagogy and the politics of culture.* Thousand Oaks, CA: Sage.

Denzin, N. K. (2006). The politics and ethics of performance pedagogy: Toward a pedagogy of hope. In D. S. Madison & J. Hamera (Eds.), *Handbook of performance studies* (pp. 325–338). Thousand Oaks, CA: Sage.

Denzin, N. K., & Giardina, M. D. (2007). Introduction: Cultural studies after 9/11. In N. K. Denzin & M. D. Giardina (Eds.), *Contesting empire, globalizing dissent: Cultural studies after 9/11* (pp. 1–19). Boulder, CO: Paradigm.

Diamond, E. (1996). *Performance and cultural politics.* New York: Routledge.

Dolan, J. (2005). *Utopia in performance: Finding hope at the theatre.* Ann Arbor: University of Michigan Press.

Edwards, P. (1999). Unstoried: Teaching literature in the age of performance studies. *Theatre Annual, 52,* 1–147.

Goldman, D. (2006). Ethnography and the politics of adaptation: Leon Forrest's *Divine Days.* In D. S. Madison & J. Hamera (Eds.), *Handbook of performance studies* (pp. 366–384). Thousand Oaks, CA: Sage.

Hamera, J. (2006a). Disruption, continuity, and the social lives of things: Navajo folk art and/as performance. *TDR: The Drama Review, 46*(4), 146–160.

Hamera, J. (Ed.). (2006b). *Opening acts: Performance in/as communication and cultural studies.* Thousand Oaks, CA: Sage.

Hamera, J. (2006c). Performance, performativity, and cultural poiesis in practices of everyday life. In D. S. Madison & J. Hamera (Eds.), *Handbook of performance studies* (pp. 46–64). Thousand Oaks, CA: Sage.

Hamera, J. (2007). *Dancing communities: Performance, difference and connection in the global city.* Basingstoke, UK: Palgrave Macmillan.

Hawes, L. C. (2006). Becoming other-wise: Conversational performance and the politics of experience. In J. Hamera (Ed.), *Opening acts: Performance in/as communication and cultural studies* (pp. 23–48). Thousand Oaks, CA: Sage.

Hurston, Z. N. (1990). *Mules and men.* New York: Harper & Row.

Hymes, D. (1981). *"In vain I tried to tell you": Essays in Native American ethnopoetics.* Philadelphia: University of Pennsylvania Press.

Jackson, S. (2004). *Professing performance: Theatre in the academy from philology to performativity.* Cambridge, UK: Cambridge University Press.

Jackson, S. (2005). *Touchable stories* and the performance of infrastructural memory. In D. Pollock (Ed.), *Remembering: Oral history performance* (pp. 46–66). New York: Palgrave Macmillan.

Jackson, S. (2009). Rhetoric in ruins: Performing literature and performance studies. *Performance Research, 14*(1), 4–15.

Johnson, E. P. (2003). *Appropriating blackness: Performance and the politics of authenticity.* Durham, NC: Duke University Press.

Kraut, A. (2008). *Choreographing the folk: The dance stagings of Zora Neale Hurston.* Minneapolis: University of Minnesota Press.

Madison, D. S. (1998). That was my occupation: Oral narrative, performance, and Black feminist thought. In D. Pollock (Ed.), *Exceptional spaces: Essays in performance and history* (pp. 319–342). Chapel Hill: University of North Carolina Press.

Madison, D. S. (2005). *Critical ethnography: Methods, ethics, and performance.* Thousand Oaks, CA: Sage.

Madison, D. S. (2006a). The dialogic performative in performance ethnography. *Text and Performance Quarterly, 26*(4), 320–324.

Madison, D. S. (2006b). Performing theory/embodied writing. In J. Hamera (Ed.), *Opening acts: Performance in/as communication and cultural studies* (pp. 243–265). Thousand Oaks, CA: Sage.

Madison, D. S. (2006c, March 2–6). *Water rites* [Multimedia performance]. Chapel Hill: University of North Carolina.

Madison, D. S. (2008). Narrative poetics and performative interventions. In N. K. Denzin, Y. S. Lincoln, & L. T. Smith (Eds.), *Handbook of critical and indigenous methodologies* (pp. 391–405). Thousand Oaks, CA: Sage.

Madison, D. S., & Hamera, J. (Eds.). (2006). *Handbook of performance studies.* Thousand Oaks, CA: Sage.

McKenzie, J. (2001a). Performance and global transference. *TDR: The Drama Review, 45*(3), 5–7.

McKenzie, J. (2001b). *Perform or else: From discipline to performance.* New York: Routledge.

Muñoz, J. E. (2006). Stages: Queers, punks, and the utopian performative. In D. S. Madison & J. Hamera (Eds.), *Handbook of performance studies* (pp. 9–20). Thousand Oaks, CA: Sage.

Olomo, O. O. O./Jones, J. L. (2006). Performance and ethnography, performing ethnography, performance ethnography. In D. S. Madison & J. Hamera (Eds.), *Handbook of performance studies* (pp. 339–345). Thousand Oaks, CA: Sage.

Pollock, D. (1990). Telling the told: Performing like a family. *The Oral History Review, 18*(2), 1–35.

Pollock, D. (2006). Marking new directions in performance ethnography. *Text and Performance Quarterly, 26*(4), 325–320.

Pollock, D. (2007). The performative "I." *Cultural Studies <=> Critical Methodologies, 7*(3), 239–255.

Roach, J. (1996). *Cities of the dead: Circum-Atlantic performance.* New York: Columbia University Press.

Schechner, R. (1985). *Between theatre and anthropology.* Philadelphia: University of Pennsylvania Press.

Spivak, G. C. (1990). *The post-colonial critic: Interviews, strategies, dialogues.* New York: Routledge.

Taylor, D. (2003). *The archive and the repertoire: Performing cultural memory in the Americas.* Durham, NC: Duke University Press.

Turner, V. (1982). *From ritual to theatre.* New York: PAJ.

Visweswaran, K. (1994). *Fictions of feminist ethnography.* Minneapolis: University of Minnesota Press.

wa Thiong'o, N. (1998). Oral power and Europhone glory: Orature, literature, and stolen legacies. In *Penpoints, gunpoints, and dreams: Towards a critical theory of the arts and the state in Africa* (pp. 103–128). Oxford, UK: Clarendon.

wa Thiong'o, N. (1999). Penpoints, gunpoints, and dreams: An interview by Charles Cantalupo. *Left Curve, 23.* Available at http://www.leftcurve.org/LC23webPages/ngugu.html

wa Thiong'o, N. (2007). Notes toward a performance theory of orature. *Performance Research, 12*(3), 4–7.

Valdez, L. (1971). *Actos.* San Juan Bautista, CA, Cucuracha Press.

van Erven, E. (1988). *Radical people's theatre.* Bloomington: Indiana University Press.

Williams, R. (1981). *Politics and letters: Interviews with* New Left Review. London: Verso.

Williams, R. (1983). *Keywords: A vocabulary of culture and society.* New York: Oxford University Press.

7

Braiding Narrative Ethnography With Memoir and Creative Nonfiction

Barbara Tedlock

Being there seeing, hearing, and meditating; being here dreaming, remembering, and inscribing. For years, I have recorded stories lurking inside my conversations with Mayan women returning from market with baskets of squawking turkeys; stories bursting forth during the sharing of a pink kola nut with a Yoruba woman on a 707 lazily circling the island of Manhattan; stories bubbling up in five gallons of red-chili deer meat on top a woodstove at the Pueblo of Zuni; stories swelling inside a Mongolian Ger filled with red-and-gold lacquered wooden chests, Chinese bronze mirrors, reindeer-hide tambourine drums, and wispy spirit placements. How does one enact such strange realities? Tapes, videos, notes, sketches, maps, and photos tell of an overanxious urge to preserve. But far more obsesses me since I have spent my time not so much in walking a particular path, but rather in spiraling along multiple alternative paths.

Writing evokes other writing and mirrors reflect other selves. The Velázquez painting *Las Meninas,* or "The Ladies in Waiting," captures a suspended moment with members of the royal court including the child Margarita, heir to the Spanish throne, staring outward implicating us as both observers and the observed. Behind and above Margarita's right shoulder hangs a painted mirror on the back wall reflecting her parents, as the king and queen in each of us. An actual mirror set up in the small room devoted to the painting at the Museo del Prado enhances the illusion; we see ourselves reflected in the vacuous center of the canvas. This creates an anomalous third space between self and other, interior and exterior, thought and emotion, truth and illusion. By creating an enchanted sacred spot, we encourage interactions in which each moment becomes two moments, history and memory, suspended in our consciousness. Such double consciousness negates the control of lineal history with its regime of cool curiosity, impersonal self-confidence, cultural completeness, ethnic purity, rational essentialism, and exoticism.

Holders of brushes and holders of cameras cannot trace a really Real reality outside the self, but instead mirror reality. As the South Indian novelist and social anthropologist Amitav Ghosh suggests, real life can only be grasped as a performance within the theater of writing that produces the presence it describes. So, why not admit that we are busy generating written mutterings? Our brush-and-camera reality creates contact zones where people meet, hauntings happen, and horizons fuse. Given our postmodern sensibility, we celebrate pop stars like Madonna and Britney with their Arabic henna hand designs and Hindu forehead *bindis* over their six chakras, seats of concealed wisdom. These cultural icons cut loose from their moorings create profound strangeness.

Field ethnographers, like street photographers, seek the magical in the quotidian: lemon-yellow flowers framed in gray-and-purple thunderstorms. Raghubir Singh, one of India's foremost ethnographic photographers, evokes the surge of life during his ongoing act of living it. In *River of Colour* (1998), he arranges his photographs tenderly yet starkly, revealing his engagement with his subjects. His rich documentation offers cultural immersion in the ongoing rush of experiencing common lifeways: cow-dung cakes drying in the morning sun, people gathering at the village well, a ragged peacock pecking at grains of millet, children shooting marbles while their fathers push carts and label shipping crates. Unlike the colonial photographers, who documented the intensely wounded life in the slums of Calcutta, his photos playfully capture the reverberating color and poetry of rural life. Walter Benjamin, if he had seen Singh's photographs, might have noticed that he had captured "a child's view of color" (Benjamin, 1996, p. 50), both as a magical substance and as an animal. Adults and children, others and ourselves, do not live in different worlds but rather live differently in the same world, tasting other ways of life in cultural co-participation, solidarity, and friendship.

Postmodern Gonzo Journalism and Ethnography

Gonzo is South Boston Irish American slang for the last person left standing after an all-night drinking marathon. Gonzo is also the title of a 1960 hit song written by James Booker, a flamboyant New Orleans rhythm and blues keyboardist famous for his raw-wired musical arrangements and heroin addiction. Bill Cardoso, a *Boston Globe* editor, invented the concept of "gonzo journalism" and applied it to Hunter Thompson's remarkable essay, "The Kentucky Derby Is Decadent and Depraved" (1970/1979). Rather than describing and honoring that year's winners of the derby, Thompson focused on himself, how bored yet frightened he felt trapped inside the huge drunk-and-disorderly crowd.

Gonzo ethnography, like gonzo journalism, is a postmodern documentary style that encourages a blend of observation with participation and rationality with altered states of consciousness. In so doing, they inscribe the Real while evoking solidarity with participants inside an exuberant unmapped performance space. An example is the cultural anthropologist Bruce Grindal's evocation of an African ritual. During his fieldwork in Ghana, he witnessed a death divination in which the corpse, sitting cross-legged on a cowhide, was propped up against the wall of his compound. Then, a praise singer danced and sang around him, until

> I began to see the *goka* [praise singer] and the corpse tied together in the undulating rhythms of the singing, the beating of the iron hoes, and the movement of feet and bodies. Then I saw the corpse jolt and occasionally pulsate, in a counterpoint to the motions of the goka. At first I thought that my mind was playing tricks with my eyes, so I cannot say when the experience first occurred; but it began with moments of anticipation and terror, as though I knew something unthinkable was about to happen. The anticipation left me breathless, gasping for air. In the pit of my stomach I felt a jolting and tightening sensation, which corresponded to moments of heightened visual awareness.
>
> What I saw in those moments was outside the realm of normal perception. From both the corpse and the goka came flashes of light so fleeting that I cannot say exactly where they originated. The hand of the goka would beat down on the iron hoe, the spit would fly from his mouth, and suddenly flashes of light flew like sparks from a fire.
>
> Then I felt my body become rigid. My jaws tightened and at the base of my skull I felt a jolt as though my head had been snapped off my spinal column. A terrible and beautiful sight burst upon me. Stretching from the amazingly delicate fingers and mouths of the *goka* strands of fibrous light played upon the head, fingers, and toes of the dead man. The corpse, shaken by spasms, then rose to its feet, spinning and dancing in frenzy. As I watched, convulsions in the pit of my stomach tied not only my eyes but also my whole being into this vortex of power. It seemed that the very floor

and walls of the compound had come to life, radiating light and power, drawing the dancers in one direction and then another. Then a most wonderful thing happened. The talking drums on the roof of the dead man's house began to glow with a light so strong that it drew the dancers to the rooftop. The corpse picked up the drumsticks and began to play. (Grindal, 1983, p. 68)

Now is the time for passionate ethnographic memoir, a blend of magical realism and a hard-driving narrative line in which a performer "is telling it like it is." Here the author is the active part of the story, a person so enthralled by hearing his own voice and listening to others telling the tale that he cannot remove himself from the narrative. The closest parallels to these memoirs are docudramas with unscripted humorous situations, POV radio, and Japanese *gakino tsukai,* or "crazy television." These and other genres create a contact zone between performers and audiences as a grittily realistic yet sacred performance space opening outward to an enchanted way of knowing and being in the world.

In the past, under the regime of colonialism, fieldwork produced two independent things: reportable nonparticipatory observation and nonreportable total participation. When ethnographers agreed to such a split, they cultivated rapport not friendship, compassion not sympathy, respect not belief, understanding not solidarity, and admiration not love. We did this, I fear, because we thought that if we cultivated friendship, sympathy, belief, solidarity, and love, we might lose it all—join history with memory and solidarity with objectivity—and "go native." Or so our tribal elders scared us into believing.

One way out of this impasse was to take the gamble and, as Australians like to say, "Go troppo!" by which they mean, "Go crazy." George Harrison, lead guitarist of the Beatles, released his album *Gone Troppo* in 1982, but it flopped. His son Dhani remastered and reissued it in 2004, and since then it has built a large international audience. Apparently, it was only a matter of timing between failure and success. This may also hold true for ethnography. Here I'm thinking about my classmate, Timothy Knab, who during the 1980s undertook linguistic research on the Nahuatl language spoken in Cuetzalan, Mexico. During his research, Tim became ensnared and ended up apprenticing himself to a group of shamans. In the early 1980s, after he wrote his doctoral dissertation, he was unable to find a publisher for his book until Harper San Francisco took the risk and released it as a work of creative nonfiction titled *The War of the Witches: A Journey Into the Underworld of the Contemporary Aztecs* (1995).

In his deeply evocative ethnography, Tim Knab unveiled how he learned to hear and tell stories and dreams in culturally recognizable ways. Later, he republished much of the same information in the genre of narrative ethnography with the University of Arizona Press, *The Dialogue of Earth and Sky: Dreams, Souls, Curing, and the Modern Aztec Underworld* (2004). These books show how his initial research as a linguist to a dying language gradually evolved into the work of apprentice to a living culture. They also reveal the strange blend of performativity and sovereignty of a nomad who learned to both live in and write about other cultural settings.

Nomadic Thought and Becoming

Undertaking documentary fieldwork in a location far from home creates radically new experiences producing a blend of wonder and shock that may result in an epiphany, or sudden reperception of reality. This leads to the understanding that one cannot simply impose one's worldview on others. If one avoids either an ethnocentric rejection or a facile assimilation of the strange, then one may reconceptualize both within a third in-between space. This space can accommodate multiple individuals with various cultural and ethnic identities who interact and in so doing change while maintaining certain of their unique qualities. When an ethnographer refuses to either occupy or conquer the third space, then nomadic thought, which does not separate differences into oppositional dualities, arises creating an overlapping dialogue based on *becoming*.

Becoming refers to a process of ongoing transformation based on multiple dynamic interactions of the type one experiences during an extended sojourn abroad. The Lithuanian-French philosopher Emmanuel Levínas (1969) envisioned travel as a return to the self in such a way that experiences with otherness did not provoke a substantive transmutation in the attitude of the traveler. A traveling ethnographer's project hinges on translating otherness without sacrificing difference to the logic of the same. Levínas's teacher, Edmund Husserl, theorized that consciousness is characterized by *intentionality,* a tendency toward owning external objects as well as internal and external psychic systems. Levínas rejected this notion of intentionality as a form of violence and pointed out that consciousness desires to conquer the world by objectifying it. He, like Jacques Derrida, rejected the notion that the Other must become the Same; instead there is a metaphysical element that remains totally strange and although it wants desperately to be heard it can never be understood. Michel Foucault (1977) admonished us to prefer difference to uniformity, flows to unities, and mobile arrangements to fixed systems.

Later, in *A Thousand Plateaus* (1987) Gilles Deleuze and Félix Guattari argued that what is real is the *becoming* that is central to the development of rhizomatic theory. In their philosophy, a rhizome, or rootlike plant stem forming an entwined spherical mass, is a metaphor for an epistemology that spreads in all directions at once. A rhizome is reducible to neither the one nor the many; it has neither a beginning nor an end, but always a middle from which it grows. The development of rhizomic thought without hierarchies produces *nomadic space,* a place where individuals are shaped by new experiences and identities that may lead to the development of double consciousness. This nomadic state of being moves beyond unified identities and affirms unique differences between people (Deleuze & Guattari, 1986).

Double Consciousness

First introduced into European philosophy by Friedrich Hegel (1807/1952), double consciousness entered American intellectual life by way of the writings of W. E. B. Du Bois. In *The Souls of Black Folk* (1903/1989), he described both the curse and the gift of African Americans who live between contradictory identities; that of "an American, a Negro; two souls, two thoughts, two unreconciled strivings; two warring ideals in one dark body, whose dogged strength alone keeps it from being torn asunder" (Du Bois, 1903, p. 215). More recently, double consciousness has been explored so as to include the worldviews of Whites and Browns. Whites live a double racial life, one colorblind and one race conscious, while Browns live suspended within a combination of whiteness and otherness (Bonilla-Silva, 2003).

As I conceptualize double consciousness, it is an equilibristic construction of identity that stresses the performativity of a nomadic subject. By endlessly citing the conventions of the social world around us, we produce our own reality through speech acts that combine language and gesture. My analysis rests on the experiential ethnographic approach pioneered by Victor and Edith Turner (1982) and practiced by a number of other ethnographers. The Turners pointed out that feeling and will, as well as thought, constitute the structure of cultural experience. To aid their students in understanding how people the world over experience the richness of their local lives, they experimented with rendering ethnography in a form of instructional theater. At the Universities of Chicago and Virginia, and New York University, they set up workshops in which members worked to acquire a kinetic understanding of other cultures. They experimented with the social dramas from their own Central African fieldwork and encouraged other ethnographers to perform dramas from their fieldwork. Stanley Walens, an ethnographer among Northwest coast Native Americans, scripted, narrated, and performed a set of rituals from his memoir *Feasting With Cannibals* (2001).

Experiential ethnographers acquire entrance into and partial enculturation within the worlds they study. During fieldwork, they may become actors and weave themselves into local cultures. Deborah Wong (2008), a Japanese American ethnographer as well as a *tako* drumming ethnomusicologist, reports that the field is simultaneously everywhere and nowhere, and thus everyone is in some sense an insider. While ethnomusicologists seem especially well suited to a performance approach, other areas of culture are also available. As the French ethnographer Jeanne Favret-Saada observed in her memoir *Deadly Words: Witchcraft in the Bocage,* "to understand the meaning of this discourse [witchcraft] there is no other solution but to practice it oneself, to become one's own informant, to penetrate one's own amnesia, and to try and make explicit what one finds unstateable in oneself" (Favret-Saada, 1980, p. 22).

Performing Ethnography

Ethnography as an enterprise consists of the examination, reflection, and shaping of human experience. Experiencing other ways of life while working and speaking with others in vulnerability and solidarity is central to the human sciences today (Tedlock, 2009). Combining participatory experience with memory and embodied performance is a rapidly emerging social practice. Performing ethnography encourages alternative strategies for the exploration, narration, celebration, writing, and rewriting of personal identities and social realities. Milton Singer's (1972) cultural performance, Victor and Edith Turner's (1982) performance ethnography, and Richard Schechner's (1989) intercultural performance merged into what we now call the "performance turn" in the social sciences (Conquergood, 1989).

Beginning in the 1980s and continuing into the early years of the 21st century, the Turners and Dwight Conquergood helped to shift ethnographers from interpretation studies toward performance studies. Dwight Conquergood performed his ethnographic work in refugee camps in Thailand and the Gaza Strip as well as among Hmong refugees in Chicago and during state executions in Texas and Indiana (Conquergood, 1985, 1992, 1998, 2002). He and others argued that social rituals draw their meaning and affective resonance from the traditions they reenact and that they never simply repeat but rather reverberate within these traditions (Schechner, 1985, pp. 36–37). These scholars advocate for performance as a "border discipline" expanding the meaning of texts by privileging embodied ethnographic research.

Performing ethnography produces a mimetic parallel or alternate instance through which the subjective is envisioned and made available to witnesses. In so doing, it creates a paradoxical location in which new possibilities for "the observation of participation" (Tedlock, 1991), or the living in while representing the world, emerges. Several recent ethnographers have centered their research and practice on the critical pedagogy and progressive politics of performative cultural studies (Alexander, 1999, 2002; Allen & Garner, 1995; Denzin, 2003; Kondo, 1997; Laughlin, 1995; Madison, 2005). Such work uses dialogue, performative writing, kinesis, and staging that directly involves the arrangement of scenery, performers, and audience members (Garoian, 1999; Schutz, 2001).

Performativity and Cultural Memory

Performativity describes the reiterative power of discourse to create and produce the phenomena it regulates and constrains. The concept was initially developed in speech-act theory by John Austin (1962, 1970). Utterances such as "I promise," "I swear," and "I do" not only describe something but they also make it happen. In feminist studies, the concept was extended by Judith Butler (1990, 1997), who theorized gender, heterosexuality, and homosexuality as acts one performs; thus, something one *does* rather than expressions of what one *is*.

During the height of Vietnam antiwar protests, in the California of the 1960s, popular theater groups, such as Bread and Puppet and El Teatro Campesino (or "The Farmworkers' Theater"), performed all over the state. These progressive collectives produced free street theater for the masses. After each show, Bread-and-Puppet performers served fresh homemade bread with strong garlic aioli to the audience as a way of creating community. Members of El Teatro Campesino stood on the flatbeds of trucks parked in the grape fields outside Delano, California. There, these predominantly Mexican migrant laborers enacted events from their own lives and those of their audiences. Luis Valdez, a member of the San Francisco Mime Troupe, supported the United Farm Workers' strike against Gallo Vineyards by producing skits for the striking workers during which they showcased their Chicano identity (Montejano, 1999).

Chicano performance culture blends the theatricality of popular performances with the performativity of historical events such as Reies Lopez Tijerina's 1967 raid on the courthouse in Tierra Amarilla, New Mexico. Like Pancho Villa's

1916 raid on Columbus, New Mexico, Reies Tijerina reasserted Mexican American ownership of the American Southwest. Villa's cunning ability to elude North American forces became part of the folklore that was rhetorically reiterated in Tijerina's later flight from U.S. authorities.

> Immediately [Tijerina] and a small band of followers became targets of the largest manhunt in New Mexico history. National Guard convoys, state police from all northern counties, local sheriffs and unofficial posses, Jicarilla Apache police and cattle inspectors, all joined the search. Equipped with two ammunition-less tanks, clattering helicopters, droning spotter planes, a hospital van, and patrolling jeeps, these forces combed every hamlet, gully, and pasture for the insurrectionists who had staged the "bold daylight raid." (Nabokov, 1970, p. 12)

Here we see Reies Tijerina *performing* Pancho Villa.

This style of performance uses a strategy that the Mexican performance artist Guillermo Gómez-Peña calls "reverse anthropology." In an interview with the philosopher Eduardo Mendieta, Gómez-Peña explained that anthropology uses the power and knowledge of the dominant culture to study marginalized others, while in reverse anthropology, "we [the marginalized others] occupy a fictional space" in order "to push the dominant culture to the margins, treat it as exotic and unfamiliar." (Mendieta & Gómez-Peña, 2001, p. 543)

Another striking example of the power of grassroots participatory performance is the work of Sistren, a Jamaican theater group that collectively wrote and produced *Lionheart Gal: Life Stories of Jamaican Women* (1987). The dramas of women's oppression they scripted and enacted were their own, including those of their director, Honor Ford-Smith, who served as a working member of the group rather than an outside researcher and director. Sistren recorded, transcribed, and edited, as a collective, dozens of life stories and enacted them publicly in theater workshops with farmworkers and slum dwellers (Sistren, 1987, pp. 14–16).

In North America, there is a long history during which native peoples were disenfranchised by means of violence, laws, and treaties. To confront this, dance-dramas based on indigenous mythology were created and performed by survivors. As Leslie Marmon Silko wrote in her novel *Almanac of the Dead*,

> The Ghost Dance has never ended, it has continued, and the people have never stopped dancing; they may call it by other names, but when they

dance, their hearts are reunited with the spirits of beloved ancestors and loved ones recently lost in the struggle. Throughout the Americas, from Chile to Canada, the people have never stopped dancing; as the living dance, they are joined again with all our ancestors before them, who cry out, who demand justice, and who call the people to take back the Americas! (1991, p. 1)

When Rosalie Jones (Daystar), a Chippewa-Cree dancer, joined the faculty of the Institute of American Indian Arts in Santa Fe, New Mexico, she began choreographing dances based on animal stories. In 1980, she formed a modern-dance company called Daystar: Classical Dance-drama of Indian America to perform and explore the spirituality behind Native American dance culture (Magill, 1998). Her dances provided the place where she connected with and communicated American Indian spiritual practices. In a masked shamanic dance she called "Wolf: A Transformation," she choreographed the *Anishinaabe* creation story in which Wolf was a companion to First Man. During the performance, a young male dancer crouched before the audience, wearing a wolf head and fur. By slowly turning his head side-to-side he connected wolfishness with humanness. Then he shed his wolf head, only to quickly reinhabit Wolf. Non-native audience members reported that as they shifted their awareness, they became active witnesses rather than passive tourists. This response is similar to Native Americans during sacred ceremonies.

Narrative Ethnography and Creative Nonfiction

Narrative is a fundamental means of imposing order on otherwise random and disconnected events and experiences. Since narratives are embedded within discourse and give shape to experience, storytelling and the self are closely linked. Narrative identity encourages a subjective sense of self-continuity while we symbolically integrate the events of our lived experience into the plot of our life stories. The pleasure of narrative is that it seamlessly translates *knowing* into *telling about* the way things really happened.

There are many narrative forms: history, drama, biography, autobiography, creative nonfiction, and narrative ethnography. Both narrative ethnography and creative nonfiction have characters, action, and shifting points of view. They follow a storylike narrative arc with a beginning, middle, and end, as well as high and low points of dramatic development including moments of tension and revelation. They also have an emotional arc consisting of inner conflict that meshes with the narrative arc. In a successful narrative ethnography, as the heroine is confronted with major decisions, dangerous threats, and emotionally powerful critiques from her family and society, we learn indirectly of her inner emotional life.

Before continuing with laying out the characteristics of narrative ethnography and creative nonfiction, I note that another, rather different, understanding of "narrative ethnography" has recently emerged in social science (Gubrium & Holstein, 2008). Here a set of methodological concepts including narrative resources, environment, embeddedness, and control are used primarily to prompt new research questions. To accomplish this, the ethnographic act and end product are collapsed into a single, highly abstract rhetorical field and reified as "an emergent method," combining epistemological, methodological, and analytical sensibilities. In so doing, the written genre is nearly erased.

The roots of the written genre of narrative ethnography lie at the crossroads between life-history and memoir. Vincent Crapanzano, in *Tuhami: Portrait of a Moroccan* (1980), documents both the life of his subject and his own responses to working with him. Over time, they evolved into reciprocal objects of transference to one another. While Tuhami was initially the main character, Crapanzano emerged in the writing process as a secondary character. The result is a psychologically rich double portrait. A similar intertwining of a biography with the story of the ethnographic encounter structured Laurel Kendall's *The Life and Hard Times of a Korean Shaman* (1988). Here, in a series of exchanges reproduced from memory and captured on tape, Kendall represents herself and her field assistant as sympathetic students of a Korean woman shaman. With the addition of personal and theoretical interludes (in typographically marked sections), we witness a female shaman actively engaging with a female ethnographer, her field assistant, and her readers.

An overlap between biography and personal memoir also structures Ruth Behar's *Translated Woman* (1993). Here she confessed how worried, yet relieved, she was when she realized that after nearly three years of studying what colonial women had said to their inquisitors and developing relationships with a number of townswomen she had let one of her subjects take over her research. Throughout the text she portrays her inner feelings by using an italic font: "*I am remembering the hurt I had felt several days before. While I was sitting in the half-open doorway reading, a boy had run past, gotten a peek at me, and yelled out with what to me sounded like venom in his voice, 'Gringa!'*" (Behar, 1993, p. 250). Since she is Cuban American, this insult from a fellow Hispanic was not only totally unexpected but also deeply painful.

What these psychologically rich intersubjective documents contribute is an unsettling of the boundaries that were once central to the notion of a self studying another. Instead, this form of border-zone cultural coproduction emerged as a new direction of ethnographic interchange and cultural inscription as a form of creative nonfiction. Creative nonfiction, like narrative ethnography, is factually accurate, and written with attention to literary style: However, the story is polyphonic with the author's voice and those of other people woven together. In creative nonfiction, the story is told using scenes rather than exposition and, as in narrative ethnography, the author-as-character is either the central figure or the central consciousness, or both. This type of artful emotional documentary discourse has emerged as a powerful literary genre infused with the rhetoric, metaphors, and other tropes that are commonly used in lyrical poetry and narrative fiction. Its sheer literariness distinguishes it from narrative ethnography.

Narrative ethnographers privilege traditional narrative techniques and include the main principles of expository writing, augments, and citing appropriate sources. Only some creative nonfiction writers use either narrative techniques or citation. Others deemphasize narrative in favor of deep reflection on experience and lyric or collage forms. An example of this tradition in creative nonfiction is *The Mirror Dance* (Krieger, 1983), a highly literary composite story told by means of a multiple-person stream of consciousness. To accomplish this, Susan Krieger constructed the account by paraphrasing her interview and documentary evidence without allowing herself any analytical commentary or even citation, as she might have if she had chosen to cast the work as a narrative ethnography. Other authors wrote creative nonfiction as a way to simultaneously refuse anonymity and authority (Eber, 1995; Tedlock, 1992). Instead, their work sought connection, intimacy, and passion. More recently, creative nonfiction has been used as a way to explore the lives of real people working in extra-legal worlds as a way of not revealing their locations and blowing their covers (Nordstrom, 2004, 2007).

Terre Humaine or Human Earth

Fifty-five years ago, Jean Malaurie, now professor of Arctic anthropology and ecology at the *École des Hautes Études en Sciences Socials* in Paris, initiated *Terre Humaine* (literally "human earth") as a literary collection. In responding to the utopian appeal of the French revolution—liberty, equality, fraternity—he encouraged authors to write directly from personal experience and commitment.

He convinced Editions Plon, at that time the second-largest publishing house in France, to accept the books he selected as a series (Balandier, 1987). Today, there are more than 85 titles that have sold over 11 million copies worldwide. The best-seller so far is *Le cheval d'orgueil: Mémoires d'un Breton du pays bigouden* by Pierre Jakez Hélias (1975). The author initially wrote in Breton, the Celtic language spoken in Brittany, then translated it himself into French for publication in the series.

The writing featured in *Terre Humaine* falls mainly into the area of creative nonfiction, which today is taught as "the fourth genre" alongside poetry, fiction, and drama in many writing programs worldwide. These literary works center on the human condition and bear witness to what each author saw, experienced, and understood. As one of the early authors, the ethnographer and folklorist Bruce Jackson, observed: "The great vision of Terre Humaine is that understanding is always a collaborative venture between those who are seen and those who are seeing, between those who speak and those who write, between those who write and those who read" (Jackson, 1999, p. 141).

The earliest books in the series were Malaurie's own Arctic travelogue *Les Derniers Rois de Thulé* (1955), and Claude Lévi-Strauss's Amazonian travelogue *Tristes Tropiques* (1955). After these successful launches, Malaurie sought out, translated, and reprinted many other examples of what he described as *la littérature du reel*, or "the literature of reality," which includes travelogues, life histories, memoirs, and autobiographies. In 1956, he found and republished Victor Segalen's remarkable documentary novel *Les immémoriaux* (1907/1956). This French naval doctor, explorer, and ethnographer of Breton origin expressed concern about the extinction of tribal civilizations in Oceania. While he presented his work as a set of harmless folkloristic recitations from ancient indigenous oral lore, it functions as an indictment of French imperialism and missionary Christianity, which nearly destroyed native Tahitian culture by a combination of mismanagement, syphilis, and drugs.

Jean Malaurie revealed his own emotional commitment to the dignity, complexity, and humanity of indigenous peoples in his five editions of *Derniers Rois*. The book steadily grew in length and complexity over the years from 328 pages of text, illustrations, and maps in the 1955 first edition to 854 pages by the final edition of 1989. He revealed his ethical stance again when he considered translating *Sun Chief: The Autobiography of a Hopi Indian* (1942). Although this remarkable life story was initially published by the American ethnographer Leo Simmons under his own name, Malaurie removed the name of Leo Simmons from the title page, returning the rightful authorship and royalties to the Hopi Indian whose life story it was, Don Talayesva (1959).

Other popular books in the series include Pierre Clastres's *Chronique des Indiens Guayaki* (1972), based on fieldwork in South America during the mid-1960s. Clastres lived among a recently contacted indigenous group in Paraguay where, although he could understand their language (since he spoke a neighboring dialect), they refused to converse with him. He hauntingly describes the situation, "they were still green," "hardly touched, hardly contaminated by the breezes of our civilization," "a society so healthy that it could not enter into a dialogue with me, with another world" (Clastres, 1972, pp. 96–97). His translator into English, the poet and prize-winning novelist Paul Auster, noted that the book is not only the true story of one man's experiences but that it is a portrait of him and that he writes with "the cunning of a novelist" (Auster, 1998, pp. 7–9).

Malaurie also selected and translated into French James Agee and Walker Evans's famous book *Let Us Now Praise Famous Men* (1941), as *Trois familles de métayers en 1936 en Alabama* (1972). At the time of their research, the writer Agee and the photographer Evans were employees of the Farm Security Administration who visited Hale County, Alabama, and became intimately acquainted with three White sharecropper families. Over a period of eight weeks, they recorded these families' struggle for survival in the aftermath of the Great Depression. The resulting book is partly documentary and partly literary, evoking the dark shacks and depleted fields of the American South.

Among the many other contributors to the series were Georges Balandier (1957), Margaret Mead (1963), Theodora Kroeber (1968), Guwa Baba and Mary Smith (1969), Bruce Jackson (1975), Alexander Alland (1984), Eric Rosny (1981), Colin Turnbull (1987), Robert Murphy (1990), Philippe Descola (1994), Roger Bastide (2000), Darcy Ribeiro (2002), Barbara Glowczewski (2004), and Barbara Tedlock (2004). Key elements in these works are firsthand experience, thick description, character development, point of view, and voice. The authors refrain from using the passive voice of a laboratory report ("it was concluded that . . ."); instead their voices are active, in the first person, passionate, and even theatrical. They portray themselves reflexively as bearing witness to both themselves and to history. Since they play important roles—be it hero, victim, or witness—they attribute motives to themselves as well as to others. Their choice of linguistic forms—including word order, tense, pronouns, and evidentials—vividly convey their points of view and cast their narrators, protagonists, and listeners in an ethically engaged performative manner.

As Bruce Jackson noted, these authors step into other worlds, stay a short while, then return to our world to bear witness. "They document their passage in ways that become for us not simply a report of experience, but an experience in itself. Their work is, in a phrase Malaurie wrote to me a letter, *plus un document qu'un documentaire*" (Jackson, 2005, p. 15). In other words, each of these works is more of a literary document than a documentary account. Each is a complex, stand-alone, three-dimensional work of art within the theater of writing rather than a simple chronological diary entry.

✶ ✶ ✶

As a child, I spent most summers and holidays in my grandmother's log home on the prairie of northern Saskatchewan. Skipping behind her on riverside trails, she pointed out dozens of living rocks and edible plants: blackberries, bearberries, deer berries, violets, mints, fiddleheads, chickweed, and wild mushrooms. Sitting together on boulders nibbling violets and mints, she told me stories of a world filled with people, only some of whom were human beings. My favorite stories were about rock persons and cumulus clouds who gave advice, and deer, badger, and bear persons who healed.

To keep her language alive in me, a half-blood child, Nokomis explained key words in her *Anishinaabe* (Ojibwe) language; rocks are *asin*, in the singular and *asiniig*, in the plural. And since the *-iig* suffix, is used only for animate possessions, this means that rocks are alive. She was certain about this since she herself had seen rocks move and heard them speak and sing. In time, she said, I might also hear and speak with rocks. She warned me though that it could only happen if I spent time in the North all alone so that my schooling could not erase the magic of the natural world. As an Anglican lay preacher and traditional Ojibwe herbalist, midwife, and storyteller, she explained to me the differences and similarities between these spiritualities—pointing out that while Christians *talked about* guardian angels, Indians *talked to* guardian spirits. "These are our brothers and sisters, the animals," she insisted. For her, the two ideas were nearly the same and she admonished me not to choose one over the other. Instead, I should walk in balance along the edges of these worlds. "There is beauty and strength in being both: a double calling, a double love."

Becoming an ethnographer, a highly suspect enterprise within most Native North American communities, has ironically enabled me to fulfill my grandmother's expectations. Today, while telling my own story alongside and entangled within the telling of others' stories, I have realized that many narrative bits are mirages, seductively real phenomena that I photograph and describe only to discover they depend upon the theater of my imagination for life. Other scraps, like rainbow spokes and wheels in air, evaporate since the shadows we cast, the ones other people see, are not accurate reflections of who we really are, were, or ever will be. The memories we hide from eventually catch us; overtake us as spiders weaving the dreamcatchers of our lives.

References

Agee, J., & Evans, W. (1972). *Louons maintenant les grands hommes: Trois familles de métayers en 1936 en Alabama.* Paris: Editions Plon, Collection Terre Humaine. (Translated into French from *Let Us Now Praise Famous Men* [1941])

Alexander, B. K. (1999). Performing culture in the classroom: An instructional (auto) ethnography. *Text and Performance Quarterly, 19,* 307–331.

Alexander, B. K. (2002). Performing culture and cultural performance in Japan: A critical (auto) ethnographic travelogue. *Theatre Annual: A Journal of Performance Studies, 55,* 1–28.

Alland, A. (1984). *La danse de l'araignée: Un ethnologue Américain chez les Abron (Côte-d'Ivoire).* Paris: Editions Plon, Collection Terre Humaine. (Translated into French from *When the Spider Danced: Notes From an African Village* [1975])

Allen, C. J., & Garner, N. (1995). Condor qatay: Anthropology in performance. *American Anthropologist, 97*(1), 69–82.

Auster, P. (1998). Translator's note. In *Chronicle of the Guayaki Indians* (pp. 7–13). New York: Zone Books.

Austin, J. L. (1962). *How to do things with words.* London: Oxford University Press.

Austin, J. L. (1970). Performative utterances. In *Philosophical papers* (pp. 233–252). London: Oxford University Press.

Baba, G., & Smith, M. F. (1969). *Baba de Karo: L'autobiographie d'une musulmane haoussa du Nigeria.* Paris: Editions Plon, Collection Terre Humaine. (Translated from the English version *Baba of Karo: A Woman of Muslim Hausa* [1954])

Balandier, G. (1957). *L'Afrique ambiquë.* Paris: Editions Plon, Collection Terre Humaine. (Translated into English as *Ambiguous Africa: Cultures in Collision* [1966])

Balandier, G. (1987). "Terre Humaine" as a literary movement. *Anthropology Today, 3,* 1–2.

Bastide, R. (2000). *Le condomblé de Bahia (Brésil).* Paris: Editions Plon, Collection Terre Humaine.

Behar, R. (1993). *Translated woman.* Boston: Beacon.

Benjamin, W. (1996). A child's view of color (1913). In M. Bullock & M. W. Jennings (Eds.), *Walter Benjamin selected writings: Vol. 1. 1913–1926.* Cambridge, MA: Harvard University Press.

Bonilla-Silva, E. (2003). *The double consciousness of Black, White, and Brown folks in the 21st century.* Paper presented at the meeting of the American Sociological Association, Atlanta, GA.

Butler, J. (1990). *Gender trouble.* New York: Routledge.

Butler, J. (1997). *Excitable speech: A politics of the performative.* London: Routledge.

Clastres, P. (1972). *Chronique des Indiens Guayaki: Ce que savent les Aché, chasseurs nomads du Paraguay.* Paris: Editions Plon, Collection Terre Humaine. (Translated into English as *Chronicle of the Guayaki Indians* [1998])

Conquergood, D. (1985). Performing as a moral act: Ethical dimensions of the ethnography of performance. *Literature in Performance, 5,* 1–13.

Conquergood, D. (1989). Poetics, play, process and power: The performance turn in anthropology. *Text and Performance Quarterly, 9,* 81–88.

Conquergood, D. (1992). Fabricating culture: The textile art of Hmong refugee women. In E. C. Fine & J. H. Speer (Eds.), *Performance, culture, and identity* (pp. 206–248). Westport, CT: Praeger.

Conquergood, D. (1998). Beyond the text: Toward a performative cultural politics. In S. J. Dailey (Ed.), *The future of performance studies: Visions and revisions* (pp. 25–36). Annandale, VA: National Communication Association.

Conquergood, D. (2002). Lethal theatre: Performance, punishment, and the death penalty. *Theatre Journal, 54,* 339–367.

Crapanzano, V. (1980). *Tuhami: Portrait of a Moroccan.* Chicago: University of Chicago Press.

Deleuze, G., & Guattari, F. (1986). *Nomadology: The war machine.* New York: Semiotext(e).

Deleuze, G., & Guattari, F. (1987). *A thousand plateaus* (B. Massumi, Trans.). Minneapolis: University of Minnesota.

Denzin, N. K. (2003). *Performance ethnography: Critical pedagogy and the politics of culture.* Thousand Oaks, CA: Sage.

Descola, P. (1994). *Les lances du crépuscule: Relations Jivaros, Haute-Amazonie.* Paris: Editions Plon, Collection Terre Humaine. (Translated into English as *The Spears of Twilight: Life and Death With the Last Free Tribe of the Amazon* [1996])

Du Bois, W. E. B. (1989). *The souls of Black folk: Essays and sketches.* New York: Penguin. (Original work published 1903)

Eber, C. (1995). *Women and alcohol in a highland Maya town.* Austin: University of Texas Press.

Favret-Saada, J. (1980). *Deadly words: Witchcraft in the Bocage.* Cambridge, UK: Cambridge University Press.

Foucault, M. (1977). Preface (R. Hurley, M. Seem & H. Lane, Trans.). In G. Deleuze & F. Guattari, *Anti-Oedipus: capitalism and schizophrenia.* New York: Viking.

Garoian, C. R. (1999). *Performing pedagogy: Toward an art of politics.* Albany: State University of New York Press.

Glowczewski, B. (2004). *Rêves en colère: La pensée en réseau des aborigènes d'Australie.* Paris: Editions Plon, Collection Terre Humaine. (Translated into English and published by Editions Plon as *Dreams in Anger* [2004])

Grindal, B. (1983). Into the heart of Sisala experience: Witnessing death divination. *Journal of Anthropological Research, 39*(1), 60–80.

Gubrium, J. F., & Holstein, J. A. (2008). Narrative ethnography. In N. Hesse-Biber & P. Leavy (Eds.), *Handbook of emergent methods* (pp. 241–264). New York: Guilford.

Hegel, G. W. F. (1952). *Phenomenology of the spirit* (A. V. Miller, Trans.). Oxford, UK: Oxford University Press. (Original work published 1807)

Hélias, P. J. (1975). *Le cheval d'orgueil: Mémoires d'un Breton du pays bigouden.* Paris: Editions Plon, Collection Terre Humaine. (Translated into English as *Horse of Pride: Life in a Breton Village* [1978])

Jackson, B. (1975). *Leurs prisons: Autobiographies de prisonniers et d'ex-détenus Américains.* Paris: Editions Plon, Collection Terre Humaine. (Translated into French from *In the Life: Versions of the Criminal Experience* [1972])

Jackson, B. (1999, October). The ethnographic voice. *Il Polo,* 139–141. Available at http://www.acsu.buffalo.edu/~bjackson/ETHNOGRAPHY.HTM

Jackson, B. (2005). "Plus un document qu'un documentaire": The voices of Terre Humaine. In M. Berne & J.-M. Terrace (Eds.), *Terre humaine: Cinquante ans d'une collection* (pp. 14–23). Paris: Bibliothèque Nationale de France.

Kendall, L. (1988). *The life and hard times of a Korean shaman: Of tales and the telling of tales.* Honolulu: University of Hawaii Press.

Knab, T. J. (1995). *The war of the witches: A journey into the underworld of the contemporary Aztecs.* San Francisco: Harper.

Knab, T. J. (2004). *The dialogue of earth and sky: Dreams, souls, curing, and the modern Aztec underworld.* Tucson: University of Arizona Press.

Kondo, D. K. (1997). *About face: Performing race in fashion and theater.* New York: Routledge.

Krieger, S. (1983). *The mirror dance: Identity in a women's community.* Philadelphia: Temple University Press.

Kroeber, T. (1968). *Ishi: Testament du dernier Indien sauvage de l'Amérique du Nord.* Paris: Editions Plon, Collection Terre Humaine. (Translated from *The Last Testament of a Wild Indian of North America* [1961])

Laughlin, R. M. (1995). "From all for all": A Tzotzil-Tzeltal tragicomedy. *American Anthropologist, 97,* 528–542.

Levínas, E. (1969). *Totality and infinity: An essay on exteriority* (A. Lingis, Trans.). Pittsburgh: Duquesne University Press.

Lévi-Strauss, C. (1955). *Tristes tropiques.* Paris: Editions Plon, Collection Terre Humaine. (Translated into English with the same title [1973])

Madison, D. S. (2005). Critical ethnography as street performance: Reflections of home, race, murder, and justice. In N. K. Denzin & Y. S. Lincoln (Eds.), *The SAGE handbook of qualitative research* (3rd ed., pp. 537–546). Thousand Oaks, CA: Sage.

Magill, G. L. (1998, August). Rosalie Jones: Guiding light of Daystar—Native American choreographer. *Dance Magazine,* 1–3.

Malaurie, J. (1955). *Les derniers rois de Thulé.* Paris: Editions Plon, Collection Terre Humaine. (Translated into English as *The Last Kings of Thule: With the Polar Eskimos, as They Face Their Destiny* [1982])

Mead, M. (1963). *Moeurs et sexualité en Océanie.* Paris: Editions Plon, Collection Terre Humaine. (Translated from the English *Manners and Sexuality in Oceania,* combining materials from her earlier books *Coming of Age in Samoa* [1928] and *Sex and Temperament in Three Primitive Societies* [1935])

Mendieta, E., & Gómez-Peña, G. (2001). A Latino philosopher interviews a Chicano performance artist. *Napantla: Views from South, 2*(3), 539–554.

Montejano, D. (1999). On the question of inclusion. In D. Montejano (Ed.), *Chicano politics and society in the late twentieth century* (pp. xi–xxvi). Austin: University of Texas Press.

Murphy, R. F. (1990). *Vivre à corps perdu: Le témoignage et le combat d'un anthropologue paralysé*. Paris: Editions Plon, Collection Terrie Humaine. (Translated into French from *The Body Silent* [1987])

Nabokov, P. (1970). *Tijerina and the courthouse raid*. Berkeley, CA: Ramparts.

Nordstrom, C. (2004). *Shadows of war: Violence, power, and international profiteering in the twenty-first century*. Berkeley: University of California Press.

Nordstrom, C. (2007). *Global outlaws: Crime, money, and power in the contemporary world*. Berkeley: University of California Press.

Ribeiro, D. (2002). *Carnets indiens: Avec les Indiens Urubus-Kaapor, Brésil*. Paris: Editions Plon, Collection Terre Humaine. (Translated from the Portuguese version, *Diarios Indios—os Urubus-Kaapor* [1996])

Rosny, E. (1981). *Les yeux de ma chèvre: Sur les pas des maîtres de la nuit en pays Douala (Cameroun)*. Paris: Editions Plon, Collection Terre Humaine. (Translated into English as *Healers in the night* [1985])

Schechner, R. (1985). *Between theater and anthropology*. Philadelphia: University of Pennsylvania Press.

Schechner, R. (1989). Intercultural themes. *Performing Arts Journal, 33/34,* 151–162.

Schutz, A. (2001). Theory as performative pedagogy: Three masks of Hannah Arendt. *Educational Theory, 51,* 127–150.

Segalen, V. (1956). *Les immémoriaux*. Paris: Editions Plon, Collection Terre Humaine. (Translated into English as *A Lapse of Memory* [1995])

Silko, L. M. (1991). *Almanac of the dead*. New York: Simon & Schuster.

Singer, M. (1972). *When a great tradition modernizes*. New York: Praeger.

Singh, R. (1998). *River of colour: The India of Raghubir Singh*. London: Phaidon.

Sistren (with Ford-Smith, H.). (1987). *Lionheart gal: Life stories of Jamaican women*. Toronto: Sister Vision.

Talayesva, D. (1959). *Soleil Hopi: L'autobiographie d'un Indien Hopi*. Paris: Editions Plon, Collection Terre Humaine. (Translated into French from *Sun Chief: The Autobiography of a Hopi Indian* [1942])

Tedlock, B. (1991). From participant observation to the observation of participation: The emergence of narrative ethnography. *Journal of Anthropological Research, 47,* 69–94.

Tedlock, B. (1992). *The beautiful and the dangerous: Encounters with the Zuni Indians*. New York: Viking.

Tedlock, B. (2004). *Rituels et pouvoirs: Les Indiens Zuñis Nouveau-Mexique*. Paris: Editions Plon, Collection Terre Humaine. (Translated into French from *The Beautiful and the Dangerous: Encounters with the Zuni Indians* [1992])

Tedlock, B. (2009). Writing a storied life: Nomadism and double consciousness in transcultural ethnography. *Etnofoor, 21*(1), 21–38.

Thompson, H. S. (1970/1979). The Kentucky Derby is decadent and depraved. In *The great shark hunt: Gonzo papers: Vol. 1. Strange tales from a strange time.* New York: Summit Books.

Turnbull, C. M. (1987). *Les Iks: Survivre par la cruauté: Nord-Ouganda.* Paris: Editions Plon, Collection Terre Humaine. (Translated into French from *The Mountain People* [1972])

Turner, V., & Turner, E. (1982). Performing ethnography. *The Drama Review, 26*(2), 33–50.

Walens, S. (2001). *Feasting with cannibals: An essay on Kwakiutl cosmology.* Princeton, NJ: Princeton University Press.

Wong, D. (2008). Moving: From performance to performative ethnography and back again. In G. Barz & T. J. Cooley (Eds.), *Shadows in the field: New perspectives for fieldwork in ethnomusicology* (pp. 76–89). New York: Oxford University Press.

8

The Constructionist Analytics of Interpretive Practice

James A. Holstein and Jaber F. Gubrium

For the last half century, qualitative inquiry has focused increasingly on the socially constructed character of lived realities (see Denzin & Lincoln, 2005; Holstein & Gubrium, 2008). Much of this has centered on the interactional constitution of meaning in everyday life, the leading principle being that the world we live in and our place in it are not simply and evidently "there," but rather variably brought into being. Everyday realities are actively constructed in and through forms of social action. The principle supplies the basis for a constructionist perspective on qualitative inquiry that is both an intellectual movement and an empirical research perspective that transcends particular disciplines.

With its growing popularity, however, the constructionist approach has become particularly expansive and amorphous. Often it seems that the term "constructionism" can be applied to virtually every research approach imaginable. James Jasper and Jeff Goodwin (2005), for example, have wryly noted, "We are all social constructionists, almost" (p. 3). But there is a drawback to this popularity, because, as Michael Lynch (2008) suggests, the perspective may have become too diverse and diffuse to adequately define or assess. In the process, constructionism sometimes loses its conceptual bearings.

Elsewhere (Holstein & Gubrium, 2008), we have argued that constructionism resists a single portrait but is better understood as a *mosaic* of research efforts, with diverse (but also shared) philosophical, theoretical, methodological, and empirical underpinnings. This does not mean, however, that just anything goes under the constructionist rubric. We should resist the temptation to conflate constructionism with other contemporary or postmodern modes of qualitative inquiry; it is not synonymous with symbolic interactionism, social phenomenology, or ethnomethodology, for example, even as it shares their abiding concerns with the dynamics of social interaction. Nor should we equate all variants of constructionism.

Darin Weinberg (2008) has argued that two important threads weave throughout the mosaic of constructionist thought: antifoundationalist sensibilities and a resistance to reification. These threads, of course, also wend through early statements of analytic philosophy, critical theory, pragmatism, and the hermeneutic tradition (see Weinberg, 2008). Joel Best (2008) traces the origins of the term "social constructionism" within sociology as far back as the early-20th century. He notes numerous appearances of the term in disciplines as varied as anthropology, history, and political science in the earlier parts of that century. At the same time, proto-constructionist sensibilities were evident in the work of a variety of scholars including W. I. Thomas (1931), George Herbert Mead (1934), Alfred Schutz (1962, 1964, 1967, 1970), and Herbert Blumer (1969), among many others. Best, however, suggests that the expansive popularity of the perspective, or perhaps the term, burst forth in the wake of the 1966 publication of Peter Berger and Thomas Luckmann's *The Social Construction of Reality: A Treatise in the Sociology of Knowledge.*

This chapter outlines the development of a constructionist analytics of interpretive practice, a particular variant of constructionist inquiry. In our view, the approach unites enough common elements to constitute a recognizable, vibrant research program. The program centers on the interactional constitution of lived realities within discernible contexts of social interaction. We use the term "analytics" because the approach and its variants produce understandings of the construction process by way of distinctive analytic vocabularies, what Blumer (1969) might have called a systematically linked set of "sensitizing concepts" spare enough not to overshadow the empirical, yet robust enough to reveal its constructionist distinctive contours. Our analytics of interpretive practice is decidedly theoretical, not just descriptive, but concertedly minimalist in its conceptual thrust. The chapter's aim is neither historic nor comprehensive. Rather, it looks more narrowly at the development of a particular strain of constructionist studies that borrows liberally, if somewhat promiscuously, from the traditions of social phenomenology, ethnomethodology, ordinary language philosophy, and Foucauldian discourse analysis.

Conceptual Sources

The constructionist analytics of interpretive practice has diverse sources. For decades, constructionist researchers have attempted to document the agentic processes—the *hows*—by which social reality is constructed, managed, and sustained. Alfred Schutz's (1962, 1964, 1967, 1970) social phenomenology, Berger and Luckmann's (1966) social constructionism, and process-oriented strains of symbolic interactionism (e.g., Blumer, 1969; Hewitt, 1997; Weigert, 1981) have offered key elements to this constructionist project. More recently, ethnomethodology and conversation analysis (CA) have arguably supplied a more communicatively detailed dimension by specifying the interactive procedures through which social order is accomplished (see Buckholdt & Gubrium, 1979; Garfinkel, 1967, 2002, 2006; Heritage, 1984; Holstein, 1993; Lynch, 1993; Maynard & Clayman, 1991; Mehan & Wood, 1975; Pollner, 1987, 1991).[1] Discursive constructionism (see Potter & Hepburn, 2008)—a variant of discourse analysis bearing strong resemblances to CA—also has emerged to examine everyday descriptions, claims, reports, assertions, and allegations as they contribute to the construction and maintenance of social order.

A related set of concerns has emerged along with ethnomethodology's traditional interest in how social action and order are accomplished, reflecting a heretofore suspended interest in *what* is being accomplished, under *what* conditions, and out of *what* resources. Such traditionally naturalistic questions have been revived, with greater analytic sophistication and with a view toward the rich, varied, and consequential contexts of social construction. Analyses of reality construction are now re-engaging questions concerning the broad cultural and the institutional contexts of meaning making and social order. The empirical horizons, while still centered on processes of social accomplishment, are increasingly viewed in terms of what we have called "interpretive practice"—the constellation of procedures, conditions, and resources through which reality is apprehended, understood, organized, and conveyed in everyday life (Gubrium & Holstein, 1997; Holstein, 1993; Holstein & Gubrium, 2000b). The idea of interpretive practice turns us to both the *hows* and the *whats* of social reality; its empirical purview relates to both how people methodically construct their experiences and their worlds and the contextual configurations of meaning and institutional life that inform and shape reality-constituting activity. This attention to both the *hows* and the *whats* of the social construction process echoes Karl Marx's (1956) maxim that people actively construct their worlds but not completely on, or in, their own terms.

This concern for constructive action-in-context not only makes it possible to understand more fully the construction process, but also foregrounds the realities themselves that enter into and are reflexively produced by the process. Attending closely to the *hows* of the construction process informs us of the mechanisms by which social forms are brought into being in everyday life, but it may shortchange the shape and distribution of these realities in their own right. The *whats* of social reality tend to be deemphasized in research that attends exclusively to the *hows* of its construction. We lose track of consequential *whats, whens,* and *wheres* that locate the concrete, yet constructed, realities that emerge.

ETHNOMETHODOLOGICAL SENSIBILITIES

Ethnomethodology is perhaps the quintessential *how* analytic enterprise in qualitative inquiry. While indebted to Edmund Husserl's (1970) philosophical phenomenology and Schutz's social phenomenology (see Holstein & Gubrium, 1994), ethnomethodology struck a new course, addressing the problem of order by combining a "phenomenological sensibility" (Maynard & Clayman, 1991) with a paramount research concern for the mechanisms of practical action (Garfinkel, 1967; Lynch, 2008). From an ethnomethodological standpoint, the social world's facticity is accomplished by way of members' discernible interactional work, the mechanics of which produces and maintains the accountable circumstances of their lives.[2] Ethnomethodologists focus on how members "do" social life, aiming in particular to document the distinct processes by which they concretely construct and sustain the objects and appearances of the life world. The central phenomenon of interest is the in situ *embodied* activity and the practical production of accounts (Maynard, 2003). This leads to inquiries into how mundane practices are actually carried out, such as doing gender (Garfinkel, 1967), counting people and things (see Martin & Lynch, 2009), or delivering good or bad news (see Maynard, 2003).

The policy of "ethnomethodological indifference" (Garfinkel & Sacks, 1970) prompts ethnomethodologists to temporarily suspend all commitments to a priori or privileged versions of the social world. This turns the researcher's attention to how members accomplish a sense of social order. Social realities such as crime or mental illness are not taken for granted; instead, belief in them is temporarily suspended in order to make visible how they become realities for those concerned. This brings into view the ordinary constitutive work that produces the locally unchallenged appearance of stable realities. This policy vigorously resists judgmental characterizations of the correctness of members' activities (see Lynch, 2008). Contrary to the common sociological tendency to ironicize and criticize commonsense formulations from the standpoint of ostensibly correct sociological understanding, ethnomethodology takes members' practical reasoning for what it is—circumstantially adequate ways of interpersonally constituting the world at hand. The abiding guideline is succinctly conveyed by Melvin Pollner's "Don't argue with the members!" (personal communication; see Gubrium & Holstein, 2011).

Ethnomethodological research is keenly attuned to naturally occurring talk and social interaction, orienting to them as constitutive elements of the settings studied (see Atkinson & Drew, 1979; Maynard, 1984, 1989, 2003; Mehan & Wood, 1975; Sacks, 1972). This has taken different empirical directions, in part depending upon whether the occasioned dynamics of social action and practical reasoning or the structure of talk is emphasized. Ethnographic studies tend to focus on locally accountable social action and the settings within which social interaction constitutes the practical realities in question. Such studies consider the situated content of talk in relation to local meaning structures (see Gubrium, 1992; Holstein, 1993; Lynch & Bogen, 1996; Miller, 1991; Pollner, 1987; Wieder, 1988). They combine attention to how social action and order is built up in everyday communication with detailed descriptions of place settings as those settings and their local understandings and perspectives serve to mediate the meaning of what is said in the course of social interaction. The texts produced from such analytics are highly descriptive of everyday life, with both conversational extracts from the settings and ethnographic accounts of interaction being used to convey the methodical production of the subject matter in question. To the extent the analysis of talk in relation to social interaction and setting is undertaken, this tends to take the form of (non-Foucauldian) discourse analysis, which more or less critically orients to how talk, conversation, and other communicative processes are used to organize social action. Variations on this analytic have also emerged in a form of discursive constructionism that resonates strongly with ethnomethodology and CA, but orients more to epistemics and knowledge construction (Potter & Hepburn, 2008; also see Nikander, 2008; Potter, 1996, 1997; Potter & Wetherell, 1987; Wodak, 2004; Wooffitt, 2005).

Studies that emphasize the structure of talk itself focus on the conversational "machinery" through which social action emerges. The focus here is on the sequential, utterance-by-utterance, socially structuring features of talk or "talk-in-interaction," a familiar term of reference in conversation analysis (see Heritage, 1984; Sacks, Schegloff, & Jefferson, 1974; Silverman, 1998; Zimmerman, 1988). The analyses produced from such studies are detailed explications of the communicative processes by which speakers methodically and sequentially construct their concerns in conversational practice. Often bereft of ethnographic detail except for brief lead-ins that describe place settings, the analytic sense conveyed is that biographical and social particulars can be understood as artifacts of the unfolding conversational machinery, although the analysis of what is called "institutional talk" or "talk at work" has struck a greater balance with place settings in this regard (see, for example, Drew & Heritage, 1992). While some contend that CA's connection to ethnomethodology is tenuous because of this lack of concern with ethnographic detail (Atkinson, 1988; Lynch, 1993; Lynch & Bogen, 1994; for counterarguments see Maynard & Clayman, 1991 and ten Have, 1990), CA clearly shares ethnomethodology's interest in the local and methodical construction of social action (Maynard & Clayman, 1991).

Recently, Garfinkel, Lynch, and others have elaborated what they refer to as a "postanalytic" ethnomethodology that is less inclined to universalistic generalizations regarding the enduring structures or machinery of social interaction (see Garfinkel, 2002, 2006; Lynch, 1993; Lynch & Bogen, 1996). This program of research centers on the highly localized competencies that constitute specific domains of everyday "work," especially the (bench)work of astronomers (Garfinkel, Lynch, & Livingston, 1981), biologists and neurologists (Lynch, 1985), forensic scientists (Lynch, Cole, McNally, & Jenkins, 2008) and mathematicians (Livingston, 1986), among many others. The aim is to document the "haecceity"—the "just thisness"—of social practices within circumscribed domains of knowledge and activity (Lynch, 1993). The practical details of the real-time work of these activities are viewed as an *incarnate* feature of the knowledges they produce. It is impossible to separate the knowledges from the highly particularized occasions of their production. The approach is theoretically minimalist in that it resists a priori conceptualization or categorization, especially historical time, while advocating detailed descriptive studies of the specific, local practices that manifest order and render it accountable (Bogen & Lynch, 1993).

Despite their success at displaying a panoply of social production practices, CA and postanalytic ethnomethodology in their separate ways tend to disregard an important balance in the conceptualizations of talk, setting, and social interaction that was evident in Garfinkel's early work and Harvey Sacks's (1992) pioneering lectures on conversational practice (see Silverman, 1998). Neither Garfinkel nor Sacks envisioned the machinery of conversation as productive of recognizable social forms in its own right. Attention to the constitutive *hows* of social realities was balanced with an eye to the meaningful *whats*. Settings, cultural understandings, and their everyday mediations were viewed as reflexively interwoven with talk and social interaction. Sacks, in particular, understood culture to be a matter of practice, something that served as a resource for discerning the possible linkages of utterances and exchanges. Whether they wrote of (Garfinkel's) "good organizational reasons" or (Sacks's) "membership categorization devices," both initially avoided the reduction of social practice to highly localized or momentary haecceities of any kind.

Some of the original promise of ethnomethodology may have been short-circuited as CA and postanalytic ethnomethodology have increasingly restricted their investigations to the relation between social practices and the immediate accounts of those practices (see Pollner 2011a, 2011b, 2011c). A broader constructionist analytics aims to retain ethnomethodology's interactional sensibilities while extending its scope to both the constitutive and constituted *whats* of everyday life. Michel Foucault, among others, is a valuable resource for such a project.

FOUCAULDIAN INSPIRATIONS

If ethnomethodology documents the accomplishment of everyday life at the interactional level, Foucault undertook a parallel project in a different empirical register. Appearing on the analytic stage at about the same time as ethnomethodology in the early 1960s, Foucault considers how historically and culturally located systems of power/knowledge construct subjects and their worlds. Foucauldians refer to these systems as "discourses," emphasizing that they are not merely bodies of ideas, ideologies, or other symbolic formulations, but are also working attitudes, modes of address, terms of reference, and courses of action suffused into social practices. Foucault (1972, p. 48) himself explains that discourses are not "a mere intersection of things and words: an obscure web of things, and a manifest, visible, colored chain of words." Rather, they are "practices that systematically form the objects [and subjects] of which they speak" (p. 49). Even the design of buildings such as prisons reveals the social logic that specifies ways of interpreting persons and the physical and social landscapes they occupy (Foucault, 1979).

Similar to the ethnomethodological view of the reflexivity of social interaction, Foucault views discourse as operating reflexively, at once both constituting and meaningfully describing the world and its subjects. But, for Foucault, the accent is as much on the constructive *whats* that discourse constitutes as it is on the *hows* of discursive technology. While this implies an analytic emphasis on the culturally "natural," Foucault's treatment of discourse as social practice suggests, in particular, the importance of understanding the practices of subjectivity. If he offers a vision of subjects and objects constituted through discourse, he also allows for an unwittingly active subject who simultaneously shapes and puts discourse to work in constructing our inner lives and social worlds (Best & Kellner, 1991; Foucault, 1988).

Foucault is particularly concerned with social locations or institutional sites—the asylum, the hospital, and the prison, for example—that specify the practical operation of discourses, linking the discourse of particular subjectivities with the construction of lived experience. Like ethnomethodology, there is an interest in the constitutive quality of systems of discourse; it is an orientation to practice that views lived experience and subjectivities as always already embedded and embodied in their discursive conventions.

Several commentators have pointed to the parallel between what Foucault (1980) refers to as systems of "power/knowledge" (or discourses) and ethnomethodology's formulation of the constitutive power of language use (Atkinson, 1995; Gubrium & Holstein, 1997; Heritage, 1997; Miller, 1997b; Potter, 1996; Prior, 1997; Silverman, 1993). The correspondence suggests that what Foucault's analytics documents historically as "discourses-in-practice" in varied institutional or cultural sites may have a counterpart in what ethnomethodology's analytics traces as "discursive practice" in varied forms of social interaction (Holstein & Gubrium, 2000b, 2003).[3] We use these terms—discourses-in-practice and discursive practice—throughout the chapter to flag the parallel concerns.

While ethnomethodologists and Foucauldians draw upon different intellectual traditions and work in distinct empirical registers, their similar concerns for social practice are evident; they both attend to the constitutive reflexivity of discourse. Neither discursive practice nor discourse-in-practice is viewed as being caused or explained by external social forces or internal motives. Rather, they are taken to be the operating mechanism of social life itself, as actually known or performed in real time and in concrete places. For both, "power" lies in the articulation of distinctive forms of social life as such, not in the application of particular resources by some to affect the lives of others. While discourses-in-practice are represented by "regimens/regimes" or lived patterns of action that broadly (historically and institutionally) "discipline" and "govern" adherents' worlds, and discursive practice is manifest in the dynamics of talk and interaction that constitute everyday life, the practices refer in common to the lived "doing" or ongoing accomplishment of society.

If ethnomethodologists emphasize *how* members use everyday methods to account for their activities and their worlds, Foucault (1979) makes us aware of the related conditions of possibility for *what* the results are likely to be. For example, in a Western postindustrial society, to seriously think of medicine and voodoo as equally viable paradigms for understanding sickness and healing would seem idiosyncratic, if not preposterous, in most conventional situations. The power of medical discourse partially lies in its ability to be "seen but unnoticed," in its ability to appear as *the* only possibility while other possibilities are outside the plausible realm.

It bears repeating that both ethnomethodological and Foucauldian approaches to empirical material are analytics, not explanatory theories in the causal sense. Conventionally understood, theory purports to explain the state of matters in question. It responds to *why* concerns, such as why the suicide rate is rising or why individuals are suffering depression. Ethnomethodology and the Foucauldian project, in contrast, aim to answer how it is that individual experience is understood in particular terms such as these. They are pretheoretical in this sense, respectively seeking to arrive at an understanding of how the subject matter of theory comes into existence in the first place, and of what the subject of theory might possibly become. The parallel lies in the common goal of documenting the practiced stuff of such realities.

Still, this remains a parallel—not a shared—scheme. Because Foucault's project (and most Foucauldian projects) operates in a historical register, real-time talk and social interaction are understandably missing from empirical materials under examination (but see Kendall & Wickham, 1999, for example). While Foucault himself points to sharp turns in the discursive formations that both shape and inform the shifting realities of varied institutional spheres, contrasting extant social forms with the "birth" of new ones, he provides little or no sense of the everyday interactional technology by which this is achieved (see Atkinson, 1995, Holstein & Gubrium, 2000b). Certainly, he elaborates the broad birth of new technologies, such as the emergence of new regimes of surveillance in medicine and modern criminal justice systems (Foucault, 1975, 1979), but he does not provide us with a view of how these operate on the ground. The everyday *hows,* in other words, are largely missing from Foucauldian analyses.

Conversely, ethnomethodology's commitment to documenting the real-time, interactive processes by which social action and order are rendered visible and accountable precludes a broad substantive perspective on constitutive resources, possibilities, and limitations. Such *whats* are largely absent in ethnomethodological work. It is one thing to show in interactive detail that our everyday encounters with reality are ongoing accomplishments, but it is quite another to derive an understanding of what the general parameters of those everyday encounters might be. The machinery of talk-in-interaction tells us little about the massive resources that are taken up in, and that guide, the operation of conversation, or about the consequences of producing particular results and not others, each of which is an important ingredient of practice. Members speak their worlds and their subjectivities, but they also articulate particular forms of life as they do so. Foucauldian considerations offer ethnomethodology an analytic sensitivity to the discursive opportunities and possibilities at work in talk and social interaction, without casting them as external templates for the everyday production of social order.

Dimensions of Constructionist Analytics

The constructionist analytics of interpretive practice reflects both ethnomethodological and Foucauldian impulses. It capitalizes on key sensibilities from their parallel projects, but it is not simply another attempt at bridging the so-called macro-micro divide. That debate usually centers on the question of how to conceptualize the relationship between preexisting larger and smaller social forms, the assumption being that these are categorically distinct and separately discernible. Issues raised in the debate perpetuate the distinction between, say, social systems on the one hand, and social interaction, on the other.

In contrast, those who consider the ethnomethodological and Foucauldian projects to be parallel operations focus their attention instead on the interactional, institutional, and cultural variabilities of socially constituting discursive practice or discourses-in-practice, as the case might be. They aim to document how the social construction process is shaped across various domains of everyday life, not in how separate theories of macro and micro domains can be linked together for a fuller account of social organization. Doctrinaire accounts of Garfinkel, Sacks, Foucault, and others may continue to sustain a variety of distinct projects, but these projects are not likely to inform one another; nor will they lead to profitable dialogue between dogmatic practitioners who insist on viewing themselves as speaking different analytic languages. In our view, what we need is an openness to new, perhaps hybridized, analytics of reality construction at the crossroads of institutions, culture, and social interaction.

BEYOND ETHNOMETHODOLOGY

Some ethnomethodologically informed varieties of CA have turned in this direction by analyzing the sequential machinery of talk-in-interaction as it is patterned by institutional context, bringing a greater concern for the *whats* of social life into the picture. Some field-based studies with ethnomethodological sensibilities have extended their concerns beyond the narrow *hows* of social interaction to include a wider interest in *what* is produced through interaction, in response to *what* social conditions. Still other forms of discourse analysis have similarly focused on the discursive resources brought to bear in situated social interaction or the kinds of objects and subjects constituted though interaction (see Wooffitt, 2005). These trends have broadened the empirical and analytic purview.

CA studies of "talk at work," for example, aim to specify how the "simplest systematics" of ordinary conversation (Sacks, Schegloff, & Jefferson, 1974) is shaped in various ways by the reflexively constructed speech environments of particular interactional regimes (see Boden & Zimmerman, 1991; Drew & Heritage, 1992). Ethnomethodologically oriented ethnographers approach the problem from another direction by asking how institutions and their respective subjectivities are brought into being, managed, and sustained in and through members' social interaction (or "reality work") (see Atkinson, 1995; Dingwall, Eekelaar, & Murray, 1983; Emerson, 1969; Emerson & Messinger, 1977; Gubrium, 1992; Holstein, 1993, Mehan, 1979; Miller, 1991, 1997a). Foucault has even been inserted explicitly into the discussion, as researchers have drawn links between everyday discursive practice and discourses-in-practice to document in local detail how the formulation of everyday texts such as psychiatric case records or coroners' reports reproduce institutional discourses (see Prior, 1997). Others taking related paths have noted how culturally and institutionally situated discourses are interactionally brought to bear, to produce social objects and institutionalized interpersonal practices (see Hepburn, 1997, and Gubrium & Holstein, 2001).

In their own fashions, these efforts consider both the *hows* and the *whats* of reality construction. But this is analytically risky business. Asking *how* questions without having an integral way of getting an analytic handle on *what* questions renders concerns with the *whats* rather arbitrary. While talk-in-interaction is locally "artful," as Garfinkel (1967) puts it, not just anything goes. On the other hand, if we swing too far analytically in the direction of contextual or cultural imperatives, we end up with the cultural, institutional, or judgmental "dopes" that Garfinkel (1967) decried.

ACCENTING ANALYTIC INTERPLAY

To broaden and enrich ethnomethodology's analytic scope and repertoire, researchers have extended its purview to the institutional and cultural *whats* that come into play in social interaction. This has not been a historical extension, such as Foucault might pursue, although that certainly is not ruled out. In our own constructionist analytics, we have resurrected a kind of "cautious" (self-conscious) naturalism that addresses the practical and sited production of everyday life (Gubrium, 1993a). More decidedly constructionist in its concern for taken-for-granted realities, this balances *how* and *what* concerns, enriching the analytic impulses of each. Such an analytics focuses on the *interplay,* not the synthesis, of discursive practice and discourses-in-practice, the tandem projects of ethnomethodology and Foucauldian discourse analysis. In doing so, the analytics assiduously avoids theorizing social forms, lest the discursive practices associated with the construction of these forms be taken for granted. By the same token, it concertedly keeps institutional or cultural discourses in view, lest they be dissolved into localized displays of practical reasoning or forms of sequential organization for talk-in-interaction. First and foremost, a constructionist analytics of interpretive practice has taken us, in real time, to the "going concerns" of everyday life, as Everett Hughes (1984) liked to call social institutions. This approach focuses attention on how members artfully put distinct discourses to work as they constitute their social worlds.

Interplay connotes the acceptance of a dynamic relationship, not a to-be-resolved tension, between the *hows* and *whats* of interpretive practice. We have intentionally avoided analytically privileging either discursive practice or discourses-in-practice. Putting it in ethnomethodological terms, in our view the aim of a constructionist analytics is to document the interplay between the practical reasoning and interactive machinery entailed in constructing a sense of everyday reality, on the one hand, and the institutional conditions, resources, and related discourses that substantively nourish and interpretively mediate interaction on the other. Putting it in Foucauldian terms, the goal is to describe the interplay between institutional discourses and the "dividing practices" that constitute local subjectivities and their domains of experience (Foucault 1965). The symmetry of real-world practice has encouraged us to give equal treatment to both its articulative and substantive engagements.

Constructionist researchers have increasingly emphasized the interplay between the two sides of interpretive practice. They are scrutinizing both the artful processes and the substantive conditions of meaning making and social order, even if the commitment to a multifaceted analytics sometimes remains implicit. Douglas Maynard (1989), for example, notes that most ethnographers have traditionally asked, "How do participants see things?" while ethnomethodologically informed discourse studies have asked, "How do participants do things?" While his own work typically begins with the later question, Maynard cautions us not to ignore the former. He explains that, in the interest of studying how members *do* things, ethnomethodological studies have tended to deemphasize factors that condition their actions. Recognizing that "external social structure is used as a resource for social interaction at the same time as it is constituted within it" (p. 139), Maynard suggests that ethnographic and discourse studies can be mutually informative, allowing researchers to better document the ways in which the "structure of interaction, while being a local production, simultaneously enacts matters whose origins are externally initiated" (p. 139). "In addition to knowing how people 'see' their workaday worlds," writes Maynard (p. 144), researchers should try to understand how people "discover and exhibit features of these worlds so that they can be 'seen.'"

Maynard (2003) goes on to note significant differences in the way talk and interaction typically are treated in conversation analytic versus more naturalistic, ethnographic approaches to social process. His own work, like many similarly grounded CA studies, exploits what Maynard terms the "limited affinity" between CA concerns and methods and more field-based ethnographic techniques and sensibilities (see Maynard, 2003, chapter 3). While a broad-based constructionist analytics would argue for a deeper, more "mutual affinity" (Maynard, 2003) between attempts to describe the *hows* and *whats* of social practice, there is clearly common ground, with much of the difference a matter of emphasis or analytic point of departure.

Expressing similar interests and concerns, Hugh Mehan has developed a discourse-oriented program of "constitutive ethnography" that puts "structure and structuring activities on an equal footing by showing *how* the social facts of the world emerge from structuring work to become external and constraining" (1979, p. 18, emphasis in the original). Mehan examines "contrastive" instances of interpretation in order to describe both the "distal" and "proximate" features of the reality-constituting work people do "within institutional, cultural, and historical contexts" (1991, pp. 73, 81).

Beginning from similar ethnomethodological and discourse analytic footings, David Silverman (1993) likewise attends to the institutional venues of talk and social construction (Silverman, 1985, 1997). Seeking a mode of qualitative inquiry that exhibits both constitutive and contextual impulses, he suggests that discourse studies that consider the varied institutional contexts of talk bring a new perspective to qualitative inquiry. Working in the same vein, Gale Miller (1994, 1997b) has proposed "ethnographies of institutional discourse" that serve to document "the ways in which setting members use discursive resources in organizing their practical actions, and how members' actions are constrained by the resources available in the settings" (Miller, 1994, p. 280). This approach makes explicit overtures to both conversation analysis and Foucauldian discourse analysis (see Miller, 1997a, and Weinberg, 2005) for rigorous empirical demonstrations of analytic interplay.

Dorothy Smith (1987, 1990a, 1990b) has been similarly explicit in addressing a version of the interplay between the *whats* and *hows* of social life from a feminist point of view, pointing to the critical consciousness made possible by the perspective. Hers has been an analytics initially informed by ethnomethodological and, increasingly, Foucauldian sensibilities. Moving beyond ethnomethodology, she calls for what she refers to as a "dialectics of discourse and the everyday" (Smith, 1990a, p. 202).

A concern for interplay, however, should not result in integrating an analytics of discursive practice with an analytics of discourse-in-practice. To integrate one with the other is to reduce the empirical purview of a parallel enterprise. Reducing the analytics of discourse-in-practice into discursive practice risks losing the lessons of attending to institutional differences and cultural configurations as they mediate, and are not "just talked into being" through, social interaction. Conversely, figuring discursive practice as the mere residue of institutional discourse risks a totalized marginalization of local artfulness.

ANALYTIC BRACKETING

A constructionist analytics that eschews synthesis or integration requires procedural flexibility and dexterity that cannot be captured in mechanical scriptures or formulas. Rather, the analytic process is more like a skilled juggling act, alternately concentrating on the myriad *hows* and *whats* of everyday life. This requires a new form of bracketing to capture the interplay between discursive practice and discourses-in-practice. We refer to this technique of oscillating indifference to the construction and realities of everyday life as "analytic bracketing" (see Gubrium & Holstein, 1997). While we have given it a name, it resonates anonymously in other constructionist analytics.

Recall that ethnomethodology's interest in the *hows* by which realities are produced requires a studied, temporary indifference to those realities. Ethnomethodologists typically begin their analysis by setting aside belief in the objectively real in order to bring into view the everyday practices by which subjects, objects, and events come to have an accountable sense of being observable, rational, and orderly. The ethnomethodological project moves forward from there, documenting how discursive practice constitutes social action and order by identifying the particular interactional mechanisms at play. Ludwig Wittgenstein (1953, p. 19) is instructive as he advocates taking language "off holiday" in order to make visible how language works to produce the objects it is otherwise viewed as principally describing.

Analytic bracketing works somewhat differently. It is employed throughout analysis, not just at the start. As analysis proceeds, the researcher intermittently orients to everyday realities as both the *products* of members reality-constructing procedures and as *resources* from which realities are reflexively constituted. At one moment, the researcher may be indifferent to the structures of everyday life in order to document their production through discursive practice. In the next analytic move, he or she brackets discursive practice in order to assess the local availability, distribution, and/or regulation of resources for reality construction. In Wittgensteinian terms, this translates into attending to both language-at-work and language-on-holiday, alternating considerations of how languages games, in particular institutional discourses, operate in everyday life and what games are likely to come into play at particular times and places. In Foucauldian terms, it leads to alternating considerations of discourses-in-practice on the one hand and the locally fine-grained documentation of related discursive practices on the other.

Analytic bracketing amounts to an orienting procedure for alternately focusing on the *whats* then the *hows* of interpretive practice (or vice versa) in order to assemble both a contextually scenic and a contextually constitutive picture of everyday language-in-use. The objective is to move back and forth between discursive practice and discourses-in-practice, documenting each in turn, and making informative references to the other in the process. Either discursive machinery or available discourses and/or constraints becomes the provisional phenomenon, while interest in the other is temporarily deferred, but not forgotten. The analysis of the constant interplay between the *hows* and *whats* of interpretive practice mirrors the lived interplay between social interaction and its immediate surroundings, resources, restraints, and going concerns.

Because discursive practice and discourses-in-practice are *mutually* constitutive, one cannot argue definitively that analysis should begin or end with either one, although there are predilections in this regard. Smith (1987, 1990a, 1990b), for example, advocates beginning "where people are"; we take her to mean the places where people are concretely located in the institutional landscape of everyday life. Conversely, conversation analysts insist on beginning with discursive practice (i.e., everyday conversation), even while a variety of unanalyzed *whats* typically inform their efforts.

Wherever one starts, neither the cultural and institutional details of discourse nor its real-time engagement in social interaction predetermines the other. If we set aside the need for an indisputable resolution to the question of which comes first, last, or has priority, we can designate a suitable point of departure and proceed from there, so long as we keep firmly in mind that the interplay within interpretive practice requires that we move back and forth analytically between its facets. In the service of not reifying the components, researchers continuously remind themselves that the analytic task centers on the *dialectics* of two fields of play, not the reproduction of one by the other.

While we advocate no rule for where to begin, we need not fret that the overall task is impossible or logically incoherent. Maynard (1998, p. 344), for example, compares analytic bracketing to "wanting to ride trains that are going in different directions, initially hopping on one and then somehow jumping to the other." He asks, "How do you jump from one train to another when they are going in different directions?" The question is, in fact, merely an elaboration of the issue of how one brackets in the first place, which is, of course, the basis for Maynard's and other ethnomethodologists' and conversation analysts' own projects. The answer is simple: knowledge of the *principle* of bracketing makes it possible. Those who bracket the lifeworld or treat it indifferently, as the case might be, readily set aside aspects of social reality every time they get to work on their respective corpuses of empirical material. It becomes as routine as rising in the morning, having breakfast, and going to the workplace.[4] On the other hand, the desire to operationalize bracketing of any kind, analytic bracketing included, into explicitly codified and sequenced procedural moves would turn bracketing into a set of recipe-like, analytic directives, something surely to be avoided. We would assume that no one, except the most recalcitrant operationalist, would want to substitute a recipe book for an analytics.[5]

The alternating focus on discursive practice and discourses-in-practice reminds us not to appropriate either one naïvely into our analysis. It helps sustain ethnomethodology's important aim of distinguishing between members' resources and our own. Analytic bracketing is always substantively temporary. It resists full-blown attention to discourses as systems of power/knowledge, separate from how these operate in lived experience. It also is enduringly empirical in that it does not take the everyday operation of discourses for granted as the truths of a setting *tout court.*[6]

RESISTING TOTALIZATION

Located at the crossroads of discursive practice and discourses-in-practice, a constructionist analytics works against analytic totalization or reduction. It accommodates the empirical realities of choice and action, allowing the analytic flexibility to capture the interplay of structure and process. It restrains the propensity of a Foucauldian analytics to view all interpretations as artifacts of particular regimes of power/knowledge. Writing in relation to the broad sweep of his "histories of the present," Foucault was inclined to overemphasize the predominance of discourses in constructing the horizons of meaning at particular times or places, conveying the sense that discourses fully detail the nuances of everyday life. A more interactionally sensitive analytics of discourse—one operating in tandem with a view to discursive practice—resists this tendency.

Because interpretive practice is mediated by discourse through institutional objectives and functioning, the operation of power/knowledge can be discerned in the myriad going concerns of everyday life. Yet, those matters that one institutional site brings to bear are not necessarily what another puts into practice. Institutions constitute distinct, yet sometimes overlapping, realities. While an organized setting may deploy a gaze that confers agency or subjectivity upon individuals, for example, another may constitute subjectivity along different lines (see, for example, Gubrium, 1992; Miller, 1997a; Weinberg, 2005).

If interpretive practice is complex and fluid, it is not socially arbitrary. In the practice of everyday life, discourse is articulated in myriad sites and is socially variegated; actors methodically build up their intersubjective realities in diverse, locally nuanced and biographically informed terms. This allows for considerable slippage in how discourses do their work; it is far removed from the apparently uniform, hegemonic regimes of power/knowledge in some Foucauldian readings. Discernible social organization nonetheless is evident in the going concerns referenced by participants, to which they hold their talk and interaction accountable.

Accordingly, a constructionist analytics deals with the perennial question of what realities and/or subjectivities are being constructed in the myriad sites of everyday life (see Hacking, 1999). In practice, diverse articulations of discourse intersect, collide, and work against the construction of common or uniform subjects, agents, and social realities. Interpretations shift in relation to the institutional and cultural markers they reference, which, in turn, fluctuate with respect to the varied settings in which social interaction unfolds. Discourses-in-practice refract one another as they are methodically adapted to practical exigencies. Local discursive practice makes totalization impossible, instead serving up innovation, diversification, and variation (see Abu-Lughod, 1991, 1993; Chase, 1995; Narayan & George, 2002).

Diverse Directions

Considering and emphasizing diverse analytic dimensions, variations on the constructionist analytics of interpretive practice continue to develop in innovative directions. Some are now "maturing," such as the "institutional ethnography" (IE) that Dorothy Smith and her colleagues have pioneered, and continue to expand. Others are of more recent vintage, such as the growth of discursive construction-ism or Gubrium and Holstein's (2009) development of a constructionist analytics for narrative practice. Old or new, in their own fashions all take up the interplay of discursive practice and discourses-in-practice, variously emphasizing the *hows* and the *whats* of everyday life.

ETHNOGRAPHY OF NARRATIVE PRACTICE

Let us begin with a recent development centered on how to analyze the inter-pretive practices associated with narrative and storytelling. Narrative analysis has become a popular mode of qualitative inquiry over the past two decades. If (almost) everyone is a constructionist, today nearly everyone also seems to be doing what they call narrative analysis. As sophisticated and insightful as the new wave of narrative analysis has become, most of this research is focused closely on texts of talk (e.g., Riessman, 1993). Researchers collect stories in interviews about myriad aspects of social life, then the stories are transcribed and analyzed for the way they emplot, thematize, and otherwise construct what they are about.

While attempts at narrative analysis have evinced constructionist sensibilities from the start, the socially situated, unfolding activeness of the narrative process has been shortchanged. The emphasis on the transcribed texts of stories tends to strip narratives of their social organization and interactional dynamics, casting narrative as a social product, not as social process. Emphasis is more on the text-based *whats* of the story and how that is organized, than on the *hows* of narrative production. Paul Atkinson (1997), among others, promotes a shift in focus:

> The ubiquity of the narrative and its centrality . . . are not license simply to privilege those forms. It is the work of anthropologists and sociologists to examine those narratives and to subject them to the same analysis as any other forms. We need to pay due attention to their construction in use: how actors improvise their personal narratives. . . . We need to attend to how socially shared resources of rhetoric and narrative are deployed to generate recognizable, plausible, and culturally well-informed accounts. (p. 341)

This reorientation encourages researchers to consider the circumstances, con-ditions, and goals of narratives—how storytellers work up and accomplish things with the accounts they produce. Adapting once more from Wittgenstein (1953, 1958), storytellers not only tell stories, they *do* things with them.

Capitalizing on Atkinson's and others suggestion, we have recently turned our brand of constructionist analytics to issues of narrative production (see Gubrium & Holstein, 2009). The challenge is to capture narrative's active, socially situated dimensions by moving outside of story texts to the occasions and practical activities of story construction and storytelling. By venturing into the domain of *narrative practice,* we gain access to the content of accounts and their internal organization, to the communicative conditions and resources surrounding how narratives are assembled, conveyed, and received, and to storytelling's everyday consequences.

The focus on practice highlights the reflexive interplay between discursive practice and discourse-in-practice. The narrative analysis of story transcripts may be perfectly adequate for capturing the internal dynamics and organization of stories, but it isolates those stories from their interactional and institutional moorings. For example, a transcript may not reveal a setting's discursive conventions, such as what is usually talked about, avoided, or discouraged under the circumstances. It may not reveal the consequences of a particular narrative told in a specific way. In order to understand how narrative operates in everyday life, we need to know the details and mediating conditions of narrative occasions. These details can only be discerned from direct consideration of the mutually constitutive interplay between what we have called "narrative work" and "narrative environments."

Narrative work refers to the interactional activity through which narratives are constructed, communicated, sustained, or reconfigured. The leading questions here are, "How can the process of constructing accounts be conceptualized?" and "How can the empirical process be analyzed?" Some of this is visible in story transcripts, but typically, narrative analysts tend to strip these transcripts of their interactional and institutional contexts and conversational character. This commonly results in the transcribed narrative appearing as a more-or-less finished, self-contained product. The in situ work of producing the narrative within the flow of conversational interaction disappears.

To recapture some of this narrative activity, we examine narrative practice for some of the ways in which narratives are activated or incited (see Holstein & Gubrium, 1995, 2000b). Working by way of analytic bracketing, these studies concentrate on conversational dynamics, machinery, and emerging sequential environments (many traditional CA concerns), while retaining sensitivity to broader contextual issues. Other studies focus on narrative linkages and composition, the ways in which horizons of meaning are narratively constructed (see Gubrium, 1993b; Gubrium & Holstein, 2009). Studies of narrative performativity document the ways in which narratives are produced and conveyed in and for particular circumstances and audiences (see Bauman, 1986; Abu-Lughod, 1993; Ochs & Capps, 2001). Collaboration and control are additional key concerns in analyzing narrative practice (see Holstein & Gubrium, 1995, 2000b; Norrick, 2000; Young, 1995). Because they are interactionally produced, narratives are eminently social accomplishments.

The other side of our analytics of narrative practice centers on narrative environments—contexts within which the work of narrative construction gets done. Narratives are assembled and told to someone, somewhere, at some time, with a variety of consequences for those concerned. (In contrast to CA, we do not limit narrative environments to the machinery of speech exchanges.) All of this has a discernible impact on how stories emerge, what is communicated, and to what ends. The environments of storytelling shape the content and internal organization of accounts, just as internal matters can have an impact on one's role as a storyteller. In turning to narrative environments, the analytic emphasis is more on the *whats* of narrative reality than on its *hows,* although, once again, analytic bracketing makes this a matter of temporary emphasis, not exclusive focus. One key question here is, "How is the meaning of a narrative influenced by the particular setting in which it is produced, with the setting's distinctive understandings, concerns, and resources, rather than in another setting, with different circumstances?" A second question is, "What are the purposes and consequences of narrating experience in particular ways?" A turn to the narrative environments of storytelling is critical for understanding what is at stake for storytellers and listeners in presenting accounts or responding to them in distinctive ways.

A growing body of work addresses such questions in relation to formal and informal settings and organizations, from families, to friendship networks, professions, and occupations (see Gubrium & Holstein, 2009). The comparative ethnographies of therapeutic organizations conducted by Miller (1997a) and Weinberg (2005) are exemplary in this regard. The influence of narrative environments is portrayed even more strikingly in *Out of Control: Family Therapy and Domestic Disorder* (Gubrium, 1992), which describes the narrative production of domestic troubles in distinctly different family therapy agencies. Susan Chase's (1995) *Ambiguous Empowerment: The Work Narratives of Women School Superintendents* and Amir Marvasti's (2003) *Being Homeless: Textual and Narrative Constructions* offer nuanced examinations of the accounts of some of society's most and least successful members, accenting the environmentally sensitive narrative work that is done to construct vastly different accounts of life and its challenges.

To move beyond transcribed texts, narrative analysis requires a methodology that captures the broad and variegated landscape of narrative practice. In essence, the researcher must be willing to move outside stories themselves and into the interactional, cultural, and institutional fields of narrative production, bringing on board a narrative ethnography of storytelling (see Gubrium & Holstein, 2008, 2009).[7] Applied to storytelling, this ethnographic approach is attuned to the discursive dynamics and contours of narrative practice. It provides opportunities for the close scrutiny of narrative circumstances, their actors, and actions in the process of constructing accounts. This clearly resonates with contextually rich work done in the ethnography of communication (Hymes, 1964), the study of orally performed narratives (Bauman, 1986; Briggs & Bauman, 1992; Ochs & Capps, 2001), and ethnographically grounded studies of folk narratives (Glassie, 1995, 2006).

Concern with the production, distribution, and circulation of stories in society requires that we step outside of narrative texts and consider questions such as who produces particular kinds of stories, where are they likely to be encountered, what are their purposes and consequences, who are the listeners, under what circumstances are particular narratives more or less accountable, how do they gain acceptance, and how are they challenged? Ethnographic fieldwork helps supply the answers. In systematically observing the construction, use, and reception of narratives, we have found that their internal organization, while important to understand in its own right, does not tell us much about how stories operate in society. This does not diminish the explanatory value of text-based narrative analysis, but instead highlights what might be added to that approach if we attended to narrative practice.

INSTITUTIONAL ETHNOGRAPHY

Another approach relating discursive practice and discourse-in-practice is Smith's "institutional ethnography" (IE) research program.[8] IE emerged out of Smith's (1987, 1990a, 1990b, 1999, 2005) feminist work that explored the ruptures between women's everyday experience and dominant forms of knowledge that, while seemingly neutral and general, concealed particular standpoints grounded in gender, race, and class (McCoy, 2008). The approach takes the everyday world as both its point of departure and its problematic. Inquiry begins with ongoing activities of actual people in the world, "starting where people are," as Smith characteristically puts it. The aim is to map the translocal processes of administration and governance that shape lives and circumstances by way of the linkages of ruling relations. Recognizing that such connections are accomplished primarily through what is often called textually mediated social organization,

IE focuses on texts-in-use in multiple settings. Across a range of locations—embodying people's everyday concerns, professional, administrative and management practices, and policy making—IE studies examine the actual activities that coordinate these interconnected sites (see DeVault & McCoy, 2002).

The dominant form of coordination is what Smith calls "ruling relations"—a mode of knowledge that involves the "continual transcription of the local and particular activities of our lives into abstracted and generalized forms . . . and the creation of a world in texts as a site of action" (Smith, 1987, p. 3). In IE, "text" orients the analyst to forms of representation (written spoken, visual, digital, or numeric) that exist materially separate from embodied consciousness. Such texts provide mediating linkages between people across time and place, making it possible to generate knowledge separate from individuals who possess such knowledge. Modern governance and large-scale coordination occur through rapidly proliferating, generalized, and generalizing, text-based forms of knowledge. These texts promote the "ruling relations [that generate] forms of consciousness and organization that are objectified in the sense that they are constituted externally to particular people and places" (Smith, 2005, p. 13). But to appreciate how texts do their coordinative work, the researcher must view them "in action" as they are produced, used, and oriented to by particular people in ongoing, institutional courses of action (see DeVault & McCoy, 2002; McCoy, 2008).

Therein lie the institutional and ethnographic dimensions of the approach. In IE, "institution" refers to coordinated and intersecting work processes and courses of action. "Ethnography" invokes concrete modes of inquiry used to discover and describe these activities. The IE researcher's goal is not to generalize about the people under study, but to identify and explain social processes that have generalizing effects. Practitioners of IE characteristically have critical or liberatory goals, an aim that we will address shortly. They pursue inquiry to elucidate the ideological and social processes that produce the experience of domination and subordination. As Smith and colleagues often point out, institutional ethnography offers a sociology *for* people not just about them (see DeVault & McCoy, 2002; McCoy, 2008; Smith, 2005).

While IE is not typically categorized as a variant of constructionism (McCoy, 2008), its conceptual antecedents and empirical interests often converge with the general constructionist project, especially with respect to the ways in which discursive resources and constraints affect social life and social forms. Centering on textually (discursively) mediated social relations, IE studies examine how forms of consciousness and organization are objectified or constituted as if they were external to particular people and places. IE analysis, however, strives to show that, at the same time, seemingly obdurate forms of social life are realized in concerted actions—produced, used, and oriented to by actual persons in ongoing, institutional courses of action (McCoy, 2008; Smith, 2005). From the standpoint of IE, the interplay between structures and agency is key to the social organization of lived experience.

As an alternative "sociology for people," IE has been adopted by researchers working in a wide variety of disciplines and settings: in education, social work, nursing and other health sciences, as well as sociology (see McCoy 2008; Smith, 2006). In a general sense, IE addresses the socially organized and organizing "work" done in varied domains of everyday life. Work is construed in a very broad sense—activities that involve conscious intent and acquired skill; including emotional and thought work as well as physical labor or communicative action. It is not confined to occupational employment, although this form of work is also ripe for analysis. Marjorie DeVault (1991), for example, has examined the work of feeding a family, while several IE studies have investigated various aspects of mothers' experience and the deeply consequential mothering work done by women in diverse domestic and organizational settings (see Brown, 2006; Griffith & Smith, 2004; Weigt, 2006). Other studies have examined the situated experience of living with HIV infection (Mykhalovskiy & McCoy, 2002), child rearing and housing (Luken & Vaughan, 2006), nursing home care (Diamond, 1992), and job training and immigrant labor (Grahame, 1998). IE investigations conducted in more formal (occupational) work settings include studies of the work performed by teachers (Manicom, 1995), security guards (Walby, 2005), social workers (De Montigny, 1995), nurses (Campbell & Jackson, 1992; Rankin & Campbell, 2006), and policing in the gay community (G. Smith, 1988). Across these IE studies, the goal is to discover how lives are socially organized and coordinated. The analytic basis for all these projects is to display the interplay between institutional practices and individual actions. If IE resists a constructionist designation, it nonetheless shares many of the sensibilities embodied in a constructionist analytics.

DISCURSIVE CONSTRUCTIONISM

Another innovative approach has been grouped loosely under the banners of discursive constructionism, or DC, and discourse analysis, or DA (see Potter, 1996; Potter & Hepburn, 2008). Its constructionist analytics also centers on the interplay of interpretive practice. As Jonathan Potter and Alexa Hepburn (2008) note, the DC label is itself a construction that supplies a particular sense of coherence to a body of more-or-less related work. If it is not singularly programmatic, it nevertheless represents a cogent analytic perspective that addresses the reflexive complexity of social interaction.

Centering attention on everyday conversations, arguments, talk-at-work, and other occasions where people are interacting, DC focuses on action and practice rather than linguistic structure. The approach emerged from the discourse analytic tradition in the sociology of scientific knowledge (e.g., Gilbert & Mulkay, 1984) and within a broader perspective developed within social psychology (e.g., Potter & Wetherell, 1987; see Hepburn, 2003). It is indebted in many ways to ethnomethodology (especially work by Harvey Sacks), and draws heavily on CA methods and findings. DC differs from CA, however, because it explicitly brings substantive issues of social construction to the fore; it is more concerned with the *whats* of social interaction than CA generally has been. While there are many other subtle distinctions, areas of overlap are substantial (Wooffitt, 2005), and in recent years DC and CA have found increasing areas of convergence (Potter & Hepburn, 2008).

DC approaches social construction in two fashions. In one, investigation aims to describe how discourse is constructed in the sense that it is assembled from a range of different resources with different degrees of structural organization. At the most basic level, these resources are words and grammatical structures, but they also include broader elements such as categories, metaphors, idioms, rhetorical conventions, and interpretive repertoires. The second approach emphasizes the constructive aspects of discourse in the sense that assemblages of words, repertoires, categories, and the like assemble and produce stabilized versions of the world and its actions and events. Central to DC is the notion that discourse does far more than describe objective states of affairs; it is used to construct versions of the world that are organized for particular purposes (Potter & Hepburn, 2008).

Following this commitment, DC treats all discourse as situated. At one level, it is located in the sequential environment of conversation (see Sacks, Schegloff, & Jefferson, 1974) and other forms of mediated interaction (e.g., turn allocation in legal or medical proceedings, screen prompts on computer displays). On another level, discourse is institutionally embedded. That is, it is generated within, and gives sense and structure to routine, ongoing practices such as family conversations, shopping transactions, and twelve-step meetings, for example. On a third level, discourse is situated rhetorically, in that discursive constructions are produced to advocate a particular version and counters possible alternatives (Potter & Hepburn, 2008). In this regard, analysis of the interest-related and consequential *whats* of discursive constructions is imperative.

While DC incorporates a view of discourse-in-practice, it stops short of the extended notion of discourse used in some of Foucault's work. DC's view of discourse is more restricted, emphasizing its use in everyday practice. Nevertheless, DC is dynamic and flexible enough to potentially address phenomena that Foucauldian analysis might also contemplate, or to conscript some of Foucault's insights about institutions, practice, and the nature of subjectivity into its own service (Potter & Hepburn, 2008). For example, Margret Wetherell (1998) argues that social identities cannot be understood apart from consideration of the discourses that provide the subject positions through which those identities are produced.

DC is not a "coherent and sealed system" (Potter & Hepburn, 2008, p. 291). Its field of interest is extremely broad, including but not restricted to, studies in discursive psychology and social psychology (e.g., Edwards, 2005; Edwards & Potter, 1992; Hepburn, 2003; Potter, 2003; Potter & Wetherell, 1987), cognition (e.g., Potter & te Molder, 2005), race and racism (e.g., Wetherell & Potter, 1992), gender (see Speer & Stokoe, in press), age (e.g., Nikander, 2002), facts (e.g., Wooffitt, 1992), and emotion (Edwards, 1999).

DC is not without its analytic tensions. For example, the issue of social structure and context remains a subject of debate. There is considerable contention regarding how the researcher might analyze utterances within conversation with an eye to identifying transcending discourses, subject positions, or repertoires. As in Foucauldian or critical discourse analysis (see, for example, Fairclough, 1995; Van Dijk, 1993; Wodak & Meyer, 2009), the issue is how critically to address the substantive *whats* of social construction while attending to the interactional dynamics and circumstances that construct them (Wooffitt, 2005). The danger in turning too fully to the study of transcendent discourse (writ large) is that it can shortchange the artful human conduct and agency involved in discursive practice (Wooffitt, 2005).

Sustaining a Critical Consciousness

This brings us to the concluding issue of how to maintain a critical consciousness in constructionist research while upholding a commitment to the neutral stance of bracketing. We have just noted that this is a desire shared by both DC and IE. But it does pose competing aims: documenting the social construction of reality, on the one hand, and critically attending to dominant and marginalized discourses and their effects on our lives, on the other. Exclusive attention to the constructive *hows* of interpretive practice cannot by itself sustain a critical consciousness.

Our way of addressing the issue comes by way of analytic bracketing. Our constructionist analytics sustains a critical consciousness by exploiting the critical potential of the analytic interplay of discourse-in-practice and discursive practice. Attending to both the constitutive *hows* and substantive *whats* of interpretive practice provides two different platforms for critique. The continuing enterprise of analytic bracketing does not keep us comfortably ensconced throughout the research process in a domain of indifference to the lived realities of experience, as phenomenological bracketing does. Nor does analytic bracketing keep us engaged in the unrepentant naturalism of documenting the world of everyday life as if it were fully objective and obdurate. Rather, it continuously rescues us from the analytic lethargies of both endeavors.

When questions of discourse-in-practice take the stage, there are grounds for problematizing or politicizing what otherwise might be too facilely viewed as socially or individualistically constructed, managed, and sustained. The persistent urgency of *what* questions cautions us not to assume that agency, artfulness, or the machinery of social interaction is the whole story. The urgency prompts us to inquire into broader environments and contingencies that are built up across time and circumstance in discursive practice. These are the contemporaneous conditions that inform and shape the construction process, and the personal and interpersonal consequences of having constituted the world in a particular way. While a constructionist view toward interpretive practice does not orient naturalistically to the "real world" as such, neither does it take everyday life as built from the ground up in talk-in-interaction on each and every communicative occasion. This allows for distinctly political observations since the analytics can point us toward matters of social organization and control that implicate matters beyond immediate interaction. It turns us to wider contexts (as constructed as they may be) in search of sources of action, control, change, or stability.

When discursive practice commands the analytic spotlight, there are grounds for critically challenging the representational hegemony of taken-for-granted realities. Researchers unsettle or deconstruct taken-for-granted realities in search of their construction to reveal the constitutive processes that produce and sustain them. Critically framed, persistent *how* questions remind us to bear in mind that the everyday realities of our lives—whether they are being normal, abnormal, law-abiding, criminal, male, female, young, or old—are realities we *do*. Having done them, they can be undone. We can move on to dismantle and reassemble realities, producing and reproducing, time and again, the world we inhabit. Politically, this recognizes that, in the world we inhabit, we could enact alternate possibilities or alternative directions, even if commonsense understandings make this seem impossible. If we make visible the constructive fluidity and malleability of social forms, we also reveal a potential for change (see Gubrium & Holstein, 1990, 1995; Holstein & Gubrium, 1994, 2000b, 2004, 2008).

The critical consciousness of a constructionist analytics deploys the continuous imperative to take issue with discourse or discursive practice when either one is foregrounded in research or seemingly obdurate in everyday life, thus turning the analytics on itself as it pursues its goals. In this sense, analytic bracketing is its own form of critical consciousness. Politically framed, the interplay of discourse-in-practice and discursive practice transforms analytic bracketing into critical bracketing, offering a basis not only for documenting interpretive practice, but also for critically commenting on its own constructions.

Notes

1. Some self-proclaimed ethnomethodologists, however, might reject the notion that ethnomethodology is in any sense a "constructionist" or "constructivist" enterprise (see Lynch, 1993, 2008). Some reviews of the ethnomethodological canon also clearly imply that constructionism is anathema to the ethnomethodological project (see Maynard, 1998; Maynard & Clayman, 1991).

2. While clearly reflecting Garfinkel's pioneering contributions, this characterization of the ethnomethodological project is perhaps closer to the version conveyed in the work of Melvin Pollner (1987, 1991) and D. Lawrence Wieder (1988) than some of the more recent "postanalytic" or conversation analytic forms of ethnomethodology. Indeed, Garfinkel (1988, 2002), Lynch (1993), and others might object to how we ourselves portray ethnomethodology. We would contend, however, that there is much to be gained from a studied "misreading" of the ethnomethodological "classics," a practice that Garfinkel himself advocates for the sociological classics more generally (see Lynch, 1993). With the figurative "death of the author" (Barthes, 1977), those attached to doctrinaire readings of the canon should have little ground for argument.

3. Other ethnomethodologists have drawn upon Foucault, but without necessarily endorsing these affinities or parallels. Lynch (1993), for example, writes that Foucault's studies can be relevant to ethnomethodological investigations in a "restricted and 'literal' way" (p. 131), and resists the generalization of discursive regimes across highly occasioned "language games." See McHoul (1986) and Lynch and Bogen (1996) for exemplary ethnomethodological appropriations of Foucauldian insights.

4. There are other useful metaphors for describing how analytic bracketing changes the focus from discourse-in-practice to discursive practice. One can liken the operation to shifting gears while driving a motor vehicle equipped with a manual transmission. One mode of analysis may prove quite productive, but it will eventually strain against the

resistance engendered by its own temporary analytic orientation. When the researcher notes that the analytic engine is laboring under, or being constrained by, the restraints of what it is currently geared to accomplish, she can decide to virtually shift analytic gears in order to gain further purchase on the aspects of interpretive interplay that were previously bracketed. Just as there can be no prescription for shifting gears while driving (i.e., one can never specify in advance at what speed one should shift up or down), changing analytic brackets always remains an artful enterprise, awaiting the empirical circumstances it encounters. Its timing cannot be prespecified. Like shifting gears while driving, changes are not arbitrary or undisciplined. Rather they respond to the analytic challenges at hand in a principled, if not predetermined, fashion.

5. This may be the very thing Lynch (1993) decries with respect to conversation analysts who attempt to formalize and professionalize CA as a "scientific" discipline.

6. Some critics (see Denzin, 1998) have worried that analytic bracketing represents a selective objectivism, a form of "ontological gerrymandering." These, of course, have become fighting words among constructionists. But we should soberly recall that Steve Woolgar and Dorothy Pawluch (1985) have suggested that carving out some sort of analytic footing may be a pervasive and unavoidable feature of any sociological commentary. Our own constant attention to the interplay between discourse-in-practice and discursive practice continually reminds us of their reflexive relationship. Gerrymanderers stand their separate ground and unreflexively deconstruct; analytic bracketing, in contrast, encourages a continual and methodical deconstruction of empirical groundings themselves. This may produce a less-than-tidy picture, but it also is designed to keep reification at bay and ungrounded signification under control.

7. The term "narrative ethnography," which is an apt designation for an ethnographic approach to narrative, is also associated with another approach to qualitative inquiry. Some researchers have applied the term to the critical analysis of representational practices in ethnography. Their aim is to work against the objectifying practices of ethnographic description. Practitioners of this form of narrative ethnography use the term to highlight researchers' narrative practices as they craft ethnographic accounts. They feature the interplay between the ethnographer's own subjectivity and the subjectivities of those whose lives and worlds are in view. Their ethnographic texts are typically derived from participant observation, but are distinctive because they take special notice of the researcher's own participation, perspective, voice, and especially his or her emotional experience as these operate in relation to the field of experience in view. Anthropologists Barbara Tedlock (1991, 1992, 2004), Ruth Behar (1993, 1996), and Kirin Narayan (1989), and sociologists Carolyn Ellis (1991), Laurel Richardson (1990a, 1990b), and others (Ellis & Flaherty, 1992; Ellis & Bochner, 1996) are important proponents of this genre. The reflexive, representational engagements of field encounters are discussed at length in H. L. Goodall's (2000) book *Writing the New Ethnography,* while Carolyn Ellis (2004) offers a description of the autoethnographic approach to narratives.

8. According to McCoy (2008), institutional ethnographers generally resist the tendency to be subsumed under the constructionist umbrella. By not affiliating with

constructionism, she argues, IE has been free to participate in constructionist conversations, but on its own terms. This independent positioning is important for the IE project that aims to begin, not from theoretical vantage points, but from the actualities of people's lives.

References

Abu-Lughod, L. (1991). Writing against culture. In R. Fox (Ed.), *Recapturing anthropology* (pp. 137–162). Santa Fe, NM: SAR Press.

Abu-Lughod, L. (1993). *Writing women's worlds: Bedouin stories.* Berkeley: University of California Press.

Atkinson, J. M., & Drew, P. (1979). *Order in court.* Atlantic Highlands, NJ: Humanities Press.

Atkinson, P. (1988). Ethnomethodology: A critical review. *Annual Review of Sociology, 14,* 441–465.

Atkinson, P. (1995). *Medical talk and medical work.* London: Sage.

Atkinson, P. (1997). Narrative turn or blind alley? *Qualitative Health Research, 7,* 325–344.

Barthes, R. (1977). *Image, music, text.* New York: Hill & Wang.

Bauman, R. (1986). *Story, performance, and event: Contextual studies of oral narrative.* Cambridge, UK: Cambridge University Press.

Behar, R. (1993). *Translated woman: Crossing the border with Esperanza's story.* Boston: Beacon.

Behar, R. (1996). *The vulnerable observer: Anthropology that breaks your heart.* Boston: Beacon.

Berger, P. L., & Luckmann, T. (1966). *The social construction of reality.* New York: Doubleday.

Best, J. (2008). Historical development and defining issues of constructionist inquiry. In J. Holstein & J. Gubrium (Eds.), *Handbook of constructionist research* (pp. 41–64). New York: Guilford.

Best, S., & Kellner, D. (1991). *Postmodern theory: Critical interrogations.* New York: Guilford.

Blumer, H. (1969). *Symbolic interactionism.* Englewood Cliffs, NJ: Prentice Hall.

Boden, D., & Zimmerman, D. (Eds.). (1991). *Talk and social structure.* Cambridge, UK: Polity.

Bogen, D., & Lynch, M. (1993). Do we need a general theory of social problems? In J. Holstein & G. Miller (Eds.), *Reconsidering social constructionism: Debates in social problems theory* (pp. 213–237). Hawthorne, NY: Aldine de Gruyter.

Briggs, C. L., & Bauman, R. (1992). Genre, intertextuality, and social power. *Journal of Linguistic Anthropology, 2,* 131–172.

Brown, D. (2006). Working the system: Re-thinking the role of mothers and the reduction of "risk" in child protection work. *Social Problems, 53,* 352–370.

Buckholdt, D. R., & Gubrium, J. F. (1979). *Caretakers: Treating emotionally disturbed children.* Beverly Hills, CA: Sage.

Campbell, M., & Jackson, N. (1992). Learning to nurse: Plans, accounts, and actions. *Qualitative Health Research, 2,* 475–496.

Chase, S. E. (1995). *Ambiguous empowerment: The work narratives of women school superintendents.* Amherst: University of Massachusetts Press.

De Montigny, G. A. J. (1995). *Social working: An ethnography of front-line practice.* Toronto: University of Toronto Press.

Denzin, N. K. (1998). The new ethnography. *Journal of Contemporary Ethnography, 27,* 405–415.

Denzin, N. K., & Lincoln, Y. S. (Eds.). (2005). *The SAGE handbook of qualitative research* (3rd ed.). Thousand Oaks, CA: Sage.

DeVault, M. L. (1991). *Feeding the family: The social organization of caring as gendered work.* Chicago: University of Chicago Press.

DeVault, M. L., & McCoy, L. (2002). Institutional ethnography: Using interviews to investigate ruling relations. In J. F. Gubrium & J. A. Holstein (Eds.), *Handbook of interview research: Context and method* (pp. 751–776). Thousand Oaks, CA: Sage.

Diamond, T. (1992). *Making gray gold: Narratives of nursing home care.* Chicago: University of Chicago Press.

Dingwall, R., Eekelaar, J., & Murray, T. (1983). *The protection of children: State intervention and family life.* Oxford, UK: Blackwell.

Drew, P., & Heritage, J. (Eds.). (1992). *Talk at work.* Cambridge, UK: Cambridge University Press.

Edwards, D. (1999). Shared knowledge as a performative and rhetorical category. In J. Verschueren (Ed.), *Pragmatics in 1998: Selected papers from the 6th International Pragmatics Conference* (Vol. 2, pp. 130–141). Antwerp, Belgium: International Pragmatics Association.

Edwards, D. (2005). Discursive psychology. In K. L. Fitch & R. E. Sanders (Eds.), *Handbook of language and social interaction* (pp. 257–273). Hillsdale, NJ: Lawrence Erlbaum.

Edwards, D., & Potter, J. (1992). *Discursive psychology.* London: Sage.

Ellis, C. (1991). Sociological introspection and emotional experience. *Symbolic Interaction, 14,* 23–50.

Ellis, C. (2004). *The ethnographic I: A methodological novel about autoethnography.* Walnut Creek, CA: AltaMira.

Ellis, C., & Bochner A. P. (Eds.). (1996). *Composing ethnography: Alternative forms of qualitative writing.* Walnut Creek, CA: AltaMira.

Ellis, C., & Flaherty, M. (Eds.). (1992). *Investigating subjectivity.* Newbury Park, CA: Sage.

Emerson, R. M. (1969). *Judging delinquents.* Chicago: Aldine de Gruyter.

Emerson, R. M., & Messinger, S. (1977). The micro-politics of trouble. *Social Problems, 25,* 121–134.

Fairclough, N. (1995). *Critical discourse analysis.* London: Longman.

Foucault, M. (1965). *Madness and civilization.* New York: Random House.

Foucault, M. (1972). *The archaeology of knowledge.* New York: Pantheon.

Foucault, M. (1975). *The birth of the clinic.* New York: Vintage.

Foucault, M. (1979). *Discipline and punish.* New York: Vintage.

Foucault, M. (1980). *Power/knowledge.* New York. Pantheon.

Foucault, M. (1988). The ethic of care for the self as a practice of freedom. In J. Bernauer & G. Rasmussen (Eds.), *The final Foucault* (pp. 1–20). Cambridge: MIT Press.

Garfinkel, H. (1967). *Studies in ethnomethodology.* Englewood Cliffs, NJ: Prentice Hall.

Garfinkel, H. (1988). Evidence for locally produced, naturally accountable phenomena of order, logic, reason, meaning, method, etc. in and as of the essential quiddity of immortal ordinary society: Vol. 1. An announcement of studies. *Sociological Theory, 6,* 103–109.

Garfinkel, H. (2002). *Ethnomethodology's program: Working out Durkheim's aphorism.* Lanham, MD: Rowman & Littlefield.

Garfinkel, H. (2006). *Seeing sociologically: The routine grounds of social action.* Boulder, CO: Paradigm Publishers.

Garfinkel, H., Lynch, M., & Livingston, E. (1981). The work of a discovering science construed with materials from the optically discovered pulsar. *Philosophy of the Social Sciences, 11,* 131–158.

Garfinkel, H., & Sacks, H. (1970). On the formal structures of practical actions. In J. C. McKinney & E. A. Tiryakian (Eds.), *Theoretical sociology* (pp. 338–366). New York: Appleton-Century-Crofts.

Gilbert, G. N., & Mulkay, M. (1984). *Opening Pandora's box: A sociological analysis of scientists' discourse.* Cambridge, UK: Cambridge University Press.

Glassie, H. H. (1995). *Passing the time in Ballymenone: Culture and history of an Ulster community.* Bloomington: Indiana University Press.

Glassie, H. H. (2006). *The stars of Ballymenone.* Bloomington: Indiana University Press.

Goodall, H. L., Jr. (2000). *Writing the new ethnography.* Walnut Creek, CA: AltaMira.

Grahame, K. M. (1998). Asian women, job training, and the social organization of immigrant labor markets. *Qualitative Sociology, 53,* 75–90.

Griffith, A. I., & Smith, D. E. (2004). *Mothering for schooling.* New York: Routledge Falmer.

Gubrium, J. F. (1992). *Out of control: Family therapy and domestic disorder.* Newbury Park, CA: Sage.

Gubrium, J. F. (1993a). For a cautious naturalism. In J. Holstein & G. Miller (Eds.), *Reconsidering social constructionism* (pp. 89–101). New York: Aldine de Gruyter.

Gubrium, J. F. (1993b). *Speaking of life: Horizons of meaning for nursing home residents.* Hawthorne, NY: Aldine de Gruyter.

Gubrium, J. F., & Holstein, J. A. (1990). *What is family?* Mountain View, CA: Mayfield.

Gubrium, J. F., & Holstein, J. A. (1995). Life course malleability: Biographical work and deprivatization. *Sociological Inquiry, 53,* 207–223.

Gubrium, J. F., & Holstein, J. A. (1997). *The new language of qualitative method.* New York: Oxford University Press.

Gubrium, J. F., & Holstein, J. A. (Eds.). (2001). *Institutional selves: Troubled identities in a postmodern world.* New York: Oxford University Press.

Gubrium, J. F., & Holstein, J. A. (2008). Narrative ethnography. In S. Hesse-Biber & P. Leavy (Eds.), *Handbook of emergent methods* (pp. 241–264). New York: Guilford.

Gubrium, J. F., & Holstein, J. A. (2009). *Analyzing narrative reality* Thousand Oaks, CA: Sage.

Gubrium, J. F., & Holstein, J. A. (2011). "Don't argue with the members." *The American Sociologist, 42.*

Hacking, I. (1999). *The social construction of what?* Cambridge, MA: Harvard University Press.

Hepburn, A. (1997). Teachers and secondary school bullying: A postmodern discourse analysis. *Discourse and Society, 8,* 27–48.

Hepburn, A. (2003). *An introduction to critical social psychology.* London: Sage.

Heritage, J. (1984). *Garfinkel and ethnomethodology.* Cambridge, UK: Polity.

Heritage, J. (1997). Conversation analysis and institutional talk: Analyzing data. In D. Silverman (Ed.), *Qualitative research: Theory, method and practice* (pp. 161–182). London: Sage.

Hewitt, J. P. (1997). *Self and society.* Boston: Allyn & Bacon.

Holstein, J. A. (1993). *Court-ordered insanity: Interpretive practice and involuntary commitment.* Hawthorne, NY: Aldine de Gruyter.

Holstein, J. A., & Gubrium, J. F. (1994). Phenomenology, ethnomethodology, and interpretive practice. In N. K. Denzin & Y. S. Lincoln (Eds.), *Handbook of qualitative research* (pp. 262–272). Newbury Park, CA: Sage.

Holstein, J. A., & Gubrium, J. F. (1995). *The active interview.* Thousand Oaks, CA: Sage.

Holstein, J. A., & Gubrium, J. F. (2000a). *Constructing the life course* (2nd ed.). Dix Hills, NY: General Hall.

Holstein, J. A., & Gubrium, J. F. (2000b). *The self we live by: Narrative identity in a postmodern world.* New York: Oxford University Press.

Holstein, J. A., & Gubrium, J. F. (2003). A constructionist analytics for social problems. In *Challenges and choices: Constructionist perspectives on social problems* (pp. 187–208). Hawthorne, NY: Aldine de Gruyter.

Holstein, J. A., & Gubrium, J. F. (2004). Context: Working it up, down, and across. In C. Seale, G. Gobo, J. F. Gubrium, & D. Silverman (Eds.), *Qualitative research practice* (pp. 297–343. London: Sage.

Holstein, J. A., & Gubrium, J. F (Eds.). (2008). *Handbook of constructionist research.* New York: Guilford.

Hughes, E. C. (1984). Going concerns: The study of American institutions. In D. Riesman & H. Becker (Eds.), *The sociological eye* (pp. 52–64). New Brunswick, NJ: Transaction Books.

Husserl, E. (1970). *Logical investigations.* New York: Humanities Press.

Hymes, D. (1964). The ethnography of communication. *American Anthropologist, 66,* 6–56.

Jasper, J. M., & Goodwin, J. (2005). From the editors. *Contexts, 4*(3), 3.

Kendall, G., & Wickham, G. (1999). *Using Foucault's methods.* London: Sage.

Livingston, E. (1986). *The ethnomethodological foundations of mathematics.* London: Routledge & Kegan Paul.

Luken, P. C., & Vaughan, S. (2006). Standardizing childrearing through housing. *Social Problems, 53,* 299–331.

Lynch, M. (1985). *Art and artifact in laboratory science.* London: Routledge & Kegan Paul.

Lynch, M. (1993). *Scientific practice and ordinary action.* Cambridge, UK: Cambridge University Press.

Lynch, M. (2008). Ethnomethodology as a provocation to constructionism. In J. A. Holstein & J. F. Gubrium (Eds.), *Handbook of constructionist research* (pp. 715–733). New York: Guilford.

Lynch, M., & Bogen, D. (1994). Harvey Sacks' primitive natural science. *Theory, Culture, and Society, 11,* 65–104.

Lynch, M., & Bogen, D. (1996). *The spectacle of history.* Durham, NC: Duke University Press.

Lynch, M., Cole, S., McNally, R., & Jenkins, K. (2008). *Truth machine: The contentious history of DNA fingerprinting.* Chicago: University of Chicago Press.

Manicom, A. (1995). What's class got to do with it? Class, gender, and teachers' work. In M. Campbell & A. Manicom (Eds.), *Knowledge, experience, and ruling relations: Studies in the social organization of knowledge* (pp. 135–148). Toronto: University of Toronto Press.

Martin, A., & Lynch, M. (2009). Counting things and people: The practices and politics of counting. *Social Problems, 56,* 243–266.

Marvasti, A. (2003). *Being homeless: Textual and narrative constructions.* Lanham, MD: Lexington Books.

Marx, K. (1956). *Selected writings in sociology and social philosophy* (T. Bottomore, Ed.). New York: McGraw-Hill.

Maynard, D. W. (1984). *Inside plea bargaining.* New York: Plenum.

Maynard, D. W. (1989). On the ethnography and analysis of discourse in institutional settings. In J. Holstein & G. Miller (Eds.), *Perspectives on social problems* (Vol. 1, pp. 127–146). Greenwich, CT: JAI.

Maynard, D. W. (1998). On qualitative inquiry and extramodernity. *Contemporary Sociology, 27,* 343–345.

Maynard, D. W. (2003). *Bad news, good news: Conversational order in everyday talk and clinical settings.* Chicago: University of Chicago Press.

Maynard, D. W., & Clayman, S. E. (1991). The diversity of ethnomethodology. *Annual Review of Sociology, 17,* 385–418.

McCoy, L. (2008). Institutional ethnography and constructionism. In J. A. Holstein & J. F. Gubrium (Eds.), *Handbook of constructionist research* (pp. 701–714). New York: Guilford.

McHoul, A. (1986). The getting of sexuality: Foucault, Garfinkel, and the analysis of sexual discourse. *Theory, Culture, and Society, 3,* 65–79.

Mead, G. H. (1934). *Mind, self, and society.* Chicago: University of Chicago Press.

Mehan, H. (1979). *Learning lessons: Social organization in the classroom.* Cambridge, MA: Harvard University Press.

Mehan, H. (1991). The school's work of sorting students. In D. Zimmerman & D. Boden (Eds.), *Talk and social structure* (pp. 71–90). Cambridge, UK: Polity.

Mehan, H., & Wood, H. (1975). *The reality of ethnomethodology.* New York: Wiley.

Miller, G. (1991). *Enforcing the work ethic.* Albany: SUNY Press.

Miller, G. (1994). Toward ethnographies of institutional discourse. *Journal of Contemporary Ethnography, 23,* 280–306.

Miller, G. (1997a). *Becoming miracle workers: Language and meaning in brief therapy.* Hawthorne, NY: Aldine de Gruyter.

Miller, G. (1997b). Building bridges: The possibility of analytic dialogue between ethnography, conversation analysis, and Foucault. In D. Silverman (Ed.), *Qualitative research: Theory, method and practice* (pp. 24–44). London: Sage.

Mykhalovskiy, E., & McCoy, L. (2002). Troubling ruling discourses of health: Using institutional ethnography in community-based research. *Critical Public Health, 12,* 17–37.

Narayan, K. (1989). *Storytellers, saints, and scoundrels: Folk narrative in Hindu religious teaching.* Philadelphia: University of Pennsylvania Press.

Narayan, K., & George, K. N. (2002). Personal and folk narrative as culture representation. In J. F. Gubrium & J. A. Holstein (Eds.), *Handbook of interview research* (pp. 815–832). Thousand Oaks, CA: Sage.

Nikander, P. (2002). *Age in action: Membership work and stages of life categories in talk.* Helsinki, Finland: Academia Scientarum Fennica.

Nikander, P. (2008). Constructionism and discourse analysis. In J. A. Holstein & J. F. Gubrium (Eds.), *Handbook of constructionist research* (pp. 413–428). New York: Guilford.

Norrick, N. R. (2000). *Conversational narrative: Storytelling in everyday talk.* Amsterdam: John Benjamins Publishing.

Ochs, E., & Capps, L. (2001). *Living narrative: Creating lives in everyday storytelling.* Cambridge, MA: Harvard University Press.

Pollner, M. (1987). *Mundane reason.* Cambridge, UK: Cambridge University Press.

Pollner, M. (1991). Left of ethnomethodology: The rise and decline of radical reflexivity. *American Sociological Review, 56,* 370–380.

Pollner, M. (2011a). The end(s) of ethnomethodology. *The American Sociologist, 42.*

Pollner, M. (2011b). Ethnomethodology from/as/to business. *The American Sociologist, 42.*

Pollner, M. (2011c). Reflections on Garfinkel and ethnomethodology's program. *The American Sociologist, 42.*

Potter, J. (1996). *Representing reality: Discourse, rhetoric, and social construction.* London: Sage.

Potter, J. (1997). Discourse analysis as a way of analyzing naturally-occurring talk. In D. Silverman (Ed.), *Qualitative research* (pp. 144–160). London: Sage.

Potter, J. (2003). Discursive psychology: Between method and paradigm. *Discourse & Society, 14,* 783–794.

Potter, J., & Hepburn, A. (2008). Discursive constructionism. In J. A. Holstein & J. F. Gubrium (Eds.), *Handbook of constructionist research* (pp. 275–294). New York: Guilford.

Potter, J., & te Molder, H. (2005). Talking cognition: Mapping and making the terrain. In H. te Molder & J. Potter (Eds.), *Conversation and cognition* (pp. 1–54). Cambridge, MA: Cambridge University Press.

Potter, J., & Wetherell, M. (1987). *Discourse and social psychology.* London: Sage.

Prior, L. (1997). Following in Foucault's footsteps: Text and context in qualitative research. In D. Silverman (Ed.), *Qualitative research: Theory, method and practice* (pp. 63–79). London: Sage.

Rankin, J. M., & Campbell, M. L. (2006.) *Managing to nurse: Inside Canada's health care reform.* Toronto: University of Toronto Press.

Richardson, L. (1990a). Narrative and sociology. *Journal of Contemporary Ethnography, 9,* 116–136.

Richardson, L. (1990b). *Writing strategies: Reaching diverse audiences.* Newbury Park, CA: Sage.

Riessman, C. K. (1993). *Narrative analysis.* Thousand Oaks, CA: Sage.

Sacks, H. (1972). An initial investigation of the usability of conversational data for doing sociology. In D. Sudnow (Ed.), *Studies in social interaction* (pp. 31–74). New York: Free Press.

Sacks, H. (1992). *Lectures on conversation* (Vols. 1 and 2). Oxford, UK: Blackwell.

Sacks, H., Schegloff, E., & Jefferson, G. (1974). A simplest systematics for the organization of turn-taking for conversation. *Language, 50,* 696–735.

Schutz, A. (1962). *The problem of social reality.* The Hague, the Netherlands: Martinus Nijhoff.

Schutz, A. (1964). *Studies in social theory.* The Hague, the Netherlands: Martinus Nijhoff.

Schutz, A. (1967). *The phenomenology of the social world.* Evanston, IL: Northwestern University Press.

Schutz, A. (1970). *On phenomenology and social relations.* Chicago: University of Chicago Press.

Silverman, D. (1985). *Qualitative methodology and sociology.* Aldershot, UK: Grower.

Silverman, D. (1993). *Interpretive qualitative data.* London: Sage.

Silverman, D. (Ed.). (1997). *Qualitative research.* London: Sage.

Silverman, D. (1998). *Harvey Sacks: Conversation analysis and social science.* New York: Oxford University Press.

Smith, D. E. (1987). *The everyday world as problematic.* Boston: Northeastern University Press.

Smith, D. E. (1990a). *The conceptual practices of power: A feminist sociology of knowledge.* Toronto: University of Toronto Press.

Smith, D. E. (1990b). *Texts, facts, and femininity.* London: Routledge.

Smith, D. E. (1999). *Writing the social: Critique, theory, and investigations.* Toronto: University of Toronto Press.

Smith, D. E. (2005). *Institutional ethnography: A sociology for people.* Lanham, MD: AltaMira.

Smith, D. E. (Ed.). (2006). *Institutional ethnography as practice.* Lanham, MD: AltaMira.

Smith, G. W. (1988). Policing the gay community: An inquiry into textually mediated relations. *International Journal of Sociology and the Law, 16,* 163–183.

Speer, S.A., & Stokoe, E. (Eds.). (in press). *Conversation and gender.* Cambridge, UK: Cambridge University Press.

Tedlock, B. (1991). From participant observation to the observation of participation: The emergence of narrative ethnography. *Journal of Anthropological Research, 47,* 69–94.

Tedlock, B. (1992). *The beautiful and the dangerous: Encounters with the Zuni Indians.* New York: Viking.

Tedlock, B. (2004). Narrative ethnography as social science discourse. *Studies in Symbolic Interaction, 27,* 23–31.

ten Have, P. (1990). Methodological issues in conversation analysis. *Bulletin de Methodolgie Sociologique, 27,* 23–51.

Thomas, W. I. (1931). *The unadjusted girl.* Boston: Little, Brown.

Van Djik, T. A. (1993). Principles of critical discourse analysis. *Discourse and Society, 4,* 249–283.

Walby, K. (2005). How closed-circuit television surveillance organizes the social: An institutional ethnography. *Canadian Journal of Sociology, 30,* 189–214.

Weigert, A. J. (1981). *Sociology of everyday life.* New York: Longman.

Weigt, J. (2006). Compromises to carework: The social organization of mothers' experiences in the low-wage labor market after welfare reform. *Social Problems, 53,* 332–351.

Weinberg, D. (2005). *Of others inside: Insanity, addiction, and belonging in America.* Philadelphia: Temple University Press.

Weinberg, D. (2008). The philosophical foundations of constructionist research. In J. A. Holstein & J. F. Gubrium (Eds.), *Handbook of constructionist research* (pp. 13–39). New York: Guilford.

Wetherell, M. (1998). Positioning and interpretive repertoires: Conversation analysis and post-structuralism in dialogue. *Discourse and Society, 9,* 387–412.

Wetherell, M., & Potter, J. (1992) *Mapping the language of racism: Discourse and the legitimation of exploitation.* New York: Columbia University Press.

Wieder, D. L. (1988). *Language and social reality.* Washington, DC: University Press of America.

Wittgenstein, L. (1953). *Philosophical investigations.* New York: Macmillan.

Wittgenstein, L. (1958). *Philosophical investigations.* New York: Macmillan.

Wodak, R. (2004). Critical discourse analysis. In C. Seale, G. Gobo, J. F. Gubrium, & D. Silverman (Eds.), *Qualitative research practice.* London: Sage.

Wodak, R., & Meyer, M. (Eds.). (2009). *Methods of critical discourse analysis.* London: Sage.

Wooffitt, R. (1992). *Telling tales of the unexpected: The organization of factual discourse.* London: Harvester/Wheatsheaf.

Wooffitt, R. (2005). *Conversation analysis and discourse analysis: A comparative and critical introduction.* London: Sage.

Woolgar, S., & Pawluch, D. (1985). Ontological gerrymandering. *Social Problems, 32,* 214–227.

Young, A. (1995). *The harmony of illusions.* Princeton, NJ: Princeton University Press.

Zimmerman, D. H. (1988). On conversation: The conversation analytic perspective. In J. A. Anderson (Ed.), *Communication yearbook* (Vol. 2, pp. 406–432). Newbury Park, CA: Sage.

9

Grounded Theory Methods in Social Justice Research

Kathy Charmaz[1]

Qualitative research has long attracted researchers who hope that their studies will matter in the public arena as well as in their disciplines. Yet many qualitative studies have been conducted that posed intriguing intellectual questions, addressed an interesting population, or explored an understudied phenomenon without raising explicit questions concerning social justice or policies that result in inequities. Such studies could often be taken a step or two further to explicate and explore social justice issues and subsequently reframe discussion of the studied phenomenon. What does social justice research entail? How can qualitative researchers move in this direction? What tools do they need?

When I speak of social justice inquiry, I mean studies that attend to inequities and equality, barriers and access, poverty and privilege, individual rights and the collective good, and their implications for suffering. Social justice inquiry also includes taking a critical stance toward social structures and processes that shape individual and collective life. I cast a wide net here across areas and levels of analysis in which questions about social justice arise. I include micro, meso, and macro levels of analysis, the local and global, as well as relationships between these levels. In the past, many social justice researchers have assumed that they must focus on macro structural relationships, but issues concerning social justice occur in micro situations and meso contexts, as well as in macro worlds and processes. Social scientists can study how the macro affects the micro and how micro processes also influence larger social entities. Global, national, and local social and economic conditions shape and are shaped by collective and individual meanings and actions. Yet when, how, and to what extent these conditions affect specific groups and individuals may not be fully recognized.

This chapter builds on my argument in the third edition of *The SAGE Handbook of Qualitative Research* (Denzin & Lincoln, 2005): Qualitative researchers can use grounded theory methods to advance social justice inquiry. These methods begin with inductive logic, use emergent strategies, rely on comparative inquiry, and are explicitly analytic. All these attributes give social justice researchers tools to sharpen and specify their analyses that will increase the analytic power and influence of their work while simultaneously expediting the research process. Grounded theory methods not only offer social justice researchers tools for developing innovative analyses but also for examining established concepts afresh. To mine the largely untapped potential of grounded theory methods for social justice inquiry, social justice researchers need to understand the logic of the method, the development of its different versions, their epistemological roots, and how they might use it.

Research in the area of social justice addresses differential power, prestige, resources, and suffering among peoples and individuals. It focuses on and furthers equitable resources, fairness, and eradication of oppression (Feagin, 1999).[2] Some reports in social justice inquiry begin with an explicit value stance and an agenda for change (see, e.g., these grounded theory studies: Karabanow, 2008; Nack, 2008; Sakamoto, Chin, Chapra, & Ricciar, 2009; Ullman & Townsend, 2008).[3] Other research reports often convey a taken-for-granted concern with social justice (e.g., Dumit, 2006; Foote-Ardah, 2003; Frohmann, 1991, 1998; Gagné, 1996; Hyde & Kammerer, 2009; Jiménez, 2008; Lio, Melzer, & Reese, 2008; Lutgen-Sandvik, 2008; Mevorach, 2008; Moore, 2005; Swahnberg, Thapar-Björkert, & Berterö, 2007; Tuason, 2008; Veale & Stavrou, 2007). Still other authors indicate that they chose a controversial topic that has social justice implications because it could illuminate a theoretical problem (Einwohner & Spencer, 2005; Ogle, Eckman & Leslie, 2003; Spencer & Triche, 1994).[4] Researchers may, however, begin their studies with an interest in a social issue rather than an impassioned commitment to changing it (Wasserman & Clair, 2010). Yet, the very process of witnessing their participants' lives and analyzing their data may elicit concerns about social justice that they had not understood earlier or anticipated.

Many researchers hold ideals of creating a good society and a better world and thus pursue empirical studies to further their ideas. For those who identify themselves as social justice researchers, "shoulds" and "oughts" are part of the research process and product. Claiming an explicit value position and studying controversial topics can result in having one's work contested. Hence, some researchers remain silent about their value commitments and instead choose to frame their studies in conceptual terms, rather than social justice concerns.

Grounded theory is a method of qualitative inquiry[5] in which data collection and analysis reciprocally inform and shape each other through an emergent iterative process. The term, "grounded theory," refers to this method and its product, a theory developed from successive conceptual analysis of data. Researchers may adopt grounded theory strategies while using a variety of data collection methods. Grounded theory studies have frequently been interview studies, and some studies have used documents (Clarke, 1998; Einwohner & Spencer, 2005; Mulcahy, 1995; Star, 1989) or ethnographic data (e.g., Casper, 1998; Thornberg, 2007; Wasserman & Clair, 2010; Wolkomir, 2001, 2006). It is often difficult, however, to discern the extent to which researchers have engaged grounded theory strategies (Charmaz, 2007, 2010; Timmermans & Tavory, 2007).

The strategies of grounded theory provide a useful toolkit for social justice researchers to employ. Grounded theory practice consists of emergent research decisions and actions that particularly fit social justice studies. The grounded theory emphases on empirical scrutiny and analytic precision fosters creating nuanced analyses of how social and economic conditions work in specific situations, whether or not researchers take their work into explicit theory construction (see, e.g., Ball, Perkins, Hollingsworth, Whittington, & King, 2009; Dixon, 2007; Jackson-Jacobs, 2004; Lazzari, Ford, & Haughey, 1996; Sixsmith, 1999; Speed & Luker, 2006). Such analyses not only contribute to knowledge, but also can inform those practices and policies that social justice researchers seek to change.

Researchers can learn how to use grounded theory guidelines and put them to use for diverse research objectives, including interrogating social justice questions. To date, few grounded theory studies in social justice inquiry demonstrate theory construction. Many, however, show how grounded theory guidelines have sharpened thematic analyses. This chapter aims to clarify the method and its evolution, illuminate how researchers have used specific grounded theory guidelines, and demonstrate how this method complements social justice inquiry.

The constructivist revision of Glaser and Strauss's (1967) classic statement of grounded theory assumes that people construct both the studied phenomenon and the research process through their actions. This approach recognizes the constraints that historical, social, and situational conditions exert on these actions and acknowledges the researcher's active role in shaping the data and analysis. The constructivist version is particularly useful in social justice inquiry because it (1) rejects claims of objectivity, (2) locates researchers' generalizations, (3) considers researchers' and participants' relative positions and standpoints, (4) emphasizes reflexivity, (5) adopts sensitizing concepts such as power, privilege, equity, and oppression, and (6) remains alert to variation and difference (see Bryant & Charmaz, 2007; Charmaz, 2006, 2009b; Clarke, 2005; Clarke & Friese, 2007).

Nonetheless, adopting strategies common to all versions of grounded theory will advance social justice studies and, therefore, I discuss works that use all versions of grounded theory.

My discussion relies on a selective review of grounded theory studies in social justice inquiry. The burgeoning number and range of relevant works across disciplines and professions precludes a comprehensive review. The selected studies (1) show connections between social justice inquiry and grounded theory, (2) reveal debates concerning grounded theory, and (3) demonstrate ways to use this method. Like other qualitative research projects, many social justice studies indicate having used grounded theory strategies only for coding and confuse developing thematic topics for theoretical categories. One purpose of this chapter is to help researchers to make informed choices about when, how, and to what extent they adopt grounded theory logic and strategies. Grounded theory strategies can help scholars with diverse pursuits without necessarily developing a grounded theory.[6] The point is to make clear decisions and to be aware of their implications.

The Logic of Grounded Theory

Grounded theory is a method of social scientific theory construction. As Glaser and Strauss (1967) first stated, the grounded theory method consists of flexible analytic guidelines that enable researchers to focus their data collection and to build middle-range theories. These guidelines emphasize studying processes in the field setting(s), engaging in simultaneous data collection and analysis, adopting comparative methods, and checking and elaborating our tentative categories. We grounded theorists begin with a systematic inductive approach to inquiry but do not stop with induction as we subject our findings and tentative categories to rigorous tests.

Fundamentally, grounded theory is an iterative, comparative, interactive, and abductive method (Bryant & Charmaz, 2007; Charmaz, 2006, 2007, 2008e; Charmaz & Henwood, 2008). The grounded theory method leads researchers to go back and forth between analysis and data collection because each informs and advances the other. By asking analytic questions during each step in the iterative process, the researcher raises the abstract level of the analysis and intensifies its power. Using comparative methods throughout the analytic—and writing—processes sharpens a researcher's emerging analysis. Moreover, using a comparative approach in an iterative process keeps grounded theorists interacting with their data by asking analytic questions of these data and emerging analyses. Thus the strength of grounded theory not only resides in its comparative methodology but moreover, in its *interactive* essence (Charmaz, 2006, 2007, 2008a, 2008e, 2009b).

The method encourages researchers to become active, engaged analysts. Abductive reasoning keeps researchers involved. As grounded theorists, we engage in abductive reasoning when we come across a surprising finding during inductive data collection. Then we consider all possible theoretical accounts for this finding, form hypotheses or questions about them, and subsequently test these explanations with new data (Peirce, 1958; Reichert, 2007; Rosenthal, 2004). Abductive reasoning advances theory construction.

What does using the method involve? Grounded theory prompts us to study and interact with our data by moving through comparative levels of analysis. First, we compare data with data as we develop codes; next, we compare data with codes; after that, we compare codes and raise significant codes to tentative categories; then, we compare data and codes with these categories; subsequently, we treat our major category(ies) as a concept(s), and last, we compare concept with concept, which may include comparing our concept with disciplinary concepts. The analytic comparisons we make during our current phase of inquiry shape what we will do in the next phase and cannot be ascertained beforehand. The method prompts us to interact with our participants, data, codes, and tentative categories. Through these interactions, our nascent analyses emerge and take form (Charmaz, 2006, 2007, 2008b, 2008c, 2008e). This comparative, interactive process of inquiry leads us to move back and forth between data collection and analysis as each informs the other (Charmaz & Henwood, 2008). The grounded theory emphasis on theory construction influences how we interact with our participants and the questions we bring to the empirical world (see Charmaz, 2009a, 2009b).

The comparisons sharpen our analyses and the iterative data collection allows us to test our ideas and to check our emerging theoretical concepts. Grounded theorizing involves imaginative interpretations and rigorous examination of our data and nascent analyses (Charmaz, 2006; Kearney, 2007; Locke, 2007). Our systematic scrutiny not only increases analytic precision but also keeps us close to the data and, thus, strengthens our claims about it. Such an approach helps social justice researchers make their work visible and their voices heard.

In short, the logic of grounded theory involves fragmenting empirical data through coding and working with resultant codes to construct abstract categories that fit these data and offer a conceptual analysis of them

(Charmaz, 2006; Glaser, 1978, 1998). Grounded theorists start with empirical specifics to move toward general statements about their emergent categories and the relationships between them. This approach allows social justice researchers to address problems in specific empirical worlds and to theorize how their categories may apply to other situations and iniquities (Dixon, 2007; Lutgen-Sandvik, 2008; Rivera, 2008; Shelley, 2001; Wolkomir, 2001).

Grounded Theory Strategies in Social Justice Inquiry

The analytic power of grounded theory offers qualitative researchers distinct advantages in pursuing social justice inquiry. Five grounded theory strengths make it a particularly useful toolkit for social justice researchers. First, this method contains tools for analyzing and situating processes. Thus, the logic of grounded theory leads to (1) defining relevant processes, (2) demonstrating their contexts, (3) specifying the conditions in which these processes occur, (4) conceptualizing their phases, (5) explicating what contributes to their stability and/or change, and (6) outlining their consequences. Adopting this logic can help social justice researchers attend to the construction of inequities and how people act toward them. Thus, grounded theory logic can lead researchers to make explicit interpretations of what is happening in the empirical world and to offer an analysis that depicts how and why it happens.

Second, grounded theory can aid researchers in explicating their participants' implicit meanings and actions (see, for example, McPhail & DiNitto, 2005). A task for social justice researchers is to see beyond the obvious. The most significant meanings and actions in a field setting are often implicit. Successive, meticulous grounded theory analysis can help researchers to define implicit meanings and actions and to theorize tentative but plausible accounts of them. Subsequently, the grounded theory guideline of checking hunches and conjectures encourages researchers to subject their tentative ideas to rigorous scrutiny and to develop more robust analyses.

Third, the purpose of grounded theory is to construct middle-range theory from data. Hence, grounded theory can aid social justice researchers to increase the abstract level of conceptualization of their analyses. Social justice researchers can then identify the conditions under which their categories emerge, specify relationships between these categories, and define the consequences. Thus, they can build complexity into their analyses that challenges conventional explanations of the studied phenomenon.

Fourth, the constructivist version of grounded theory attends to context, positions, discourses, and meanings and actions and thus can be used to advance understandings of how power, oppression, and inequities differentially affect individuals, groups, and categories of people. Last, but extremely significant, grounded theory methods provide tools to reveal links between concrete experiences of suffering and social structure, culture, and social practices or policies (Charmaz, 2007; Choi & Holroyd, 2007; Einwohner & Spencer, 2005; Rier, 2007; Sandstrom, 1990, 1998).

To date, few researchers who adopt grounded theory methods have explicitly framed their work as contributions to social justice inquiry or made social justice issues a central focus (but see Mitchell & McCusker, 2008; Sakamoto et al., 2009; Tuason, 2008). Implicit concerns about justice, however, form a silent frame in numerous grounded theory studies. Many researchers' studies assume the significance of social justice goals (see, e.g., Carter, 2003; Ciambrone, 2007; Hyde & Kammerer, 2009; Jones, 2003; Karabanow, 2008; Mcintyre, 2002; Roxas, 2008; Scott, 2005; Scott, London, & Gross, 2007; Wasserman & Clair, 2010), and other studies advance these goals through the content of their analyses (Frohmann, 1998; Quint, 1965; Sakamoto et al., 2009; Sixsmith, 1999; Swahnberg et al., 2007; Ullman & Townsend, 2008; Valdez & Flores, 2005; Veale & Stavrou, 2007). In keeping with grounded theory logic, social justice issues may arise through grappling with data *analysis* as well as through learning what is happening during data collection or starting from an explicit standpoint of pursuing social justice.

Researchers who pursue social justice goals enrich the contributions of development of the grounded theory method. Their attentiveness to context, constraint, power, and inequality advances attending to structural, temporal, and situational contexts in qualitative research generally and in grounded theory studies specifically. Social justice researchers are attuned to the silent workings of structure and power. They can offer grounded theorists important reminders of how historical conditions and larger social conditions shape current situations.

The critical stance of social justice inquiry combined with its structural focus can aid grounded theorists to locate subjective and collective experience in larger structures and increase understanding of how these structures work (Charmaz, 2005; Clarke, 2003, 2005; Maines, 2001; Rivera, 2008). The narrow focus and small size of many grounded theory studies have militated against the authors finding variation in their data, much less seeing how structure and historical process affect both the data and analysis. Like most qualitative researchers over the past 50 years, grounded theorists have often concentrated on overt processes and overt statements. A social justice standpoint brings critical inquiry to covert processes and invisible structures. Thus, we can discover contradictions between rhetoric and realities, ends and means, and goals and outcomes. This stance furthers understandings of the tacit, the liminal, and the marginal that otherwise might remain unseen and ignored, such as latent sources of conflict. The critical edge of social justice inquiry can help us subject our data to new tests and create new connections in our theories (Charmaz, 2005).

Recent grounded theory studies show increased engagement with social justice issues. To varying degrees, these studies address power, agency, structural constraints, resources, and analyze a wide range of questions including specific problems of impoverished, oppressed, stigmatized, and disenfranchised people (Choi & Holroyd, 2007; Ciambrone, 2007; Hyde & Kammerer, 2009; Mevorach, 2008; Ryder, 2007; Scott et al., 2007; Sixsmith, 1999; Tuason, 2008; Ullman & Townsend, 2008; Veale & Stavrou, 2007; Wilson & Luker, 2006; Wolkomir, 2001) as well as those that interrogate relationships between a social justice issue and social structure (Gunter, 2005; McDermott, 2007; Mitchell & McCusker, 2008). To date, the latter frequently emerge in the implications of studying a pressing issue or small group of people who suffer multiple and cumulative effects of iniquities (e.g., Dixon, 2007; Jiménez, 2008; Valadez, 2008; Wasserman & Clair, 2010; Wolkomir, 2001, 2006; Zieghan & Hinchman, 1999). Researchers in diverse disciplines and professions have primarily used grounded theory methods for small studies of individual behavior, as have researchers using other qualitative approaches. That does not, however, preclude adopting grounded theory to develop organizational and structural studies, as studies in organizations (O'Connor, Rice, Peters, & Veryzer, 2003; Scott, 2005; Vandenburgh, 2001) and the sociology of science have already shown (Casper, 1998; Clarke, 1998; Star, 1989). Grounded theory methods have gained a foothold in participatory action research (PAR) (Dick, 2007; Foster-Fishman, Nowell, Deacon, Nievar, & McCann, 2005; Kemmis & McTaggart, 2005; McIntyre, 2002; Poonamallee, 2009; Sakamoto et al., 2009; Teram, Schachter, & Stalker, 2005), a method that holds powerful potential for re-envisioning life and thus for advancing emancipatory change.

Reconstructing Grounded Theory

GROUNDED THEORY AS A SPECIFIC, GENERAL, AND GENERALIZED METHOD

Grounded theory is simultaneously a method that invokes specific strategies, a general method with guidelines that has informed qualitative inquiry, and a method whose strategies have become generalized, reconstructed, and contested. Strauss and Corbin (1994) observed over 15 years ago that grounded theory has become a general qualitative method. Grounded theory methodological strategies of simultaneous data collection and analysis, inductive coding, and memo writing have permeated qualitative research. Authors who claim to use grounded theory may, however, be conducting a more general form of qualitative research. Some authors' claims to be using grounded theory are attempts to legitimize inductive qualitative research; others result from naïve readings of the method. The abstract guidelines and dense writing in the early grounded theory texts led to misunderstandings of the method and confused readers (Piantanida, Tananis, & Grubs, 2004).

As grounded theory has become a general method, researchers may only adopt one or two grounded theory strategies (Foster-Fishman et al., 2005; Mitakidou, Tressou, & Karagianni, 2008). Other researchers may adopt more strategies but misunderstand them. And consistent with Virginia Olesen's (2007) statement about her work, some researchers may understand grounded theory strategies but their research questions and objectives lead them to combine grounded theory strategies with other qualitative approaches. Researchers frequently combine grounded theory strategies, especially coding, with narrative and thematic analyses (see, e.g., Cohn, Dyson, & Wessley, 2008; Hansen, Walters, & Baker, 2007; Harry, Sturges, & Klingner, 2005; Mathieson & Stam, 1995; Moreno, 2008; Salander, 2002; Sakamoto et al., 2009; Somerville, Featherstone, Hemingway, Timmis, & Feder, 2008; Tuason, 2008; Williamson, 2006; Wilson & Luker, 2006).

Naïve misunderstandings of grounded theory can prevent researchers from realizing its analytic power. In brief, misunderstandings about grounded theory arise in three main areas: coding, theoretical sampling,[7] and theory construction. I outline these misunderstandings and describe principles of grounded theory coding here but discuss them more thoroughly elsewhere (Charmaz, 2006, 2007, 2008b, 2008c). Cathy Urquhart (2003) questions whether grounded theory is, in essence, a coding technique. Coding is crucial but grounded theory is much more than a coding technique. Many researchers, however, use it for just that and appear to rely on CAQDAS (Computer Assisted Qualitative Data Analysis Software) to do their coding (see Bong, 2007, for problems of grounded theory coding with CAQDAS).

Grounded theory coding strategies include sorting, synthesizing, and summarizing data but, moreover, surpass these forms of data management. Rather, the fundamental characteristic of grounded theory coding involves taking data apart and defining how they are constituted. By asking what is happening in small segments of data and questioning what theoretical category each segment indicates, grounded theorists can take a fresh look at their data and create codes that lead to innovative analyses. By simultaneously raising questions about power and connections with larger social units, social justice researchers can show how data are constituted in ways that elude most grounded theorists.

Early grounded theory works (Glaser, 1978; Glaser & Strauss, 1967) lack clarity on what theoretical sampling means and how to conduct it. This lack of clarity combined with researchers' preconceptions of the term "sampling" created frequent misunderstandings. Theoretical sampling occurs *after* the initial data collection and analysis. It means sampling data to fill out the properties of an emergent conceptual category (Charmaz, 2006; Glaser, 1978, 1998; Morse, 2007). This strategy also helps a researcher to discover variation in the category and differences between categories. Thus, grounded theorists conduct theoretical sampling *after* they have developed tentative categories of data, *not* before they begin to collect data.

The objective of theoretical sampling is theory construction. Jane Hood (2007) contends that textbook authors often mistake theoretical sampling for purposive sampling, which sets criteria for representation of key attributes when planning initial data collection. Sharon Nepstad's (2007) methodological statement assumes this common misunderstanding: "Then I contacted staff members at these solidarity organizations and with their input I constructed a purposive theoretical sample (Glaser & Strauss, 1967) to ensure a diverse representation of geographic regions, age range, gender, and levels of participation in the movement" (p. 474).

In another area of common misunderstanding, many grounded theorists claim to construct theory but neglect to explicate what they assume theory encompasses. As I (Charmaz, 2006, p. 133) have argued, their assumptions about what constitutes theory suggest a range of meanings that include (1) a description, (2) an empirical generalization, (3) relationships between variables, and (4) an abstract understanding of relationships between concepts. If we define theory as either explaining the relationships between concepts or offering an abstract understanding of them, most studies that purport to have produced theory actually do not. Their authors assert that they construct theory but their analyses attest to their efforts to synthesize data and condense themes. Despite lofty claims to the contrary, most grounded theorists do not produce theory, although some move toward theory construction. And numerous authors produce mundane descriptions under the guise of doing grounded theory. The potential of grounded theory for theory construction has yet to be fully explored and exploited.

GROUNDED THEORY AS A SPECIFIC METHOD

We can discern convergent approaches between recognized grounded theorists that undergird grounded theory as a specific method. *How* grounded theorists use their methodological strategies differs from other qualitative researchers who study topics and structures instead of actions and processes. How we collect data and what we do with it matters. Research *actions* distinguish grounded theory from other types of qualitative inquiry (Charmaz, 2010). Grounded theorists representing each version engage in the following actions:

1. Conduct data collection and analysis simultaneously in an iterative process

2. Analyze actions and processes rather than themes and structure

3. Use comparative methods

4. Draw on data (e.g. narratives and descriptions) in service of developing new conceptual categories

5. Develop inductive categories through systematic data analysis

6. Emphasize theory construction rather than description or application of current theories

7. Engage in theoretical sampling

8. Search for variation in the studied categories or process

9. Pursue developing a category rather than covering a specific empirical topic (Charmaz, 2010)

Researchers who engage in the first five actions give their studies a distinctive analytic cast that differs from that of other qualitative works, particularly those that remain descriptive. Studies by grounded theorists reach across individuals and events to reveal a collective analytic story. Detailing conceptual categories takes precedence over participants' accounts and summarized data. A grounded theorist presents excerpts and summaries of data to demonstrate the connection between data and category and to offer evidence for the robustness of the category. A much smaller number of researchers engage in the remaining actions but they move their analyses into theory construction (Charmaz, 2010).

Despite agreement about these nine research actions, what stands as a bona fide grounded theory study may remain ambiguous (Charmaz, 2008e, 2010; Timmermans & Tavory, 2007). Methods statements in published works seldom address analytic strategies, much less detail them.[8] Certain studies such as Qin and Lykes (2006), Roschelle and Kaufman (2004), and Wolkomir (2001) illustrate distinctive grounded theory logic because they conceptualize a problematic process, construct analytic categories from inductive, comparative coding of data, define the properties of the categories, specify the relationships between categories, and outline the consequences of the processes.

If readers cannot discern distinctive grounded theory logic in the analysis, then it becomes difficult to determine whether authors' claims to using grounded theory methods are mistaken or are aimed to legitimize inductive qualitative research. Nonetheless, some authors' analyses may not indicate a grounded theory approach but their methodological descriptions reveal a sophisticated understanding of the method. Consider Henry Vandenburgh's (2001) statement in his study of organizational deviance:

> I followed the stages suggested by Turner (1981) in interpreting Strauss, first developing categories that used available data to suggest nominal classifications fitting these data closely. I then saturated these categories by accumulating all of the examples I could from my interview data that fit each category. Next, I then abstracted a definition for each category by stating the criteria for putting further instances of this specific type of phenomena into the category. I continued to use the categories by making follow-up calls based upon some of the questions raised. I then further exploited the categories by inspecting them to see if they suggested additional categories, suggested more general or specific instances, or suggested their opposites. I noted and developed links between categories by becoming aware of the patterned relationships between them, and by developing [a] hypothesis about these links. Finally, I considered the conditions under which the links held by theorizing about these relationships and the contexts that conditioned them. I then made conditions to existing theory. (2001, p. 62)

Like Vandenburgh, other grounded theorists may reveal their use of the method in their methodological discussions rather than in their analyses. Monica Casper (1997, 2007) and Robert Thornberg (Thornberg & Charmaz, in press) each have telling discussions that illuminate their studies (see Casper, 1998; Thornberg, 2007, 2009).

GROUNDED THEORY AS CONTESTED FROM WITHIN

Grounded theory is a contested method from both within and without (see Boychuk, Duchscher, & Morgan, 2004; Charmaz, 2006, 2009a; Kelle, 2005).[9] The contested status of the method further complicates what stands as a grounded theory study today. Since its inception in 1967, the grounded theory method has undergone both clarification and change by all of its major proponents.

Grounded theory has become an evolving *general* qualitative method with three versions: constructivist, objectivist, and postpositivist. Major texts that teach readers how to use grounded theory represent each version of grounded theory (Bryant & Charmaz, 2007; Charmaz, 2006; Corbin & Strauss, 2008; Glaser, 1978, 1998; Strauss & Corbin, 1990, 1998).

Constructivist grounded theory adopts the methodological strategies of Glaser and Strauss's classic statement but integrates relativity and reflexivity throughout the research process. As such, this approach loosens grounded theory from its positivist, objectivist roots and brings the researcher's roles and actions into view. Constructivist grounded theory uses methodological strategies developed by Barney Glaser, the spokesperson for objectivist grounded theory, yet builds on the social constructionism inherent in Anselm Strauss's symbolic interactionist perspective (Charmaz, 2006; 2007, 2008). Constructivist grounded theory views knowledge as located in time, space, and situation and takes into account the researcher's construction of emergent concepts.

Objectivist grounded theory shares an emphasis on constructing emergent concepts but emphasizes positivist empiricism with researcher neutrality while aiming for abstract generalizations independent of time, place, and specific people (Glaser, 1978, 1998, 2001). Unlike many positivists of the past, however, Glaser evinces little concern for establishing criteria for data collection or for evaluating its quality. He maintains that "all is data" (2001, p. 145) but leaves unexamined what researchers may define as "all." For Glaser, a concern with data reflects the "worrisome accuracy" (Glaser, 2002, para. 2) characterizing the conventional qualitative research that he argues against. Phyllis Noerager Stern (2007), a major proponent of Glaserian grounded theory, finds that a small number of cases is sufficient to saturate the researcher's emerging analytic categories. Glaser contends that examining many cases through the comparative process renders data objective. His previous view that research participants will tell researchers their main concern about what is happening in their setting (Glaser, 1992) likely contributed to the notion of discovering theory in the data, as though it simply resided there.[10] I have long argued that we cannot assume that participants' overt statements represent the most significant data (Charmaz, 1990, 1995, 2000). Instead their statements may take for granted fundamental processes that shape their lives or provide a strategic rhetoric to manage an impression (Charmaz, 1990, 2000, 2008f). Constructivist grounded theory contrasts with its objectivist predecessor in several fundamental ways, as I indicate above and summarize below. Postpositivist grounded theory (Corbin & Strauss, 2008; Strauss & Corbin, 1990, 1998) takes a middle ground between the two versions. It places less emphasis on emergence than the objectivist and constructivist approaches, as it provides preconceived coding and analytic frameworks to apply to data. Yet postpositivist grounded theory views reality as fluid, evolving, and open to change. Strauss and Corbin's early books made grounded theory a method of application rather than innovation (Charmaz, 2007).

In her recent reflection, however, Juliet Corbin (2009) outlines how her approach to research has changed. She describes having been imbued with methodological prescriptions of earlier decades that shaped writing the first two editions of *Basics of Qualitative Research* (Strauss & Corbin, 1990, 1998). These prescriptions led qualitative researchers to (1) study data to find the theory embedded in them; (2) maintain objectivity; (3) avoid "going native"; and (4) capture a semblance of "reality" in data and present them as "theoretical findings," while simultaneously believing that no one truth existed (Corbin, 2009, pp. 36–37). Corbin's list combined with the technical procedures in Strauss and Corbin's (1990, 1998) *Basics of Qualitative Research* confirms my earlier contentions (Charmaz, 2000, 2002) that their earlier editions contain objectivist threads. Corbin (2009) now, however, endorses engaging in reflexivity, takes a value stance that furthers social justice, believes in multiple realities, and disavows rigid application of technical procedures. These changes mark the updated third edition of *Basics of Qualitative Research* (Corbin & Strauss, 2008) and bring it closer to constructivist grounded theory.

The three versions of grounded theory share commitments to conceptualizing qualitative data through analyzing these data, constructing theoretical analyses, and adopting key grounded theory strategies. Each version emphasizes systematic inquiry using transparent strategies, begins with an inductive logic, emphasizes constructing theory, and aims to construct useful analyses for research participants, policy makers, and relevant practitioners (Charmaz, 2009b). Which strategies each version adopts, creates, or discards often differ in crucial ways that reflect more than favored or disfavored techniques. Differences in epistemology and ontology come into play.

EPISTEMOLOGICAL DIFFERENCES IN VERSIONS OF GROUNDED THEORY

Grounded theory contained the seeds of divergence from its beginnings. Glaser's Columbia University positivism and theoretical background in structural-functionalism[11] and Strauss's University of Chicago pragmatism[12] drew on conflicting philosophical and methodological presuppositions about the nature of reality, objectives of inquiry, and the research process and practice. The legacy of

Anselm Strauss rests on pragmatism and its development in symbolic interactionism (Charmaz, 2008d). Differences between a grounded theory informed by positivism and one informed by pragmatism appear most starkly in the contrast between objectivist grounded theory and constructivist grounded theory articulated in the second edition of this handbook (Charmaz, 2000; see also Bryant, 2002; Bryant & Charmaz, 2007, in press; Charmaz, 2002, 2006, 2007, 2008e, 2009b; Charmaz & Bryant, 2011; Charmaz & Henwood, 2008).

Objectivist grounded theory assumes that a neutral observer discovers data in a unitary external world. In this view, researchers can separate their values from "facts" residing in this world and suggests what Kelle (2007) calls "epistemological fundamentalism" (p. 205). In this approach, data gathering does not raise questions about researchers' tacit assumptions, privileged statuses, or the particular locations from which they view studied life. The researcher stands outside the studied phenomenon. Data are "there" rather than constructed. Researchers can add reflexivity about data collection and their roles, if they wish. Ordinarily, however, the neutral but passive observer simply gathers data to analyze as the authoritative expert and active analyst. In the objectivist logic, the number of cases corrects the researcher's possible biases. This approach gives priority to the researcher's voice and analysis and treats the researcher's representation of participants as straightforward, not as inherently problematic. A hazard is that researchers may import their unacknowledged presuppositions into the research process and product. Objectivist grounded theory aims for parsimonious abstract generalizations about relationships between variables that explain empirical phenomena. These generalizations constitute a middle-range theory explaining the studied phenomenon.

Constructivist grounded theory adopts a contrasting relativist approach that shifts its ontological and epistemological grounds (Charmaz, 2009b) and aligns them with the pragmatist tradition of Anselm Strauss (see Charmaz, 2008a, 2008d, 2009b; Reichert, 2007; Strübing, 2007). Here, realities are multiple and the viewer is part of what is viewed. Subjectivities matter. Values shape what stands as fact. To the extent possible, constructivist grounded theorists enter the studied phenomenon and attempt to see it from the inside. Researchers and participants co-construct the data through interaction. Data reflect their historical, social, and situational locations, including those of the researcher (Charmaz, 2009a, 2009b). Representations of the data are inherently problematic and partial. These concerns involve constructivist grounded theorists in reflexivity throughout inquiry as an integral part of the research process (see also Mruck & Mey, 2007; Neill, 2006). Rather than aiming for theoretical generalizations, constructivist grounded theory aims for interpretive understanding. The quest for generalizations erases difference and obscures variation (see also Clarke, 2003, 2005, 2006; Clarke & Friese, 2007). For constructivists, generalizations remain partial, conditional, and situated. Moreover, generalizations are not neutral. As Norman Denzin (2007) avows, interpretation is inherently political.

All these contrasts alter the processes and products of inquiry, as do differences in grounded theory practice, such as the contested place of the literature review. Glaser (1978, 1998, 2003) advocates conducting the literature review after developing an independent analysis to avoid forcing the data into preconceived categories and theories. However, few doctoral students and professional researchers begin their studies without knowledge of their fields (Charmaz, 2006; Lempert, 2007). They must include thorough literature reviews in dissertation proposals, grant applications, and today even in some human subjects IRB (institutional review board) applications. Karen Henwood and Nick Pidgeon's (2003) concept of theoretical agnosticism makes more sense than theoretical innocence. They argue that researchers need to subject all possible theoretical explanations of a phenomenon to rigorous scrutiny—whether from the literature or their own analysis. Perhaps most significantly, constructivist grounded theorists contend that researchers' starting points and standpoints, including those occurring throughout inquiry, influence the research process and product.

Grounded Theory in Mixed Methods Social Justice Inquiry

Researchers have identified grounded theory as a useful qualitative method to adopt in mixed methods research. Despite the growing number of studies that purport to use grounded theory studies in mixed methods to increase knowledge of the studied topic, few of these studies have a clear focus on social justice. The place of grounded theory in mixed methods social justice inquiry has yet to be developed. Thus, I offer brief concerns about mixed methods here that grounded theory social justice researchers might consider.

Mixed methods research usually means using both quantitative and qualitative methods to gain more, and a more nuanced, analysis of the research problem. Definitions of mixed methods and what they mean for inquiry are, however, contested and multiple. For mixed methods specialists (see, e.g., Cameron, 2009; Creswell, 2003; Morgan, 2007), the rapid rise of mixed methods is a movement heralding a paradigm shift analogous to the qualitative revolution that Denzin and Lincoln proclaimed in 1994. For many researchers, mixed methods are tools that produce findings, regardless of their reasons for adopting these tools, analyzing the findings, and deciding whether and to what extent to use each of the subsequent analyses. For a few researchers, mixed methods simply means using more than one method, whether or not these methods mix quantitative and qualitative research.[13] R. Burke Johnson, Anthony J. Onwuegbuzie, and Lisa A. Turner (2007) view mixed methods as combining qualitative and quantitative approaches including their respective perspectives, analyses, and forms of inference. They point out that mixed methods mean combining elements of methods for "breadth and depth of understanding and corroboration" (p. 123).

The discussion of mixed methods takes into account Norman Denzin's (1970) early call for triangulation (Greene, 2006; Morse, 1991; Tashakkori & Teddlie, 2003). Numerous researchers advocate methodological pluralism. Others take a more skeptical view and see the quantitative data and analysis as not only dominating mixed methods projects, but also "quantitizing" qualitative data by transforming them into numbers (Sandelowski, Voils, & Knafl, 2009).[14] However, Creswell, Shope, Plano Clark, and Green (2006) and Creswell and Plano Clark (2007) argue that qualitative methods extend mixed methods practice and may be given priority in mixed methods projects. In practice, researchers use mixed methods for varied purposes including to (1) construct instruments, (2) corroborate findings, (3) reduce cultural and investigator biases, (4) improve clinical trials, (5) address research participants' experience, (6) demonstrate credibility, (7) increase generalizability, and (8) inform professional practice and/or public policy.

Questions arise about integrating the results and analyses in mixed methods studies. To what extent should integration of quantitative and qualitative findings be a major methodological goal? What should be done when the qualitative and quantitative data have conflicting results? Bryman (2007) finds that mixed methods researchers often dismiss the qualitative analyses. He contends that "the key issue is whether in a mixed methods project, the end product is more than the sum of the individual quantitative and qualitative parts" (p. 8). In practice, that may not occur, nor may it have been the researchers' intent, as Bryman observes.

Mixed methods research designs often consist of complicated procedures and hence require team efforts. Grounded theory mixed methods projects are steadily increasing in fields such as education and health in which funded team research is common. Social justice research, especially in its explicit forms, is less likely to be a funded team project staffed by an array of methodological specialists having different but complementary skills. Few researchers are equally skilled in both quantitative and qualitative methods. Social justice research is likely to be an unfunded individual pursuit or a participatory action research project in which the researchers are members of and responsible to local communities.

Thomas W. Christ (2009) correctly observes that the goals of mixed methods research typically contrast with those in transformative inquiry in which social justice goals dominate. As he points out, researchers conduct critical and transformative research "to improve communities or reduce oppression, not to generalize results from a non-representative sample to a larger population" (p. 293). However, Donna Mertens (2007, 2010) argues eloquently for using mixed methods in a transformative paradigm to further social justice and Deborah K. Padgett (2009) states, "Social justice values do not have to be sidelined" (p. 101). Their purposes are explicit rather than hidden under a bland— and exclusive—term like "public sociology" (Burawoy, 2004).

Because social justice researchers may face skeptical audiences, presenting multiple forms of data in an integrated analysis may buttress their reports. The emerging philosophical foundations for mixed methods would support their efforts. Discussions are occurring that position mixed methods in pragmatism, and thus fit grounded theory research in social justice (see, e.g., Duemer & Zebidi, 2009; Feilzer, 2010; Morgan, 2007).

Researchers in education are among the most attuned to using grounded theory in mixed methods studies for social justice goals. As is evident in other studies, however, other researchers may assume, rather than state, social justice goals and use grounded theory in limited or extensive ways. To cite one interesting example, Sahin-Hodoglugil et al. (2009) used mixed methods in a randomized controlled clinical trial to study the effect of a low-cost HIV prevention method, the diaphragm. This method gave women control because they could use it without their male partners' knowledge. The authors invoked an iterative process in which both quantitative data and qualitative findings informed each other. Sahin-Hodoglugil et al. used insights about covert diaphragm use from the qualitative analysis to inform the analytic framework for the quantitative data and then subsequently explored some findings in the quantitative portion by gathering qualitative data. These researchers discovered that covert use was more complicated than they had anticipated and occurred along a continuum with disclosure.

In short, social justice researchers who can bring multiple types of solid data to their analyses make their reports less easy to dismiss. The test of mixed methods studies resides in doing credible work in all adopted methods to answer the research questions, fulfill the research goals, and convince relevant audiences of the significance of the reports.

Using Grounded Theory
Strategies in Social Justice Inquiry

In this section, I offer several specific examples of grounded theory in practice. Coding, memo writing, theoretical sampling and saturation, sorting memos are all part of the process. These grounded theory strategies have been described elsewhere in detail (Charmaz, 1990, 2001, 2002, 2005, 2006; Corbin & Strauss, 2008; Glaser, 1978, 1998, 2001, 2003; Strauss, 1987; Strauss & Corbin, 1990, 1998), so I merely introduce several examples of how constructing grounded theory analyses animate social justice inquiry.

CODING FOR PROCESSES

By using gerunds to code for actions, grounded theorists make individual or collective action and process visible and tangible. Social justice researchers can use grounded theory coding strategies to show how people enact injustice and inequity.[15] Gerunds define actions and enable grounded theorists to envision implicit actions and to identify how they are linked (see, e.g., Schwalbe, 2005; Schwalbe, Godwin, Schrock, Thompson, & Wolkomir, 2000).

Coding data for actions and mining the theoretical potential of both data and codes make grounded theory distinctive (Charmaz, 2006, 2008b, 2008c). Coding with gerunds pinpoints actions and thus helps grounded theorists to define what is happening in a fragment of data or a description of an incident. Gerunds enable grounded theorists to see implicit processes, to make connections between codes, and to keep their analyses active and emergent. In contrast, coding for topics and themes helps the researcher to sort and synthesize the data but neither breaks them apart as readily as grounded theory coding for actions nor fosters seeing implicit relationships between topics and themes.

Line-by-line coding, the initial grounded theory coding with gerunds, is a heuristic device to bring the researcher into the data, interact with it, and study each fragment of it (see Box 9.1). This type of coding helps to define implicit meanings and actions, gives researchers directions to explore, spurs making comparisons between data, and suggests emergent links between processes in the data to pursue and check. The data excerpts in the textboxes tell the story of a middle-aged woman with lupus erythematosus whose friends rushed her to a doctor to reassess her medications during a medical crisis. These medications often cause multiple side effects including confusion, depression, blurred vision, and inappropriate emotional responses. After two hospital transfers, this woman's medical crisis became redefined as a psychiatric crisis. Subsequently, her claims of having physical symptoms were unacknowledged and her requests for lupus medications went unheeded. She aroused the doctor's ire when he discovered another patient helping her complete the detailed confidential intake survey. Getting help with the survey broke hospital rules but this woman's vision problems meant that she could not read the survey and so just filled circles randomly after her doctor forbade her from having help. Her actions in one incident after another made sense given her situation, but fit neither hospital protocol nor her treatment program. Nevertheless, she attempted to present her views and to become her own advocate while her illness worsened. A psychiatrist who was unaware of her medical history or ignored it could invoke the same incidents as justifying his treatment approach. In this case, the grounded theory codes chronicle the woman's progressive loss of control over her life and her illness. Thus, the initial codes in the excerpt become the details substantiating a more general code, "resisting spiraling powerlessness."

Box 9.1a   Initial Coding for Topics and Themes

Examples of Codes	Narrative Data to Be Coded
Friends' support	P: They called the clinic to see if they could see me, if they would reevaluate some of my meds and stuff,
Hospitalization	and they said, "Oh yeah." When I got there they decided that they were going to put me in, put me
Conflict with doctor	away or whatever. And I ended up with a really bad doctor. Really bad. I even brought charges against him, but I lost.
Hospital transfer	I: What did he do?
Loss of choice of doctor	P: They put me in this one place, then the next day they sent me over to West Valley [hospital 60 miles away],
Conflict with doctor	and they didn't have any female doctors there, they only had male, so you didn't have a choice, and you get one and that's who you get the whole time you're
Physician control	there. For some reason he just took a disliking, I guess, and I tried to tell him about some of the problems

Threats Powerlessness Lack of physical care	I had with my Lupus and stuff, and angered him. [He had ordered her to take off her dark glasses.] And I wore [dark] glasses all the time and I tried to tell him, you know, that if he would turn off the fluorescent lights, I would take off the glasses. And he felt I was just being stubborn. I gave him the name and number of my doctor that makes the glasses and he just ripped it up in front of me and threw it away. And you have to go to group sessions all the time while you're there. I went, I just didn't speak to anybody. But I went. I went to everything they said I had to. And everyday he'd say that he was going to lock me up again. After ten days he did. He called me in to this little room and there were these two big guys there and they grabbed me and put me on a gurney and tied me down. And he sent me to a lockup ward, wouldn't let me make a call or do anything. And my potassium was down really bad and, I mean my whole–I was *sick*. They weren't giving me the pills that I needed and he just wouldn't even acknowledge that I had Lupus. It was bad.

Box 9.1b   Initial Grounded Theory Coding

Examples of Codes	Initial Narrative Data to Be Coded
Receiving friends' help in seeking care Requesting regimen reevaluation Gaining medical access Being admitted to hospital Getting a "bad" doctor Taking action against MD	P: They [her friends] called the clinic to see if they could see me, if they would reevaluate some of my meds and stuff, and they said, "Oh yeah." When I got there they decided that they were going to put me in, put me away or whatever. And I ended up with a really bad doctor. Really bad. I even brought charges against him, but I lost.

(Continued)

(Continued)

Being sent away Preferring a female MD Losing choice; dwindling control Getting stuck with MD Accounting for MD's behavior Trying to gain a voice—explaining symptoms Remaining unheard Asserting self Attempting to bargain Being misjudged Countering the judgment Offering evidence, being discounted Facing forced attendance Maintaining silence "Following" orders Receiving daily threats MD acting on threat Being overpowered Experiencing physical constraints Experiencing immediate loss of control Witnessing one's deterioration Being denied medication MD rejecting illness claims	I: What did he do? P: They put me in this one place, then the next day they sent me over to West Valley [hospital 60 miles away], and they didn't have any female doctors there, they only had male, so you didn't have a choice, and you get one and that's who you get the whole time you're there. For some reason he just took a disliking, I guess, and I tried to tell him about some of the problems I had with my Lupus and stuff, and angered him. [He had ordered her to take off her dark glasses.] And I wore [dark] glasses all the time [because of her photosensitivity] and I tried to tell him, you know, that if he would turn off the fluorescent lights, I would take off the glasses. And he felt I was just being stubborn. I gave him the name and number of my doctor that makes the glasses and he just ripped it up in front of me and threw it away. And you have to go to group sessions all the time while you're there. I went, I just didn't speak to anybody. But I went. I went to everything they said I had to. And everyday he'd say that he was going to lock me up again. After ten days he did. He called me in to this little room and there were these two big guys there and they grabbed me and put me on a gurney and tied me down. And he sent me to a lockup ward, wouldn't let me make a call or do anything. And my potassium was down really bad and, I mean my whole—I was *sick*. They weren't giving me the pills that I needed and he just wouldn't even acknowledge that I had Lupus. It was bad.

Comparing the codes in the boxes demonstrates that grounded theory codes preserve the character of the data, provide a precise handle on the material, and point to places that need further elucidation. Coding gives the researcher leads to pursue in subsequent data collection. In vivo codes use research participants' terms as codes to uncover their meanings and understand their emergent actions. Zieghan and Hinchman's (1999) in vivo codes: "breaking the ice," "figuring out how to help," "trying to understand" gave form to their study of college students who tutored adult learners. Note that they code in gerunds and thus portray the tutors' actions as they wrestled with dealing with their situations. Despite the student tutors increased awareness of poverty and lack of opportunity, the authors learned "that the border between campus life and the adult literacy community is a site of reproduction rather than transformation" (p. 99).

If coding in gerunds is so fruitful, why don't more researchers use them? In my view, the English language favors thinking in structures, topics, and themes rather than thinking in actions and processes. In addition, Strauss and Corbin's (1990, 1998) books have instructed thousands of researchers but emphasize gerunds less than Charmaz's (1990, 2006, 2008c) and Glaser's (1978, 1998) works. Many researchers report beginning with open coding, the initial coding in which the researcher examines and categorizes the data. Some turn next to axial coding, a type of coding to relate categories to subcategories, or to thematic coding but do not build fresh conceptual categories. Those following Strauss and Corbin (1990, 1998) often adopt complicated coding procedures to generate themes (Ball et al., 2009; Morrow & Smith, 1995; Sakamoto et al., 2009; Ullman & Townsend, 2008). Ullman and Townsend's (2008) coding procedures generated themes such as "Definitions of Feminist/Empowerment Approaches," "Importance of Control," "Techniques for Empowerment," and "Advocate Versus Agency Orientations," rather than a theory or conceptualized process. Although many authors found Strauss and Corbin's coding procedures to be helpful, some like Judy Kendall (1999) did not. She states, "I became so distracted by working the model to its natural conclusion that I stopped thinking about what the data were telling me in regard to the research question" (p. 753).

Grounded theory coding need not be complex. By engaging in thorough coding early in the research process and comparing data and codes, the researcher can identify which codes to explore as tentative categories. In turn, selecting categories expedites inquiry because the researcher then uses these categories to sort large batches of data. This approach is particularly useful in social justice research projects that address pressing social issues and policies. Grounded theory coding preserves empirical detail and simultaneously moves the project toward completion.

CONSIDERING CAQDAS

Increasingly, grounded theorists turn to one of the CAQDAS programs for coding the data. Several CAQDAS programs aim to be compatible with grounded theory logic and treat qualitative inquiry as interchangeable with grounded theory, or their conception of grounded theory. Software developers may have been criticized for their reliance on grounded theory. Ironically, however, their products may fit general qualitative coding for topics and themes more than coding for processes and engaging in comparative analysis. Grounded theory coding involves more than merely applying labels, identifying topics, and labeling themes, although many researchers do not realize it.

Depending on the grounded theorist's skills and objectives, advantages of using CAQDAS may include (1) relative ease of searching, retrieving, sorting, separating, and categorizing data and codes, (2) the ability to work at multiple levels of analysis simultaneously, (3) visibility of both the data and analytic processes, (4) document-sharing capacities for team research, and (5) management and organization of the data and emerging analysis. Since the advent of CAQDAS, numerous researchers (see, e.g., Fielding & Lee, 1998; Glaser, 2003; Weitzman, 2000) have raised varied questions concerning the conceivable advantages of using CAQDAS. Their concerns included users becoming too close or too distanced from their data, software design driving the analysis, and users being able to produce results without understanding the analytic process or range of analytic approaches. CAQDAS has gained much wider audiences since the early years and the software supports more intricate functions (Fielding & Lee, 2002). As the software becomes more sophisticated, its effects on knowledge production may change. Bringer, Johnston, and Brackenridge (2006) state that effective use of the grounded theory method holds greater significance than whether or not a software package is adopted. Konopásek (2008) avers that "The software . . . extends the researcher's mental capabilities to organise, to remember, and to be systematic. But while doing so it essentially remains a stupid instrument" (para. 2). Yet for Konopásek, the software not only consists of tools but also a virtual environment in which a set of mediations and embodied and practice-based knowledge production occurs.

Udo Kelle (2004) argues that CAQDAS requires its users to explicate their data management strategies and subsequently to think about their methodological and epistemological significance (p. 473). Does it? To what extent? Kelle acknowledges that CAQDAS could be viewed as a step in the rationalization and mechanization of qualitative research with the production of trivial results. The plethora of simplistic CAQDAS papers written under the guise of grounded theory confirms that this problem exists. However, Kelle contends that CAQDAS helps users to gain clarity about the processes involved in theory construction. Yet many researchers use CAQDAS—and grounded theory—primarily for coding without venturing into theory construction. Nonetheless, Kelle presents a worthy goal. But first, researchers need to learn to use the method.

DEFINING EXTANT CONCEPTS THROUGH DATA ANALYSIS

Social justice researchers use concepts that reflect structural arrangements and collective forces. They could adopt grounded theory strategies to refine or redefine these concepts by their empirical properties. In this sense, they can subject a sensitizing concept to rigorous *empirical* analysis. In the following example, I examined my data about the experience of illness and used marginalization as a sensitizing concept (Blumer, 1969; van den Hoonaard, 1997) from which to begin analysis. A 46-year old woman I call Marilyn (Charmaz, 2008f) recounted becoming ill and disabled with chronic fatigue syndrome and environmental illness.

Marilyn compares and contrasts her now unending saga of illness with the story of her past successes.

> I did a lot of things that were very challenging, and, you know, I used to work 50, 60 hours a week, and made good money and had great benefits, and had a life and all of that stuff changed one year—really abruptly in one year. And since then, everything is gone—from the financial to memory to—and everything in between. (p. 7)

Marilyn planned to testify at a city council meeting to restrict wood burning because of its devastating effects on people with lung disease, asthma, and chemical sensitivities. Because she anticipated possible discomfort from odors in a packed, closed room, she arrived 15 minutes before the time for community members to speak, but she had a long wait. Marilyn recounted:

> I had to wear my mask and by two hours the charcoal [filter in the mask] was shot and by the time I got up to speak, you know, my voice was going, my brain was starting to go, I was having problems formulating words, so it's, and then of course when you wear a mask, people, you know, you've seen mothers kind of pull their kids close to them. (pp. 8–9)

In her first statement, Marilyn is making identity claims about who she had been. Her second statement reveals the combined effects of appearance and of losing control over timing. The subsequent increasing visibility of Marilyn's difference led to her being discredited, devalued—othered. As I coded data and compared incidents, it was apparent that visible difference marginalized people with illnesses and disabilities. But what did marginalization mean? Through coding data, I identified properties of marginalization that linked its social origins with subjective experience and thus stated, "Marginalization means boundaries or barriers, distance or separation, and division or difference. Disconnection, devaluation, discrimination, and deprivation exemplify experiences of marginalization" (Charmaz, 2008f, p. 9). Moreover, I showed how people enacted marginalization.

Using grounded theory strategies in similar ways can assist social justice researchers to infuse taken-for-granted concepts with specific meanings.[16] Furthermore, it can help them avoid reifying, objectifying, and universalizing ideas without putting them to the test.

DEVELOPING CATEGORIES AND DISCOVERING MEANINGS

Grounded theory has long been touted as a method of discovery—of data and of theory. The constructivist critique argues that such "discoveries" are constructions located in space, time, and situation. Yet grounded theory can give us tools for constructing new understandings. Learning how participants define their situations, attempting to grasp what they assume, and understanding the problems that confront them become major sources of our "discoveries" and of the categories through which we conceptualize these discoveries. In his study of street youth, Jeff Karabanow (2008) discovered what leaving the street meant to these young people. He explains a crucial category and part of the process of leaving the streets as "cutting street ties."

> Cutting street ties meant leaving friends, surrogate families, and a culture associated with the downtown core. For many young people, friends and surrogate families were forged as a result of, or during, very stressful survival situations. (p. 781)

Karabanow's category speaks to meanings of the past as well as of the present and future. Cutting street ties meant more than merely leaving the streets. It occurred in a complex context in which the streets often held greater appeal to the young people than having shelter. Karabanow's analysis has resonance and power not only because of the clarity of his analysis but also because of the strength of his data: 128 interviews with street youth, 50 interviews with service providers, lengthy experience with the topic, and the help of two research assistants who lived on the streets.

Note that Karabanow's category, cutting street ties is a precondition for the larger process of leaving the streets. Grounded theory analyses gain this kind of specificity when researchers scrutinize the data to explicate the conditions that produce the studied process or phenomenon. In their study of women who had suffered childhood sexual abuse, Susan L. Morrow and Mary Lee Smith (1995) looked for causal conditions that led to the abuse. They identify two strategies that their research participants had used to cope with it: "keeping from being overwhelmed by threatening or dangerous feelings," and "managing helplessness, powerlessness, and lack of control" (pp. 27–28). Morrow and Smith find that these women had had few resources available for help and thus had adopted psychological strategies that focused inward on self and emotions such as reducing the intensity of troubling feelings, avoiding or escaping feelings, or using self-induced physical pain to override emotional pain.

As Morrow and Smith learned what these women had done to cope with their situations, they also learned the meanings the women had held. Social justice inquiry often focuses on people who experience horrendous coercion and oppression. Not surprisingly their categories reflect the untenable situations they observe. Angela Veale and Aki Stavrou (2007) studied the reintegration of Ugandan child abductees who had been forced to fight against the Uganda People's Defense Force (UPDF), their own people. Veale and Stavrou state that the child abductees are part rebel soldier, part a child of his or her village but yet identified as "external to it— as the aggressor" (p. 284). Veale and Stavrou's category depicting this conflicted identity is "Managing Contradictions." Veale and Stavrou state,

> The UPDF is Ugandan, and fighting the UPDF is a source of sadness, because they fought to kill the enemy in order to survive. Victor expressed the conflict as follows:
>
> *Victor:*   When fighting against the Ugandan Army, I felt partly as army, partly as civilian.
>
> *Interviewer:*   You used to steal food from Ugandan families. What did you feel when you steal food?
>
> *Victor:*   I feel very bad 'cause the food I am going to steal is [from] my father or guardian, my brothers' or sisters' guardian.
>
> For these youth, this dual role as soldier–abductee could not be resolved. (p. 285)

The irony of Veale and Stavrou's category resides in the impossibility of resolution: The contradictions exceeded the confronted reality and yet these very contradictions were the reality.

Each of the categories discussed above remain close to the studied experience and address what is happening in the data. Grounded theorists construct theoretical categories, in contrast, as they ask what theoretical questions and concepts the data indicate and Michelle Wolkomir's (2001) analysis suggests below.

CONCEPTUALIZING A PROCESS

The emphasis on coding in action terms enables grounded theorists to discern processes that might otherwise remain invisible. Scrutinizing these processes can help social justice researchers refine their concepts, form nuanced analyses, see how powerful cultural scripts are acted upon, and become attuned to possibilities for change. In her study of gay and ex-gay Christian men in a support group, Michelle Wolkomir (2001) outlines how the men engaged in "ideological maneuvering" (p. 407) to evade and subvert Christian ideology that condemned their sexuality and viewed them as "egregious sinners" (p. 408). She argues that such ideological revision requires sustained effort, particularly when conducted by marginalized groups without power.

Consistent with a grounded theory emphasis on analyzing social and social psychological processes, Wolkomir's major conceptual category, ideological maneuvering, is a process. She developed her analysis of this process through studying the men's actions and observing the tensions they faced from their perspectives. How could they avoid stigma and claim moral Christian identities? Wolkomir's (2001) guiding analytic question for her article asks, "Under what conditions is such change [ideological change] likely to occur, and how is it accomplished?" (p. 407). By raising such questions and defining these conditions, Wolkomir brings analytic precision to her analysis. Moreover, her work provides a theoretical concept that can be transported and tested in other empirical studies.

Wolkomir's article reveals the underpinnings of her grounded theory analysis while simultaneously providing an insightful analysis of the overall process and major conceptual category. Wolkomir states that the process of ideological maneuvering entails three subprocesses: (1) "selective dismantling of existing ideology to open new interpretive space; (2) constructing a new affirming ideology; and (3) authenticating new self-meanings" (p. 408). She treats these subprocesses as analytic categories and then demonstrates the actions constituting each one. Note that Wolkomir's categories are active, specific, and rooted in the data. Her categories depict how the men dealt with the Christian ideology that condemned and excluded them. Wolkomir found that for one support group, dismantling the existing ideology explicitly included "redefining sin" (p. 413). These men discovered new scriptural reasons to believe that the significance of homosexual sin had been exaggerated and "concluded that their homosexual sin was no worse than selfishness or gossip" (p. 414).

Not only does Wolkomir show how these men challenged and shifted reigning ideas and hierarchical relationships but she also specifies the conditions under which changes occur. Wolkomir's analysis does not end with successful ideological maneuvering. Instead, she positions her analysis in relation to its larger implications of her study. Wolkomir concludes that inequalities limit such ideological revision and, in turn, ideological maneuvering reproduces inequality because it allows the larger oppressive ideology to remain intact. In short, Wolkomir's grounded theory analysis advances our understanding of how ideological change can occur while simultaneously specifying its limits.

Wolkomir's processual analysis demonstrates grounded theory in practice. Her approach reveals how people confer meaning on their situation and enact ideological stances. Yet Wolkomir's analysis does more. It contains strong links between detailed ethnographic description, substantive processual categories, and development of a theoretical concept, ideological maneuvering. Wolkomir then situates her concept and frames her article in the larger theoretical discourse on ideology, and by doing so offers a dynamic analysis of relationships between agency and structure. Wolkomir's nuanced theoretical account contributes to knowledge in a substantive area, theoretical ideas in her discipline, and useful understandings for social justice scholars and activists.

DEFINING VARIATION

Defining variation in a process or phenomenon is an important grounded theory goal, particularly of the postpositivist and constructivist versions. Researchers who conduct thorough research may discover variation within their findings and subsequent analyses. Learning how to handle variation analytically and how to write about it strengthens the analytic precision and usefulness of the grounded theory.

Grounded theorists compare their analyses with the extant literature, which can serve as data to illuminate the properties of emergent categories. Ordinarily, grounded theorists develop their analyses first and then use the relevant literature for comparative analysis. Researchers who gain intimate knowledge of their participants and settings may, however, define sharp differences with the literature early in their research. They may then construct their analyses from this position. Both Wasserman and Clair (2010) and Roschelle and Kaufman (2004) discovered that homelessness was not monolithic and sought to demonstrate the variation they found. Roschelle and Kaufman focused on homeless kids in their ethnographic study of an organization that served and sheltered homeless families. They offered new representations of these children that challenged earlier conclusions of homeless children having developmental and psychiatric problems. In a similar logic, Wasserman and Clair argued that homeless men who had networks on the streets were safer than those who used shelters.

The features of the setting and context of the studied phenomenon thus shape behavior and events. Curtis Jackson-Jacobs (2004) realized that he had found a strategic site that challenged earlier knowledge about crack cocaine uses and their worlds. He analyzed the settings and context of crack cocaine use among four college students as a strategic site and made systematic comparisons between it and previously reported sites of crack use.

Following Glaser and Strauss's (1967) guidelines, Jackson-Jacobs (2004) treated the literature as data to analyze the variation between his strategic site to arrive at causal generalizations and thus build theory. Jackson-Jacobs revealed that two conditions in his study contrasted with prior research on crack cocaine use and altered our knowledge of it. First, college student crack cocaine users could keep their drug use bounded because they (1) had resources, (2) wanted to avoid being identified as crack users, (3) treated smoking crack as a leisure pursuit, (4) purchased crack from friends, and (5) gave higher priority to their conventional involvements.[17] Second, these students had substantial residential mobility within a "safe" area where college students lived, not where drug dealers and users hung out. The residential location gave the men a benign environment that camouflaged hard drug use. Mobility allowed them to move if tensions arose or when they feared being identified.

By following the men over time, Jackson-Jacobs witnessed the explanatory power of the two conditions he had specified. One man lost control of his drug use and suffered the stigma of his friends' viewing him as a failure and of his mother discovering his crack habit. Another man's situation changed upon moving home. Location matters. This man no longer had the safety and relative anonymity afforded by his former neighborhood. He and his suburban friends now had to buy rock cocaine in the nearby urban ghetto, which changed the conditions, meanings, and consequences of drug use. They got into trouble with the dealers and police and experienced violence at the hands of both.

Comparative Analysis With Extant Literatures

In the above ethnographies, the authors report that they were struck by the difference between the portrayals of their studied phenomenon in the literature and what they later observed. In conventional grounded theory practice, researchers develop their analyses first and then return to the literature, whether to position their studies or to use the literature as data. Roz Dixon (2007) delineates how she developed her analysis in her exploratory study of the early school experiences and peer relationships of 35 deaf adults. Early coding revealed that deaf children's classmates subjected them to physical and psychological attacks. Dixon's early codes consisted of incidents such as "pulled my hearing aids out," "damaged hearing aids," and "banged my ears." The children not only rejected a deaf classmate, but also colluded so that this child broke group norms, as the following account indicates:

Bryony: If there was a lot of noise, I didn't stand a hope of hearing anything . . . and frequently when things were going on and (the teachers) were trying to tell things, people would start drumming desks (*she demonstrates making the sound of very gentle knocking on the table top*).

Interviewer: So that you couldn't hear?

Bryony: So that I couldn't hear. . . . I wouldn't know what (had been said) . . . and the teacher would get pissed off with having to keep repeating, you know, "How many times do I have to tell you" sort of thing, and you'd say "Sorry, I didn't hear" . . . "Well, it's funny you heard for the last half hour." . . . and, you know, and I think the teachers were very suspicious of me." (Dixon, 2007, p. 12)

Apparently, Bryony had had no troubles with friendships at school until classmates excluded her after she became deaf. Dixon does not specify how the teacher's exasperated response contributed to the simultaneous processes of experiencing ostracism and harassment. The teacher likely gave her students license to break classroom deportment rules and further harass Bryony.[18] Dixon's detailed grounded theory coding of her interview data revealed signs of ostracism such as in Bryony's interview. Subsequently, Dixon used the literature as data to identify general properties of ostracism, the properties of temporary coercive ostracism, and the properties of actual exclusion. She states:

It was during the process of subsequently organizing the codes that some codes seemed particularly suggestive of ostracism. To test this hypothesis, a literature review was conducted to clarify the nature, function and parameters of ostracism. A set of codes was developed describing behaviours and contextual factors which might be seen in the interview data if ostracism had been at work. All data was reanalyzed. (2007, p. 9)

Consistent with conventional grounded theory practice, Dixon first coded her data and studied her codes. Subsequently, she examined and coded how other authors treated ostracism. This coding enabled her to define types of ostracism as well as the "generic features of ostracism" (pp. 13–14), which she tested with her data. While acknowledging inherent limitations of using retrospective accounts, Dixon distinguishes conditions that link ostracism and bullying and specifies conditions under which ostracism may be desirable.[19] Dixon's grounded theory analysis led her to define both problems related to ostracism by children and creative interventions for handling it.

Summary and Conclusions

The implications of the above discussion are fivefold. First, the review of grounded theory clarifies strategies and approaches that grounded theorists share. These strategies and approaches distinguish the method from other types of qualitative research. Simultaneously, the influence of grounded theory on the development of qualitative methods becomes more apparent.

Second, delineating the similarities between versions of grounded theory and juxtaposing their differences creates a space for methodological explication of foundational assumptions and of research practice. Grounded theory studies range between objectivist and constructionist approaches and often contain elements of both. Yet attending to foundational assumptions and to research practice constitute pivotal turns toward engaging in reflexivity. And that may heighten awareness of our research choices and actions and, moreover, deeper understandings of our research participants' situations because we see them in new light.

Third, the constructivist version reclaims grounded theory from being a method of application to a method of innovation. Wolkomir's (2001) analysis exemplifies the difference between application and innovation. She uses the method to learn about her participants' views and concerns, not to apply a set of rules to her data. Under these conditions, grounded theory remains an emergent method. Both the form and specific content of the method arise as the researcher grapples with the problems at hand. Thus, the emergent character of the method contributes to its flexibility. This flexibility gives social justice researchers a mutable frame for their studies that they can adapt to fit their research problems and budding analyses.

Fourth, constructivist grounded theory acknowledges the foundations of its production, calls for reproduction of the method on new grounds, and moves inquiry beyond what is overt and obvious. In these ways, constructivist grounded theory answers earlier criticisms of objectivist grounded theory that emanate from feminist scholarship (Olesen, 2007), postmodernism, performance, and interpretive ethnography (Denzin, 2007), as well as critiques by qualitative methodologists.[20] Constructivist grounded theory challenges positivist elements that ignore reflexivity, overlook ethical issues, disregard issues of representation, and do not attend to researchers' agency in constructing and interpreting data (Olesen, 2007).

Fifth, constructivist grounded theory acknowledges the dual roots of the method in positivism and pragmatism and seeks to develop the emphasis on pragmatism. Consistent with pragmatism, constructivist grounded theory acknowledges multiple perspectives and multiple forms of knowledge. Its practitioners become attuned to nuances in empirical worlds that elude researchers who assume a unitary method and unitary knowledge and thus are ill-quipped to grasp such nuances as the unheard voice of dissent and the silence of suffering. Both may remain imperceptible when researchers use objectivist grounded theory or, for that matter, conventional research methods. Classic grounded theory set forth tools for developing theoretical sensitivity. Constructivist grounded theory adds tools for increasing critical sensitivity and thus holds considerable potential for social justice inquiry.

The constructivist turn in grounded theory has clarified the strategies of the classic statements and generated a resurgence of interest in the method. It complements new developments such as Adele E. Clarke's (2005) situational analysis and incorporates methodological developments. It offers mixed methods researchers a set of useful tools and holds promise of informing software development. Constructivist grounded theory is and will be a method for the 21st century.

Notes

1. I thank Adele E. Clarke, Norman K. Denzin, and the following members of the Sonoma State University Faculty Writing Program—Sheila Katz, Lena McQuade, Suzanne Rivoire, Tom Rosin, and Richard Senghas—for their helpful comments on an earlier version of this chapter.

2. Such emphases often start with pressing social problems, collective concerns, and impassioned voices. In contrast, Rawls's (1971) emphasis on fairness begins from a distanced position of theorizing individual rights and risks from the standpoint of the rational actor under hypothetical conditions. Conceptions of social justice must take

into account both collective goods and individual rights and recognize that definitions of rationality as well as of "rational" actors are situated in time, space, and culture—and both can change. To foster justice, Nussbaum (2000, p. 234) argues that promoting a collective good must not subordinate the ends of some individuals over others. She observes that women suffer when a collective good is promoted without taking into account the internal power and opportunity hierarchies within a group.

3. Throughout my discussion, I focus on studies that identify grounded theory as their method of inquiry.

4. Their approach may follow conventions of framing research for academic consumption rather than indicating a stance on social justice.

5. One of the originators of grounded theory, Barney Glaser, has consistently argued that researchers can use the method for quantitative as well as qualitative research, and his recent book (2008) reaffirms this argument. To date, few researchers have acted on it.

6. But see earlier contentious arguments about purism in methods (Glaser, 1992; Greckhamer & Koro-Ljungberg, 2005; May, 1996; Stern, 1994; Wilson & Hutchinson, 1996).

7. Theoretical sampling means sampling to develop the properties of a theoretical category, not to sample for representation of a population.

8. The task of offering methodological discussions has been taken up in other venues, such as this handbook. Publishers' qualitative methods lists, journals such as *Qualitative Inquiry* and *International Journal of Social Research Methods,* as well as methodological articles in substantive journals bring methodological proclivities and practices into view. Where once methodological confessional tales focused on what happened in the research site, now authors such as Wasserman and Clair (2010), Suddaby and Greenwood (2005), and Harry, Sturges, and Klingner (2005) reveal remarkable candor in making their analytic strategies transparent. These authors invert the backstage of analytic work and bring it to the front stage of discussion. Although I view each discussion as only partly grounded theory (but see Suddaby's [2006] astute depiction of what is not grounded theory), I admire their candor and willingness to enter the methodological fray.

9. I have addressed criticisms of grounded theory in the third edition of this handbook in some detail, so I will only present those from within grounded theory here.

10. Over the years, Glaser (2001, 2003) has changed his view and now states that the researcher conceptualizes participants' main concern.

11. Structural-functionalism was the reigning theory of the 1950s. It invokes a biological metaphor, addresses the structure of social institutions, and evaluates how well they accomplished key societal tasks such as socializing children and controlling crime. Structural-functionalism assumes consensus between individuals and segments of society, studies social order, and emphasizes social roles within institutions (see Merton, 1957; Parsons, 1951).

12. Pragmatism not only informed Strauss's work, but also he stayed within and developed the pragmatist tradition through symbolic interactionism. This perspective emphasizes interaction, language, and culture as shaping the construction of meaning and action. It assumes a dynamic relationship between agentic, reflective actors and

society and thus sees social institutions and society as constructed, not as given (see Blumer, 1969; Reynolds & Herman, 2003; Strauss, 1959/1969, 1993).

13. Fielding and Cisneros-Puebla (2010) integrate CAQDAS and GIS (geographic information system) methods in an innovative mixed methods approach.

14. These authors affirm that "qualitizing" quantitative data also occurs.

15. Schwalbe et al.'s (2000) article and Harris's (2001, 2006a, 2006b) studies exemplify how inequalities are enacted.

16. At the time I worked on this analysis, the literature contained many studies that used marginalization as a significant concept. However, authors left its meanings implicit and understood rather than taking them as problematic.

17. This last point resonates with Patrick Biernacki's (1986) grounded theory of natural recovery from heroin use. Based on his findings, Biernacki constructs an analysis of identity. Relinquishing heroin use without treatment turned on the significance of having and maintaining conventional identities.

18. For a grounded theory of how school rules are enacted, see Thornberg (2007).

19. The reciprocal effects of interactional dynamics come into play here. Not all children who were ostracized were bullied. Dixon found that temporary ostracism by peers kept some children's angry outbursts in check and manageable.

20. See Charmaz (2005) for these critiques and my responses.

References

Ball, M. M., Perkins, M. M., Hollingsworth, C., Whittington, F. J., & King, S. V. (2009). Pathways to assisted living: The influence of race and class. *Journal of Applied Gerontology, 28,* 81–108.

Biernacki, P. L. (1986). *Pathways from heroin addition: Recovery without treatment.* Philadelphia: Temple University Press.

Blumer, H. (1969). *Symbolic interactionism.* Englewood Cliffs, NJ: Prentice Hall.

Bong, S. A. (2007). Debunking myths in CAQDAS use and coding in qualitative data analysis: Experiences with and reflections on grounded theory methodology. *Historical Social Research, 32*(Suppl. 19), 258–275.

Boychuk Duchscher, J. E., & Morgan, D. (2004). Grounded theory: Reflections on the emergence vs. forcing debate. *Journal of Advanced Nursing, 48*(6), 605–612.

Bringer, J. D., Johnston, L. H., & Brackenridge, C. H. (2006). Using computer-assisted qualitative data analysis software to develop a grounded theory project. *Field Methods, 18*(3), 245–266.

Bryant, A. (2002). Re-grounding grounded theory. *The Journal of Information Technology Theory and Application, 4,* 25–42.

Bryant, A., & Charmaz, K. (2007). Grounded theory in historical perspective: An epistemological account. In A. Bryant & K. Charmaz (Eds.), *The SAGE handbook of grounded theory* (pp. 31–57). London: Sage.

Bryant, A., & Charmaz, K. (in press). Grounded theory. In P. Vogt & M. Williams (Eds.), *The SAGE handbook of methodological innovations in the social sciences.* London: Sage.

Bryman, A. (2007). Barriers to integrating quantitative and qualitative research. *Journal of Mixed Methods Research, 1*(1), 8–22.

Burawoy, M. (2004). For public sociology. *American Sociological Review, 70*(1), 4–28.

Cameron, R. (2009). A sequential mixed model research design: Design, analytical and display issues. *International Journal of Multiple Research Approaches, 3*(2), 140–152.

Carter, P. L. (2003). Black cultural capital, status positioning, and schooling conflicts for low-income African-American youth. *Social Problems, 50*(1), 136–155.

Casper, M. J. (1997). Feminist politics and fetal surgery: Adventures of a research cowgirl on the reproductive frontier. *Feminist Studies, 23*(2), 232–262.

Casper, M. J. (1998). *The making of the unborn patient: A social anatomy of fetal surgery.* New Brunswick, NJ: Rutgers University Press.

Casper, M. J. (2007). Fetal surgery then and now. *Conscience 28*(3), 24–28.

Charmaz, K. (1990). "Discovering" chronic illness: Using grounded theory. *Social Science and Medicine, 30*(11), 1161–1172.

Charmaz, K. (1995). Between positivism and postmodernism: Implications for methods. In N. K. Denzin (Ed.), *Studies in symbolic interaction, 17,* 43–72.

Charmaz, K. (2000). Constructivist and objectivist grounded theory. In N. K. Denzin & Y. S. Lincoln (Eds.), *The SAGE handbook of qualitative research* (2nd ed., pp. 509–535). Thousand Oaks CA: Sage.

Charmaz, K. (2002). Grounded theory analysis. In J. F. Gubrium & J. A. Holstein (Eds.), *The SAGE handbook of interview research* (pp. 675–694). Thousand Oaks, CA: Sage.

Charmaz, K. (2005). Grounded theory in the 21st century: Applications for advancing social justice studies. In N. K. Denzin & Y. S. Lincoln (Eds.), *The SAGE handbook of qualitative research* (3rd ed., pp. 507–535). Thousand Oaks, CA: Sage.

Charmaz, K. (2006). *Constructing grounded theory: A practical guide through qualitative analysis.* London: Sage.

Charmaz, K. (2007). Constructionism and grounded theory. In J. A. Holstein & J. F. Gubrium (Eds.), *Handbook of constructionist research* (pp. 319–412). New York: Guilford.

Charmaz, K. (2008a). A future for symbolic interactionism. In N. K. Denzin (Ed.), *Studies in symbolic interaction, 32,* 51–59.

Charmaz, K. (2008b). Grounded theory. In J. A. Smith (Ed.), *Qualitative psychology: A practical guide to research methods* (2nd ed., pp. 81–110). London: Sage. (Revised and updated version of the 2003 chapter)

Charmaz, K. (2008c). Grounded theory as an emergent method. In S. N. Hesse-Biber & P. Leavy (Eds.), *The handbook of emergent methods* (pp. 155–170). New York: Guilford.

Charmaz, K. (2008d). The legacy of Anselm Strauss for constructivist grounded theory. In N. K. Denzin (ed.), *Studies in symbolic interaction, 32,* 127–141.

Charmaz, K. (2008e). Reconstructing grounded theory. In L. Bickman, P. Alasuutari, & J. Brannen (Eds.), *The SAGE handbook of social research methods* (pp. 461–478). London: Sage.

Charmaz, K. (2008f). Views from the margins: Voices, silences, and suffering. *Qualitative Research in Psychology, 5*(1), 7–18.

Charmaz, K. (2009a). Recollecting good and bad days. In W. Shaffir, A. Puddephatt, & S. Kleinknecht (Eds.), *Ethnographies revisited: The stories behind the story.* New York: Routledge.

Charmaz, K. (2009b). Shifting the grounds: Constructivist grounded theory methods for the twenty-first century. In J. M. Morse, P. N. Stern, J. Corbin, B. Bowers, K. Charmaz, & A. E. Clarke, *Developing grounded theory: The second generation* (pp. 127–154). Walnut Creek, CA: Left Coast Press.

Charmaz, K. (2010). Studying the experience of chronic illness through grounded theory. In G. Scambler & S. Scambler (Eds.), *New directions in the sociology of chronic and disabling conditions: Assaults on the lifeworld* (pp. 8–36). London: Palgrave.

Charmaz, K., & Bryant, A. (2010). Grounded theory. In B. McGaw, E. Baker, & P. P. Peterson (Eds.), *The international encyclopedia of education* (pp. 401–406). Oxford, UK, Elsevier.

Charmaz, K., & Henwood, K. (2008). Grounded theory in psychology. In C. Willig & W. Stainton-Rogers (Eds.), *The SAGE handbook of qualitative research in psychology* (pp. 240–260). London: Sage.

Choi, S. Y. P., & Holroyd, E. (2007). The influence of power, poverty and agency in the negotiation of condom use for female sex workers in Mainland China. *Culture, Health and Sexuality, 9*(5), 489–503.

Christ, T. W. (2009). Designing, teaching, and evaluating two complementary mixed methods research courses. *Journal of Mixed Methods Research, 3*(4), 292–325.

Ciambrone, D. (2007). Illness and other assaults on self: The relative impact of HIV/AIDS on women's lives. *Sociology of Health & Illness, 23*(4), 517–540.

Clarke, A. E. (1998). *Disciplining reproduction: Modernity, American life sciences and the "problem of sex."* Berkeley: University of California Press.

Clarke, A. E. (2003). Situational analyses: Grounded theory mapping after the postmodern turn. *Symbolic Interaction 26,* 553–576.

Clarke, A. E. (2005). *Situational analysis: Grounded theory after the postmodern turn.* Thousand Oaks, CA: Sage.

Clarke, A. E. (2006). Feminisms, grounded theory, and situational analysis. In S. Hess-Biber & D. Leckenby (Eds.), *The SAGE handbook of feminist research methods* (pp. 345–370). Thousand Oaks, CA: Sage.

Clarke, A. E., & Friese, C. (2007). Situational analysis: Going beyond traditional grounded theory. In K. Charmaz & A. Bryant (Eds.), *The SAGE handbook of grounded theory* (pp. 694–743). London: Sage.

Cohn, S., Dyson, C., & Wessley, S. (2008). Early accounts of Gulf War illness and the construction of narratives in UK service personnel. *Social Science & Medicine, 67,* 1641–1649.

Corbin, J. (2009). Taking an analytic journey. In J. M. Morse, P. N. Stern, J. Corbin, B. Bowers, K. Charmaz, & A. E. Clarke, *Developing grounded theory: The second generation* (pp. 35–53). Walnut Creek, CA: Left Coast Press.

Corbin, J., & Strauss, A. (2008). *Basics of qualitative research* (3rd ed.). Thousand Oaks, CA: Sage.

Creswell, J. W. (2003). *Research design: Qualitative, quantitative, and mixed methods design* (2nd ed.). Thousand Oaks, CA: Sage.

Creswell, J. W., & Plano Clark, V. L. (2007). *Designing and conducting mixed methods research.* Thousand Oaks, CA: Sage.

Creswell, J. W., Shope, R., Plano Clark, V. L., & Green, D. O. (2006). How interpretive qualitative research extends mixed methods research. *Research in the Schools, 13*(1), 1–11.

Denzin, N. K. (1970). *The research act: A theoretical introduction to sociological methods.* Chicago: Aldine.

Denzin, N. K. (2007). Grounded theory and the politics of interpretation. In A. Bryant & K. Charmaz (Eds.), *The SAGE handbook of grounded theory* (pp. 454–471). London: Sage.

Denzin, N. K., & Lincoln, Y. S. (1994). Preface. In N. K. Denzin & Y. S. Lincoln (Eds.), *Handbook of qualitative research* (pp. ix–xii). Thousand Oaks, CA: Sage.

Denzin, N. K., & Lincoln, Y. S. (2005). *The SAGE handbook of qualitative research* (3rd ed.). Thousand Parks, CA: Sage.

Dick, B. (2007). What can grounded theorists and action researchers learn from each other? In A. Bryant & K. Charmaz (Eds.), *The SAGE handbook of grounded theory* (pp. 398–416). London: Sage.

Dixon, R. (2007). Ostracism: One of the many causes of bullying in groups? *Journal of School Violence, 6*(3), 3–26.

Duemer, L S., & Zebidi, A. (2009). The pragmatic paradigm: An epistemological framework for mixed methods research. *Journal of Philosophy and History of Education, 59,* 164–168.

Dumit, Joseph. (2006). Illnesses you have to fight to get: Facts as forces in uncertain, emergent illnesses. *Social Science & Medicine, 62*(3), 577–590.

Einwohner, R. L., & Spencer, J. W. (2005). That's how we do things here: The construction of sweatshops and anti-sweatshop activism in two campus communities. *Sociological Inquiry, 75*(2), 249–272.

Feagin, J. R. (1999). Social justice and sociology: Agendas for the twenty-first century. *American Sociological Review, 66*(1), 1–20.

Feilzer, M. V. (2010). Doing mixed methods research pragmatically: Implications for the rediscovery of pragmatism as a research paradigm. *Journal of Mixed Methods Research, 4*(4), 6–16.

Fielding, N., & Cisneros-Puebla, C. (2010). CAQDAS-GIS convergence: Toward a new integrated mixed method research practice. *Journal of Mixed Methods Research, 3*(4), 349–370.

Fielding, N., & Lee, R. M. (1998). *Computer analysis and qualitative field research.* London: Sage.

Fielding, N., & Lee, R. M. (2002). New patterns in the adoption and use of qualitative software. *Field Methods, 14*(2), 197–216.

Foote-Ardah, C. E. (2003). The meaning of complementary and alternative medicine practices among people with HIV in the United States: Strategies for managing everyday life. *Sociology of Health & Illness, 25*(5), 481–500.

Foster-Fishman, P., Nowell, B., Deacon, Z., Nievar, M. A., & McCann, P. (2005). Using methods that matter: The impact of reflection, dialogue, and voice. *American Journal of Community Psychology, 36*(3/4), 275–291.

Frohmann, L. (1991). Discrediting victims' allegations of sexual assault: Prosecutorial accounts of case rejections. *Social Problems, 38*(2), 213–226.

Frohmann, L. (1998). Constituting power in sexual assault cases: Prosecutorial strategies for victim management. *Social Problems, 45*(3), 393–407.

Gagné. P. (1996). Identity, strategy and feminist politics: Clemency for women who kill. *Social Problems, 43*(1), 77–93.

Glaser, B. G. (1978). *Theoretical sensitivity.* Mill Valley, CA: Sociology Press.

Glaser, B. G. (1992). *Basics of grounded theory analysis.* Mill Valley, CA: Sociology Press.

Glaser, B. G. (1998). *Doing grounded theory: Issues and discussions.* Mill Valley, CA: Sociology Press.

Glaser, B. G. (2001). *The grounded theory perspective: Conceptualization contrasted with description.* Mill Valley, CA: Sociology Press.

Glaser, B. G. (2002). Constructivist grounded theory? *Forum: Qualitative Sozialforschung/ Qualitative Social Research, 3*(3). Available at http://www.qualitative-research.net/ index.php/fqs/article/view/825

Glaser, B. G. (2003). *The grounded theory perspective II: Description's remodeling of grounded theory methodology.* Mill Valley, CA: Sociology Press.

Glaser, B. G. (2008). *Doing quantitative grounded theory.* Mill Valley, CA: Sociology Press.

Glaser, B. G., & Strauss, A. L. (1967). *The discovery of grounded theory.* Chicago: Aldine.

Greckhamer, T., & Koro-Ljungberg, M. (2005). The erosion of a method: Examples from grounded theory. *International Journal of Qualitative Studies in Education, 18*(6), 729–750.

Greene, J. C. (2006). Toward a methodology of mixed methods social inquiry. *Research in the Schools, 13*(1), 94–99.

Gunter, V. J. (2005). News media and technological risks: The case of pesticides after *Silent Spring. The Sociological Quarterly, 46*(4), 671–698.

Hansen, E. C., Walters, J., & Baker, R. W. (2007). Explaining chronic obstructive pulmonary disease (COPD): Perceptions of the role played by smoking. *Sociology of Health & Illness, 29*(5), 730–749.

Harris, S. R. (2001). What can interactionism contribute to the study of inequality? The case of marriage and beyond. *Symbolic Interaction, 24*(4), 455–480.

Harris, S. R. (2006a). *The meanings of marital equality.* Albany: State University of New York Press.

Harris, S. R. (2006b). Social constructionism and social inequality: An introduction to a special issue of JCE. *Journal of Contemporary Ethnography, 35*(3), 223–235.

Harry, B., Sturges, K. M., & Klingner, J. K. (2005). Mapping the process: An exemplar of process and challenge in grounded theory analysis. *Educational Researcher, 34*(2), 3–13.

Henwood, K., & Pidgeon, N. (2003). Grounded theory in psychological research. In P. M. Camic, J. E. Rhodes, & L. Yardley (Eds.), *Qualitative research in psychology: Expanding perspectives in methodology and design* (pp. 131–155). Washington, DC: American Psychological Association.

Hood, J. (2007). Orthodoxy vs. power: The defining traits of grounded theory. In A. Bryant & K. Charmaz (Eds.), *The SAGE handbook of grounded theory* (pp. 151–164). London: Sage.

Hyde, J., & Kammerer, N. (2009). Adolescents' perspectives on placement moves and congregate settings: Complex and cumulative instabilities in out-of-home care. *Children and Youth Services Review, 31*, 265–273.

Jackson-Jacobs, C. (2004). Hard drugs in a soft context: Managing trouble and crack use on a college campus. *Sociological Quarterly, 45*(4), 835–856.

Jiménez, T. R. (2008). Mexican immigrant replenishment and the continuing significance of ethnicity and race. *American Journal of Sociology, 113*(6), 1527–1567.

Johnson, R. B., Onwuegbuzie, A. J., & Turner, L. A. (2007). Toward a definition of mixed methods research. *Journal of Mixed Methods Research, 1*, 112–133.

Jones, S. J. (2003). Complex subjectivities: Class, ethnicity, and race in women's narratives of upward mobility. *Journal of Social Issues, 50*(4), 804–820.

Karabanow, J. (2008). Getting off the street: Exploring the processes of young people's street exits. *American Behavioral Scientist, 51*(6), 772–788.

Kearney, M. H. (2007). From the sublime to the meticulous: The continuing evolution of grounded formal theory. In A. Bryant & K. Charmaz (Eds.), *The SAGE handbook of grounded theory* (pp. 127–150). London: Sage.

Kelle, U. (2004). Computer-assisted qualitative data analysis. In C. Seale, G. Gobo, J. F. Gubrium, & D. Silverman (Eds.), *Qualitative research practice* (pp. 473–489). London: Sage.

Kelle, U. (2005, May). Emergence vs. forcing: A crucial problem of "grounded theory" reconsidered. *Forum: Qualitative Sozialforsung/Qualitative Sociology, 6*(2). Available at http://www.qualitative-research.net/index.php/fqs/article/view/467

Kelle, U. (2007). The development of categories: Different approaches of grounded theory. In A. Bryant & K. Charmaz (Eds.), *The SAGE handbook of grounded theory* (pp. 191–213). London: Sage.

Kemmis, S., & McTaggart, R. (2005). Participatory action research: Communicative action and the public sphere. In N. K. Denzin & Y. S. Lincoln (Eds.), *The SAGE handbook of qualitative research* (3rd ed., pp. 559–603). Thousand Oaks, CA: Sage.

Kendall, J. (1999). Axial coding and the grounded theory controversy. *Western Journal of Nursing Research, 21*(6), 743–757.

Konopásek, Z. (2008). Making thinking visible with Atlas.ti: Computer assisted qualitative analysis as textual practices. *Forum: Qualitative Sozialforschung/Qualitative Social Research, 9*(2). Available at http://nbn-resolving.de/urn:nbn:de:0114-fqs0802124

Lazzari, M. M., Ford, H. R., & Haughey, K. J. (1996). Making a difference: Women of action in the community. *Social Work, 41*(2), 197–205.

Lempert, L. B. (2007). Asking questions of the data: Memo writing in the grounded theory tradition. In A. Bryant & K. Charmaz (Eds.), *The SAGE handbook of grounded theory* (pp. 245–264). London: Sage.

Lio, S., Melzer, S., & Reese, E. (2008). Constructing threat and appropriating "civil rights": Rhetorical strategies of gun rights and English only leaders. *Symbolic Interaction, 31*(1), 5–31.

Locke, K. (2007). Rational control and irrational free-play: Dual-thinking modes as necessary tension in grounded theorizing. In A. Bryant & K. Charmaz (Eds.), *The SAGE handbook of grounded theory* (pp. 565–579). London: Sage.

Lutgen-Sandvik, P. (2008). Intensive remedial identity work: Responses to workplace bullying trauma and stigmatization. *Organization, 15*(1) 97–119.

Maines, D. R. (2001). *The faultline of consciousness: A view of interactionism in sociology.* New York: Aldine.

Mathieson, C., & Stam, H. (1995). Renegotiating identity: Cancer narratives. *Sociology of Health & Illness, 17*(3): 283–306.

May, K. (1996). Diffusion, dilution or distillation? The case of grounded theory method. *Qualitative Health Research, 6*(3), 309–311.

McDermott, K. A. (2007). "Expanding the moral community" or "blaming the victim"? *American Education Research Association Journal, 44*(1), 77–111.

Mcintyre, A. (2002). Women researching their lives: Exploring violence and identity in Belfast, the North of Ireland. *Qualitative Research, 2*(3), 387–409.

McPhail, B. A., & DiNitto, D. M. (2005). Prosecutorial perspectives on gender-bias hate crimes. *Violence Against Women, 11*(9), 1162–1185.

Mertens, D. M. (2007). Transformative paradigm: Mixed methods and social justice. *Journal of Mixed Methods Research, 1*(3), 212–235.

Mertens, D. M. (2010). *Research and evaluation in education and psychology: Integrating diversity with quantitative, qualitative, and mixed methods.* Thousand Oaks, CA: Sage.

Merton, R. K. (1957). *Social theory and social structure.* Glencoe, IL: Free Press.

Mevorach, M. (2008). Do preschool teachers perceive young children from immigrant families differently? *Journal of Early Childhood Teacher Education, 29,* 146–156.

Mitakidou, S., Tressou, E., & Karagianni, P. (2008). Students' reflections on social exclusion. *The International Journal of Diversity in Organisations, Communities and Nations, 8*(5), 191–198.

Mitchell, R. C., & McCusker, S. (2008). Theorising the UN convention on the rights of the child within Canadian post-secondary education: A grounded theory approach. *International Journal of Children's Rights, 16,* 159–176.

Moore, D. L. (2005). Expanding the view: The lives of women with severe work disabilities in context. *Journal of Counseling and Development, 83*(3), 343–348.

Moreno, M. (2008). Lessons of belonging and citizenship among hijas/os de inmigrantes Mexicanos. *Social Justice, 35*(1), 50–75.

Morgan, D. (2007). Paradigms lost and pragmatism regained: Methodological implications of combining qualitative and quantitative research. *Journal of Mixed Methods Research 1*(1): 48-76.

Morrow, S. L., & Smith, M. L. (1995). Constructions of survival and coping by women who have survived childhood sexual abuse. *Journal of Counseling Psychology, 42*(1), 24–33.

Morse, J. M. (1991). Approaches to qualitative-quantitative methodological triangulation. *Nursing Research, 40*(2), 120–123.

Morse, J. M. (2007). Sampling in grounded theory. In A. Bryant & K. Charmaz (Eds.), *The SAGE handbook of grounded theory* (pp. 229–254). London: Sage.

Mruck, K., & Mey, G. (2007). Grounded theory and reflexivity. In A. Bryant & K. Charmaz (Eds.), *The SAGE handbook of grounded theory* (pp. 515–538). London: Sage.

Mulcahy, A. (1995). Claims-making and the construction of legitimacy: Press coverage of the 1981 Northern Irish hunger strike. *Social Problems, 42*(4), 449–467.

Nack, A. (2008). *Damaged goods? Women living with incurable sexually transmitted diseases.* Philadelphia: Temple University Press.

Neill, S. J. (2006). Grounded theory sampling: The contribution of reflexivity. *Journal of Research in Nursing, 11*(3), 253–260.

Nepstad, S. E. (2007). Oppositional consciousness among the privileged: Remaking religion in the Central America solidarity movement. *Critical Sociology, 33*(4), 661–688.

Nussbaum, M. C. (2000). Women's capabilities and social justice. *Journal of Human Development, 1,* 219–247.

O'Connor, G. C., Rice, M. P., Peters, L., & Veryzer, R. W. (2003). Managing interdisciplinary, longitudinal research teams: Extending grounded theory-building methodologies. *Organization Science, 14*(4), 353–373.

Ogle, J. P., Eckman, M., & Leslie, C. A. (2003). Appearance cues and the shootings at Columbine High: Construction of a social problem in the print media. *Sociological Inquiry, 73*(1), 1–27.

Olesen, V. (2007). Feminist qualitative research and grounded theory. In A. Bryant & K. Charmaz (Eds.), *The SAGE handbook of grounded theory* (pp. 417–435). London: Sage.

Padgett, D. K. (2009). Qualitative and mixed methods in social work knowledge development. *Social Work, 54*(1), 101–105.

Parsons, T. (1951). *The social system.* Glencoe, IL: Free Press.

Peirce, C. S. (1958). *Collected papers.* Cambridge, MA: Harvard University Press.

Piantanida, M., Tananis, C. A., & Grubs, R. E. (2004). Generating grounded theory of/for educational practice: The journey of three epistemorphs. *International Journal of Qualitative Studies in Education, 17*(3), 325–346.

Poonamallee, L. (2009). Building grounded theory in action research through the interplay of subjective ontology and objective epistemology. *Action Research, 7*(1), 69–83.

Qin, D., & Lykes, M. B. (2006). Reweaving a fragmented self: A grounded theory of self-understanding among Chinese women students in the United States of America. *International Journal of Qualitative Studies in Education, 19*(2), 177–200.

Quint, J. C. (1965). Institutionalized practices of information control. *Psychiatry, 28*(May), 119–132.

Rawls, J. (1971). *A theory of justice.* Cambridge, MA: Belknap.

Reichert, J. (2007). Abduction: The logic of discovery in grounded theory. In A. Bryant & K. Charmaz (Eds.), *The SAGE handbook of grounded theory* (pp. 214–228). London: Sage.

Reynolds, L. T., & Herman, N. J. (Eds.). (2003). *Handbook of symbolic interaction.* Walnut Creek, CA: AltaMira.

Rier, D. (2007). Internet social support groups as moral agents: The ethical dynamics of HIV+ status disclosure. *Sociology of Health & Illness, 29*(7), 1–16.

Rivera, L. A. (2008). Managing "spoiled" national identity: War, tourism, and memory in Croatia. *American Sociological Review, 73*(4), 613–634.

Roschelle, A. R., & Kaufman, P. (2004). Fitting in and fighting back: Stigma management strategies among homeless kids. *Symbolic Interaction, 27*(1), 23–46.

Rosenthal, G. (2004). Biographical research. In C. Seale, G. Gobo, J. F. Gubrium, & D. Silverman (Eds.), *Qualitative research practice* (pp. 48–64). London: Sage.

Roxas, K. (2008). Who dares to dream the American dream? *Multicultural Education, 16*(2), 2–9.

Ryder, J. A. (2007). "I wasn't really bonded with my family": Attachment, loss and violence among adolescent female offenders. *Critical Criminology, 15*(1), 19–40.

Sahin-Hodoglugil, N. N., vander Straten, A., Cheng, H., Montgomery, E. T., Kcanek, D., Mtetewa, S., et al. (2009). A study of women's covert use of the diaphragm in an HIV prevention trial in sub-Saharan Africa. *Social Science & Medicine, 69,* 1547–1555.

Sakamoto, I., Chin, M., Chapra, A., & Ricciar, J. (2009). A "normative" homeless woman? Marginalisation, emotional injury and social support of transwomen experiencing homelessness. *Gay and Lesbian Issues and Psychology Review, 5*(1), 2–19.

Salander, P. (2002). Bad news from the patient's perspective: An analysis of the written narratives of newly diagnosed cancer patients. *Social Science & Medicine, 55,* 721–732.

Sandelowski, M., Voils, C. I., & Knafl, G. (2009). On quantitizing. *Journal of Mixed Methods Research, 3,* 208–222.

Sandstrom, K. L. (1990). Confronting deadly disease: The drama of identity construction among gay men with AIDS. *Journal of Contemporary Ethnography, 19,* 271–294.

Sandstrom, K. L. (1998). Preserving a vital and valued self in the face of AIDS. *Sociological Inquiry, 68*(3), 354–371.

Schwalbe, M. (2005). Identity stakes, manhood acts, and the dynamics of accountability. In N. K. Denzin (Ed.), *Studies in symbolic interaction 28,* 65–81. Bingley, UK: Emerald Publishing Group.

Schwalbe, M., Godwin, S., Holden, D., Schrock, D., Thompson, S., & Wolkomir, M. (2000). Generic processes in the reproduction of inequality: An interactionist analysis. *Social Forces, 79,* 419–452.

Scott, E. K. (2005). Beyond tokenism: The making of racially diverse feminist organizations. *Social Problems, 52*(2), 232–254.

Scott, E. K., London, A. S., & Gross, G. (2007). "I try not to depend on anyone but me": Welfare-reliant women's perspectives on self-sufficiency, work, and marriage. *Sociological Inquiry, 77*(4), 601–625.

Shelley, N. M. (2001). Building community from "scratch": Forces at work among urban Vietnamese refugees in Milwaukee. *Sociological Inquiry, 71*(4), 473–492.

Sixsmith, J. A. (1999). Working in the hidden economy: The experience of unemployed men in the UK. *Community, Work and Family, 2*(3), 257–277.

Somerville, C., Featherstone, K., Hemingway, H., Timmis, A., & Feder, G. S. (2008). Performing stable angina pectoris: An ethnographic study. *Social Science & Medicine, 66*(7), 1497–1508.

Speed, S., & Luker, K. A. (2006). Getting a visit: How district nurses and general practitioners "organise" each other in primary care. *Sociology of Health & Illness, 28*(7), 883–902.

Spencer, J. W., & Triche, E. (1994). Media constructions of risk and safety: Differential framings of hazard events. *Sociological Inquiry, 64*(2), 199–213.

Star, S. L. (1989). *Regions of the mind: Brain research and the quest for scientific certainty.* Stanford, CA: Stanford University Press.

Stern, P. N. (1994). Eroding grounded theory. In J. Morse (Ed.), *Critical issues in qualitative research methods* (pp. 212–223). Thousand Oaks, CA: Sage.

Stern, P. N. (2007). On solid ground: Essential properties for growing grounded theory. In A. Bryant & K. Charmaz (Eds.), *The SAGE handbook of grounded theory* (pp. 114–126). London: Sage.

Stern, P. N. (2009). Glaserian grounded theory. In J. M. Morse, P. N. Stern, J. Corbin, B. Bowers, K. Charmaz, & A. E. Clarke, *Developing grounded theory: The second generation* (pp. 23–29). Walnut Creek, CA: Left Coast Press.

Strauss, A. L. (1969). *Mirrors and masks: The search for identity.* Mill Valley, CA: Sociology Press. (Original work published 1959)

Strauss, A. L. (1987). *Qualitative analysis for social scientists.* New York: Cambridge University Press.

Strauss, A. L. (1993). *Continual permutations of action.* New York: Aldine.

Strauss, A., & Corbin, J. (1990). *Basics of qualitative research: Grounded theory procedures and techniques.* Newbury Park, CA: Sage.

Strauss, A., & Corbin, J. (1994). Grounded theory methodology: An overview. In N. K. Denzin & Y. S. Lincoln (Eds.), *Handbook of qualitative research* (pp. 273–285). Thousand Oaks, CA: Sage.

Strauss, A., & Corbin, J. (1998). *Basics of qualitative research: Grounded theory procedures and techniques* (2nd ed.). Thousand Oaks, CA: Sage.

Strübing, J. (2007). Research as pragmatic problem-solving: The pragmatist roots of empirically grounded theorizing. In A. Bryant & K. Charmaz (Eds.), *The SAGE handbook of grounded theory* (pp. 580–601). London: Sage.

Suddaby, R. (2006). From the editors: What grounded theory is not. *Academy of Management Journal, 49*(4), 633–642.

Suddaby, R., & Greenwood, R. (2005). Rhetorical strategies of legitimacy. *Administrative Science Quarterly, 50*(1), 35–67.

Swahnberg, K., Thapar-Björkert, S., & Berterö, C. (2007). Nullified: Women's perceptions of being abused in health care. *Journal of Psychosomatic Obstetrics and Gynecology, 28*(3), 161–167.

Tashakkori, A., & Teddlie, C. (2003). The past and future of mixed methods research: From data triangulation to mixed model designs. In A. Tashakkori & C. Teddlie (Eds.), *Handbook of mixed methods in social & behavioral research* (pp. 671–701). Thousand Oaks, CA: Sage.

Teram, E., Schachter, C. L., & Stalker, C. A. (2005). The case for integrating grounded theory and participatory action research: Empowering clients to inform professional practice. *Qualitative Health Research, 15*(8), 1129–1140.

Thornberg, R. (2007). Inconsistencies in everyday patterns of school rules. *Ethnography and Education, 2*(3), 401–416.

Thornberg, R. (2009). The moral construction of the good pupil embedded in school rules. *Education, Citizenship and Social Justice, 4*(3), 245–261.

Thornberg, R., & Charmaz, K. (in press). Grounded theory. In S. Lapan, M. Quartaroli, & F. Riemer (Eds.), *Qualitative research: An introduction to methods and designs.* San Francisco: Jossey-Bass.

Timmermans, S., & Tavory, I. (2007). Advancing ethnographic research through grounded theory practice. In A. Bryant & K. Charmaz (Eds.), *The SAGE handbook of grounded theory* (pp. 493–512). London: Sage.

Tuason, M. T. G. (2008). Those who were born poor: A qualitative study of Philippine poverty. *Journal of Counseling Psychology, 55*(2), 158–171.

Turner, B. A. (1981). Some practical aspects of qualitative data analysis: One way of organizing the cognitive processes associated with the generation of grounded theory. *Quantity and Quality, 15,* 225–247.

Ullman, S. E., & Townsend, S. M. (2008). What is an empowerment approach to working with sexual assault survivors? *Journal of Community Psychology, 36*(3), 299–312.

Urquhart C. (2003). Re-grounding grounded theory-or reinforcing old prejudices? A brief response to Bryant. *Journal of Information Technology Theory and Application, 4*(3), 43–54.

Valadez, J. R. (2008). Shaping the educational decisions of Mexican immigrant high school students. *American Educational Research Journal, 45*(4), 834–860.

Valdez, A., & Flores, R. (2005). A situational analysis of dating violence among Mexican American females associated with street gangs. *Sociological Focus, 38*(2), 95–114.

Vandenburgh, H. (2001). Physician stipends as organizational deviance in for-profit psychiatric hospitals. *Critical Sociology, 27*(1), 56–76.

van den Hoonaard, W. C. (1997). *Working with sensitizing concepts: Analytical field research.* Thousand Oaks, CA: Sage.

Veale, A., & Stavrou, A. (2007). Former Lord's Resistance Army child soldier abductees: Explorations of identity in reintegration and reconciliation. *Peace and Conflict: Journal of Peace Psychology, 13*(3): 273–292.

Wasserman, J. A., & Claire, J. M. (2010). *At home on the street: People, poverty, and a hidden culture of homelessness.* New York: Lynne Rienner.

Weitzman, E. A. (2000). Software and qualitative research. In N. K. Denzin & Y. S. Lincoln (Eds.), *The SAGE handbook of qualitative research* (2nd ed., pp. 803–820). Thousand Oaks, CA: Sage.

Williamson, K. (2006). Research in constructivist frameworks using ethnographic techniques. *Library Trends, 55*(1), 83–101.

Wilson, H. S., & Hutchinson, S. A. (1996). Methodologic mistakes in grounded theory. *Nursing Research, 45*(2), 122–124.

Wilson, K., & Luker, K. A. (2006). At home in hospital? Interaction and stigma in people affected by cancer. *Social Science & Medicine, 62,* 1616–1627.

Wolkomir, M. (2001). Wrestling with the angels of meaning: The revisionist ideological work of gay and ex-gay Christian men. *Symbolic Interaction, 24*(4), 407–424.

Wolkomir. M. (2006). *Be not deceived: The sacred and sexual struggles of gay and ex-gay Christian men.* New Brunswick, NJ: Rutgers University Press.

Ziegahn, L., & Hinchman, K. A. (1999). Liberation or reproduction: Exploring meaning in college students' adult literacy tutoring. *Qualitative Studies in Education, 12*(1), 85–101.

10

In the Name of
Human Rights

I Say (How) You (Should) Speak (Before I Listen)[1]

Antjie Krog

It is the year 1872. A Bushman shaman called //Kabbo narrates an incident to a German philologist Wilhelm Bleek in Cape Town, South Africa. In the narration, which took Bleek from April 13 to September 19 to record and translate from/Xam into English, the following two paragraphs appear, describing how a young woman tracks down her nomadic family:

> She [the young widow] arrives with her children at the water hole. There she sees her younger brother's footprints by the water. She sees her mother's footprint by the water. She sees her brother's wife's spoor by the water.
> She tells her children: "Grandfather's people's footprints are here; they had been carrying dead springbok to the water so that people can drink on their way back with the game. The house is near. We shall follow the footprints because the footprints are new. We must look for the house. We must follow the footprints. For the people's footprints were made today; the people fetched water shortly before we came." (Lewis-Williams, 2002, p. 61)

For more than a hundred years, these words seemed like just another interesting detail in an old Bushmen story, until researcher Louis Liebenberg went to live among modern Bushmen. In his book, *The Art of Tracking: The Origin of Science*

(1990), Liebenberg insists that what seems to be an instinctive capacity to track a spoor, is actually the Bushmen using intricate decoding, contextual sign analysis to create hypotheses.

Liebenberg distinguishes three levels of tracking among the Bushmen: first, simple tracking that just follows footprints. Second, systematic tracking involving the gathering of information from signs until a detailed indication is built up of the action. Third, speculative tracking that involves the creation of a working hypothesis on the basis of (1) the initial interpretation of signs, (2) a knowledge of behavior, and (3) a knowledge of the terrain. According to Liebenberg, these skills of tracking are akin to those of Western intellectual analysis, and he suggests that all science actually started with tracking (Brown, 2006, p. 25).

Returning to the opening two paragraphs, one sees that the young widow effortlessly does all three kinds of tracking identified by Liebenberg. She identifies the makers of the footprints, their coming and going, that they were carrying something heavy and/or bleeding, that they were thirsty, that they drank water on the way back from hunting, she identifies the game as a springbok, she establishes when the tracks were made and then puts forward a hypothesis of what they were doing and where and how she will find her family that very day.

The question I want to pose here is: Is it justified to regard Wilhelm Bleek (as the recorder of the narration), Louis Liebenberg (as a scholar of tracking), and myself (for applying the tracking theory to the narration) as the scholars/ academics, while //Kabbo (Bushman narrator) and the woman in the story (reading the tracks) are "raw material"?

How does this division respect Article 19 of the Universal Declaration of Human Rights of the United Nations?

> Everyone has the right to freedom of opinion and expression; this right includes freedom to hold opinions without interference *and to seek, receive and impart information and ideas through any media and regardless of frontiers.* (emphasis added; available at http://www.un.org/en/documents/udhr/)

WHO MAY ENTER THE DISCOURSE?

The rights of two groups will be discussed in this essay: First, the rights of those living in marginalized areas but who produce virtually on a daily basis intricate knowledge systems of survival. Second, the rights of scholars coming from those marginalized places, but who can only enter the world of acknowledged knowledge in languages not their own and within discourses based on foreign and estrang-*ing* structures.

Although Gayatri Spivak describes the one group as subaltern, she deals with both of these groups in her famous essay, "Can the Subaltern Speak?" suggesting that the moment that the subaltern finds herself in conditions in which she can be heard, "her status as a subaltern would be changed utterly; she would cease to be subaltern" (Williams & Chrisman, 1994, p. 190).

"MRS. KHONELE" AS SUBALTERN

During the two years of hearings conducted by the South African Truth and Reconciliation Commission (TRC), 2,000 testimonies were given in public. Instead of listening to the impressive stories of well-known activists, the commission went out of its way to provide a forum for the most marginalized narratives from rural areas given in indigenous languages. In this way, these lives and previously unacknowledged narratives were made audible and could be listened to through translation to become the first entry into the South African psyche of what Spivak so aptly calls in her piece, *Subaltern Studies—Deconstructing Historiography,* "news of the consciousness of the subaltern" (Williams & Chrisman, 1994, p. 203).

Covering the hearings of the truth commission for national radio, one woman's testimony stayed with me as the most incoherent testimony I had to report on. I considered the possibility that one needed special tools to make sense of it and wondered whether clarification could be found in the original Xhosa, or was the woman actually mentally disturbed, or were there vestiges of "cultural supremacy" in me that prevented me from hearing her?

Trying to find her testimony later on the truth commission's website proved fruitless. There was no trace of her name in the index. Under the heading of the Gugulethu Seven incident, her surname was given incorrectly as "Khonele," and she was the only mother in this group to be presented without a first name. Her real name was Notrose Nobomvu Konile, but I later found that even in her official identity document her second name was given incorrectly as "Nobovu." (Notrose Konile's TRC testimony is available online at http://www.justice.gov.za/trc/hrvtrans/heide/ct00100.htm.)

One might well ask: Is it at all possible to hear this unmentioned, incorrectly identified, misspelled, incoherently testifying, translated, and carelessly transcribed woman from the deep rural areas of South Africa?

I asked two colleagues at the University of the Western Cape—Nosisi Mpolweni from the Xhosa department, and Professor Kopano Ratele from the psychology department and women and gender studies—to join me in a reading of the testimony. Mpolweni and Ratele immediately became interested. Using the original Xhosa recording, we started off by transcribing and retranslating. Then we applied different theoretical frameworks (Elaine Scarry, Cathy Garuth, Soshana Felman, Dori Laub, G. Bennington, etc.) to interpret the text; and, finally, we visited and reinterviewed Konile. What started out as a casual teatime discussion became a project of two and a half years and finally a book: *There Was This Goat—Investigating the Truth Commission Testimony of Notrose Nobomvu Konile* (Krog, Mpolweni, & Ratele, 2009).

But first, some concepts need to be introduced that play a role the moment that the voice of the subaltern becomes audible.

THE FLUKE OF "RAW MATERIAL"

I was proud to be appointed by a university that, during apartheid, deliberately ignored the demands of privileged White academia and focused unabashedly on the oppressed communities surrounding the campus. The university prided itself, and rightly so, on being the University of the Left and threw all its resources behind the poor.

Since the first democratic election in 1994, South Africa has been trying to become part of what is sometimes called "a normal dispensation." Some months after my appointment at the university five years ago, I was asked to send a list of what I had published that year. Fortunately, or so I thought, I was quite active: a nonfiction book, poetry, controversial newspaper pieces, and more. So imagine my surprise to receive an e-mail saying that none of the listed writings "counted."

I went to see the dean of research. The conversation went like this:

"Why do my publications not count?"

"It's not peer reviewed."

"It was reviewed in all the newspapers!"

"But not by peers."

Wondering why the professors teaching literature would not be regarded as my peers I asked, "So who are my peers?"

"Of course you are peerless," this was said somewhat snottily, "but I mean the people in your field."

"So what is my field?"

"The people working . . . ," and his hands fluttered, "in the areas about which you write."

"Well," I said, "when I look at their work I see that they all quote me."

His face suddenly beamed: "So you see! You are raw material!"

Initially, I thought nothing of the remark, but gradually came to realize how contentious, judgmental, and excluding the term "raw material" was. Who decides who is raw material? Are Konile and //Kabbo and the Bushman woman "raw material"? Looking back on our project, I found myself asking, why did we three colleagues so easily assume that Konile was "raw material" and not a cowriter of our text? Why are her two testimonies and one interview in which she constructs and analyzes, deduces and concludes, less of an academic endeavor than our contribution? Her survival skills after the devastating loss of her son were not perchance remarks, but careful calculations and tested experiences from her side. During our interview, we even asked her to interpret her text. Why should she enter our book and the academic domain as raw material? Should she not be properly credited as a cotext producer on the cover like the three of us?

I began wondering: What would be the questions another Gugulethu mother would ask Konile? Or to move to another realm: How would one cattle herder interview another cattle herder? How would one cattle herder analyze and appraise the words of a fellow cattle herder? How would such an interview differ from me interviewing that cattle herder? And, finally, how can these experiences enter the academic discourse *without* the conduit of a well-meaning scholar? How shall we ever enter any new realm if we insist that all information must be processed by ourselves for ourselves?

THE FLUKE OF DISCIPLINE

After being downgraded to "raw material," I duly applied to attend a workshop on how to write "un-raw" material in order to meet one's peers through unread but accredited journals. The workshop had been organized by the university after it became clear that our new democratic government wanted universities to come up with fundable research. We were obliged to compete with the established and excellently resourced former White universities and their impressive research histories.

I walked into this organized workshop. There were about 40 of us. I was the only White person. During smoke breaks, the stories poured out. The professor in math told the following:

One Sunday a member of the congregation told me that he was installing science laboratories in the schools of the new South Africa, that it was very interesting because every school was different. So this went on every Sunday until I said to him that he should write it down. So after I had completely forgotten about it, he pitched up [arrived] with a manuscript this thick [about four inches] and joked: Is this not a MA thesis? I looked and indeed it was new, it was methodically researched and systematically set out and riveting to read. So where to now? I said it was not math so he should take it to the science department. Science said it was more history than science. History said no . . . and so forth.

The group that attended the workshop was by no means subaltern, but first-generation educated men and women from formerly disadvantaged communities in apartheid South Africa. As we attended subsequent workshops in writing academic papers, one became aware of how the quality of "on-the-ground experience" was being crushed into a dispirited nothingness through weak English and the specific format of academic papers. We learned how easily an important story died within the corset of an academic paper, how a crucial observation was nothing without a theory, and how a valuable experience dissolved outside a discipline.

THE FLUKE OF THEORY

The last story is about a seminar I attended on the Black body. Opening the seminar, the professor said that when he was invited, he thought that the paper he was preparing would already have been accepted by an accredited journal and the discussion could then have taken place together with the peer reviews. The journal had, however, rejected the piece, so . . . maybe the discussion should start from scratch.

The paper he presented was indeed weak. As he was speaking, one had the distinct feeling of seeing a little boat rowing with all its might past waves and fish and flotillas and big ships and fluttering sails to a little island called Hegel. The oar was kept aloft until, until. . . . At last, the oar touched Hegel. Then the rowing continued desperately until the oar could just-just touch the island called Freud or Foucault. In the meantime, you want to say, forget these islands, show us what is in your boat, point out the fish that you know, how did you sidestep that big ship, where did you get these remarkable sails?

The discussion afterward was extraordinary. Suddenly, the professor was released from his paper and the Black students and lecturers found their tongues and it became a fantastic South African analysis. Afterward, I asked the professor: "Why didn't you write what you have just said?" He answered, "Because I can't find a link between what I know and existing literature. It's a Catch-22 situation: I cannot analyze my rural mother if it is assumed that there is no difference between her mind and the average North American or Swedish mind. On the other hand, my analysis of my rural mother will only be heard and understood if it is presented on the basis of the North American and Swedish mind."

Academics From Marginalized Communities

Both of my colleagues, Nosisi Mpolweni and Kopano Ratele, were the first in their families to be tertiary educated, while I was the fourth generation of university-educated women. Right through our collective interpretative analysis on the testimony of Konile, the power relations among us changed. The project started with my initiative, but I quickly became the one who knew the least. Ratele was the best educated of us three, having already published academically. Nosisi made an invaluable input with her translations and knowledge about Xhosa culture. I could write well, but not academically well. English was our language, but only Ratele could speak it properly. During our field trip to interview Konile, the power swung completely to Nosisi, while I, not understanding Xhosa, had no clout during our fieldwork excursions.

However, during our discussions, I became aware that while we were talking my colleagues had these moments of perfect formulation—a sort of spinning toward that sentence that finally says it all. We would stop and realize: Yes, this was it. This was the grasp we were working toward, but when we returned with written texts, these core sentences were nowhere to be seen in the work.

For one of our sessions, I brought a tape recorder. We were discussing why Konile so obsessively used the word "I" within her rural collective worldview. I transcribed the conversation, sent everybody chunks, and here is the text returned by Ratele:

> Mrs. Konile dreamt about the goat the night before she heard that her son was killed. The TRC however was not a forum for dreams, but for the truth about human rights abuses. I suggest that through telling about the dream, Mrs. Konile was signaling to the TRC her connection to the ancestral worlds.
>
> The dream revealed that she was still whole, that she was in contact with the living and the dead and she clearly experienced little existential loneliness. . . . Her son's death is what introduced her to a loneliness, a being an

"I." She had become an individual through the death of her son—selected, cut off, as it were to become an individual. She was saying: "I am suffering, because I had been forced to become an individual." The word "I" was not talking about her real psychological individuality. Mrs. Konile was using "I" as a form of complaint. She was saying: "I don't want to be I. I want to be us, but the killing of my son, made me into an 'I.'" (Krog et al., 2009, pp. 61–62)

As a White person steeped in individuality, I initially did not even notice the frequency of the word "I," but when I did it merely confirmed to me that the notion of African collective-*ness* was overrated, despite the emphasis it receives from people like Nelson Mandela and Archbishop Desmond Tutu. The conclusion Ratele reached, however, was the opposite, and it was a conclusion I could not have reached, and, up until now, also one that no other White TRC analyst had reached.

For me, this was the big breakthrough not only for our book, not only in TRC analysis, but also in our method of working. The confidence of the spoken tone, a confidence originating from the fact that somebody was talking from within and out of a world he knows intimately, had been successfully carried over onto paper. Ratele was crossing "frontiers" to get past all the barriers lodged in education, race, background, structure, language, and academic discipline to interpret his own world from out of its postcolonial, postmodern past and racial awarenesses with a valid confidence that speaks into and even beyond exclusive and prescriptive frameworks.

My guess is that my colleague would never have been able to write this particular formulation without first talking it, and talking it to us—a Black woman who understood him and a White woman who did not.

We wrote an essay about Konile's dream in our three different voices, but the piece was rejected by a South African journal for allowing contradictory viewpoints to "be" in the essay, for having a tone that seemed oral, for not producing any theory that could prove that Konile was somehow different from other human beings, and so on. The piece was, however, I am glad to say, accepted by Norman Denzin, Yvonna Lincoln, and Linda Smith for their book on indigenous methodologies.

Conclusion: Research as Reconciliatory Change

These examples, ranging from a Bushman shaman to a Black professor of psychology, expose the complexities of doing research in a country emerging from divided histories and cultures. It also poses ethical questions about the conditions we set for people to enter academic discourse. Spivak indeed stresses that ethics is not a problem of knowledge but a call of relationship (Williams & Chrisman, 1994, p. 190). When she claims that the subaltern "cannot speak," she means that the subaltern as such cannot be heard by the privileged of either the first or third worlds. If the subaltern were able to make herself heard, then her status as a subaltern would be changed utterly; she would cease to be subaltern. But is that not the goal of our research, "that the subaltern, the most oppressed and invisible constituencies, as such might cease to exist" (Williams & Chrisman, 1994, p. 5)?

French philosopher Deleuze rightly remarks that the power of minorities "is not measured by their capacity to enter into and make themselves felt within the majority system" (Deleuze & Quattari, 1987, p. 520). At the same time, Deleuze points out that it is precisely these different forms of minority-becoming that provide the impulse for change, but change can only occur to the extent that there is adaptation and incorporation on the side of the standard or the majority.

We have to find ways in which the marginalized can enter our discourses in their own genres and their own terms so that we can learn to hear them. They have a universal right to *impart information and ideas through any media and regardless of frontiers,* and we have a duty to listen and understand them through engaging in new acts of becoming.

Note

1. This chapter extends and inserts itself into the discussion of *testimonio,* as given in John Beverley's article, "*Testimonio,* Subalternity, and Narrative Authority" (Denzin & Lincoln, 2005, pp. 547–558).

References

Brown, D. (2006). *To speak of this land—Identity and belonging in South Africa and beyond.* Scottsville, South Africa: University of KwaZulu-Natal Press.

Deleuze, G., & Quattari, F. (1987). *Thousand plateaus: Capitalism and schizophrenia* (B. Massumi, Trans.). Minneapolis: University of Minnesota Press.

Denzin, N. K., & Lincoln, Y. S. (Eds.). (2005). *The SAGE handbook of qualitative research* (3rd ed.). Thousand Oaks, CA: Sage.

Denzin, N. K., Lincoln, Y. S., & Smith, L. T. (Eds.). (2008). *Handbook of critical and indigenous methodologies.* Thousand Oaks, CA: Sage.

Krog, A., Mpolweni, N., & Ratele, K. (2009). *There was this goat—Investigating the truth commission testimony of Notrose Nobomvu Konile.* Scottsville, South Africa: University of KwaZulu-Natal Press.

Lewis-Williams, J. D. (Ed.). (2000). *Stories that float from afar—Ancestral folklore of the San of Southern Africa.* Cape Town, South Africa: David Philip.

Liebenberg, L. (1990). *The art of tracking: The origin of science.* Cape Town, South Africa: David Philip.

Spivak, G. C. (1988). Can the subaltern speak? In C. Nelson & L. Grossberg (Eds.), *Marxism and the interpretation of culture.* New York: Macmillan.

Williams, P., & Chrisman, L. (Eds.). (1994). *Colonial discourse and post-colonial theory: A reader.* New York: Harvester Wheatsheaf.

11

Jazz and the Banyan Tree

Roots and Riffs on Participatory Action Research

Mary Brydon-Miller, Michael Kral,
Patricia Maguire, Susan Noffke, and Anu Sabhlok[1]

When Charles Mingus, Charlie Parker, Dizzy Gillespie, Max Roach, and Bud Powell took the stage at Massey Hall in 1953 playing *Perdido*, it seemed effortless, as if this incredible music just exploded from the stage to engulf the audience. But the truth is that this apparently spontaneous eruption of perfectly crafted music was the result of rigorous training—an integration of music theory and years of practice. Genuine improvisation is only possible when the players understand that each voice contributes a vital component to the overall structure of the piece. The willingness to innovate and explore that is the heart of great jazz music is made possible by the individual expertise of the musicians and their respect for one another's differing contributions.

Participatory action research (PAR) is like jazz.[2] It is built upon the notion that knowledge generation is a collaborative process in which each participant's diverse experiences and skills are critical to the outcome of the work. PAR combines theory and practice in cycles of action and reflection that are aimed toward solving concrete community problems while deepening understanding of the broader social, economic, and political forces that shape these issues. And PAR is responsive to changing circumstances, adapting its methods, and drawing on the resources of all participants to address the needs of the community.

347

Participatory action research is also like the banyan tree. The great Indian poet Rabindranath Tagore immortalized the "shaggy-headed banyan tree," a symbol of learning, meditation, reflection, and enlightenment in both Hindu and Buddhist traditions. But the banyan tree is also a gathering place of common people, a place of community discussion and decision making. By spreading out its branches and putting down deep roots, the banyan tree extends its reach and creates new spaces for living and learning. Similarly, the participatory action research process provides a space within which community partners can come together and a process by which they can critically examine the issues facing them, generating knowledge and taking action to address these concerns.

In this chapter, we draw upon the power of metaphor and narrative to provide readers new to participatory action research a framework for understanding and appreciating this practice, while at the same time, we hope, providing those already familiar with PAR some unexpected insights into this approach. We begin by defining participatory action research and by locating this approach within the broader context of action research practice. We then provide a brief historical overview of participatory action research and the major contributors to the development of this practice. Following this, we consider the relationship between some of the theoretical frameworks that have informed participatory action research and the ways in which methodological choices both reflect and deepen our understanding of theory, including a discussion of new frameworks for conceptualizing research ethics in the context of PAR. We then provide three exemplars from recent projects to illustrate how PAR works in practice and to identify common themes and concerns rising out of the process. We highlight these research narratives because we believe that these descriptions best demonstrate the reach of participatory action research, the diversity of issues that are being addressed, and the wealth of approaches that have been developed to create new knowledge and to bring about meaningful change in communities. And because these narratives bring to life the most important element of PAR—the people involved in doing it. We close with a discussion of pedagogical strategies for deepening understanding and improving practice in both classroom and community settings and a reconsideration of our metaphors and their implications for the future.

Defining Participatory Action Research

Participatory action research is the sum of its individual terms, which have had and continue to have multiple combinations and meanings, as well as a particular set of assumptions and processes. Most important to this chapter are the intentions behind the terms, as well as the particular historical and contemporary meanings these convey. Participation is a major characteristic of this work, not only in the sense of collaboration, but in the claim that all people in a particular context (for both epistemological and, with it, political reasons) need to be involved in the whole of the project undertaken. Action is interwoven into the process because change, from a situation of injustice toward envisioning and enacting a "better" life (as understood from those in the situation) is a primary goal of the work. Research as a social process of gathering knowledge and asserting wisdom belongs to all people, and has always been part of the struggle toward greater social and economic justice locally and globally. While participatory action research falls under the broader framework of action research approaches, all of which share a belief that knowledge is generated through reflection on actions designed to create change (Reason & Bradbury, 2008), PAR is distinct in its focus on collaboration, political engagement, and an explicit commitment to social justice.

Exploring the Roots of Participatory Action Research

It is always problematic to construct a history of PAR, whose roots, like those of the banyan tree, are deep and wide. Distinguished by a collaborative ethos, any origins narrative of PAR involves the tension between giving credit to seminal individuals' work while avoiding the "one great expert" trap. As McDermott (2007) notes, the theoretical underpinnings and the practical methodologies of PAR "resisted traditional models of knowledge construction which privilege expert knowledge" (p. 405), so we endeavor here to place the history of PAR within the global social and political contexts both within and outside the academy that framed its creation, while acknowledging some of the key contributors to this development.

All approaches to knowledge production or inquiry are shaped by the historical contexts in which they emerge. The seeds of PAR were sown in the early 20th century as the social sciences emerged as new disciplines. African American and feminist voices (DuBois, 1973; Lengerman & Niebrugge-Brantley, 1998; Reinharz, 1992) were part of a broad effort to create new forms of inquiry deeply connected to collective action for social justice (Greenwood, personal communication; see also Messer-Davidow, 2002; Price, 2004). Meanwhile critiques of positivist social science research exposed claims to values-free knowledge production as untenable and challenged the basic tenets of objectivity and generalizability

(Fay, 1975; Kuhn, 1970; Mills, 1961), laying the groundwork for more politically informed and socially engaged forms of knowledge creation. PAR has also been deeply influenced by feminist critiques of the social construction of knowledge (Calloway, 1981; Maguire, 1987, 2001a; Mies, 1982; Reid & Frisby, 2007; Reinharz, 1992; Smith, 1989), acknowledging that the identities and positionalities of those involved in knowledge creation affect its processes and outcomes.

Affirming the notion that ordinary people can understand and change their own lives through research, education, and action, PAR emerged with other challenges to existing structures of power by fostering opportunities for the development of more participatory and democratic solutions to social problems. PAR's development has been informed by numerous social struggles and movements, including workers' movements (Adams, 1975), women's movements (Maguire, 2001b), and human rights and peace movements (Tandon, 1996). One such influence was the postcolonial reconceptualization of international development assistance in the 1960s and 1970s in response to a quarter century of failed development policies (Frank, 1973; Furtado, 1973).

Much of the early development of PAR took place outside of traditional academic settings, particularly in the "south," or third world, away from Western European and North American contexts. In the early 1970s, Marja-Liis Swantz, a Finnish social scientist with the Tanzanian Bureau of Land Use and Productivity, and her students at the University of Dar es Salaam used the term "participant research" to describe their participatory development and research work with Tanzanian villagers (Swantz, 1974, 2008; see also Hall, 1993). During the same period, Orlando Fals Borda and other Latin American sociologists were using the term *investigation yaccion*—participatory action research—to describe "research that involved investigating reality in order to transform it" (quoted in de Souza, 1988, p. 35; see also Fals Borda, 1977, 1979).

Another key contribution to the development of PAR was the reframing of adult education as an empowering alternative to traditional and colonial education to unsettle relationships based on dominance (Freire, 1970; Horton & Freire, 1990; Kindervatter, 1979; Nyerere, 1969). Confronting "contradictions between their philosophy of adult education and their practice of research methodology" (Tandon, 1988, p. 5), adult educators sought to develop research approaches that reflected the same democratic and collaborative values that informed their pedagogy. Paulo Freire's literacy work in Brazil (1970), the Scandinavian folkschool movement, the contributions of Myles Horton and the other founders of the Highlander Research and Education Center (Horton & Freire, 1990; Lewis, 2001), and regional participatory research networks, such as the Society for Participatory Research in Asia (see Tandon, 2005), which grew out of the International Council for Adult Education funded Participatory Research Project (PRP) under the directorship of Budd Hall (2001), all contributed to the further growth of critical pedagogy and participatory action research.

These international connections and networks, formal and informal, provided an important opportunity for links between the long-standing tradition of action research in education and other social research areas. For example, in the action research emerging in Australia in the mid 1980s, Kemmis and McTaggart, through the suggestion of Giovanna di Chiro, formed connections to the work of Fals Borda, describing their work as participatory action research. This explicitly socially critical perspective on action research also built on participatory norms developed in the literacy work of Marie Brennan and Lynton Brown (Kemmis & McTaggart, personal correspondence; see also Kemmis & McTaggart, 2005).

Following the United Nations' Convention on the Rights of the Child (1989), which recognized children's right to participate in projects affecting them, there has been considerable growth of PAR involving young people as agents rather than objects of research (Fine & Torre, 2005). Whether in community-based organizations or school-related projects, young people often frame problems—and solutions—differently from adults in those settings (Cammarota & Fine, 2008; Fernández, 2002; Groundwater-Smith & Downes, 1999; Guishard, 2009; Hutzel, 2007; Lewis, 2007; McIntyre, 2000; Morgan et al., 2004; Tuck, 2009).

Taken together, these varied "origins" of PAR show distinct characteristics. One is that of continued challenges to forms of knowledge generation that position nondominant groups as outsiders. Popular knowledge generation is a crucial element to PAR. But perhaps most important is that PAR has grown from and with social movements (Mies, 1982). PAR's emergence within the academy came from discipline-specific activist scholarship. The social struggles of literacy and development workers, feminists, labor activists, civil rights workers, and activist academics all informed the foundation of PAR, and are an essential part of considering its use in contemporary social research.

THEORETICAL AND METHODOLOGICAL FRAMEWORKS

In participatory action research, the distinction between theory and method is challenged by the assumption that theory is informed by practice and practice a reflection on theory. Methods for collecting, analyzing, understanding, and distributing data cannot be separated from the epistemologies, social theories, and ethical stances that shape our understanding of the issues we seek to address.

While the theories, methods, and the methodologies in PAR are varied and evolve differently within every context, it is the belief in collaboration and respect for local knowledge, the commitment to social justice, and trust in the ability of democratic processes to lead to positive personal, organizational, and community transformation that provide the common set of principles that guide this work (Brydon-Miller, Greenwood, & Maguire, 2003). PAR stems from the understanding that knowledge(s) are plural and that those who have been systematically excluded from knowledge generation need to be active participants in the research process, especially when it is about them. The nature of the data collected, the methods of analysis, and the resulting reflections and actions emerge out of a collaborative engagement within a community and often, but not always, with an academic researcher as a partner in the process. In order to reflect the principles of PAR, this academic researcher must be willing to embrace the hard work of examining how his or her multiple identities shape and inform engagement with community members.

This critical examination of issues of identity requires an analysis of the dynamics of power and privilege. From the outset, reflection on these aspects of the research relationship has informed the practice of participatory action research. The early Gramscian and feminist-informed PAR work were developed as responses to the political agendas and social contexts of their time. The critiques of colonialism embedded in these works (Fals Borda & Mora-Osejo, 2003) and the role of women's groups in the efforts toward social reconstruction (Mies, 1982) must be seen as efforts toward theorizing power relations. In the contemporary context, these would be recognized as part of postcolonial theorizing, and PAR workers in that era were aware of the emergent writings of Freire and his analysis of systems of oppression (1970). While other social theories have been employed in relation to PAR, the integral connection between social theory and social action has been an essential part of participatory action research strategies. Theoretical frames are seen as integrally connected to politics, meaning not only in the examination of the workings of power, but also the nature of participation, and in activism as a contributor to the fight for social justice. One example of current resonances between social struggle and social research is reflected in the use of narratives within PAR and the prominence of counter narrative within critical race theory (Brydon-Miller, 2004; Ladson-Billings & Tate, 1995). As Delgado notes, "stories can shatter complacency and challenge the status quo" (2000, p. 61), key objectives of the participatory action research process as well. Another emergent intersection between an existing theoretical framework and PAR is in the exploration of the ways in which the notion of borderlands scholarship (Anzaldúa, 2007; Torre & Ayala, 2009a) can deepen the practice of PAR.

There is also an important component of reciprocity in the relationship with both critical race theory and borderlands scholarship, in that PAR offers concrete strategies for making manifest the critical perspectives and demands for social justice embodied in these frameworks (Brydon-Miller, 2004; Torre & Ayala, 2009b).

Recent social theory also emphasizes agency, subjectivity, and pragmatism. Toulmin (1988) described the more recent philosophical turn from universal, general, and timeless thinking to oral, particular, local, and timely investigations. Writers from the later Frankfurt School challenged positivist inquiry by looking at local and contextualized meanings, as well as moral, historical, and political realities needing to be tied to research methodology (Rabinow & Sullivan, 1985). Ortner (2006) argues for the need to incorporate subjectivity, agency, and power into social research, what Burke (2005) calls the return of the actor. In PAR, the research subject becomes this actor, whose contexts and communities are woven into the research tapestry. And PAR argues for including diverse actors in the process. It is an indigenizing of research practice, and indigenous organizations such as the National Aboriginal Health Organization (NAHO) of Canada have developed ethical principles calling for deep community participation in, and shared ownership of, all aspects of research projects (NAHO, 2007; Royal Commission on Aboriginal Peoples, 1993; Smith, 1999). In many indigenous communities, researchers have made a bad name for themselves. Linda Tuhiwai Smith (1999) writes that research "is probably one of the dirtiest words in the indigenous world's vocabulary" (p. 1). This is because, like the colonizers, researchers have, too many times, come into indigenous communities to collect their stories to disappear without a word coming back or any benefit returning to the community. This has been experienced by many indigenous communities as another form of dispossession. Some researchers have come as ethnographers who were later seen as spies working with "informants" (see Deloria, 1997). The natives are now talking back, in the contexts of decolonization and reclamation of control over their lives, part of self-representation and what is now being called indigenism (Niezen, 2003).

Asad (1993) referred to such practices as the reconstitution of colonized subjectivities. Increasingly, the addition of collaboration, reciprocity, consultation, and public engagement are entering the social research agenda. A public anthropology is on the rise, which includes public participation and empowerment in research directed toward solving problems in the world (Lamphere, 2004; Rylko-Bauer, Singer, & Van Willigen, 2006). This practical or pragmatic emphasis is also appearing in methodological texts (Creswell & Plano Clark, 2007; Maxwell, 2005).

The openness and willingness to allow for multiple knowledge(s) within the PAR process, as well as the rejection of the assumptions embedded in a positivist worldview and the emphasis on critical reflection, open the doors to an eclectic approach to using existing methods as well as the development of methodological innovations. PAR draws upon both quantitative (Krzywkowski-Mohn, 2008; Merrifield, 1993; Schulz et al., 1998) and qualitative approaches, adhering to the belief that the issues facing the community and the research questions they generate to address these issues should drive the method. But, for the most part, the focus is on creating dialogue and generating knowledge through interaction. Often, PAR researchers use methods and communication strategies that have a "hands-on" nature (Kindon, Pain, & Kesby, 2007), especially when working with marginalized communities.

One area of particular note is in the use of arts as a way of both generating and recording the PAR process. PAR's emphasis on multiple ways of knowing creates fertile ground for experimentation and innovation with arts-based methodologies. Art offers both a means of expression and the potential to challenge and change. Arts-based methods employ a wide repertoire including storytelling (Sangtin Writers & Nagar, 2006), visual arts (Bastos & Brydon-Miller, 2004; Hutzel, 2007), photography (McIntyre & Lykes, 2004; Wang, 1999), performance (Boal, 1985; Guhathakurta, 2008; Pratt, 2004), fiber arts, indigenous arts (Lykes, 2001), and newer forms of media art. In addition, new technologies such as geographic information systems (GIS), which allow users to gather, synthesize, and represent information relating phenomena such as environmental hazards, health outcomes, income and educational disparities, or the incidence of crime to a location (Mapedza, Wright, & Fawcett, 2003), afford opportunities for innovative PAR methods that can help communities to re-envision change. These innovative data collection techniques must be seen in light of the epistemological shifts ongoing in research strategies. The use of the arts, of graphic organizers, and other techniques were not developed as ways to gain greater access to information for the "outside" researchers to analyze and interpret. Rather, the "methods" within PAR are determined not only to gain a richer understanding, but to generate new ways to consider actions within the socio-political sphere (Cammarota & Fine, 2008). Importantly, the "action" part of PAR has been a way to develop both the strategies for change in oppressive social situations as well as a sense of hope and agency among participants (Mies, 1996).

Clearly, there is a wealth of approaches available to researchers and community partners to carry out a PAR process, but whichever specific methods are selected, they emerge from the context, the interactions between the "outsider" and community knowledge forms, the questions to be addressed, the nature of actions, and the way the project evolves. The process is as critical as the product; and while the research results are important, PAR researchers pay careful attention to developing the skills and capacities of the community participants through the research process (Kesby, Kindon, & Pain, 2005; Maguire, 1987).

The theory and methods of PAR require a fundamental reconsideration of research ethics as well. The current system relies upon a contractual model of research ethics with an emphasis on informed consent and the academic researcher's ownership and control of data. This model reinforces the power and authority of the academic researcher and abets what Newkirk (1996) has referred to as the seduction and betrayal of research subjects lured into revealing intimate aspects of their lives only to have those details made public through the interpretations and representations of the researcher. The current model of research ethics also calls into question the principles of caring and commitment that are at the heart of participatory action research by recasting these relationships as potential sites of coercion.

An alternative model builds instead upon the notion of covenantal ethics, "an ethical stance enacted through relationship and commitment to working for the good of others" (Brydon-Miller, 2009, p. 244; see also Hilsen, 2006; May, 2000). The ethical grounding of participatory action research might be best conceived of as a system of community covenantal ethics framed by relationships of reciprocal responsibility, collaborative decision making, and power sharing (Brydon-Miller, 2007). This framework draws upon feminist research ethics (Brabeck, 2000) and is consistent with the current efforts within many indigenous communities to establish community-based systems of research ethics guidelines (Battiste, 2007). In Canada, the Royal Commission on Aboriginal Peoples (1993) published ethical guidelines for research where participation is key: "Researchers shall establish collaborative procedures to enable community representatives to participate in the planning, execution, and evaluation of research results" (p. 39). The National Aboriginal Health Organization (NAHO, 2007) also has a document on ethical research practices in indigenous communities arguing, "all partners are involved in the entire scope of the research project through the planning, implementation, data analysis and reporting stages" (p. 2). The challenge now before us is to synthesize these various efforts to reconceptualize research ethics and to clearly articulate criteria by which the ethics of participatory action research might be examined.

Variations on the Theme of Participatory Action Research

The following exemplars present PAR projects in very different communities around the world, dealing with issues as diverse as youth suicide, response to and recovery from natural disasters, and the reclamation of local knowledge to enhance health outcomes for school-aged children. The methods used in these studies also highlight the range of ways in which PAR can be practiced. But all three demonstrate the commitment of the researchers to developing close and trusting relationships with community partners, their shared dedication to working for positive social change, and their willingness to reflect upon the challenges and contradictions of participatory action research.

Welcoming the Uninvited Guest: Participatory Action Research and the Self Employed Women's Association

ANU SABHLOK

My perceived vulnerability, especially the fact that I was pregnant, created unforeseen advantages for me as a researcher. I was welcomed, well almost forced into homes. Immediately groups of women gathered around me. Ah! I thought I didn't have to work very hard towards getting respondents. But again, I was in for surprises. Before I could ask any of my questions I was fielding theirs, "what makes you come here in a pregnant state? Where is your husband, how did your family allow you to travel? Why is your nose not pierced?"—it was almost as if the gaze was reversed. I was the subject and they were the researchers. Sharing with them my stories, however, did help form a bond and created a space where research became a dialogue rather than a one-way interview.

—Anu Sabhlok, excerpts from my fieldnotes, 2001

Dissertations usually are very individualistic ventures—it is your question, your research, and eventually your degree. However, as my experience during my dissertation work in Gujarat shows, the dynamics of more participatory, community-centered research are difficult to predict and often unfold in surprising ways during the process. Gujarat, a state in western India, witnessed a massive earthquake in 2001, the year I started my doctoral work on earthquake rehabilitation. In 2002, violent Hindu-Muslim riots broke out resulting in more than 50,000 people having to flee to relief camps, primarily from the minority Muslim communities.

My initial agenda as I embarked upon this project as an architecture and geography student was to work on post-earthquake structures and temporary relief housing. However, many discussions with the local populations revealed that it was not the number of houses constructed or amount of money received in aid that was important; rather there were questions of access, corruption, economic liberalization (pulling out of the welfare state), religious ideology, and power that needed to be addressed. Thus, the research focus shifted to understanding the multiple meanings of relief work from the perspective of those that perform relief and those that receive it.

Sometimes "experts" are invited by development agencies to conduct PAR, other times an organic collaboration develops between the academics and the community. In my case, I wanted to do research that was participatory, that had a social justice agenda, and that dismantled the researcher-researched hierarchy. This desire stemmed from my feminist epistemological position and training. The collaboration was not organic and I was not invited—how then does one become part of a community and engage with them collaboratively toward a common agenda?

It is also important to address the question of distance—both geographic and social. How does engaged, participatory action research happen across 10,000 miles? I established e-mail contact with an organization that I admired, SEWA: Self Employed Women's Association. With roots in Marxist and Gandhian struggles, SEWA is the world's largest trade union of poor, informal-sector women workers. SEWA women had adopted five relief camps and had initiated *Shantipath Kendras* (centers of peace) to cultivate dialogue among the diverse religious communities. Through my work, I wanted to express solidarity with SEWA. Ironically, SEWA women, busy in their grassroots work, did not welcome me in easily. Bridging the gap with the working-class women in SEWA seemed almost impossible. However, I think our shared commitment toward building a more just, more peaceful, and a more democratic country (and Gujarat State in particular) paved the way for a collaborative process.

Eventually, after two months of visiting SEWA offices, I was accepted as a volunteer in SEWA academy. SEWA academy is the research section of SEWA and has been conducting grassroots research for the past 30 years. SEWA academy trains poor, often illiterate, women in the tools of research and helps them form a team of what they call "barefoot researchers." These teams go into urban and rural homes to identify and document issues relevant to informal-sector poor women. SEWA women also produce participatory videos to make their voices heard in the public domain. After a few "sharing sessions," we decided to document the multiple meanings of relief for those at the grassroots. Initially, we organized focus groups where collective and individual experiences of relief work were shared. Then, accompanied by one or two SEWA women, I started conducting in-depth interviews and life-story sharing sessions with individual

SEWA women. At the end of every week, we would again have a "sharing session" at the SEWA academy, where I would present an analysis of the interviews and the SEWA team would share results from the survey research they were conducting. A day before I returned to the United States, SEWA academy conducted an "experience sharing" session wherein we reflected upon the collaborative experience and attempted to make sense of the data. This process of collecting and exchanging understandings of relief efforts deepened and complicated our collective understanding of relief on both the individual and community levels. Through discussions, there emerged a collectively generated analysis of the relief process that not only outlined the numbers of those affected and resources distributed but also revealed how power (at the international, national, and local levels) and issues of identity (particularly religious, gender, class, and caste) play out during the relief process.

Back in the United States in 2005, I transcribed, translated, and re-analyzed the interviews and discussions and wrote out a 300-page document that was "my" dissertation. While we retained intermittent contact during the writing phase, there was very little collaboration with SEWA. I graduated in 2007 with a doctoral degree in geography and women's studies from Pennsylvania State University (Sabhlok, 2007). I struggle with numerous questions as I write this section: To what extent was this process PAR? While the research questions emerged out of a dialogue and we collaborated and shared the data collection with a collective agenda of social justice through research, yet the written product was my analysis and my writing. I struggle with questions of belonging—I was sometimes accepted as an insider (we shared similar commitments) and at other times my outsider position (differences in class and educational background) was made apparent. While the theoretical analysis in my dissertation might be of little use to SEWA women, I think it was the process of collaborative research, sharing, and reflection that enriched their and my perspectives (and therefore action) on disaster relief among other seemingly mundane things. This example brings to light some of the challenges that surface when academics engage with organizations that are independently deeply immersed in PAR processes.

SEWA's website shows a banyan tree. The top part of the tree shows thick foliage as its members, and the numerous roots stemming from branches represent the cooperatives, the social security organizations, the SEWA academy, and the various unions in SEWA. The interconnectedness of the roots gives the tree its strength and the new branches and roots that emerge create new spaces for SEWA's collective engagement and actions. Looking back, I see myself as part of these new roots that grow independently and yet are always connected to the tree. Looking ahead, I visualize that connection growing stronger. The dissertation as I see it was just the starting point for a long-term engagement with women in SEWA.

"Don't Worry—Our Community's Been Gardening for Centuries": Youth Participatory Action Research in a School Setting

PATRICIA MAGUIRE, FROM THE WORK OF ALICIA FITZPATRICK AND HER STUDENTS

In this exemplar, Alicia Fitzpatrick, a high school teacher, and 15 students used participatory action research to create new spaces in school for learning and living (Eriacho et al., 2007; Fitzpatrick et al., 2007). A former Peace Corps volunteer, Alicia taught science for three years in an alternative high school on an American Indian nation in the southwestern United States. She was also a graduate student in a teacher education master's program that promoted critical reflection and action research with transformative intentions. During the program, teachers engage in action research (AR) to improve their own practices and to more deeply understand—and attempt to unsettle—the inequitable power arrangements and relationships that shape U.S. schooling (Maguire & Horwitz, 2005).

It was in the context of taking my teacher action research course, that this PAR project emerged from Alicia's conversation with a student. Reflecting on changes she had already made to her teaching practices, Alicia noted of her classroom lab activities, "I was still uncomfortable with the fact that the students were finding solutions to problems that had already been solved" (Eriacho et al., 2007, p. 6). While grappling with teaching practices she might improve through action research, one of her students, Alex, talked with her about the quality of school lunches. Noting widespread problems of diabetes and obesity, he thought school lunches should include fresh produce and vegetarian options. Reporting on this conversation, Alex noted two things. First, Ms. Fitzpatrick actually listened; and second, she asked him, "How do you see a solution to this problem?" (Eriacho et al., 2007, p. 7). His reply, that the school should grow its own food, framed the problem to be addressed by students and teacher through PAR.

Building on Alex's suggestion to develop an agricultural management elective, 15 students (with Ms. Fitzpatrick's facilitation and extensive inclusion of community members as resources) used a series of research-action cycles to codevelop the agricultural course curriculum through which they planned, built, and operated a school greenhouse and traditional garden. The core group of nine male and five female students included teen parents, students who had been expelled from other schools, and students identified for special education services. As they began, Richelle, one of the students, noted that the community viewed students from the alternative school as "bad influences" who would never graduate (Eriacho et al., 2007, p. 14). The project slowly unsettled this perception as students demonstrated leadership qualities while interacting with community members.

Alicia and these students studied what was happening for them as they codeveloped the agricultural class, school greenhouse, and garden. They maintained reflection journals and analyzed photographs of their work using Photovoice protocols (Wang, 1999). A group of students and Alicia cowrote the final paper for her graduate AR course (Eriacho et al., 2007). They were the first student-teacher team to ever copresent at the New Mexico Center for Teaching Excellence's annual Teacher Action Research conference (Fitzpatrick et al., 2007).

While PAR has increasingly been utilized with youth in community organizations, development projects, and after-school programs (Fernández, 2002; Hutzel, 2007; McIntyre, 2000; Nairn, Higgins, & Sligo, 2007), school-based teacher-student PAR is less common. Indeed, Groundwater-Smith and Downes (1999) have criticized the teacher-as-researcher movement, in which teachers examine their own practices, for positioning students as objects of teachers' studies rather than collaborators in classroom AR. In the school greenhouse and garden project, Fitzpatrick intentionally created processes for meaningful student leadership and decision making. This was challenging as the structures needed to support students as coresearchers are not well represented in teacher action research literature (Brydon-Miller & Maguire, 2009). Throughout the AR course, Alicia continuously talked with other teachers—and her students—about how to create processes and spaces for students' control of the project and agricultural class.

Fitzpatrick and her students worked to move up Hart's Ladder of Child Participation (1997; see also Arnstein, 1969), from the bottom rungs of manipulated or token student participation to more meaningful youth-initiated and -directed participation. This movement required the teacher to share power and control with the students and community members in ways quite uncommon in the wake of No Child Left Behind mandates. Initially, Alicia was reluctant to even take on creation of the agricultural course, noting that she did not know much about gardening. Alex reassured her, "Don't worry—our community's been gardening for centuries." The students knew that given a framework, they could tap into the vast and long-term, community-held knowledge of traditional gardening practices in the arid Southwest. The teens were likewise required to stretch out of their comfort zones to develop curriculum, initiate contact with community resources, speak before public officials, and keep regular school attendance.

Teacher and students moved into another uncomfortable zone when they confronted the inequitable power arrangements of gender at play in the project.

Alicia noticed that when students initially divided up the work, the boys took on greenhouse construction while the girls worked on the project website. She was also aware of the dominance of male voices in the classroom. "I instantly started to brainstorm ways in which females could speak up ... not ... strategies that would help the males become active listeners." She realized her teacher silence condoned male dominance and was surprised that her first impulse had been "to fix the girls" (personal communication, February 5, 2007). Despite her intellectual understanding of schools as raced, classed, and gendered spaces (Maguire & Berge, 2009), Alicia, a community outsider, was reluctant to start a conversation about project gender issues. But given space and structures, students did it themselves through Photovoice. For example, Farrah wrote about the time when analyzing photographs, a male student pointed out that there were only boys in one photo and only girls in another. "Once that was brought up, Ms. Fitzpatrick started asking questions about why that was. I said I would have liked to join the guys but then I would have been the only girl and I would have felt out of place" (Eriacho, et al., 2007, p. 23). Alicia continued the narrative: "After Farrah shared her thoughts . . . a male student sitting next to her said, 'What? You felt like this?' She looked at him and said, 'Yes.'" Only the girls had been aware of the very visible gender divisions. This is not unusual in PAR projects when gender is a quality assigned to females but not males and the gendering mechanisms at work are ignored (Maguire, 2001b). After the discussion, two girls joined the previously all-male construction group.

The greenhouse and garden project is an example of combining PAR and a greening project to change school landscapes into "learnscapes" (Lewis, 2007). As Lewis (2004) noted, the school grounds offered a rare uncolonized *third space* in schools where participatory research and education projects could take root.

"I'm Doing This From My Heart": Inuit Suicide Prevention and Reclamation in Nunavut, Canada

MICHAEL KRAL

Suicide among indigenous youth is an epidemic in the circumpolar north. Canadian Inuit have among the highest suicide rates in the world. Why suicide? A brief history puts this in perspective. Nunavut is an Inuit political territory established in 1999 in the central and eastern Canadian Arctic. It is about the size of India, with 26 communities and a population of about 27,000. Almost all community members are Inuit, speaking Inuktitut and English. Significant contact by outsiders or *Qallunaat* began with Scottish and American whalers in the late 19th and early 20th centuries, and continued with the trinity of the fur trade, missionaries, and police. The most colossal change in Inuit history began in the 1950s, when the Canadian government tried to help Inuit during a tuberculosis epidemic and time of hunger. Inuit were moved from their family camps to aggregated settlements, children were placed in day or residential/boarding schools where they were not allowed to speak their language. *Qallunaat* Northern Service Officers ran the settlements and established a foreign electoral system, gender roles changed particularly for men, the new welfare state created poverty, and intergenerational segregation began for a people for whom kinship was at the center of social organization. Many of those children grew up without proper parenting skills and traditional ways, and their children began killing themselves in the 1980s in numbers that have only continued to grow (see Brody, 2000; Condon, 1988; Kral & Idlout, 2009; Wenzel, 1991).

In 1994, I attended a national conference on suicide prevention in Iqaluit, now the capital of Nunavut, Canada. This was my first visit to the Arctic. I was asked to chair a panel on suicide research based on my involvement with the Canadian Association for Suicide Prevention, which was hosting the conference. I was the only *Qallunaat* on that panel. Most of those attending were Inuit, and discussions were in Inuktitut and English with simultaneous translation. At this session, Inuit from many communities spoke about what they needed to know to prevent suicide among their youth. One older woman stood up and began a discussion in Inuktitut by saying, "In my community we have many suicides. My relative lives in another community and they have no suicides. We need to learn from that community. We need to ask about wellness." Inuit also spoke about how to gather this information. This gathering of knowledge would need to take an oral and collective angle, in keeping with Inuit culture. Sharing was emphasized. Elders and youth should be involved with other community members. On the last day of the conference as a number of us sat around a table, I suggested we put these ideas into a project.

I was nervous as an outsider, not wanting to be seen as yet another colonial researcher taking advantage. I asked an Inuit elder with a translator what she thought of my being involved with them in such a project. Her response was that if my heart is in it, this is good. We developed a project over the next three years. An Inuit steering committee was organized by Eva Adams, an Inuk (Inuit) living in Nunavut, and I put together an academic research team. Our work together was based on the research questions and methodology offered by Inuit at the conference. We applied for and received a grant, and conducted our first study with two Nunavut communities, primarily with members of their youth committees, who helped shape the questions and how the research would take place. Elders finalized the open-ended interview, with Anthony Qrunnut volunteering as a test interviewee. I was greatly relieved when at the end, after an anxious (for me) pause, he smiled and said those were the questions he would ask. The Inuit steering committee provided the most direction during planning and data collection. We completed our report in 2003 with our grant money having expired years earlier, but the time taken was worth it. This work cannot be rushed. This is where I first learned about PAR, which emerged as an indigenous methodology.

Many Inuit have been involved in our participatory research, and we have a core group of four Inuit and myself. I am still the only *Qallunaat* in our Nunavut research group, and am honored to be so accepted. Not everyone in the Inuit communities accepts me, however, and this is a reality I live with. Yet my Inuit partners acknowledge that I can provide a helpful outsider's perspective. My main partner has been Lori Idlout, executive director of the Embrace Life Council, an Inuit organization devoted to suicide prevention and community wellness in Nunavut. Lori believes in PAR and cannot see us working any other way, telling me, "PAR is the most culturally sensitive form of academic research in social sciences when working with Inuit. The methodology is such that decision making is collaborative between the researcher and the community involved." (Idlout, personal communication, June 2010). The participatory process has been directed by Inuit in our research through their local knowledge and expertise. It is the process that has been the product, the most important factor.

Natar Ungalaq, our coresearcher in Igloolik, Nunavut, has long been involved in helping youth in his community. He said that money was not his priority when we were discussing people getting paid from our grant. "I'm doing this from my heart." This is the enduring spirit of our collaborative research on a difficult topic, which has now turned into individual and community success stories. Inuit have been decolonizing, moving to reclaim control over their lives, and our research aligns with this (Kral, Wiebe, Nisbet, Dallas, Okalik, Enuaraq, & Cinotta, 2009). Our research is Inuit-driven yet a true collaboration of minds, hearts, and cultures with love of life, people and community, and Inuit pride, as our motivating forces.

Local Riffs on Common Themes

These exemplars highlight a number of issues related to the practice of participatory action research. The question of the roles and relationships of the researcher and the community members involved in the process are often cast in terms of insider/outsider dynamics, but this kind of dichotomizing overlooks the complex nature of these relationships and the possibility that the researcher might occupy multiple positions simultaneously. Anu's position as a young Indian woman brings her into the homes of the people in the community, but her caste, class, and educational status set her apart. Alicia's status as outsider necessitates a shift in her role as teacher to that of learner challenging the traditional systems of power and authority embedded in our educational practices. And while Michael is clearly identified as an outsider, a *Qallunaat,* which leads some members of the community to question his participation, his long-term commitment to working to address critical community concerns has led to the development of effective interventions as well as warm friendships (see also Humphrey, 2007; Johns, 2008).

The importance of community knowledge and expertise and the question of who owns and controls that knowledge and who benefits from the research are also central concerns in PAR. Alex's reassurances to Alicia that the understanding of effective agricultural techniques already resides in his community and her willingness to respect that knowledge and to put her own skills and resources to work on behalf of the community represents the kinds of genuine partnerships that are at the heart of participatory action research. Likewise, in Michael's exemplar, his research partner Lori notes that PAR is more resonant with local culture and mores than other forms of social research. PAR is in keeping with indigenous cosmologies where relationships are at the center, a form of research that is "evaluated by participant-driven criteria" (Denzin & Lincoln, 2008, p. 11). It is a decolonizing of methods and of academia, a political stance in the redistribution of power with a focus on sharing and mutual respect. Fine, Tuck, and Zeller-Berkman (2008) show that "participatory methods respond to these crises in politics by deliberately inverting who constructs research questions, designs, methods, interpretations, and products, as well as who engages in surveillance" (pp. 160–161).

The action side of PAR is to make the findings useful, and there is clear benefit to the communities participating in these projects. The impact of community-based programs in reducing youth suicide in Inuit communities is testament to the ability of participatory action research to create positive change. Likewise, Alicia's students benefit not only by having access to healthier food, but in developing stronger academic skills and deepening their sense of pride and their acceptance as contributing members of their communities. And even as Anu questions her effectiveness in bringing about change it is clear that her partners have acquired new skills and new understandings and that her on-going commitment to working for positive social change will continue to benefit the community.

At the same time it is important to acknowledge broader implications of PAR and the importance of transferability of knowledge to other researchers, other communities, and other settings. In each case the research being conducted by these scholars—and this includes both the academic and community-based researchers—deepens our collective understanding of important issues and provides strategies for others to draw upon in working to address similar concerns. Michael's work with his partners is already being expanded to other communities in the circumpolar region while Alicia's project provides an opportunity for other teachers to consider ways in which they might bring the knowledge already extant in their communities into their classrooms to enrich their students'—and their own—learning experiences. Anu's work enables an alternative narrative to government and international non-governmental organizational studies on disaster relief, one that is constructed in partnership with those that perform the hard on-the-ground labor of providing relief.

Each of these exemplars also reflects the criteria of the system of community covenantal ethics described earlier: reciprocal responsibility, collaborative decision making, and power sharing. Michael's project is explicitly founded in systems of indigenous research ethics that inform this understanding of research ethics. And by partnering with SEWA and responding to the questions and concerns of that community Anu also reflects these values. Sharing power with her students and working together to reach decisions regarding the process, Alicia allows them to create a project that is both personally and culturally meaningful to them. Drawing upon such work provides clear models for the further development of this notion of community convenantal ethics and compelling demonstrations of how they might be applied in practice.

Practical Pedagogical Issues of Implementation

Jazz challenges assumptions about what music is, how it works, and what makes it beautiful. In teaching participatory action research, as with jazz, the first step is in challenging the dominant aesthetic of positivist research and traditional teaching methods in order to find beauty and productivity in the unpredictable and polyvocal processes of collaboration and group work. As a former student, Beverly Eby, noted after completing a year-long participatory action research course, "it took a whole quarter to learn that it was okay to do this."

Participatory action research provides spaces and specific processes where people, whatever their "instrument" or level of skill, can work together to "make music." The participants, whether expert or novice, must do the work of critical self-reflection, examining their own identities, positions of power and privilege, and interaction styles, as well as how these continuously impact the research process. The pedagogy of PAR must be congruent with these underlying values, proactively inviting and facilitating the contributions of and dialogue among diverse learners (Maguire, 2001b). This is as potentially scary as it is exciting because it means relinquishing control in the classroom to allow students to take the lead.

Participatory action research has been described as the intersection of popular education, community-based research, and collaborative action aimed at achieving positive social change (Brydon-Miller, 2001; Hall, 1993). PAR draws from nonformal and experiential education and community participatory appraisal techniques (Chambers, 1980; Kindervatter, 1979). Teaching PAR, whether this takes place in a university classroom or in a community center or other informal educational setting, must also combine these three elements. Traditional forms of "banking education" (Freire, 1970) must give way to more generative forms of exploration, discovery, and play while at the same time remaining attentive to the well-articulated theoretical and methodological foundations of this approach. Challenging accepted pedagogical practices in this way creates a "constructive disruption" (Cochran-Smith & Lytle, 2009, p. 86) of the basic structures of education by shifting power from the instructor to a system that actively encourages participation and ownership by all participants, whether they are students in a classroom or community partners.

Conclusion

Using metaphors, if done uncritically, can be tricky. In closing, let us consider some of the limitations of the jazz and banyan tree metaphors and the way they might provide a more nuanced understanding of some of the issues of power and privilege that are at the heart of participatory action research (PAR). The Bania, a subcaste of Indian traders who sat under banyan trees to strategize and plan, have been accused of making heavy profits at the cost of the peasantry (Kumar, 1983). While not the fault of the banyan tree, which merely offers its shade, digging just below the surface of the metaphor raises issues of cooptation and expropriation. Who benefits from the strategizing taking place in the shade of the banyan, and for what and whose purposes? In a similar vein, we are concerned about the potential for participatory action research methods to be coopted by those using the language of collaboration and community control to encourage participation in processes that ultimately serve the interests of those in power in political, economic, as well as academic spheres.

From its inception, jazz has been criticized as being a male-dominated musical form, in which cultural and gender constraints colluded to keep many women out and to keep those women instrumentalists who made it in, under-recognized. Race solidarity did not trump gender discrimination. Tucker (n.d.) asked, "If women have played jazz all along, why don't we know more about them?" The reasons for our limited knowledge of African American women's and other women's contributions to the world of jazz are similar to reasons that at one time we knew little of the extensive contributions of women to the early development of PAR. The historical records that become the canon were often written by men, about their male colleagues, citing their male colleagues' publications (Maguire, Brydon-Miller, & McIntyre, 2004). There was little professional expectation that male social scientists or project directors would be well-versed in evolving feminist scholarship or women working in projects.

For great jazz music and banyan trees to endure, they have had to grow and change. The banyan extends its reach by sending down shoots that take root and become new trees. And musicians such as Charles Mingus and the others had to welcome on stage new generations of jazz musicians and even entirely new musical forms. So, too, PAR grows, changes, and expands with each new group of practitioners. Anu, Michael, Alicia, and the other students and younger scholars working in the field represent those new forms and new voices in participatory action research. The commitment of these individuals to their community partners and their dedication to tackling tough issues and to working to achieve meaningful social change reflect the influence and values of their predecessors. At the same time, their theoretical and methodological innovations, including an increased access to technology and the opportunity for increased international dialogue and the exchange of experiences and practices this makes possible, create fertile ground for further growth and development of the field. What comes next is therefore integrally connected to the social struggles evident in the global and local contexts and how those at the local level use the methods of research to understand and change the world.

We believe passionately in the power of participatory action research to push us to challenge and unsettle existing structures of power and privilege, to provide opportunities for those least often heard to share their knowledge and wisdom, and for people to work together to bring about positive social change and to create more just and equitable political and social systems.

Notes

1. The authors are listed in alphabetical order and have contributed equally to this work.

2. We wish to thank Mary's former student, Warren Foster, for first suggesting the jazz metaphor. It is also worth noting here that we chose this moment in jazz history because, to quote Rick VanMatre, director of Jazz Studies at the College-Conservatory of Music at the University of Cincinnati, "most modern jazz musicians still consider Mingus, Parker, and the others on this Massey Hall concert to be at the highest level of artistry and collaboration." VanMatre goes on to note that "the principles of working your butt off, studying, analyzing, and achieving a personal best, then allowing your more intuitive, right brain, collaborative nature to help you interact with others to create a whole greater than the sum of its parts, is common to all great jazz, and all great collaborative research" (personal communication). While jazz forms, like participatory action research methods, evolve, this dedication to artistry and collaboration remain as the most crucial elements of both practices. We thank Norman Denzin and Rick VanMatre for their insights and reflections on the history of jazz and the connections between jazz and PAR.

References

Adams, F. (1975). *Unearthing seeds of fire: The idea of Highlander.* Winston-Salem, NC: John F. Blair.

Anzaldúa, G. (2007). *Borderlands/La Frontera: The new Mestiza* (3rd ed.). San Francisco: Aunt Lute Books.

Arnstein, S. R. (1969). A ladder of citizen participation. *Journal of the American Planning Association, 35*(4), 216–224.

Asad, T. (1993). Afterword: From the history of colonial anthropology to the anthropology of Western hegemony. In G. W. Stocking (Ed.), *Colonial situations: Essays on the contextualization of ethnographic knowledge* (pp. 314–324). Madison: University of Wisconsin Press.

Bastos, F., & Brydon-Miller, M. (2004). Speaking through art: Subalternity and refugee women artists. In B. M. Lucas & A. B. Lopez (Eds.), *Global neo-imperialism and national resistance: Approaches from postcolonial studies* (pp. 107–118). Vigo, Spain: Universidade de Vigo.

Battiste, M. (2007). Research ethics for protecting indigenous knowledge and heritage: Institutional and researcher responsibilities. In N. K. Denzin & M. D. Giardina (Eds.), *Ethical futures in qualitative research: Decolonizing the politics of knowledge* (pp. 111–132). Walnut Creek, CA: Left Coast Press.

Boal, A. (1985). *Theatre of the oppressed.* London: Pluto.

Brabeck, M. M. (Ed.). (2000). *Practicing feminist ethics in psychology.* Washington, DC: American Psychological Association.

Brody, H. (2000). *The other side of Eden: Hunters, farmers, and the shaping of the world.* New York: North Point Press/Farrar, Straus & Giroux.

Brydon-Miller, M. (2001). Education, research, and action: Theory and methods of participatory action research. In D. L. Tolman & M. Brydon-Miller (Eds.), *From subjects to subjectivities: A handbook of interpretive and participatory methods* (pp. 76–89). New York: New York University Press.

Brydon-Miller, M. (2004). The terrifying truth: Interrogating systems of power and privilege and choosing to act. In M. Brydon-Miller, P. Maguire, & A. McIntyre (Eds.), *Traveling companions: Feminism, teaching, and action research* (pp. 3–19). Westport, CT: Praeger.

Brydon-Miller, M. (2007, September). *The community covenant: Understanding the ethical challenges of participatory action research.* Paper presented at Arbeidsforskning sinstituttet/Work Research Institute, Oslo, Norway.

Brydon-Miller, M. (2009). Covenantal ethics and action research: Exploring a common foundation for social research. In D. Mertens & P. Ginsberg (Eds.), *Handbook of social research ethics* (pp. 243–258). Thousand Oaks, CA: Sage.

Brydon-Miller, M., Greenwood, D., & Maguire, P. (2003). Why action research? *Action Research, 1*(1), 9–28.

Brydon-Miller, M., & Maguire, P. (2009). Participatory action research: Contributions to the development of practitioner inquiry in education. *Educational Action Research, 17*(1), 79–93.

Burke, P. (2005). *History and social theory.* Ithaca, NY: Cornell University Press.

Calloway, H. (1981). Women's perspective: Research as re-vision. In P. Reason & J. Rowan (Eds.), *Human Inquiry* (pp. 457–472). New York: John Wiley.

Cammarota, J., & Fine, M. (Eds.). (2008). *Revolutionizing education: Youth participatory action research in motion.* New York: Routledge.

Chambers, R. (1980). *Rapid rural appraisal: Rationale and repertoire* (IDS Discussion Paper No. 155). Brighton, UK: University of Sussex, Institute of Development Studies.

Cochran-Smith, M., & Lytle, S. (2009). *Inquiry as stance: Practitioner research for the next generation.* New York: Teachers College Press.

Condon, R. G. (1988). *Inuit youth: Growth and change in the Canadian Arctic.* New Brunswick, NJ: Rutgers University Press.

Creswell, J. W., & Plano Clark, V. L. (2007). *Designing and conducting mixed methods research.* Thousand Oaks, CA: Sage.

Delgado, R. (2000). Storytelling for oppositionists and others: A plea for narrative. In R. Delgado & J. Stefancic (Eds.), *Critical race theory: The cutting edge* (pp. 60–70). Philadelphia: Temple University Press.

Deloria, V., Jr. (1997). Anthros, Indians, and planetary reality. In T. Biolsi & L. J. Zimmerman (Eds.), *Indians and anthropologists: Vine Deloria Jr. and the critique of anthropology* (pp. 209–221). Tucson: University of Arizona Press.

Denzin, N. K., & Lincoln, Y. S. (2008). Introduction: Critical methodologies and indigenous inquiry. In N. K. Denzin, Y. S. Lincoln, & L. T. Smith (Eds.), *Handbook of critical & indigenous methodologies* (pp. 1–20). Thousand Oaks, CA: Sage.

de Souza, J. F. (1988). A perspective of participatory research in Latin America. *Convergence, 21*(2/3), 29–38.

DuBois, W. E. B. (1973). *The education of Black people: Ten critiques.* Amherst: University of Massachusetts Press.

Eriacho, R., Fitzpatrick, A., Jamon, A., Lahaleon, T., LaRue, F., Lewis, K., Poncho, G., Quam, R., & Tsethlikai, G., & Tsethlikai, S. (2007). *A student initiative to improve school lunch by practicing traditional agricultural and modern greenhouse management practices.* Unpublished manuscript, Western New Mexico University, Gallup Graduate Studies Center, Silver City, NM.

Fals Borda, O. (1977). *For praxis: The problem of how to investigate reality in order to transform it.* Paper presented at the Cartagena Symposium on Action Research and Scientific Analysis, Cartagena, Colombia.

Fals Borda, O. (1979). Investigating reality in order to transform it. *Dialectical Anthropology, 4*(1), 33–55.

Fals Borda, O., & Mora-Osejo, L. (2003) Context and diffusion of knowledge: A critique of Eurocentrism. *Action Research, 1*(1), 20–37.

Fay, B. (1975). *Social theory and political practice.* London: George Allen and Unwin.

Fernández, M. (2002). *Creating community change: Challenges and tensions in community youth research* (JGC Issues Brief). Stanford, CA: John W. Gardner Center for Youth and Their Communities.

Fine, M., & Torre, M. (2005). Resisting and researching: Youth participatory action research. In S. Ginwright, J. Cammarota, & P. Noguera (Eds.), *Social justice, youth, and their communities* (pp. 269–285). New York: Routledge.

Fine, M., Tuck, E., & Zeller-Berkman, S. (2008). Do you believe in Geneva? Methods and ethics at the global-local nexus. In N. K. Denzin, Y. S. Lincoln, & L. T. Smith (Eds.), *Handbook of critical & indigenous methodologies* (pp. 157–180). Thousand Oaks, CA: Sage.

Fitzpatrick, A., Concho, G., Jamon, A., Lahaleon, T., LaRue, F., Tsethlikai, G., & Tsethlikai, S. (2007, June 8). *Youth action research for sustainable agriculture in a rural Southwest USA schoolyard.* Paper presented at the Center for Teaching Excellence Fifteenth Annual Action Research Conference at Eastern New Mexico University, Portales, NM.

Frank, A. (1973). The development of underdevelopment. In C. K. Wilber (Ed.), *The political economy of development and underdevelopment* (pp. 94–103). New York: Random House.

Freire, P. (1970). *Pedagogy of the oppressed.* New York: Seabury.

Furtado, C. (1973). The concept of external dependence. In C. K. Wilber (Ed.), *The political economy of development and underdevelopment* (pp. 118–123). New York: Random House.

Groundwater-Smith, S., & Downes, T. (1999). *Students: From informants to co-researchers.* Paper presented at the Australian Association of Research in Education Annual

Conference, Melbourne, Australia. Available at http://www.aare.edu.au/99pap/gro99031.htm

Guhathakurta, M. (2008). Theatre in participatory action research: Experiences from Bangladesh. In P. Reason & H. Bradbury (Eds.), *The SAGE handbook of action research: Participative inquiry and practice* (2nd ed., pp. 510–521). London: Sage.

Guishard, M. (2009). The false paths, the endless labors, the turns now this way and now that: Participatory action research, mutual vulnerability, and the politics of inquiry. *Urban Review, 41,* 85–105.

Hall, B. (1993). Introduction. In P. Park, M. Brydon-Miller, B. Hall, & T. Jackson (Eds.), *Voices of change: Participatory research in the United States and Canada* (pp. xiii–xxii). Westport, CT: Bergin and Garvey.

Hall, B. (2001, December 5). *In from the cold? Reflections on participatory research from 1970–2002.* Inaugural Professorial Lecture, University of Victoria, Victoria, British Columbia, Canada.

Hart, R. (1997). *Children's participation: The theory and practice of involving young citizens in community development and environmental care.* New York: UNICEF/Earthscan.

Hilsen, A. I. (2006). And they shall be known by their deeds: Ethics and politics in action research. *Action Research, 4*(1), 23–36.

Horton, M., & Freire, P. (1990). *We make the road by walking: Conversations on education and social change.* Philadelphia: Temple University Press.

Humphrey, C. (2007). Insider-outsider: Activating the hyphen. *Action Research, 5*(1), 11–26.

Hutzel, K. (2007). Reconstructing a community, reclaiming a playground: A participatory action research study. *Studies in Art Education, 48*(3), 299–320.

Johns, T. (2008). Learning to love our black selves: Healing from internalized oppressions. In P. Reason & H. Bradbury (Eds.), *The SAGE handbook of action research: Participative inquiry and practice* (2nd ed., pp. 473–486). London: Sage.

Kemmis, S., & McTaggart, R. (2005). Participatory action research: Communicative action and the public sphere. In N. K. Denzin & Y. S. Lincoln (Eds.), *The SAGE handbook of qualitative research* (3rd ed., pp. 559–603). Thousand Oaks, CA: Sage.

Kesby, M., Kindon, S., & Pain, R. (2005). "Participatory" approaches and diagramming techniques. In R. Flowerdew & D. Martin (Eds.), *Methods in human geography: A guide for students doing a research project* (pp. 144–166). London: Pearson Prentice Hall.

Kindervatter, S. (1979). *Nonformal education as an empowering process.* Amherst: University of Massachusetts, Center for International Education.

Kindon, S., Pain, R., & Kesby, M. (Eds.). (2007). *Participatory action research approaches and methods.* London: Routledge.

Kral, M. J., & Idlout, L. (2009). Community wellness and social action in the Canadian Arctic: Collective agency as subjective well-being. In L. J. Kirmayer & G. G. Valaskakis (Eds.), *Healing traditions: The mental health of aboriginal peoples in Canada* (pp. 315–334). Vancouver: University of British Columbia Press.

Kral, M. J., Wiebe, P., Nisbet, K., Dallas, C., Okalik, L., Enuaraq, N., & Cinotta, J. (2009). Canadian Inuit community engagement in suicide prevention. *International Journal of Circumpolar Health, 68,* 91–107.

Krzywkowski-Mohn, S. (2008). *Diabetic control and patient perception of the Scheduled in Group Medical Appointment at the Cincinnati Veterans Administration Medical Center.* Unpublished doctoral dissertation, University of Cincinnati, OH.

Kuhn, T. (1970). *The structures of scientific revolutions* (2nd ed.). Chicago: University of Chicago Press.

Kumar, K. (1983). Peasants' perception of Gandhi and his program: Oudh, 1920–1922. *Social Scientist, 11*(5), 16–30.

Ladson-Billings, G., & Tate, W. F. (1995). Towards a critical race theory of education. *Teachers College Record, 97*(1), 47–69.

Lamphere, L. (2004). The convergence of applied, practicing, and public anthropology in the 21st century. *Human Organization, 63,* 431–443.

Lengermann, P., & Niebrugge-Brantley, J. (1998). *The women founders: Sociology and social theory: 1830–1930.* Boston: McGraw-Hill.

Lewis, H. (2001). Participatory research and education for social change: Highlander Research and Education Center. In P. Reason & H. Bradbury (Eds.), *Handbook of action research: Participative inquiry and practice* (pp. 356–362). London: Sage.

Lewis, M. E. (2004). A teacher's schoolyard tale: Illuminating the vagaries of practicing participatory action research (PAR) pedagogy. *Environmental Education Research, 10*(1), 89–115.

Lewis, M. E. (2007, April). *Developing and practicing participatory action research (PAR) pedagogy in a NYC high school greenhouse project: An insider's narrative inquiry.* Presentation at the annual meeting of the American Educational Research Association, Chicago, IL.

Lykes, M. B. (in collaboration with the Association of Maya Ixil women—New Dawn, Chajul, Guatemala). (2001). *Creative arts and photography in participatory action research in Guatemala.* In P. Reason & H. Bradbury (Eds.), *Handbook of action research: Participative inquiry and practice* (pp. 363–371). Thousand Oaks, CA: Sage.

Maguire, P. (1987). *Doing participatory research: A feminist approach.* Amherst: University of Massachusetts, Center for International Education.

Maguire, P. (2001a). The congruency thing: Transforming psychological research and pedagogy. In D. Tolman & M. Brydon-Miller (Eds.), *From subjects to subjectivities: A handbook of interpretive and participatory methods* (pp. 276–289). New York: New York University Press.

Maguire, P. (2001b). Uneven ground: Feminisms and action research. In P. Reason & H. Bradbury (Eds.), *Handbook of action research: Participative inquiry and practice* (pp. 59–69). London: Sage.

Maguire, P., & Berge, B.-M. (2009). Elbows out, arms linked: Claiming spaces for feminisms and gender equity in educational action research. In B. Somekh & S. Noffke (Eds.), *Handbook of educational action research* (pp. 398–408). London: Sage.

Maguire, P., Brydon-Miller, M., & McIntyre, A. (2004). Introduction. In M. Brydon-Miller, P. Maguire, & A. McIntyre (Eds.), *Traveling companions: Feminism, teaching, and action research* (pp. ix–xix). Westport, CT: Praeger.

Maguire, P., & Horwitz, J. (2005, April 11). *Nurturing transformative teacher action research in a teacher education program: Possibilities and tension.* Paper presented at the annual meeting of the American Education Research Association, Montreal, Canada.

Mapedza, E., Wright, J., & Fawcett, R. (2003). An investigation of land cover change in Mafungautsi Forest, Zimbabwe, using GIS and participatory mapping. *Applied Geography, 23*(1), 1–21.

Maxwell, J. A. (2005). *Qualitative research design: An interactive approach* (2nd ed.). Thousand Oaks, CA: Sage.

May, W. F. (2000). *The physician's covenant: Images of the healer in medical ethics* (2nd ed.). Louisville, KY: Westminster John Knox Press.

McDermott, C. (2007, June 6–9). Teaching to be radical: The women activist educators of Highlander. In L. Servage & T. Fenwick (Eds.), *Proceedings of the joint international conference of the Adult Education Research Conference and the Canadian Association for the Study of Adult Education* (pp. 403–408), Mount Saint Vincent University, Halifax, Nova Scotia, Canada.

McIntyre, A. (2000). *Inner-city kids: Adolescents confront life and violence in an urban community.* New York: New York University Press.

McIntyre, A., & Lykes, M. B. (2004). Weaving words and pictures in/through feminist participatory action research. In M. Brydon-Miller, P. Maguire, & A. McIntyre (Eds.), *Traveling companions: Feminism, teaching, and action research* (pp. 57–77). Westport, CT: Praeger.

Merrifield, J. (1993). Putting scientists in their place: Participatory research in environmental and occupational health. In P. Park, M. Brydon-Miller, B. Hall, & T. Jackson (Eds.), *Voices of change: Participatory research in the United States and Canada* (pp. 65–84). Westport, CT: Bergin and Garvey.

Messer-Davidow, E. (2002). *Feminism: From social activism to academic discourse.* Durham, NC: Duke University Press.

Mies, M. (1982). *Fighting on two fronts: Women's struggles and research.* The Hague, the Netherlands: Institute of Social Studies.

Mies, M. (1996). Liberating women, liberating knowledge: Reflections on two decades of feminist action research. *Atlantis, 21*(6), 10–24.

Mills, C. W. (1961). *The sociological imagination.* New York: Grove.

Morgan, D., Pacheco, V., Rodriguez, C., Vazquez, E., Berg, M., & Schensul, J. (2004). Youth participatory action research on hustling and its consequences: A report from the field. *Children, Youth, and Environments, 14*(2), 201–228. Available at http://www.colorado.edu/journals/cye

Nairn, K., Higgins, J., & Sligo, J. (2007, June 9). Youth researching youth: "Trading on" subcultural capital in peer research methodologies. *Teachers College Record.* Available at http://www.tcrecord.org/content.asp?contentid=14515

National Aboriginal Health Organization (NAHO). (2007). *Considerations and templates for ethical research practices.* Ottawa, Ontario, Canada: Author.

Newkirk, T. (1996). Seduction and betrayal in qualitative research. In P. Mortensen & G. Kirsch (Eds.), *Ethics and representation in qualitative studies of literacy* (pp. 3–16). Urbana, IL: National Council of Teachers of English.

Niezen, R. (2003). *The origins of indigenism.* Berkeley: University of California Press.

Nyerere, J. (1969). Education for self-reliance. *Convergence, 3*(1), 3–7.

Ortner, S. B. (2006). *Anthropology and social theory: Culture, power, and the acting subject.* Durham, NC: Duke University Press.

Pratt, G. (2004). *Working feminism.* Philadelphia: Temple University Press.

Price, D. (2004). *Threatening anthropology.* Durham, NC: Duke University Press.

Rabinow, P., & Sullivan, W. M. (1985). *Interpretive social science: A second look.* Berkeley: University of California Press.

Reason, P., & Bradbury, H. (2008). *The SAGE handbook of action research: Participative inquiry and practice* (2nd ed.). Thousand Oaks, CA: Sage.

Reid, C., & Frisby, W. (2007). Continuing the journey: Articulating dimensions of feminist participatory action research (FPAR). In P. Reason & H. Bradbury (Eds.), *The SAGE handbook of action research: Participative inquiry and practice* (2nd ed., pp. 93–105). London: Sage.

Reinharz, S. (1992). *Feminist methods in social research.* New York: Oxford University Press.

Royal Commission on Aboriginal Peoples. (1993). *Integrated research plan: Appendix B. Ethical guidelines for research.* Ottawa, Ontario, Canada: Office of the Solicitor General.

Rylko-Bauer, B., Singer, M., & Van Willigen, J. (2006). Reclaiming applied anthropology: Its past, present, and future. *American Anthropologist, 108,* 178–190.

Sabhlok, A. (2007). *SEWA in relief: Gendered geographies of disaster relief in Gujarat, India.* Unpublished doctoral dissertation, Pennsylvania State University, State College.

Sangtin Writers, & Nagar, R. (2006). *Playing with fire: Feminist thought and activism through seven lives in India.* Minneapolis: University of Minnesota Press.

Schulz, A. J., Parker, E. A., Israel, B. A., Becker, A. B., Maciak, B. J., & Hollis, R. (1998). Conducting a participatory community-based survey for a community health intervention on Detroit's East Side. *Journal of Public Health Management and Practice, 4*(2), 10–24.

Smith, D. E. (1989). *The everyday world as problematic: A feminist sociology.* Boston: Northeastern University Press.

Smith, L. T. (1999). *Decolonizing methodologies: Research and indigenous people.* London: Zed.

Swantz, M. L. (1974). *Participant role of research in development.* Unpublished manuscript, Bureau of Resource Assessment and Land Use Planning, University of Dar es Salaam, Tanzania.

Swantz, M. L. (2008). Participatory action research as practice. In P. Reason & H. Bradbury (Eds.), *The SAGE handbook of action research: Participative inquiry and practice* (2nd ed., pp. 31–48). London: Sage.

Tandon, R. (1988). Social transformation and participatory research. *Convergence, 21*(2/3), 5–18.

Tandon, R. (1996). The historical roots and contemporary tendencies in participatory research. In K. de Koning & M. Martin (Eds.), *Participatory research in health* (pp. 19–26). Johannesburg, South Africa: Zed.

Tandon, R. (2005). *Participatory research: Revisiting the roots.* New Delhi, India: Mosaic Books.

Torre, M., & Ayala, J. (2009a). Envisioning participatory action research entremundos. *Feminism and Psychology, 19*(3), 387–393.

Torre, M., & Ayala, J. (2009b, August). *Participatory echoes of Chataway: A symposium reflecting on the social change legacy of Cynthia Joy Chataway.* Paper presented at the annual meeting of the American Psychological Association, Toronto, Ontario, Canada.

Toulmin, S. (1988). The recovery of practical philosophy. *The American Scholar, 57,* 337–352.

Tuck, E. (2009). Re-visioning action: Participatory action research and indigenous theories of change. *Urban Review, 41,* 47–65.

Tucker, S. (n.d.). *Women in jazz.* Available at http://www.pbs.org/jazz/time/time_women .htm

United Nations. (1989). *Convention on the rights of the child.* New York: Author.

Wang, C. (1999). Photovoice: A participatory action research strategy applied to women's health. *Journal of Women's Health, 8,* 185–192.

Wenzel, G. W. (1991). *Animal rights, human rights: Ecology, economy and ideology in the Canadian Arctic.* Toronto, Ontario, Canada: University of Toronto Press.

12

What Is Qualitative Health Research?

Janice M. Morse

What is qualitative *health* research? And why do qualitative health research-ers need their own courses, insist on their own journals, and require specialized methodological texts? Surely knowing qualitative inquiry and being adept in qualitative methods is all that is required to be a good qualitative health researcher? No?

In this chapter, I argue that the complexities encountered by qualitative researchers in the context of health care, the seriousness of the conditions of their participants, the life-and-death nature of the topics that they study, and the clini-cal significance of their findings, make the qualitative health researcher distinct from researchers who do other forms of qualitative inquiry, and the product, qualitative health research, distinct. Here, I consider the origins, content, and scope of qualitative health research. Then, from a content analysis of all articles published in 2009 in *Qualitative Health Research* (Volume 19, *N* = 142 articles), I discuss the current areas of emphases, clinical application, and the contribution of these articles to the medical and allied health care fields. In the final section, I discuss why and how qualitative methods must be adapted for use with the ill and in the clinical setting, and close by making an argument that qualitative health research is developing as an important disciplinary subfield in its own right.

Classical Foundations

Qualitative inquiry has had a presence in hospitals and health care institutions and clinics since the 1950s, when ethnographies (conducted mainly by sociologists) began to appear. Some of this work endures as classics. It includes the study of the socialization of medical students, *Boys in White* (Becker, Geer, Hughes, & Strauss, 1961); Erving Goffman's *Asylums* (1961), a study of "mental patients and other inmates" in Washington, D.C.; Barney Glaser and Anselm Strauss's *Awareness of Dying* (1965); Jeanne Quint's (1967) *The Nurse and the Dying Patient;* and Talcott Parsons's *The Sick Role and the Role of the Physician Reconsidered* (1975). At the University of California, San Francisco, in the 1970s, the student collaborators of Glaser and Strauss—Julie Corbin, Shizuko Fagerhaugh, David Maines, Barbara Suczek, and Carolyn Weiner—published *Chronic Illness and the Quality of Life* (Strauss et al., 1975), building an important foundation for qualitative health research. In nursing, qualitative inquiry was dependent on methodological texts from other disciplines such as anthropology and sociology. From the mid 1980s, they commenced writing their own methods texts, and moved away from other disciplines to be more centrally established into nursing. They also conducted significant qualitative inquiry situated in health. Of this work, Carole Germain's *The Cancer Unit* (1979) and Patricia Benner's *From Novice to Expert* (1984) have been influential. In medicine, the early work of Arthur Kleinman (*Patients and Healers in the Context of Culture* [1980]) was groundbreaking. Most of these studies used ethnography, with the exception of the work at the University of California, San Francisco, where Barney Glaser and Anslem Strauss (1967) were developing grounded theory, and this work continues development through the "second generation" of their students, Phyllis Stern, Julie Corbin, Barbara Stevens, Kathy Charmaz, and Adele Clarke (Morse et al., 2009).

In phenomenology, Jan van den Berg's *The Psychology of the Sick Bed* (1960) was significant. Then, mainly through the work of Max van Manen—his methodological text (van Manen, 1990), the Human Science Conferences, and the journal, *Phenomenology and Pedagogy* (Vols. 1–10, 1983–1992)—phenomenology gained importance in North America. Van Manen, primarily with his students from nursing, developed the phenomenology of illness as an important area, investigating *meaning* in the embodiment of illness.

Ben Crabtree and Will Miller's *Doing Qualitative Research* (1992) and the Family Practice Qualitative Interest Group annual conferences and publications of edited books were important in moving qualitative inquiry into medicine. Narrative inquiry in medicine began with Arthur Kleinman's *The Illness Narratives* (1986) and Howard Brody's *Stories of Sickness* (1987), bringing the patients' experience into medicine (see Engel, Zarconi, Pethtel, & Missimi, 2008) for the evaluation of care. Since the late 1990s, focus groups as a method and now mixed method design have gained significance, particularly in psychiatry and family medicine.

Qualitative inquiry, as a method and a way to approach research, moved into health care first through the work of a group of nurse anthropologists, most notably Madeleine Leininger, Pamela Brink, Margarita Kay, Eleanor Bowens, and Noel Chrisman, who, through the American Anthropological Association's Council of Nurse-Anthropologists (CONAA), provided a supportive forum for qualitative research. In the mid 1980s, qualitative texts began to appear (Field & Morse, 1985; Leininger 1985), courses were offered in graduate programs, and the National Institutes of Health's National Center for Nursing Research (now NINR, National Institute for Nursing Research) was urged to fund qualitative research. Publication of qualitative health research was scattered among several journals, such as *Social Science in Medicine,* or in disciplinary specialist journals, such as *Medical Anthropology* or *Symbolic Interaction.* In 1991, *Qualitative Health Research* (QHR) was launched as a quarterly journal, and it has continued to expand to its current 12 issues annually.

Gaining this acceptance has not been easy for qualitative researchers. Health care research was, and is still, dominated by medical research with an agenda of treatment and cure, using experimental clinical trials, rather than the more subjective, experiential agenda of qualitative inquiry. Medical researchers tend to focus on disease, rather than the person, and with their limited contact with the patient in practice, they have backstaged "the patient's experience." Further, medical research funding agencies historically have been heavily—if not solely—populated by quantitative researchers who had little or no understanding of or appreciation for the principles of qualitative inquiry, so that gaining recognition was slow.

Even today, in medicine, qualitative research continues to be devalued. In Britain, the Cochrane criteria (Cochrane, 1972 /1989; Sackett, 1993) are used to evaluate evidence in medicine. This system establishes a hierarchy of evidence that assigns the most credibility to the clinical trial, and the lowest to "mere opinion." While I do not believe that Cochrane intended to include qualitative inquiry in this hierarchy, researchers tended to assign qualitative inquiry to the lowest rank, categorizing it as "mere opinion." The result of this classification was that qualitative inquiry was denigrated as invalid and of little worth. For instance, in the 1990s in Australia, where the Cochrane system was used by the National Health and Medical Research Council (NHMRC) to make funding decisions, qualitative inquiry was ranked as noncompetitive, and this took considerable energy to successfully reverse. Today, the NHMRC does fund qualitative inquiry, supporting workshops and was commissioning qualitative research. In Britain in the 1990s, likewise, qualitative inquiry was not considered generalizable, and was inappropriate for Cochrane reviews. It took a committee (led by Jennie Popay) to have qualitative inquiry recognized as an adequately rigorous method to be included in reviews to determine evidence. The *British Medical Journal* (*BMJ*) now publishes a regular column on qualitative methods, and in the United States, the occasional qualitative article appears in the *New England Journal of Medicine* and in *JAMA*, the *Journal of the American Medical Association.*

To support the development of qualitative inquiry, the International Institute of Qualitative Methodology (IIQM) was established in 1997 at the University of Alberta, Canada, and funded by a grant from the Alberta Heritage Foundation for Medical Research.[1] In an effort to establish qualitative inquiry as a discipline, the IIQM sponsored the annual Qualitative Health and Advances in Qualitative Methods research conferences in North America and internationally, held lecture and workshop series (called *Thinking Qualitatively*), and consequently facilitated training for a generation of qualitative health researchers. The IIQM developed and supported a multilingual, open-access, online journal called the *International Journal of Qualitative Methods* (*IJQM*), supported *Qualitative Health Research* (a Sage monthly international journal), initiated the *Qual Press* (publishing monographs), and a postdoc and predoc training program (EQUIPP, Enhancing Qualitative Understanding of Illness Process and Prevention), which provided an internship for international trainees. National and international outreach included links with 115 universities through hubs of eight international sites, which in turn spawned additional research, centers, conferences, and organizations internationally.

Where are we today, in 2011? Qualitative health research is now published in the major medical journals, although such articles still remain in the minority. Qualitative inquiry is considered an essential part of graduate research training in many universities, although it is not on an equal basis with quantitative inquiry. We still have some distance to go, and as recently as 2008, qualitative research was excluded from a Canadian urology conference (Morse, 2008). An earlier crisis, that is, the lack of mentors and supervisors to support new qualitative researchers, is easing as competence is gained and more researchers become experienced in qualitative inquiry, and issues of quality and standards are resolved. There is no doubt that the field is maturing. It simply takes time.

What Do Qualitative Health Researchers Study?

Presently, qualitative health research is taking place in all areas where health care is administered: in the hospitals and nursing homes; in the clinics, schools, and workplaces; and in the community—on the streets, in the parks, and at people's homes. It focuses on the experiences of illness, on patient states and behaviors, on the healthy and the sick. It includes accidents, acute onset, and chronicity. The caregivers' experiences, including both lay and professional caregivers and their interactions with the sick person, is an important area. Qualitative inquiry examined cultural perception of disease and responses to illness. The focus was generally on the individual, the family, or groups. Qualitative health research also encompasses the education of health care professionals, and health care information provided the patients and their families.

To illustrate, using some concrete examples of the nature of the scope of qualitative health research, in the next section I provide a broad overview from *Qualitative Health Research*, Volume 19, Issues 1–12, 2009.[2]

The Contributions of *Qualitative Health Research*

Research focused on health using qualitative methods can be broadly classified several ways. One may, for instance, classify participants by age group, ethnicity, medical specialty, or disease—or by behavioral concept or type of research method. For the purposes of this chapter, however, I will classify studies by the broadest system, that is, by *use*—categories used in clinical application, educational topics, and groups of subsequent research. These categories are examining the identification of health care needs, barriers and access to health care, processes of seeking health care, responses to illness, adjusting to being ill, living with illness, responses to treatment, behaviors and experiences of professional care providers, experiences of lay caregivers, perspectives of professional caregivers, and experiences of both lay and professional caregivers. There is also considerable research emphasis on studying support systems in illness and experiences of recovering from illness. Research that contributes to medicine, nursing, and other allied health professions is also important, assisting with delineating symptoms. Finally, I address evaluating health care, and aspects of teaching health care to patients as well as the education of members of the health professions.

The processes of recognizing that one is ill (or the responses to an acute episode or accident), the processes of seeking and receiving care, and the processes of recovering are presented in Table 12.1.

1. *The identification of health care needs*
Research in this category identifies silent or emerging health care problems that are not presently addressed, or poorly addressed, within the system. These

Table 12.1 Categories and Examples of Articles in *Qualitative Health Research* in 2009

Article Title (abbreviated)	Author(s)	Citation
The identification of health care needs		
Perceptions of food insecurity among rural and urban Oregonians	De Marco et al.	*19*, 1010–1024
Menopause: Mapping the complexities of coping strategies	Kafanelis et al.	*19*, 30–41
Identifying patterns of seeking health care		
Cancer patients' accounts of negotiating a plurality of therapeutic options	Broom	*19*, 1050–1059
Treatment seeking by Samoan people in Samoa and New Zealand	Norris et al.	*19*, 1466–1475
The experience of involuntarily childless Turkish immigrants in the Netherlands	Van Rooij et al.	*19*, 621–632
Describing the illness experience		
Disclosing a cancer diagnosis to friends and family	Hilton et al.	*19*, 744–754
Dignity violation in health care	Jacobson	*19*, 1536–1547
Illness meanings of AIDs among women with HIV: Merging immunology and life experience	Scott	19, 454-465
The culture of pediatric palliative care	Davies et al.	*19*, 5–16
Adjusting to illness/Living with illness		
Adjusting to life after esophagectomy	McCorry et al.	*19*,1485–1494
Making sense of living under the shadow of death	Kenne Sarenmalm et al.	*19*, 1116–1130
Social support and unsolicited advice in a bipolar disorder online forum	Vayreda & Antaki	*19*, 931–942
Pill taking from the perspective of HIV-infected women who are vulnerable to antiretroviral failure	Stevens & Hildebrandt	*19*, 593–604

Article Title (abbreviated)	Author(s)	Citation
Disclosure outcomes, coping strategies, and life changes among women living with HIV in Uganda	Medley et al.	*19,* 1744–1754
Breast cancer patients' experiences of external-beam radiotherapy	Schnur et al.	*19,* 668–676
Experiences of kidney graft failure	Ouellette et al.	*19,* 1131–1138
Experiences and practices of professional care providers		
Birth talk in second stage labor	Bergstrom et al.	*19,* 954–964
Positions in doctors' questions during psychiatric interview	Ziółkowska	*19,* 1621–1631
Experiences and practices of lay caregivers		
Hope experience of older bereaved women who cared for a spouse with terminal cancer	Holtslander & Duggleby	*19,* 388–400
Perspectives of both lay and professional caregivers		
Encounter between informal and professional care at the end of life	James et al.	*19,* 258–271
Empathy and empowerment in general practitioners who have been patients	Fox et al.	*19,* 1580–1588
Identification and analysis of support systems		
Being there for another with serious mental illness	Champlin	*19,* 1525–1535
Family presence during resuscitation and invasive procedures: Perceptions of nurses	Miller & Stiles	*19,* 1431–1442
Reflections on the Illness Experience		
The paradox of childhood cancer survivorship	Cantrell & Conte	*19,* 312–322
Normalization strategies of children with asthma	Protudjer et al.	*19,* 94–104
Dreams of my daughter: An ectopic pregnancy	Lahman	*19,* 272–278

problems may be sorted into subcategories with certain common factors that are jeopardizing health; they may be factors that the health care system overlooks; they may be factors in the environment that impair health. In these studies, authors point out inequities or health problems, usually using ethnographic or interview methods. For instance, one of De Marco, Thorburn, and Kue's (2009) malnourished participants said, "in a country as affluent as America, people should be eating." Not surprisingly, poor health, low income, and unemployment were contributors to poor nutrition, but these studies documented the importance of nutrition assistance programs, alternative food sources, and social support ("godsends") to supplement diets. The authors recommend that policy should focus on increasing human capital for the prevention of malnutrition.

Does this recommendation sound obvious? By way of contrast, let us examine the descriptions of the complexities of coping with menopause in Australian women (Kafanelis, Kostanski, Komesaroff, & Stojanovska, 2009). These authors wrote that women's responses "surged and ebbed in intensity, leaving women to stumble, collapse, shift, settle, and meander from one episode or event to the next.... This fluidity allowed women to create, uncover and reinterpret their experiences ... which enabled women to maintain, consolidate and stabilize various coping strategies" (p. 39). Kafanelis et al. identify three styles of responses from such confusion: inventive (able to respond in an effective manner and work through their experiences), troubled (women who responded with anxiety, negativity, and increased conflict), and reactive (women who were determined, active, well-informed, and optimistic). This study illustrates the power of qualitative inquiry in its ability to mirror life, to reveal the implicit, and to be of use for those providing care. It is apparent that in good qualitative inquiry, mundane questions can produce significant findings.

2. *Identifying patterns of seeking health care*

The Western model of providing care is simple: The patient suspects that he/she may have a health problem, and comes to the physician for care. The physician diagnoses the problem, gives treatment recommendations to the patient, who then complies with the treatment and recovers. But this model collapses with some patients, when barriers to care impede access.

Different processes and choices acted upon when ill, the interpretation of the illness symptoms, and the effects of the input of others from the family were described by a team of New Zealand and Samoan researchers, explaining how Samoans choose to use the Western (*palagi*) or the traditional Samoan health care and healing resources—or both. The fact that the individual may select one course of action, and still be overruled by the family, has important implications for all cultures in which the family is the unit for treatment decisions (Norris,

Fa'alau, Va'ai, Churchward, & Arroll, 2009). The model can break down even when the patient gets to the physician. In the United States, the patient is asked his or her preferences for therapy, and the advantages, effectiveness, and side effects of each alternative is explained. The multiple options for treatment can be overwhelming, yet the Western system expects patients to be involved in decisions about treatment options. Compounding the patient's choice among these therapeutic options are the number of complementary medicines available. Broom (2009) describes patients "piecing together" therapies from both the Western and the complementary systems, using "intuitive" and "objective" scientific knowledge, and making their own decisions to assess therapeutic effectiveness of their treatments.

3. *The illness experience*

This category forms the main component of qualitative health research as a subdiscipline (and accounts for the majority of articles published in *QHR*). It includes response to illness, adjusting to illness, and living with illness.

Researchers are fascinated with the worlds of the acutely and chronically ill—the dramatic change in one's self, to one's lifestyle, and to one's being. Illness impacts and alters the core of the self (Jacobson, 2009). Becoming ill involves breaking the bad news to loved ones (Hilton, Emslie, Hunt, Chapple, & Ziebland, 2009), and their distress in turn compounds the suffering of the ill person.

In an article from Uganda, Medley, Kennedy, Lynyolo, and Sweat (2009) examined how women with HIV cope with the changes after learning their diagnosis. Stevens and Hildebrandt (2009) provide interesting perspectives of women who "had difficulty" taking their antiretroviral medications. Taking this medication "produced existential angst, interfered with functioning or caused a loss of self." Whenever they took their medications, they were reminded that they had HIV—in fact *not* taking their medications was viewed as a "positive thing—it enabled them to feel fully human, dignified" and "pleased that they managed to take at least some of their medications some of the time" (p. 601).

The complex emotions associated with being told that cancer has recurred were vividly described by Kenne Sarenmalm, Thorén-Jönsson, Gaston-Johansson, and Öhlén (2009). The feelings of "shock, fear, anxiety, sadness and depression, apathy and listlessness" were overwhelming for these women. The losses were acute—women felt "like a nothing" with the loss of femininity, loss of their physical appearance, and their attractiveness. "I usually feel like an 'it' on legs." They experienced a loss of self, a loss of control, loss of power to influence the situation, loss of independence, and of being dependent on others (p. 1121).

Schnur, Ouellette, Bovbjerg, and Montgomery (2009) described the experiences of women with breast cancer receiving external beam radiotherapy. The side effects experienced were not "just" side effects. In addition to being considered as a "problem with treatment," side effects were evaluated as an "omen of symptoms to come" or as an "indicator of personal unworthiness." For instance, fatigue may be "expected and considered normal to the physician," but is a sign of "weakness" to the women. Skin toxicity may be seen as "sunburn" to others, but to the women it would be considered "hideous." Women were self-critical ("self-downing"), and had difficulty in giving themselves permission to "take it easy." They were "merciless" and the self-criticism went beyond their treatment and pervaded their "self-identity as a conscious worker, a good parent, a good patient, and an attractive woman" (p. 673).

Treatments are not always "successful," as Ouelette, Achille, and Pâquet (2009) note. Kidney patients whose grafts had failed and who were forced to return to dialysis appeared to redefine their "representation of reality." How well they achieved that depended on their comparison with others, and how they sought normalcy. How well they were able to regain a sense of control of their lives depended on individual characteristics and the time since graft failure.

These articles uncover nuances of the illness experience, reinvestigating needs and opportunities for interaction and interventions.

4. *Experiences and practices of professional care providers*

Illness brings dependency, a reliance on others for assistance with the most intimate and private functions. Professional caregiving is easier for the patient to accept than intimate care provided by, perhaps, one's children. But dependency on the professional caregiver involves more than just being a recipient of physical care. Bergstrom, Richards, Proctor, Bohrer, Morse, & Roberts (2009) describe how "talking through"—providing "comfort talk" to women in second stage labor—can assist women to overcome the terror of the second stage of labor, to regain control, and cooperate with caregivers. A caregiver's therapeutic use of self is crucial for the women to have a safe labor experience.

The impact of the ill person's experiences on the caregiver is profound and extends after the patient's death. Holtslander and Duggleby (2009) explored the concept of *hope* in older bereaved women who had cared for their spouse with terminal cancer. When one's spouse is diagnosed with cancer, the loss of confidence, loss of security in the future, and overwhelming losses accompanied the loss of hope. Without hope, "one doesn't want to go on, this reality doesn't matter." "They don't care." The trick is to "search for a new hope" to fill the void, and this will enable them to "go on."

Interviews with both lay *and* professional caregivers provide us with two types of perspectives: (1) those comparing and contrasting lay and professional caregivers and (2) those studying professionals who had also been patients. The experience of being a patient changes the way a physician subsequently interacts with patients—in the realms of empathy, self-disclosure, and recognition of the "disempowering" role of being a patient. Fox et al. (2009) recommend that this content be introduced into medical students' curricula.

Family caregivers have a specialized knowledge. They are experts and protectors, possessing practical knowledge about "what care is best" (or "least harmful") for their loved one. Yet, when the loved one is transferred into the hospital, they are forced back to the sidelines, hovering and observing care, waiting for death (James, Andershed, & Ternestedt, 2009).

5. *Recovering from illness*

The course of rehabilitation has various patterns: rapid and complete, partial or prolonged. In the last, the person lives in the community as a disabled person. Champlin (2009, p. 1525) describes the process of the continuing care for a mentally ill person as one of both accepting and grieving for the changed person, accepting the challenge of caregiving, and recognizing it as never-ending and unpredictable, feeling isolated and ambiguous about the caregiving charge, yet knowing the other well and accepting the responsibility.

Is recovery ever complete? Cantrell and Conte (2009) describes the experiences of childhood cancer, in which the adolescents have the paradoxical experiences of their current state of functioning and, at the same time, being off treatment and having survived. They had to learn to refocus from the uncertainty of illness and treatment, to the fact that they could now dream, hope, and plan, and to reorient from "losses and missed opportunity to what they could accomplish and experience in the future" (p. 320).

6. *Research that contributes to the examination of nursing and other professions*

The original compendium of medical signs and symptoms in medicine came from careful observations of the single patient—qualitative observations. This contribution formed the very basis of medicine, and this role of symptom identification still continues. Qualitative inquiry assists with delineating symptoms, and also identifying new syndromes.

But the conundrum of diagnoses—particularly psychiatric diagnoses—continues. In an article examining beliefs, sensations, and symptoms of PTSD (post-traumatic stress disorder), Spoont and her colleagues (2009) use narrative to explore post-trauma suffering of veterans, and the process by which they themselves came to label their suffering as PTSD. While the experiences of some veterans were clear and validating (and treatment options available), the experiences of others were more ambiguous, and the veterans were uncertain about both the diagnostic label and treatment options. The lack of clarity with the diagnostic label left veterans unable to validate their own suffering as PTSD, unsure how they should proceed with seeking care, and "even contributed to a denial of their suffering." The authors conclude that the diagnostic label of PTSD serves to "provide meaning and validation for those who experience trauma-related suffering" and yet concerns about "possible malingering (i.e., feigning illness for personal gain)" exist (p. 1463).

7. *"Knowing the patient"*

This is an important category, with qualitative research targeting specific information that will be used in patient assessment and subsequent interventions. As shown in some of the studies mentioned in Table 12.2, these assessments are not included in routine assessment protocol, but rather they are investigated for further

Table 12.2   Examples of Articles Making Substantive Contributions to Improving Medicine and Nursing in *Qualitative Health Research* in 2009

Article Title (abbreviated)	Author(s)	Citation
Children's pain assessment in Northern Thailand	Forgeron et al.	*19, 71–81*
Development of a health screening questionnaire for women in welfare transition programs	Lutz et al.	*19, 105–115*
Ecological validity of neuropsychological testing	Gioia	*19, 1495–1503*
Mind and body strategies for chronic pain and rheumatoid arthritis	Shariff et al.	*19, 1037–1049*
PTSD: Beliefs about sensations, symptoms, and mental illness	Spoont et al.	*19, 1456–1465*
Considering culture in physician–patient communication during colorectal screening	Gao et al.	*19, 778–789*
Exploring tuberculosis patients' adherence to treatment regimens and prevention programs	Naidoo et al.	*19, 55–70*
Helping direct and indirect victims of national terror: Experiences of Israeli social workers	Shamai & Ron	*19, 42–54*

understanding of signs and symptoms (see, for instance, Spoont et al., 2009, for PTSD), as groundwork for developing assessment tools (see, for instance, Forgeron et al., 2009, for work with children's pain in Northern Thailand), or to develop models, such as Shariff et al.'s (2009) research in managing the pain of arthritis.

These articles promote important applicable information that may be transferred to the clinical arena or contribute directly to the development of quantitative tools. For instance, medicine used careful observation to establish a compendium of signs and symptoms as early as the 18th century; this effort continues today. Spoont et al.'s (2009) article on post-traumatic stress disorder jumps into the debate about the disorder (Is it a natural response to extreme trauma, or a psychiatric disorder?) with interviews with veterans who had submitted disability claims. Approximately half of the 40 participants were currently in mental health treatment, and all had had a period of military service. The sample included males and females. All were extremely distressed. Determining if their symptoms were consistent with the prototypical description of PTSD, or if they had an ambiguous presentation with symptoms varying in intensity, resulted in self-recognition of the symptoms and difficulty in diagnosis. When considered in context, veterans struggled with the normalcy of the symptoms versus the psychiatric-illness presentation. The ambiguous nature of the syndrome both helped and hindered veterans. Spoont et al. (2009) noted that on one hand it validated their suffering while on the other hand the lack of clarity regarding the diagnostic label left them uncertain whether or not they should seek treatment.

8. *Health care evaluation*

Qualitative inquiry is excellent for evaluation, and evaluations range from health in the community, to the evaluations of health care institutions, to patient self-evaluations of care (see Table 12.3). These articles pertain to the health care system, rather than patient symptoms, as in the previous category. An example of using ethnographic methods to determine local explanatory models of how mothers perceive diarrheal disease in young children in Northern Thailand was published by Pylypa (2009). Mothers believed that diarrhea *(thai su)* was necessary to "lighten the body" so that infants could achieve a new developmental stage, such as sitting, standing, or walking. Therefore, she concluded, "mothers do not direct much attention to prevention, nor manage diarrheal cases in a manner consistent with biomedical recommendations" (p. 965), and it is "unlikely that health education will eliminate this strongly held ethnomedical belief" (p. 974). Importantly, the author notes that this information was "only accessible as a result of the use of an in-depth, qualitative approach to interviewing that has been largely absent from Thai studies of diarrheal disease" (p. 974).

Table 12.3 Examples of Articles on Health Care Evaluation in *Qualitative Health Research* in 2009

Article Title (abbreviated)	Author(s)	Citation
Gaps between patients, media, and academic medicine in discourses on gender and depression	Johansson et al.	*19, 633–644*
Creating a quality improvement dialogue: Utilizing knowledge from frontline staff, managers, and experts to foster health care quality improvement	Parker et al.	*19, 229–242*
Elder authority and situational diagnosis of diarrheal diseases as normal infant development in Northeast Thailand	Pylypa	*19, 965–975*
From trauma to PTSD: Beliefs about sensations, symptoms, and mental illness	Spoont et al.	*19, 1456–1465*

Parker et al. (2009) combined the approaches of the local and the "expert" quality improvement personnel to provide a comprehensive perspective on quality improvement. These researchers noted that as dialogue must be established with the frontline managers and staff members, the best method for such conversations to take place is face to face, and the focus of these discussions sometimes differed (for instance, workload versus costs). Participants in this study felt the project was worth the time and effort. Further, health care organizations must be prepared not only to pay staff to care for patients, but also to work toward improvement in that care.

9. *Teaching health care to patients and the education of health professionals*
Articles in this category (see Table 12.4) address teaching techniques and strategies used by the health professions, including unique programs (Oman, Moulds, & Usher, 2009) and the development of models for teaching (Jenkins, Mabbett, Surridge, Warring, & Gwynn, 2009). Teaching in medicine and nursing has some unique characteristics. Rounds are used, and this necessarily involves patients. Care to an individual patient is provided by different practitioners and different specialties, and these professionals are responsible for different aspects of care. Qualitative inquiry reveals the strengths and weaknesses inherent in the utilization, evaluation, and improvement of such unique teaching structures.

Table 12.4 Examples of Articles on Education and Models in *Qualitative Health Research* in 2009

Article Title (abbreviated)	Author(s)	Citation
Medical education		
Patients' involvement in hospital bedside teaching encounters	Monrouxe et al.	*19,* 918–930
Medical programs		
Professional satisfaction and dissatisfaction among Fiji specialist trainees: What are the implications for preventing migration?	Oman et al.	*19,* 1246–1258
Communication channels in general internal medicine: Improved interprofessional collaboration	Gotlib Conn et al.	*19,* 943–953
Health education		
Health materials and strategies for the prevention of immigrants' weight-related problems	Ferrari et al.	*19,* 1259–1272
Models for nursing		
Cooperative inquiry into action learning and praxis development in a community nursing module	Jenkins et al.	*19,* 1303–1320

From the above variety of contexts, perspectives, and conditions that were the focus of the research, we will now explore the question of necessary adaptations to qualitative methods to be used in health care research.

Doing Clinical Qualitative Health Research

The process of trying to "get inside" the world of the ill, the disabled, and the dying evokes special ethical and methodological problems: ethically because the impact of the illness leaves little room for participation, and methodologically because of the restrictions of the illness process on the participants. Each of these two aspects will be discussed.

IRB QUANDARIES WITH QHR

Qualitative research may be considered invasive and intrusive in participant's lives. As IRBs (institutional review boards) consider these factors during review, sometimes they seek to protect participants by arguing that patients do not have the energy, inclination, or the time to participate in qualitative research (McIntosh & Morse, 2009). For example, if a patient is in pain, or struggling for breath, IRBs sometimes consider that they should not be "disturbed" for research, for the consent procedures, to be interviewed, or even have their privacy interrupted with the presence of an observer. If a patient is dying, qualitative research takes precious time that the patient should be spending with his or her family, or used productively to complete tasks they must accomplish while they are able. The research is considered to have limited benefit for the participant and their family, and the "benefit" of qualitative inquiry for subsequent patients is also considered limited if the generalizability of findings is questioned. Thus, IRBs are frequently reticent to approve requests for access, even when the interviewer is a nurse accustomed to working with the ill (Morse, 2002).

However, researchers report that these perceptions about patients not wanting to participate are incorrect, and participants appreciate the support, the opportunity to talk and to be listened to, and accept the presence of an observer. Patient's report they can see the benefit of research to others, and do not consider the research process as an invasion of their privacy. If the IRBs' concerns are correct and some patients do not wish to be involved in research, certainly some do wish to participate, and the concern regarding patients' time should not be the consideration for nonapproval. Patients themselves should be given the opportunity to choose if they wish to participate or not.

One area that has not been well studied is emergency care, in which treatment takes precedence over consent procedures. Medical research involving drug trials and other treatments has special regulations to allow the research to continue without consent, with the patient's consent replaced by the consent of two physicians. Such dispensation has not been obtained for qualitative inquiry, even though it does not generally involve treatments or impact care.

The cast of thousands. The complexity of care and the number of people involved directly or indirectly with patient care, even in one 8- or 12-hour shift, make the obtaining of consents for the conduct of observational research using videos very difficult. If the focus of the research is the patient, consent must be also obtained from all of those who interact with the patient, who come in contact with the patient, from the physician to the cleaning staff and the person who delivers the newspaper, as they will be on the tape. In one project involving videotaping trauma care, we obtained as many consents as possible before the project started—this involved EMTs (emergency medical technicians), a number of medical specialties, all staff who wished to participate, and the auxiliary staff, such as radiologists and the cleaning staff. Then, when we were actually taping, we posted signs on the door stating the we were taping for research purposes, and stood by the door, reminding people as they rushed in that we were collecting research data. Any person, including the patient, could ask for the video recorder to be switched off at any time. The tapes were secured until the patient was able to give consent or declined to be in the study, and in the latter case the tapes were immediately erased. This demonstrates that such research can be conducted, but certainly not easily.

Vulnerable participants. Research conducted with institutionalized patients is considered a risk, as patients are *vulnerable.* Therefore, all research that is to be conducted in an institution is subject to IRB approval, and a review of the clinical areas may be conducted with respect to research burden—that is, are too many projects being conducted in the same area, resulting in too much "work" for the patient participants or too much time involvement for staff?

Participant vulnerability is clear when the patients are cognitively impaired (and unable to provide consent, but may be required to *assent,* and the guardian *consent*), or are minors (and the child is expected to provide *assent* to the research, and the parents to provide *consent).*

Consent becomes an issue with institutionalized patients. When the person obtaining consent (or conducting the research) is the same as the one providing care, the perceived coercive effects are considered a risk. The potential participant may ask, "What if care will be withheld if I do not participate?" Therefore, an explanation of the study, or the consent itself, is usually obtained by someone who is not involved with direct patient care, and the fact that the patient may withdraw from the project at any time without penalty is stressed. Staff must know who is participating in research, and usually a copy of the consent form is placed in the patient's file. Many institutions employ an ombudsman to oversee research projects and to manage questions or complaints, if any.

Privacy laws. Once the researcher has permission to conduct research in a hospital, locating patients with the necessary characteristics may be an issue. In the United States, federal privacy legislation HIPPA (Health Insurance Portability and Accountability Act of 1966, available at http://www.hhs.gov/ocr/privacy/), may prohibit contact. Canada has two federal privacy laws, the Privacy Act and the Personal Information Protection and Electronic Documents Act (PIPEDA; available at http://www.priv.gc.ca/fs-fi/02_05_d_15_e.cfm#contenttop), and many provinces have their own privacy laws. For instance, Alberta has FOIP (Freedom of Information and Protection of Privacy Act Canada; available at http://foip.alberta.ca/legislation/index.cfm), which prevents staff from releasing names and any other information to nonstaff without obtaining the patient's permission. This means that those who are eligible to participate in a study must be first contacted by a staff member, or a letter sent from the hospital to the patients, asking if they would be interested in hearing about and possibly participating in the study.

Access/gatekeepers/"getting in." Unfortunately, having administrative approval does not ensure that the researcher has access to patients. Some institutions require "administrative approval" from the physician and the head of the department. First, the physician: Even if your research does not involve treatments, it is a courtesy to inform the physician about the project. If the research does involve treatments—or perhaps involves identifying former patients—try to get the physician interested in your research, and perhaps involve him as a collaborator. The physician's permission will be essential before you invite patients to participate in your research.

Getting permission of the charge nurse is important. The nurses will be helping to ease you into the setting, to "learn the ropes," and if necessary, to assist you with patient identification and in gaining the cooperation of the staff. She (or he) will be setting up meetings for you with the staff to explain your study and to gain their interest, because whether or not they are involved, they must know who you are and why you are there, and when you are (or are not) on the unit. Be certain to learn the names of all staff members, including support staff. Take donuts to staff meetings—they are the currency of the hospital—and show your appreciation on special occasions and when withdrawing by taking a special cake for the staff (Kayser-Jones, 2003).

Empowered patients. Occasionally, you will be in a long-term care unit in which patient governance is significant and strong. In this case, it is important to have the patients' governing body's permission before you proceed. This may involve a meeting with the executive committee or even the council president to explain your study and get them interested. In turn, they will invite you to the next general meeting to explain your study, answer questions, and to get their permission to proceed. Again, this group has the power to provide you with permission for entry or to block your access.

The fear of documentation. The greatest fear of documenting clinical practice for staff is the fear of evaluation. This ranges from an informal discomfort (staff have asked, "Please hire non-nurses to monitor the cameras" so they would not feel their care was being evaluated), to a worry that a staff member may be recognized in your data, and embarrassed, or reprimanded for "doing something wrong," to a fear that the data may subpoenaed and used against the staff member. This makes clinical data "highly sensitive," and issues of trust, confidentiality, and anonymity very important.

This brings another issue to the fore: What happens if the researcher observes suboptimal care practices? Are they obligated to become a whistleblower? At what point does the researcher intervene?

The costs of intervening are always high—the researcher may, very likely, lose the research site. Of course, it depends on what the problem is; remember that the researcher's first obligation is always to the patient. An excellent model for discussion of such a problem is the fieldwork of Kayser-Jones (2002). When studying the hydration and nutrition of Alzheimer's patients in a nursing home, she and her research team meticulously documented the food intake of residents, weighing patients and recording the timing of their feedings. But at the same time, the researchers did not hesitate to give patients food and water if they so requested, but documented these actions, making it a part of the data. They also discussed the problems of thirst and hunger with the nursing home administrators in an attempt to elicit change—and, in addition to publishing their findings, gave testimony to government.

Ownership of data. If you are conducting research in a clinical setting, to whom does your research data belong? If the research is funded by an external agency, the research data belongs to the university (to whom the grant was awarded); in obtaining permission to conduct the research, the institution in which the research is being conducted relinquishes rights to those data. However, the researcher has the responsibility to protect these data. Data are always sensitive—names must be removed from transcripts, and code numbers assigned as pseudonyms. Data should not be reported case by case, as the more identifying tags are listed, the easier it is to identify each participant. Data must be kept in a locked cabinet, in a locked space. Similarly, the identity of the research site should not be revealed, and perhaps not even the city in which the study was conducted. Some institutions will ask to see articles for approval, prior to publication—this is a very awkward situation in which to find yourself—do not agree to such a requirement, for you may be asked to alter or adjust your report, which is a type of censorship.

If your data are sensitive, they may be subpoenaed—patients may wish to use information to sue caregivers, or a third party may want to use it as evidence. Researchers can protect their data (and therefore their participants) by applying for a NIH Certificate of Confidentiality (available at http://grants1.nih.gov/grants/policy/coc/background.htm). These certificates are available even to researchers who are not funded by the National Institutes of Health.

DIFFICULTY IN CONDUCTING RESEARCH WITH THE ACUTELY ILL AND DYING

Qualitative inquiry is often delimited by the domain in which care is provided: in the hospital, sometimes limited to one department, patient unit, physician's office, or patient's room; in the community clinic; school office; or the patient's home. These studies are usually ethnographic or participant observation. While the research may center on the patient, it often includes the patient's family, the caregiver, or the interaction between the patient and the caregiver. Because of the way hospitals are organized, with patients with a similar condition sharing the same space—such as patients in a cardiac unit, undergoing renal dialysis, or chemotherapy—it is often difficult to get a private space to conduct an interview.

Silenced by disease. Patients are silenced by disease. They may be unconscious or on a respirator and unable to talk, have had oral surgery, or a dry mouth and unable to articulate. They may be confused, or mentally ill, and unable to express themselves coherently. They may have too much pain to be able to focus on the interview. They may be too fatigued or too sleepy to participate. Treatment also mutes patients—the patient may have an oral brace, may have gone through surgery, or may lack dentures and be unable to speak. They may have medications to make them drowsy, be very breathless, or lack the will to talk. Sometimes patients are stunned by shock and pain, and unable to comprehend anything but the overwhelming agony.

Confusing their physical state, patients are psychologically trying to grapple with their injuries or illness. Patients are too bewildered to make sense of whatever is going on with them, let alone report it to a researcher.

Instability/rapid change/inaccessibility. Often, if the patient's condition is unstable, it may rapidly deteriorate, so that nurses and physicians must try to resuscitate the person. While the researcher may interview the patient about the resuscitation afterward, drugs administered may erase the patient's memory. Again, patients grapple to make sense of what has happened to them, and often are unable to report the changes to another.

In this setting, the urgency/pace of care and the number of people involved in the care means that the researcher may not even be able to see the patient, let alone collect data. Participants may die, be transferred, be in a condition that suddenly deteriorates, or be discharged. When one can start data collection, interviews may be difficult. Patients lack time, have no privacy, and no quiet, uninterrupted space to participate in an interview. Finally, the bodily smells, the sounds of agony, and the sight of injuries, may combine to make the researcher feel faint, or nauseated, and unable to continue collecting data. If such feelings occur, leave the setting before you become an additional person for the staff to care for.

Does Qualitative Health Research Require Modification of Methods?

Qualitative inquiry traditionally used orthodox qualitative methods, and in the 1970s and 1980s, qualitative health researchers used the same texts as researchers in anthropology, sociology, and education. The only exception was grounded theory, developed at the University of California, San Francisco, School of Nursing, and later adopted by other disciplines. Thus, until the mid 1980s, there was some methodological consistency between disciplines.

Given that patients and institutions by their very nature interfere with data collection, it is surprising that any qualitative research is conducted in the hospital. Certainly, interview research is difficult. Some types of observational research are easier, provided one can actually see the patient. But when using observational methods alone, the researcher may have difficulty in interpreting the patient's experience. What did that waving of her hand in the air actually *mean?*

Given these limitations and difficulties, there are some strategies that work to make clinical qualitative research possible, or almost possible.

1. Do retrospective interviews: Interestingly, patients never forget (or forget very slowly) about significant events. Illness and hospitalization is one of those events that is hard to forget. In fact, asking patients to recall after the fact is often a more effective design than repeating interviews throughout the event. If

patients have had time to reflect on the illness and learn what effect it has on their lives, to move from the suppression of emotions in enduring to emotional reflection and suffering, then the interviews will be of much better quality. The patients will have the emotional expression needed to do good qualitative description. Remember that the emotions felt in recalling the event mirror the emotions felt when the event was originally experienced, thus the interviews retain their validity. Furthermore, the "retrospective" methods work well with grounded theory, placing events in sequential order, an organization that simplifies the ordering of the process.

2. If one has difficulty in accessing the patient due to privacy or treatment constraints, collect data for shorter, more delineated periods of real time, modifying the topic accordingly. For instance, the topic of "breaking bad news" may be easily accomplished by audio- or videotaping consultations. Such recordings may be analyzed using conversational analysis, and later be combined with interviews to obtain a more rounded perspective.

3. Another perspective may be to involve the caregivers as coinvestigators, as some type of participatory action research (PAR). The caregiver may supplement ongoing data collection with stories of other cases, of other incidents, thus developing your database. Similarly, a patient's relative or caregiver may be an excellent source of observational data.

4. The most important piece of advice is to "take your time." Make the effort to spend time in the clinical setting, and to get to know the staff and the patients.

Conclusion

I began this chapter by asking, Is qualitative health research a subdiscipline within the area of qualitative inquiry? And what are those features that make qualitative health research different?

The nature of illness itself gives people a different perspective on life. The ill may experience pain, immobility, a changed *self*. Socially, they may experience a loss of employment, changes in financial status, dependency on others (sometimes even for intimate functions), restrictions on day-to-day living, and perhaps an inability to eat or breathe without assistance. The time that must be allotted to therapies and medical appointments, and the threat of limited life remaining, demands that personal time be prioritized before an external researcher's request for interviews and/or observation. For the researcher, illness produces a different world, with a very different atmosphere from the day-to-day world "outside." This changed environment contains the intensity of birth and death, of pain, of suffering, and the joy of surviving. The researcher does not have priority in this world, and the researcher must take a back seat to the individual's treatment/healing agenda. Furthermore, to do such research requires additional skills and specialized knowledge: The researcher must know the formal rules and codes of conduct in hospitals, yet be empathetic toward the ill, and not become overwhelmed and upset by stories of dying or sights and smells in hospitals. The researcher must have the knowledge and skills to understand the acutely ill, in order, for instance, to break the interview into manageable chunks to prevent fatigue, or to manage the emotions of acute distress.

Julianne Cheek (personal communication, 2010) asked an interesting question: Are the features of the illness experience and health care environment the same for qualitative or quantitative research? If so, does that give qualitative and quantitative health research more in common than when both are compared to another discipline's research, such as educational research? In other words, does the environment and topic differentiate research more than differences in the research method itself?

I conclude "not entirely," for we must also consider the fact that quantitative researchers can more easily—and are expected to—remain detached from their subjects and "objective" in their approach to the topic. This means that they are not emotionally involved with their participants and their topic, and in this regard, quantitative methods, therefore, cannot be grouped with qualitative methods.

Where is the discipline likely to go in the future? As the numbers of students using qualitative health research methods increase and these students graduate, so does the present problem of inadequate numbers of supervisors and mentors dissipate, and the subdiscipline itself become stronger. The numbers of texts, courses, and workshops increase and qualitative heath research becomes mainstream. This push will be helped by unexpected sources—for instance, the push for evaluation and for mixed methods will help qualitative inquiry in places that the influx of qualitative inquiry per se may be slower.

Thus, I conclude by maintaining that qualitative health research is a specialized form of qualitative research. The emotional components of qualitative health research are different enough, and the ethical issues separate enough, that qualitative inquiry has its own needs for education, training, methods, and dissemination of knowledge. The conditions in the institutions and the features of ill participants are different enough substantively for qualitative health research to be considered a "specialty," requiring specialized knowledge, research design, and modification of methods.

Notes

1. AHFMR, as an establishment grant to Janice Morse.

2. *QHR* is published monthly, with approximately 12 to 14 articles per issue. The content analysis here was derived from the 142 articles published in Volume 19 in 2009.

References

Becker, H. S., Geer, B., Hughes, E. C., & Strauss, A. L. (1961). *Boys in white: Student culture in medical school.* Chicago: University of Chicago Press.

Benner, P. (1984). *From novice to expert: Excellence and power in clinical nursing practice.* Englewood Cliffs, NJ: Prentice Hall.

Bergstrom, L., Richards, L., Proctor, A., Bohrer Avila, L., Morse, J. M., & Roberts, J. E. (2009). Birth talk in second stage labor. *Qualitative Health Research, 19,* 954–964.

Brody, H. (1987). *Stories of sickness.* New York: Oxford University Press.

Broom, A. (2009). Intuition, subjectivity, and le bricoleur: Cancer patients' accounts of negotiating a plurality of therapeutic options. *Qualitative Health Research, 19,* 1050–1059.

Cantrell, M. A., & Conte, T. M. (2009). Between being cured and being healed: The paradox of childhood cancer survivorship. *Qualitative Health Research, 19,* 312–322.

Champlin, B. E. (2009). Being there for another with a serious mental illness. *Qualitative Health Research, 19,* 1525–1535.

Cochrane, A. L. (1972/1989). *Effectiveness and efficiency: Random reflections on health services.* London: British Medical Journal. [Original publication London: Nuffield Provincial Hospitals Trust, 1972]

Crabtree, B. F., & Miller, W. L. (1992). *Doing qualitative research.* Thousand Oaks, CA: Sage.

Davies, B., Larson, J., Contro, N., Reyes-Hailey, C., Ablin, A. R., Chesla, C. A., et al. (2009). Conducting a qualitative culture study of pediatric palliative care. *Qualitative Health Research, 19,* 5–16.

De Marco, M., Thorburn, S., & Kue, J. (2009). "In a country as affluent as America, people should be eating": Experiences with and perceptions of food insecurity among rural and urban Oregonians. *Qualitative Health Research, 19*(7), 1010–1024.

Engel, J. D., Zarconi, J., Pethtel, L. L., & Missimi, S. A. (2008). *Narrative in health care: Healing patients, practitioners, profession, and community.* Oxford, UK: Radcliffe.

Ferrari, M., Tweed, S., Rummens, J. A., Skinner, H. A., & McVey, G. (2009). Health materials and strategies for the prevention of immigrants' weight-related problems. *Qualitative Health Research, 19,* 1259–1272.

Field, P. A., & Morse, J. M. (1985). *Nursing research: The application of qualitative approaches.* London: Croom Helm.

Forgeron, P. A., Jongudomkarn, D., Evans, J., Finley, G. A., Thienthong, S., Siripul, P., et al. (2009). Children's pain assessment in Northeastern Thailand: Perspectives of health professionals. *Qualitative Health Research, 19,* 71–81.

Fox, F. E., Rodham, K. J., Harris, M. F., Taylor, G. J., Sutton, J., Scott, J., et al. (2009). Experiencing "The other side": A study of empathy and empowerment in general practitioners who have been patients. *Qualitative Health Research, 19,* 1580–1588.

Gao, G., Burke, N., Somkin, C. P., & Pasick, R. (2009). Considering culture in physician-patient communication during colorectal cancer screening. *Qualitative Health Research, 19,* 778–789.

Germain, C. P. (1979). *The cancer unit: An ethnography.* Wakefield, MA: Nursing Resources.

Gioia, D. (2009). Understanding the ecological validity of neuropsychological testing using an ethnographic approach. *Qualitative Health Research, 19,* 1495–1503.

Glaser, B. G., & Strauss, A. (1965). *Awareness of dying.* Chicago: Aldine.

Glaser, B. G., & Strauss, A. (1967). *Discovery of grounded theory.* Chicago: Aldine.

Goffman, E. (1961). *Asylums: Essays on the social situation of mental patients and other inmates.* New York: Anchor Books, Doubleday.

Gotlib Conn, L., Lingard, L., Reeves, S., Miller, K., Russell, A., & Zwarenstein, M. (2009). Communication channels in general internal medicine: A description of baseline patterns for improved interprofessional collaboration. *Qualitative Health Research, 19,* 943–953.

Hilton, S., Emslie, C., Hunt, K., Chapple, A., & Ziebland, S. (2009). Disclosing a cancer diagnosis to friends and family: A gendered analysis of young men's and women's experiences. *Qualitative Health Research, 19,* 744–754.

Holtslander, L. F., & Duggleby, W. D. (2009). The hope experience of older bereaved women who cared for a spouse with terminal cancer. *Qualitative Health Research, 19,* 388–400.

Jacobson, N. (2009). Dignity violation in health care. *Qualitative Health Research, 19,* 1536–1547.

James, I., Andershed, B., & Ternestedt, B.-M. (2009). The encounter between informal and professional care at the end of life. *Qualitative Health Research, 19,* 258–271.

Jenkins, E. R., Mabbett, G. M., Surridge, A. G., Warring, J., & Gwynn, E. D. (2009). A cooperative inquiry into action learning and praxis development in a community nursing module. *Qualitative Health Research, 19,* 1303–1320.

Johansson, E. E., Bengs, C., Danielsson, U., Lehti, A., & Hammarström, A. (2009). Gaps between patients, media, and academic medicine in discourses on gender and depression: A metasynthesis. *Qualitative Health Research, 19,* 633–644.

Kafanelis, B. E., Kostanski, M., Komesaroff, P. A., & Stojanovska, L. (2009). Being in the script of menopause: Mapping the complexities of coping strategies. *Qualitative Health Research, 19,* 30–41.

Kayser-Jones, J. (2002). Malnutrition, dehydration, and starvation in the midst of plenty: The political impact of qualitative inquiry. *Qualitative Health Research, 12,* 1391–1405.

Kayser-Jones, J. (2003). Continuing to conduct research in nursing homes despite controversial findings: Reflections by a research scientist. *Qualitative Health Research, 13*, 114–128.

Kenne Sarenmalm, E., Thorén-Jönsson, A.-L., Gaston-Johansson, F., & Öhlén, J. (2009). Making sense of living under the shadow of death: Adjusting to a recurrent breast cancer illness. *Qualitative Health Research, 19*, 1116–1130.

Kleinman, A. (1980). *Patients and healers in the context of culture.* Berkeley: University of California Press.

Kleinman, A. (1986). *The illness narratives.* New York: Basic Books.

Lahman, M. K. E. (2009). Dreams of my daughter: An ectopic pregnancy. *Qualitative Health Research, 19*, 272–278.

Leininger, M. M. (1985). *Qualitative research methods in nursing.* New York: Grune & Stratton.

Lutz, B. J., Kneipp, S., & Means, D. (2009). Development of a health screening questionnaire for women in welfare transition programs in the United States. *Qualitative Health Research, 19*, 105–115.

McCorry, N. K., Dempster, M., Clarke, C., & Doyle, R. (2009). Adjusting to life after esophagectomy: The experience of survivors and carers. *Qualitative Health Research, 19*, 1485–1494.

McIntosh, M., & Morse, J. M. (2009). Institutional review boards and the ethics of emotion. In N. K. Denzin & M. D. Gardina (Eds.), *Qualitative inquiry and social justice* (pp. 81–107). Walnut Creek, CA: Left Coast Press.

Medley, A. M., Kennedy, C. E., Lynyolo, S., & Sweat, M. D. (2009). Disclosure outcomes, coping strategies, and life changes among women living with HIV in Uganda. *Qualitative Health Research, 19*, 1744–1754.

Miller, J. H., & Stiles, A. (2009). Family presence during resuscitation and invasive procedures: The nurse experience. *Qualitative Health Research, 19*, 1431–1442.

Monrouxe, L. V., Rees, C. E., & Bradley, P. (2009). The construction of patients' involvement in hospital bedside teaching encounters. *Qualitative Health Research, 19*, 918–930.

Morse, J. M. (2002). Interviewing the ill. In J. Gubrium & J. Holstein (Eds.), *Handbook of interview research* (pp. 317–330). Thousand Oaks, CA: Sage.

Morse, J. M. (2008). Excluding qualitative inquiry: An open letter to the Canadian Urological Association [Editorial]. *Qualitative Health Research, 18*(6), 583.

Morse, J. M., Stern, P. N., Corbin, J., Bowers, B., Charmaz, K., & Clarke, A. (2009) *Grounded theory: The second generation.* Walnut Creek, CA: Left Coast Press.

Naidoo, P., Dick, J., & Cooper, D. (2009). Exploring tuberculosis patients' adherence to treatment regimens and prevention programs at a public health site. *Qualitative Health Research, 19*, 55–70.

Norris, P., Fa'alau, F., Va'ai, C., Churchward, M., & Arroll, B. (2009). Navigating between illness paradigms: Treatment seeking by Samoan people in Samoa and New Zealand. *Qualitative Health Research, 19*, 1466–1475.

Oman, K. M., Moulds, R., & Usher, K. (2009). Professional satisfaction and dissatisfaction among Fiji specialist trainees: What are the implications for preventing migration? *Qualitative Health Research, 19,* 1246–1258.

Ouellette, A., Achille, M., & Pâquet, M. (2009). The experience of kidney graft failure: Patients' perspectives. *Qualitative Health Research, 19,* 1131–1138.

Parker, L. E., Kirchner, J. E., Bonner, L., Fickel, J. J., Ritchie, M. J., Simons, C. E., et al. (2009). Creating a quality improvement dialogue: Utilizing knowledge from frontline staff, managers, and experts to foster health care quality improvement. *Qualitative Health Research, 19,* 229–242.

Parsons, T. (1975). The sick role and the role of the physician reconsidered. *The Millbank Memorial Fund Quarterly. Health and Society, 53*(3), 257–278.

Protudjer, J. L. P., Kozyrskyj, A. L., Becker, A. B., & Marchessault, G. (2009). Normalization strategies of children with asthma. *Qualitative Health Research, 19,* 94–104.

Pylypa, J. (2009). Elder authority and situational diagnosis of diarrheal diseases as normal infant development in Northeast Thailand. *Qualitative Health Research, 19,* 965–975.

Quint, J. (1967). *The nurse and the dying patient.* New York: Macmillan.

Sackett, D. L. (1993). Rules of evidence and clinical recommendations. *Canadian Journal of Cardiology, 9*(6), 487–489.

Schnur, J. B., Ouellette, S. C., Bovbjerg, D. H., & Montgomery, G. H. (2009). Breast cancer patients' experiences of external-beam radiotherapy. *Qualitative Health Research, 19,* 668–676.

Scott, A. (2009). Illness meanings of AIDS among women with HIV: Merging immunology and life experience. *Qualitative Health Research, 19,* 454–465.

Shamai, M., & Ron, P. (2009). Helping direct and indirect victims of national terror: Experiences of Israeli social workers. *Qualitative Health Research, 19,* 42–54.

Shariff, F., Carter, J., Dow, C., Polley, M., Salinas, M., & Ridge, D. (2009). Mind and body management strategies for chronic pain and rheumatoid arthritis. *Qualitative Health Research, 19,* 1037–1049.

Spoont, M. R., Sayer, N., Friedemann-Sanchez, G., Parker, L. E., Murdoch, M., & Chiros, C. (2009). From trauma to PTSD: Beliefs about sensations, symptoms, and mental illness. *Qualitative Health Research, 19,* 1456–1465.

Stevens, P. E., & Hildebrandt, E. (2009). Pill taking from the perspective of HIV-infected women who are vulnerable to antiretroviral treatment failure. *Qualitative Health Research, 19,* 593–604.

Strauss, A., Corbin, J. S., Fagerhaugh, S., Glaser, B., Maines, D., Suczek, B., & Weiner, C. (1975). *Chronic illness and the quality of life.* St. Louis, MO: Mosby.

van den Berg, J. H. (1960). *The psychology of the sick bed.* Pittsburgh, PA: Duquesne University Press.

van Manen, M. (1990). *Researching the lived experience.* London, Ontario, Canada: Althouse Press.

Van Rooij, F. B., van Balen, F., & Hermanns, J. M. A. (2009). The experiences of involuntarily childless Turkish immigrants in the Netherlands. *Qualitative Health Research, 19,* 621–632.

Vayreda, A., & Antaki, C. (2009). Social support and unsolicited advice in a bipolar disorder online forum. *Qualitative Health Research, 19,* 931–942.

Ziółkowska, J. (2009). Positions in doctors' questions during psychiatric interviews. *Qualitative Health Research, 19,* 1621–1631.

Author Index

Page numbers in italics indicate tables.

Subject Index

Page numbers in italics indicate tables.

⊛SAGE research**methods**

The essential online tool for researchers from the world's leading methods publisher

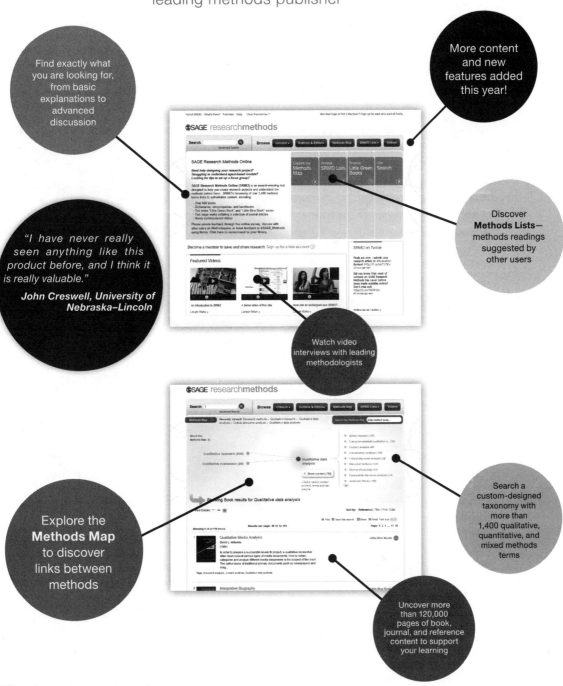

Find exactly what you are looking for, from basic explanations to advanced discussion

More content and new features added this year!

Discover **Methods Lists**— methods readings suggested by other users

"*I have never really seen anything like this product before, and I think it is really valuable.*"

John Creswell, University of Nebraska–Lincoln

Watch video interviews with leading methodologists

Explore the **Methods Map** to discover links between methods

Search a custom-designed taxonomy with more than 1,400 qualitative, quantitative, and mixed methods terms

Uncover more than 120,000 pages of book, journal, and reference content to support your learning

Find out more at
www.sageresearchmethods.com